*Law and Transaction Costs
in the Ancient Economy*

LAW AND SOCIETY IN THE ANCIENT WORLD

SERIES EDITORS:

Dennis P. Kehoe, Tulane University
Cynthia J. Bannon, Indiana University
Matthew R. Christ, Indiana University

The study of law in ancient societies has a distinguished tradition in both Anglo-American and continental scholarship. Many of our fundamental ideas about ancient society were built on research into legal sources. These traditions continue to provide a foundation for newer approaches to law and society. More recent scholarship draws on a range of methodologies to analyze legal practices, including critical legal studies, sociology of law, economics, and literary criticism.

This series, distinguished by its emphasis on interdisciplinary approaches to law and society, seeks out innovative approaches to ancient legal studies that bring new perspectives to legal topics as well as to broader questions concerning the impact of law on commercial, political, and cultural practices in the ancient world.

Law and Transaction Costs in the Ancient Economy

Dennis Kehoe, David M. Ratzan,
and Uri Yiftach, editors

UNIVERSITY OF MICHIGAN PRESS

ANN ARBOR

Published in the United States of America by the
University of Michigan Press
Manufactured in the United States of America
♾ Printed on acid-free paper

2018   2017   2016   2015   4   3   2   1

A CIP catalog record for this book is available from the British Library.

Legal Documents in Ancient Societies (Conference) (2nd : 2009 : Washington, D.C.)
    Law and transaction costs in the ancient economy / Dennis P. Kehoe, David
Ratzan, and Uri Yiftach, editors.
        pages   cm — (Law and society in the ancient world)
    "The papers in this collection are the product of a conference titled 'Transaction
Costs in the Ancient World' organized by David Ratzan and Uri Yiftach. The
conference was held on 27–29 July 2009 at the Center for Hellenic Studies of
Harvard University in Washington, DC, with the financial support of the Institute
for the Study of the Ancient World (ISAW) of New York University. This
conference was one in a series of colloquia held since 2008 by the research group
Legal Documents in Ancient Societies (LDAS)." — Acknowledgments.
    Includes bibliographical references and index.
    ISBN 978-0-472-11960-8 (hardcover : alk. paper)
    1. Law and economics—History—To 1500—Congresses.   2. Transaction costs—
History—To 1500—Congresses.   3. Roman law—Economic aspects—
Congresses.   4. Law, Greek—Economic aspects—Congresses.   5. Law, Egyptian—
Economic aspects—Congresses.   I. Kehoe, Dennis P., editor.   II. Ratzan, David
M., editor.   III. Yiftach, Uri., editor.   IV. Center for Hellenic Studies (Washington,
D.C.), sponsoring body.   V. New York University. Institute for the Study of the
Ancient World, sponsoring body.   VI. Title.

KL8022.5.L44   2015
340.5'3—dc23

                                                            2015017644

Contents

Acknowledgments

The papers in this collection are the product of a conference titled "Transaction Costs in the Ancient World," organized by David Ratzan and Uri Yiftach. The conference was held on 27–29 July 2009 at the Center for Hellenic Studies of Harvard University in Washington, DC, with the financial support of the Institute for the Study of the Ancient World (ISAW) of New York University. This conference was one in a series of colloquia held since 2008 by the research group Legal Documents in Ancient Societies (LDAS). We are very grateful to Prof. Gregory Nagy of Harvard University, the director of the Center for Hellenic Studies, for offering us the use of the facilities of the center; to the staff of the center for its hospitality; and to Prof. Roger Bagnall of ISAW for his continuing support for the LDAS colloquia. The papers from the LDAS colloquia are intended for publication, and several volumes have already appeared. The present volume represents LDAS II.

We are grateful to Ellen Bauerle of the University of Michigan Press for supporting this publication and to the referees for the press for their many helpful comments. We are also grateful to Mary Hashman, our copy editor, for her skill and patience in preparing the volume for publication. Finally, we thank Prof. Giuseppe Dari-Mattiacci of the Amsterdam Center for Law and Economics at the University of Amsterdam for agreeing to write the concluding chapter to the volume.

Abbreviations

The abbreviation FIRA I² refers to "Leges," part 1 of *Fontes Iuris Romani Ante-justiniani*, ed. S. Riccobono, 2nd ed. (Florence, 1941). References to papyri follow the conventions of the *Checklist of Editions of Greek, Latin, Demotic, and Coptic Papyri, Ostraca and Tablets* (June 2011), http://papyri.info/docs/checklist. Abbreviations of journals in classical studies follow the style of *L'Année philologique*. Standard abbreviations are used for inscriptions.

Introduction

Transaction Costs, Ancient History, and the Law

Dennis Kehoe, David M. Ratzan, and Uri Yiftach

Adam Smith's assertion of a basic human "propensity to truck, barter and exchange one thing for another" has never seemed so true as it does today, given the relentless drive to increase the types, frequency, and value of economic transactions over the past two centuries.[1] To take but a single index of the accelerating pace of transactions, the New York Stock Exchange alone executed an average of over 4.5 million trades per day in April 2014. This represents a staggering volume increase of 6,615 percent over the daily average (just under sixty-nine thousand trades) on the NYSE in April 1990, a period, however, in which the exchange accounted for a far greater percentage of all U.S. stock transactions than it does today.[2] One might object that this is an anomaly—that far from being representative of the larger economy, this sort of hypertrophic transactional growth is instead an index of the extent to which the finance industry has succeeded in unmooring itself from any underlying economic reality, helped by new computer technology that supports runaway high-frequency trading. While one may debate the social value of such trading, it is no anomaly when seen from the vantage point of the last two hun-

---

1. *Wealth of Nations*, bk. 1, chap. 2 (Smith [1776] 2000: 14).
2. NYSE Statistics Archive, http://www.nyse.com/financials/1022221393023.html#.

dred years: systematic legal and moral deregulation and intensive capital investment to increase transactional fluidity are the historical norm in the
modern West. Indeed, one of the defining differences between premodern and
modern economies is precisely the number of jobs and occupations in the latter that are devoted to organizing and facilitating transactions.[3]

The obvious quantitative changes in our economic lives since the late
eighteenth century and the institutional innovations and technologies that
have enabled them have led—not surprisingly—to concomitant qualitative
changes in the social organization and experience of life. These social and
psychological transformations are more subtle but not any less profound
than the conspicuous changes in our material condition. We live, one might
say, increasingly transactional lives, a fact that has been continuously cele-
brated or lamented by philosophers, economists, sociologists, and cultural
critics since the publication of the *Wealth of Nations*.[4] It is therefore only natural that our transactional society has rendered us alert—perhaps even hyper-
sensitive—to the interposition of "transaction costs" in our daily lives.[5] Most
of us, of course, have an intuitive, thoroughly unscientific notion of the "costs
of doing business," often thinking of them not as real costs but, rather, as an-
noying and unnecessary add-ons to the "real" price of a good or service, such
as paying a real estate agent's commission on top of the price for a home.
However, if we once again step back to consider our economic lives from a
historical perspective, the nickel-and-diming of these ubiquitous and intrusive transaction costs are revealed as the price we pay for a sophisticated and
powerful economy.

Given the absolute economic growth of the last hundred years and the
relative growth in what one might call the "transaction sector" (Wallis and
North 1986), it is little wonder that economists turned to the study of transac-

---

3. See Wallis and North 1986 for an attempt to measure the growth of the "transaction sector"
    in the American economy from 1870 to 1970. Of course, comparable data for the ancient
    world hardly exist, though one might consider tracing the development of an ancient
    "transaction sector" at certain periods through the study of proxies.
4. In January 2014, Nicholas Lemann offered a meditation on this theme, entitled "The Trans-
    action Society," as part of his Tanner Lectures at Stanford University. Videos of the lectures
    are available at https://ethicsinsociety.stanford.edu/events/past-events.
5. One cannot help but simultaneously identify with and be repulsed by the advertisement
    directed by Kinka Usher for Visa Inc. entitled "Transactional Fluidity" (http://www.colori-
    bus.com/focus/kinka-ushers-best-works/8817255/), in which individuals are envisioned as en-
    thusiastic cogs in a giant, precision, Technicolor transaction machine, with Visa lubricating
    our automatic consumption because "Life takes faster money; life takes VISA."

tion costs in the second half of the twentieth century.[6] It is a commonplace now to cite Ronald Coase's classic article "The Nature of the Firm" (1937) as the *fons et origo* of transaction cost economics, and it is just as commonplace to note that the term *transaction cost* does not actually appear in his work until several decades later. For our purposes, the intellectual history matters less than the conceptual framework that has now developed around the idea and the question of what it might mean to study transaction costs in ancient history.

Transaction costs (henceforth TC) are, as George Stigler (1972: 12) put it, the "friction" in any economic system, so their analysis is vital to understanding institutional design and economic performance. Their importance has long been appreciated by economists, legal scholars, and economic historians, among them two recent Nobel Prize winners, Douglass C. North and Oliver Williamson, who are pioneers in transaction cost economics, or what has been called the "new institutional economics."[7] The questions such scholars wrestle with include:

1. Why are some transactions organized as exchanges on an open market, while others are formalized as contracts, and yet still others integrated into a hierarchical organizations, like a firm?
2. What explains modern economic growth and disparities in economic performance and outcomes in different regional or historical economies?
3. How and why do seemingly inefficient institutions not only survive but even persist over time?
4. What is the role of the state in promoting growth or efficient institutions?
5. What is the economic impact of the law?

These and other similar questions are of immediate interest and obvious relevance to the ancient historian, but the first has rarely been asked, while the rest have not yet been systematically explored by those sufficiently well

---

6. See Klaes 2000a and 2000b for the intellectual history of the concept of the transaction cost.
7. See Eggertsson 1990: 3–32 for a (still) excellent summary of current approaches to the ways in which institutions are analyzed in economics, including the new institutional economics.

acquainted with the evidence.[8] Although the ancient economy has been a subject of study for well over a century now, one is nevertheless justified in saying that the proper economic analysis of ancient institutions, especially the law, is still in its infancy, a state that is reflected by the literature: to date, there are a handful of helpful introductions to the basic concepts (notably Frier and Kehoe 2007) but only a relatively small number of institutional studies by the theoretical avant-garde.[9]

The purpose of this book is to explore the concept of "transaction costs" in ancient economic history, with a particular emphasis on the role of the state and one of its primary organs, the law. It is the first of its kind to collect a number of small-bore studies from the TC perspective, with essays spanning broad chronological, cultural, and evidentiary boundaries (no attempt, however, was made to be comprehensive: there is, for instance, no essay focusing on the Roman Republic). A secondary aim of the volume is to provide an equally broad spectrum of scholarly voices. To that end, the reader will find herein contributions from leading practitioners of TC analysis in ancient history as well as from established scholars with more traditional methodological perspectives and younger scholars experimenting with the approach. The remainder of this introduction aims to ground the following chapters in both the larger framework of TC analysis and the more specific context of the economic analysis and history of law.

What Is a "Transaction Cost"?

Despite the prodigious volume of transaction cost literature and the emergence of more than one school of transaction cost economics, it remains a curious fact that the core concept of the transaction cost remains notoriously ill defined.[10] Coase's basic definition (1937: 390) is that it is "the cost of using the price mechanism," essentially costs associated with making exchanges on an open market. This would seem simple enough, but economists have tended to study two very different types of TC. Some studies (generally the

---

8. See, e.g., the brief and wholly inadequate summary of the "Roman" economy in North 1981: 107–9 and the equally unsatisfactory treatment in North, Wallis, and Weingast 2009: 33, 44–49, 159–60, 195. Cf. also the text accompanying n. 24 below.
9. E.g., Kehoe 2007; Ober 2008; Manning 2010. Cf. Bang 2009 and also below.
10. See the recent overview of the literature in Wang 2007.

earliest ones) focus on concrete opportunity costs, such as brokerage fees. Such costs are, in the end, merely costs: individuals and firms incur them as they do any other cost, duly factoring them into their calculations when they decide which opportunities to pursue and how.

The other tradition, which sprang up in the 1960s and 1970s, understands transaction costs as arising from the cost of information, as Coase seemed to do in his seminal paper "The Problem of Social Cost" (1960: 15).

> In order to carry out a market transaction it is necessary to discover who it is that one wishes to deal with, to inform people that one wishes to deal and on what terms, to conduct negotiations leading up to a bargain, to draw up the contract, to undertake the inspection needed to make sure that the terms of the contract are being observed, and so on.

The framing of TC as intimately related to information costs has been made more explicitly by other economists, including Douglass C. North (1990: 27).

> The costliness of information is the key to the costs of transacting, which consist of the costs of measuring the valuable attributes of what is being exchanged and the costs of protecting rights and policing and enforcing agreements.

The scope of inquiry thus expanded beyond an initial interest in the optimal cost levels associated with using the market mechanism per se to a more explicitly comparative mode of analysis, with the objective of studying the relative TC regimes associated with different types of exchange. In this light, TC may be seen more broadly, in line with Kenneth Arrow's well-known definition, as "the costs of running an economic system" (cf. Stigler 1972: 12, previously cited).[11] This broader view of TC postulates, first, that all transactions are organized or "governed" by a specific set of institutional arrangements and, second, that each institutional environment—be it a spot market, a contractual relationship, or a hierarchy (e.g., a firm or government agency) in the contemporary United States, nineteenth-century Malaysia, or fourth-century B.C.E. Athens—is characterized by a particular set of corresponding TC.

Although the first type of TC clearly may be understood as but a species

---

11. Cf. Klaes 2000b on the development of TC out of an earlier economic discourse of friction.

of the genus captured in the second definition, an essential difference between the two stems from the fact that the wider conception of TC springs from the desire to explain imperfections in the neoclassical model. The TC of the first sort do not, by definition, impede transacting, except at the margin. We know of such costs precisely because they are not so high as to prevent markets from forming—indeed, as already mentioned, they help make markets (which is not the same thing as saying that they are necessarily always efficient or set at the optimal level). TC of the second sort represent a residual category in the neoclassical theory, an x-factor meant to explain various "failures." Such was the impetus behind Coase's initial work (1937), which asked why there are firms at all: if markets are so efficient, why is there not one big market? Similarly, one of Oliver Williamson's seminal articles (1971) is an attempt to reform antitrust law by rehabilitating vertical integration (i.e., monopolies) as a reasonable and predictable response to various forms of "market failure" induced by TC.[12]

This point of departure largely explains the fuzziness of the TC concept, an endemic problem for any residual category, and one quickly discovers a host of second-order definitional and empirical questions as soon as one attempts to work with TC in a systematic way. For example, are all TC really information costs? Conversely, are all information costs TC? Do TC drive institutional evolution, do institutions create TC, or is there a complex dynamic relationship between the two? Which are the important TC, the ones with explanatory power, driving economic behavior and institutional change?

The last question is important, since there would seem to be several possible ways to categorize TC.[13] For instance, one may establish a chronological typology centered on the transaction, classifying TC by the stage at which they are incurred, that is, the prebargain (often denoted in the literature as *ex ante*), bargain, or postbargain (*ex post*) phase of the transaction. Thus one may recognize search costs (prebargain); negotiating and decision costs (bargain); and monitoring, policing, and enforcement costs (postbargain). Alternatively, one may adopt a "functional" perspective, categorizing TC by "the type of impediment that the person who incurred the cost was seeking to overcome" (Ellickson 1989: 613). Robert Ellickson (1989: 615) suggests the following categories on the basis of a functional analysis: get-together costs, decision and execution costs, and information costs.

---

12. See Carroll and Teece 1999 for discussion of the place of this article in the development of Williamson's thinking and TC economics more generally.
13. See Ellickson 1989.

Get-together costs are the burdens of arranging . . . connections among transacting parties. They include the costs of establishing lines of communication, setting up meetings, and transporting parties and goods.

Decision and execution costs are the costs, apart from information costs, that parties who have gotten together incur to actualize their agreement. Decision costs are in evidence when an individual wants to "mull over" an opportunity to trade . . . In many contexts, such as ordering at a restaurant, an individual's decision costs are likely to be trivial. Decision costs are likely to be nontrivial, however, when a transacting party is either a nonhierarchical group of two or more persons who must coordinate together or a hierarchical organization with a multi-person decision-making structure. Execution costs include the costs of documenting a deal.

Information costs, the broadest of the three functional categories, warrant further subdivision . . . :

- information on the item's *quality* (the attributes that a full owner of the item would enjoy);
- information on the item's *title* (that is, on the existence of third-party claims that might limit the transferor's capacity to pass full ownership of the item);
- information on the *price and terms* that the transferor will ultimately charge; and
- information about the *transferor* that would help the acquirer predict the transferor's behavior in subsequent dealings.

To return to our question, which set of TC are the most important? Those incurred *ex ante* or those incurred *ex post*? What if, as is often true, anticipation of *ex post* costs drives *ex ante* costs in a sort of feedback loop? Or is it better to understand TC functionally, as arising out of specific problems associated with transacting? Should we understand information costs as a type of TC, or are TC best defined in a more limited fashion, as, for example, the "resources used to establish and maintain property rights" (Allen 1991), in which case they arise from the costliness of information but are not identical with information costs? Or should our frame of reference, our taxonomy, respond to the particular aspects or dimensions of specific transactions and the institutional regimes in which they take place, such as the relationship between the parties, the nature of the good or service exchanged, the default rights granted under the law, the enforcement options available, and so on?

If so, are we really talking about a unitary concept or phenomenon?[14] These difficult and frequently debated questions have exposed TC economics to sharp criticism, even by those who believe the concept to be useful.

This definitional problem engenders the further difficulty of measurement. Precision and ease of quantification recommend the more limited definition of TC: by simple observation, one can easily measure the economic value of brokerage fees and other discrete costs, such as the spread between bid and ask prices. But assigning values to real-world search, bargaining, and enforcement costs is a tricky business, partly because such an operation depends on one's categories (as previously discussed) and partly because many of the most significant costs are never actually incurred. If we recall that these TC are, by definition, those that are (or are perceived to be) large enough to push parties into transactions with relatively lower TC or to forestall exchange altogether, measurement necessarily depends on discovering proxies for counterfactual situations, that is, what the costs would have been for the roads not taken.

Transaction Costs and Ancient History

Despite the inherent problems previously outlined, the second conceptualization of TC has appealed to a wide variety of thinkers, in different fields and disciplines, who share a common interest in the intersection of economics, organizations, and institutions. More important, because, as the essays in this volume show, TC had a demonstrable impact in the ancient world, we are obliged to take TC into account in our study of ancient history. Although it may be fashionable in some quarters to say so, the previous sentence is not an anachronism.[15] While our transactional society may render TC more visible and more palpable to us, TC were an unavoidable feature of the economic lives of ancient people simply by virtue of those people's engagement in exchange. However, it is incumbent on us to be more precise as to the specific features of "exchanges" in the ancient world that lead to TC.

The question before us is whether, when examining the evidence we have

---

14. It is worth noting that the preceding discussion does not exhaust the possible and proposed taxonomies of TC. See, e.g., Klaes 2000a: 577–83 on the distinction between "technological" and "institutional" TC , as well as Lerouxel's essay in this volume (chapter 7) for another typology that mirrors those already discussed.
15. Boldizzoni 2011.

for ancient economic life, we can recognize the following fundamental features of exchanges that generate TC:

1. Information is not free.
2. The goods exchanged are alterable and variable in quality.
3. A plurality of partners must seek (and be known to seek) to extract value from opposite parties in exchanges while simultaneously seeking (and being known to seek) to protect or retain value they themselves control.[16]

These are not controversial propositions for the ancient world. In fact, not only did all of these preconditions for TC obtain in antiquity, but the first two were, if anything, more pronounced in antiquity than in the twentieth or twenty-first centuries, suggesting that the average levels of TC were higher in antiquity than today.

The first proposition is necessary to state only because the traditional neoclassical model does not take into account the cost of information. To say that it takes resources to acquire and deploy information is a truism for all time—though perhaps truer for antiquity than today. While there is certainly vastly more to know in the information age, modern search technology has lowered the cost of information exponentially. In the ancient world, however, information was a truly costly resource, especially as most of what one could acquire beyond one's own direct experience or immediate circle of friends was not "branded" as it is today by government imprimatur or the information market. Several of the essays in this volume explicitly engage with the economic and institutional implications of costly information in the ancient world.

The second proposition is an essential precondition for the emergence of TC because the variability of goods is one major source of information asymmetry and, consequently, a major source of expense as parties attempt to mitigate that asymmetry. Again, while it is true that most goods and services exchanged in the ancient Mediterranean were not as complex as they are today and therefore had fewer potential latent defects (think of all that may go wrong in an automobile or laptop), it is also true that the standardization of even the most basic commodities was, for all intents and purposes, unknown in classical Greece and only marginally more advanced in the Roman peri-

---

16. Adapted from Allen 1991.

od.[17] The ancient condition was one of radical variability at all levels, such that to speak in terms of "commodities" is misleading in many cases.

The last precondition is perhaps more controversial. If the variability of goods leads to information asymmetry, so does variability in trading partners. People are bigger, darker "black boxes" than goods: they have different skill sets, different capacities for making good on promises (e.g., one would like to know how solvent a potential debtor is), different propensities and motivations for trading or keeping promises (hence the importance of reputation), and so on. Yet the third proposition does not refer to this variability, which is taken for granted. Instead, the precondition makes a stronger claim about the way in which people approach exchange: namely, that it is a basic feature of human nature to suspect that other parties may act opportunistically, even if one does not act opportunistically oneself.[18] For this condition to hold, parties need not act opportunistically all of the time, in every exchange, or always to the same degree; rather, one needs merely the awareness or recognition of the ever-present possibility of opportunistic behavior, taking precautions against which entails a certain cost. This precondition thus asserts that trading is an inherently ambiguous moment—one of potential cooperation, confrontation, or, more likely, both—and that it is always implicitly, if not explicitly, approached agonistically. This ambiguity is the ineluctable product of our innate theory of mind: we human beings cannot help but enter into an exchange with the knowledge that there is another human being on the other side with a mind and a motivation all his or her own and therefore unknowable to us, such that the possibility of the other person taking advantage of existing information asymmetries (i.e., "cheating") can never be fully discounted.[19] Blanket statements about human nature are

---

17. Cf. Johnstone 2011.
18. One might justly qualify this by saying that it is an attribute of an *experienced* human nature.
19. Readers with even a cursory knowledge of game theory will find this a familiar axiom. The point here is that one is conscious of never having complete and perfect information concerning all relevant aspects of an exchange, though this is naturally more important in some exchanges than in others (e.g., in employment contracts, where one party, the employee, always retains an unsettling amount of private, unverifiable information regarding his or her efforts and diligence). Many now see TC economics as an informal and inferior version of game theory. Posner (1993) has been famously critical; cf. Calvert's (1995) stimulating attempt to "game out" institutions. More generous and profitably engaged with the two approaches is Kreps 1999. That said, the basic criticism that there are many cases in which game theory deals better with problems of asymmetric information while avoiding the definitional and measurement problems already outlined is justified and therefore represents another potentially profitable method that ancient historians should pursue.

justly to be eschewed as dangerous generalizations, but in this book we need not go so far as to extend the problem of opportunism to every culture that ever traded: we need only assert that it was a problem for the ancient Mediterranean in order for this proposition to hold. One does not need to look far to find evidence of a deep-seated anxiety about "immoral" economic opportunism in ancient Mediterranean cultures.

We therefore have all the ingredients for the imposition of TC in the ancient world: expensive information, structural information asymmetries (e.g., highly variable goods), and the perceived potential for taking advantage of those asymmetries (i.e., opportunism). What, then, are some of the advantages of meditating on these dynamics in the ancient world and the TC that arise from them?

First, the mode of analysis is comparative without being normative. The tired debate between the "primitivist" and "modernist" views of the ancient economy depended on a normative comparison with the "modern" economy. This explains, in part, Finley's construction of an essentially "ancient" economy. Thankfully, the study of ancient economies since the late 1980s has moved beyond this essentializing dichotomy, shifting to a more nuanced focus on describing and explaining economic performance (Scheidel, Morris, and Saller 2007b; cf. Saller 2002). In meditating on TC in ancient economic settings, we take another step in this direction beyond normative models by building from the inside out. In focusing on the transaction, we attempt to articulate the strategies and choices available to ancient agents and organizations, thereby inviting our historical imaginations to inhabit the practical challenges ancient people faced in their economic lives as we attempt to recover the meanings of their decisions. We do not need to commit ourselves to any specific economic mentality when we do so: opportunism and the recognition of opportunism in economic exchange fit equally well with maximizing and satisficing behaviors.[20] It is thus a methodology that asks us to model economic behavior from the bottom up, keeping us close to our evidence, while committing us to a minimum number of a priori theoretical assumptions.

Second, by asking us to consider a range of possible alternatives at the

---

20. A "satisficing" decision or strategy is one that does not necessarily make the optimum use of all resources (something that is generally impossible to determine given our limited knowledge) but is sufficient to accomplish a goal. For this concept, see especially Simon 1983: 84–85. Ober discusses the concept in chapter 2 of this volume.

strategic and institutional levels, TC analysis encourages the building of explicit hypotheses and models. To understand a transaction properly, one must put it in context by considering the possible alternative routes, and must explain, to the extent possible, why the transaction was structured the way it was. One way to reconstruct this original continuum is to attempt to trace the TC associated with each alternative route one posits. This systematic re-creation of ancient problem solving helps to break down potentially artificial divisions and categories imposed on the evidence and facilitates the forging of productive new connections. It also creates a space for testable hypotheses. For example, if one suggests that the costs of transaction or policy x are higher than y because of z, one establishes a set of potentially falsifiable relations between institutions and agents if one subsequently discovers people choosing x in the continued presence of z or after the costs of z have demonstrably diminished.

If one is not careful, of course, one can fall into practicing a nonsensical counterfactual history: historians can only draw evidence from the world that actually existed, and the TC landscape would almost certainly have been different had one of the proposed alternatives actually been the state of the world.[21] To avoid falling into this fallacy, one must find actual states of the world that represent the alternatives. Two essays in this collection practice this method. François Lerouxel (chapter 7) studies the impact of the creation of the βιβλιοθήκη ἐγκτήσεων, a property register of the Roman imperial period, on credit markets. This is a simple before-and-after comparison, controlling for one variable (the establishment of the βιβλιοθήκη) and measuring its impact on the TC involved in structuring credit transactions. David Ratzan (chapter 8) builds a synchronic set of alternative routes for parties in Roman Egypt attempting to assign temporary property rights over people.[22] He does so by assembling a group of typical transactions (wet-nursing, apprenticeship, and service contracts), which have traditionally been studied as distinct contract types, into a superclass of contracts, justified by the fact that all deal with the same basic assignment problem. Taken together, these contracts suggest a set of available solutions to parties negotiating an underlying

21. Fischer 1970: 15–21; cf. Boldizzoni 2011: 13–15.
22. Ratzan is thus one of the only contributors to take a Williamsonian (synchronic) approach. Most other contributors are interested in pursuing the question of institutional performance over time, which is more of a Northian question. On the differences between these two approaches, see Hirsch and Lounsbury 1996.

property right in people (e.g., why do the nurses "lease" the slave children they raise instead of the owners hiring the nurses under employment contracts, which were used for other service relationships in the same period?). As with Lerouxel's case, the alternatives here are all taken from the world as it was. The extent to which parties actively "chose" between these alternatives is up for debate, but it is hard to see how changing the way in which apprenticeship contracts were drafted would have had an effect on the drafting of service contracts. A truly counterfactual—and thus impossible— question would be to ask what would have been the case had the default fundamental property rights in third-party dependents been other than what they were.

Perhaps the most important advantage that a TC approach provides to students of ancient economic history is a framework for thinking about the role of institutions in the economy, not simply how institutions might affect economic performance over time, but why they might exist in the first place. To take the issue of economic performance over time, the underlying assumption in this volume is that institutions were crucial to economic performance, although one must acknowledge the basic constraints on any ancient economy represented by population and technology, a theme emphasized in *The Cambridge Economic History of the Greco-Roman World*.[23] In other words, it is quite possible for two societies with the same basic endowment of population and technology to experience very different economic performances, and the issue is what role institutions might play in shaping different economic outcomes.[24]

From one perspective, we might expect institutions that hampered economic activity to disappear over time, giving way to more "efficient" institutions that allow resources to find their highest valued use (a theme addressed in Kehoe's essay in chapter 9). However, in historical societies, matters were never so simple. Many economic institutions persist despite their "inefficiency," because they promote the interests of powerful, well-connected groups. These are the people who are powerful enough to influence the design of institutions, and they would oppose any institutional changes that

---

23. Scheidel, Morris, and Saller 2007a.
24. This problem describes not only a historical research agenda in new institutional economics but also a comparative one in understanding differences in the economic performance and outcomes between contemporary economies. See, e.g., Harriss, Hunter, and Lewis 1995.

might threaten their privileges. Powerful groups can perpetuate institutions that would be swept away into the dustbin of history if "efficiency" were the only factor influencing institutional change. This is a theme emphasized by Sheilagh Ogilvie (2007) in an important article on medieval economic institutions, one that is cited in several essays in this volume, and Ogilvie's conclusions surely hold true for many ancient societies.

For example, in this volume Joseph Manning (chapter 4) discusses how the Ptolemaic monarchy fused its own bureaucratic institutions with already existing ones that were controlled by native Egyptian elites: the purpose of the monarchy was certainly not to promote anything recognizable as economic efficiency as we would understand it today but to capture revenues and maintain the stability of its rule. The monarchy required steady sources of revenue to maintain itself, but to gain the support of crucial elites, including very powerful priesthoods, it allowed local officials and temples to participate in its fiscal system by serving as loosely controlled agents. Thus numerous levels of government in Egypt exacted revenues and also worked to maintain a system from which they profited, probably at some considerable expense to society as a whole. That this system affected economic performance is strongly suggested by Andrew Monson's (2012) analysis of the changes in fiscal policy that the Romans implemented when they took over Egypt. Beginning in the first century C.E., the Romans replaced the Ptolemaic system of taxing agriculture with a simpler system, one that established fixed amounts of tax for most categories of land and at more modest levels than the Ptolemies had exacted. The result was that the private ownership of land grew in Roman Egypt, so that, over time, in terms of investment in private estates, Roman Egypt resembled most other provinces in the eastern part of the Roman Empire, with a class of landowners in major cities capable of holding civic offices much as the landowning classes did in other cities in the eastern part of the Roman Empire. In effect, the Romans reduced the TC for acquiring private land (which was possible under the Ptolemies), while at the same time removing some of the incentives of wealthier people to seek the offices in existence under the Ptolemies that allowed them to exact revenues.

So, in broad terms, the Roman administration in Egypt substantially changed the TC connected with the ownership of land, with historically crucial implications for the history of the region. It is difficult to determine whether the Roman system promoted a more widespread prosperity of the population of Egypt as a whole or, rather, mainly served the interests of a wealthy class of landowners who were expected to take up local offices as in other provinces. One could, for instance, argue that the Ptolemies and the pharaohs before them maintained direct control over land precisely to promote a more egalitarian distribution of wealth among Egypt's farming population. The example of Egypt suggests how the broad institutional structure of an ancient state could affect the organization and performance of the economy. Even structures that reduced transaction costs could affect the economic interests of different segments of society in markedly different ways. But by examining economic institutions in ancient societies in terms of TC, we can come to a better understanding of the capacity of an ancient economy to grow or at least to perform to its full potential, while at the same time appreciate the likely effects of institutional arrangements on people across society. A TC approach to ancient economic history, then, provides us with a deeper understanding of the relationships that characterized the economies of ancient societies.

Transaction Costs and Ancient Law

TC are also important at the level of the individual transactions involving private parties. In this connection, one of the major questions addressed by the essays in this volume concerns the role that ancient states made in establishing legal norms and institutions that affected transaction costs. It in not impossible to imagine that an ancient state could be wholly unaware of or indifferent to the need to facilitate economic activity.[25] The issue, then, is what role law and legal institutions played in society. We can usefully approach this issue by considering the case of the Roman Empire, both because of its rich legal tradition and because the role of law in the Roman Empire and the possible effects it had on the economy have been the subject of a great deal of recent debate.

In broad terms, one must recognize that neither the Roman Empire nor any ancient state represented an "open-access society," in the formulation of North, Wallis, and Weingast in their recent book *Violence and Social Orders* (2009). In such societies, represented today by the United States, Canada, and western Europe, economic and legal relationships can be viewed as "imper-

---

25. Cf. the debate about why ancient states minted coins: see Howgego 1990; cf. van Alfen 2012.

sonal," to the extent that access to the protection of the law does not depend on patronage or other personal connections. In the view of North, Wallis, and Weingast, such societies are capable of supporting organizations that play important economic and political roles but that exist independently from any state support. In their analysis, Rome, like other ancient states, is a "natural state," one dominated by elite coalitions that cooperated to share social, political, and economic privileges.

Such a view is consistent with the way in which many ancient historians view the Roman Empire. For example, Peter Bang (2008) analyzes Rome as a "tributary empire," one whose essential purpose is to exact revenues from the empire's subjects to benefit a ruling elite. As such, the Roman Empire and other ancient polities could be viewed as "predatory states," and to the extent to which they took a long-term view to stabilizing their sources of revenues, the Roman Empire and other ancient states would be "stationary predators."[26] The ruling coalition that would benefit from such policies includes the emperor, the senatorial and equestrian classes, and the wealthy landowners who comprised the town councils across the empire. From this perspective, the law would serve mainly to benefit these elites, establishing or reinforcing structures that would help to maintain their economic, political, and social privileges. One could extend this conception of the "predatory state" to other ancient states as well. For example, Manning's essay in this volume (chapter 4) shows how the Ptolemaic monarchy organized its administration of Egypt in such a way as to capture revenues and left in place structures that it inherited to preserve the revenues of temple elites, a policy by means of which the Ptolemies hoped to gain the support of traditional Egyptian elites. The notion of the predatory state can be applied to specific policies. Thus, Alain Bresson in his essay (chapter 5), shows in detail how the monetary policy of the Ptolemies was designed to garner substantial revenues from foreign merchants doing business in Egypt.

From another perspective, we might consider how law and legal institutions can be viewed as serving a more impartial purpose, one of promoting social order without a direct agenda to support the interests of certain well-connected groups. In his recent and monumental study of the Roman jurists, Aldo Schiavone (2012) traces how the profession of Roman jurisprudence developed independently of politics. The jurists, professional legal experts, struggled to maintain their independence from political life until the late

---

26. See Barzel 2002.

principate, when they became part of the administration of the empire. In their work to refine Roman law, the jurists were guided by many forces, including current intellectual movements and their own senses of justice. Certainly, their views were affected by the interests of the elite classes from which they came, but it would be a gross oversimplification to argue that their work aimed simply at promoting the interests of the empire's elite classes. The question is, then, whether Roman law contributed to the economy by establishing contractual forms and legal remedies to resolve disputes in such a way as to facilitate efforts to enter into and maintain productive business relationships. The alternative is that the law did not do this, either because, in developing it, the jurists and other legal authorities were unaware of or indifferent to societal needs or because the law did not have such a broad reach, in that it did not establish the rules by which commercial relations in the Roman Empire were carried out.

If we broaden our historical perspective for a moment, it is certainly possible to detect efforts to make the law authoritative and predictable in other ancient societies besides Rome. To take the case of classical Athens, Edward Harris (2013) argues that procedures were established to assure that trials were conducted in accordance with the laws and not simply left to the judgment or caprice of the jurors. Before a case ever came to trial, the plaintiff had to declare the specific laws on the basis of which he was bringing his suit; the defendant could prepare his suit on this basis. As Josiah Ober points out in his essay in this volume (chapter 2), the fourth-century Athenians established special courts, δικαὶ ἐμπορικαί, for cases involving foreign merchants trading in Athens. In such courts, foreigners had standing to sue, and Adriaan Lanni (2006) argues that trials there were more predictable in their outcomes than in other Athenian courts, where social considerations might affect the jury's verdict (Harris and Lanni have very contrasting views of Athenian courts). The point was that these courts helped to attract foreign merchants to Athens by providing them with greater assurance that they would be able to protect their property rights while doing business there.[27] The impartial Athenian procedures for testing silver coinage that Ober discusses also contributed to this effort. Likewise, the relatively low costs that the Athenians established for bringing lawsuits, as discussed by Thür (chapter 1), helped to keep the courts accessible to people of modest wealth.

---

27. Cf. Ober 2010 on the connections between this expansion of legal access, the development of an ethic of impartiality, and the fourth-century Athenian belief in the "increased instrumental value of foreigners."

Certainly, many ancient states sought to establish procedures that made the law more accessible and predictable, and they also established institutions that could encourage economic activity. Take the example of the "archive of acquisitions," or βιβλιοθήκη ἐγκτήσεων, discussed by Lerouxel in chapter 7 and also by Uri Yiftach in chapter 6. The Roman administration in Egypt created this registry as a place in which the precise legal status of real estate, with all the obligations encumbering it, would be recorded. Such a registry reduced the uncertainty about title to land, which generally represented people's most valuable asset. As a consequence, as Lerouxel argues, landowners could capitalize their land more efficiently and realize more of its value, since the property registry created more transparency for creditors. Whether the loans that people took out on the security of their property tended to be used for productive purposes or were simply "consumer" loans is, of course, difficult to determine.

Perhaps a more important issue in understanding the role that law might play in transaction costs is whether it served to help private parties to contractual arrangements structure their agreements in relatively low-cost ways that allowed them to define their property rights and thus to reduce uncertainty. In the case of Roman law, the crucial issues concern the extent to which the Roman legal authorities responded to social needs in formulating the rules of private law, as well as the extent to which the Roman legal system was authoritative enough to establish the "rules of the game" for economic activity across society. On the one hand, the Roman Empire encompassed a wide variety of legal systems, including various forms of Greek law in the eastern provinces, as well as Greco-Egyptian law in Egypt,[28] and many arrangements were conducted in accordance with local laws or customs for which we have little evidence. On the other hand, the Roman emperor was the final arbiter of the law, and one of the basic functions of the emperor, at least by the Severan period, was to respond to petitions on matters of private law. The Romans established a whole office, headed by a high-ranking official called the a libellis, to handle such petitions. The Roman chancery's responses to such petitions, as preserved in the sixth-century Code of Justinian, are formulated in terms of Roman private law. In handling such petitions, the Roman chancery could not decide issues of fact, but it would decide how the law was to be applied, and the successful petitioner could use the emperor's

---

28. See now, e.g., Keenan, Manning, and Yiftach-Firanko 2014.

rescript to press his or her claim before a court back home. In addition, the emperor could use the process of responding to petitions to modify existing law, as emperors did in numerous areas of the law.[29] In the third century, after the promulgation of the *Constitutio Antoniniana* in 212 C.E., all free people in the Roman Empire were Roman citizens and thus, at least in theory, subject to Roman law. As Serena Connolly (2010) shows in her study of the responses that the imperial chancery under the emperor Diocletian made to such petitions in the years 293–94, the petitioners represented a broad range of social statuses and certainly included many people from outside the elite. Clearly, these people had confidence that the process of petitioning the emperor was worth their while. In the case of Roman Egypt, where the papyri preserve numerous petitions to the prefect or governor as well as to numerous local officials, the process of petitioning was central to people's efforts to protect their interests.[30] All of this suggests that the Roman legal system was authoritative enough to establish the "rules of the game" for economic activity across society. Without an authoritative system of law to establish rules by which to structure economic activities, people would have been left to their own devices to find ways to formulate and enforce agreements. So one of the major questions to consider when one evaluates the role of transaction costs in ancient economies is the interplay between private and public efforts to control transaction costs.

The authority of the legal institutions supporting Roman law does not rule out private solutions to the problem of transaction costs. If the costs of ascertaining and protecting property rights represent an impediment to economic activity by making it more expensive for people to enter into contracts, then logically the parties to a potential contract will have an incentive to reduce these costs to the extent possible. As Giuseppe Dari-Mattiacci points out in his concluding chapter to this volume, the parties to a contract will sometimes negotiate provisions that result in their sharing information, or they might structure contracts in such a way as to make the two parties' compliance with the provisions of the contract as transparent as possible. These are phenomena seen in the nursing and apprenticeship contracts in Roman Egypt analyzed in this volume by Ratzan (chapter 8).

Private ordering of contracts, backed up by self-help, represents part of

---

29. On the emperor as legislator, see Coriat 1997.
30. On petitions in Egypt, see Kelly 2011.

the solution to reducing transaction costs without the direct involvement or support of the state. But a broader issue concerns how people gain access to markets in the first place, that is, how they gain the information necessary to allow them to pursue potentially lucrative opportunities. Presumably, the parties to apprenticeship contracts in Roman Egypt knew one another, at least by reputation, and so had some assurance from the outset that the provisions of the contract would be honored. At the same time, the concentration of certain types of transactions, such as animal sales, at particular markets would tend to make it easier for trading partners to acquire information, as would their membership in trading associations (see below). But what would happen when people were engaging in trade or other commercial ventures on a larger scale, particularly ones that involved contracts with partners in distant locations? How did parties gain the information about potential trading partners that would encourage them to make a deal with the confidence that the partner would honor his or her obligations? In societies not characterized by open access, the capacity to enter into a trading relationship often depended on personal connections. As the Princeton economist Avinash Dixit argues in his book *Lawlessness and Economics: Alternative Modes of Governance* (2004), commercial enterprises in such a society usually revolve around personal relationships; it can be difficult for an outsider to enter into a market without a personal connection, either a business partner or even simply someone to vouch for his or her trustworthiness.

Whether or not the notion of a "natural state" as formulated by North, Wallis, and Weingast can usefully be applied to the Roman Empire, it seems clear that commercial and legal relationships in the Roman world were anything but impersonal and that much contracting was "relational," in the sense discussed by Dixit. Uncertainty about the reputation of potential trading partners would represent a transaction cost for economic actors (as discussed in the previous two sections above), and this would tend to make their property rights less certain. If there were impediments to seeking the protection of the law and legal institutions, these costs would be even greater, since property rights would be even less certain. In this situation, economic actors might develop methods to identify reliable trading partners, as well their own rules either to bolster the protections offered by the formal law or to maneuver around inconvenient legal institutions.

In his recent study of trading communities in the Roman Empire, Taco Terpstra (2013) emphasizes the key role that networks of individuals bound together by common business interests or even ethnic identity could play in commercial life. For Terpstra, these networks were vitally important to establish contacts and facilitate deal making. But they were also significant because they provided a means of enforcing contracts. This particular function of such networks was crucial, as Terpstra argues, because Roman law provided merchants with very weak protections. Since the state did not directly enforce contracts, it was basically left up to merchants to find private means to accomplish this purpose.[31] A major part of the solution, in Terpstra's view, was to create trading communities as more or less permanent institutions in cities with substantial interregional commerce. These would be communities of foreign traders at important commercial cities, such as communities of Syrians and other groups at the Campanian port of Puteoli, similar communities at Ostia and Rome, and communities of Roman merchants in commercially important cities in Asia Minor. Such communities would provide an entry into commercial life to fellow countrymen, while they would also function together to gain protection for people who otherwise might be marginal outsiders. Terpstra draws on Avner Greif's (2006) analysis of trading communities in the early medieval period, particularly the community that existed among the Maghrebi traders, Jewish merchants who had settled in various locations around the Mediterranean, especially in Sicily, Tunisia, and Egypt, as documented in the Cairo Geniza. The Jewish traders created their own "merchants' law" as a means of enforcing contracts and commercial relationships, and presumably trading communities in the ancient Mediterranean world did as well. Merchants' law would represent rules that a discrete community might create to enforce norms of behavior. For commercial relationships, one could imagine that the rules would enforce honest dealing in contracts, paying back debts when called on to do so, and perhaps providing other services, such as guaranteeing loans, for other members of the community. The reputation of members of the community would be crucial to their ability to conduct business.

The difference between the medieval world that Greif examines and the Roman Empire is that, in the former, the merchants' law of the Maghrebi traders compensated, to some extent, for the lack of a uniform set of laws to enforce the types of contracts involved in overseas commercial ventures. It

31. The weakness of the Roman state's enforcement of contracts is also a theme emphasized in Bang 2008.

would certainly be an exaggeration to claim that the Roman Empire had uniform commercial law across the Mediterranean. However, it also seems clear that the protections provided by Roman and provincial courts were more reliable than what one would expect in the early medieval period, since there was one overarching power structure in the Roman Empire. For dispute resolution, it seems likely that many groups develop their own private methods that operate independently from formal state-enforced law, even in societies in which the state's legal institutions are strong and authoritative. One famous example involves Shasta County in northern California, where Robert Ellickson (1991) has analyzed the informal methods, particularly social sanctions, that neighboring ranchers and farmers used to resolve disputes, specifically those arising when livestock caused damage to property belonging to farmers. Informal methods of dispute resolution did not completely supplant more formal ones; rather, they functioned as presumably low-cost methods of addressing disputes that did not involve great stakes. But the same people who dealt with their neighbors in a fashion that preserved harmony in the community could turn to the courts when more serious issues arose.

We should imagine that many groups of people in the ancient world established their own sets of norms that guided business relationships. In the Roman Empire, such groups would include the foreign merchants discussed by Terpstra, associations of people in various professions (e.g., weavers, documented by papyrological evidence from Roman Egypt), and even members of religious groups.[32] After all, the Roman senator Pliny the Younger, when investigating Christians in his role as governor of the province of Bithynia-Pontus, found out from two *ministrae* ("deaconesses") questioned under torture that Christians promised, among other things, not to deceive one another in business and not to refuse to return property held on deposit (*Ep.* 10.96.7). Somewhat earlier, Paul had recommended to the Christian community at Corinth that its members settle disputes informally among themselves rather than resorting to the courts and the scrutiny of pagans (1 Cor. 6.1–7). This is the type of mutual loyalty and support we would expect to see in many social groups. But the solidarity of a community and its preference to settle differ-

---

32. For various aspects of *collegia*, see van Nijf 1997; Liu 2009; Venticinque 2010; Hawkins 2012: 186–93.

ences involving its members does not mean that the law of the state played no role in establishing how economic activity would be organized.

Concerning Roman law, we can gain a better perspective on the complementary roles of formal law enforced by the state and the informal rules established by trading networks by considering the Murecine tablets, which preserve the archive of the Sulpicii. The Sulpicii were a group of bankers active at the busy port city of Puteoli at least from the twenties until the early sixties C.E., and their activities are a focal point of Terpstra's analysis of the trading communities at Puteoli. We know about their activities because of a collection of wax tablets recording various types of agreements and matters connected with lawsuits and settlements that was stored in a house at Pompeii, apparently still under some kind of renovation when Mt. Vesuvius erupted in August of 79.[33] The archive reveals that the Sulpicii, themselves freedmen, were involved in many business deals at Puteoli, involving other freedmen, including some from the imperial household, as well as other private individuals. The people with whom they did business included foreigners resident at Puteoli, many of whom were of peregrine status. What is striking about the archive is that all the contracts and other proceedings were arranged in accordance with Roman law. In fact, as Wolf (2001) observes, the Sulpicii could call on expert knowledge of the law when they arranged business deals.

It is likely that the law played a fundamental role in organizing the commercial life at Puteoli and, presumably, at many other cities in the Roman Empire. Roman law was authoritative for merchants and other people engaging in commerce because it provided a kind of infrastructure for supporting contracts and other commercial arrangements that private parties or even a community would be hard pressed to invent on their own. Consider what is likely to happen when people negotiate a contract for a business venture. It is often beyond the capacity of parties to a contract to negotiate all contingencies at the outset, because there are circumstances that are either unforeseeable or envisioned as not very likely to occur. In such circumstances, it would simply be too costly for the parties to spend time providing for all possible contingencies. Such contracts—and indeed to some extent all contracts—may be considered "incomplete," and disputes typically result when circum-

---

33. For discussion of the archive of the Sulpicii, which has produced a substantial bibliography, see especially Wolf 2001; Terpstra 2013: 9–49. The fullest publication of the archive is in Camodeca 1999.

stances arise that are not specifically envisioned by either party at the time when they entered into the contract. It is in precisely this situation that law and legal institutions can play a crucial role in reducing transaction costs.

The law can do this by establishing "default" rules to contracts, that is, rules on which the parties to a contract can fall back when circumstances arise for which they had not made a specific provision. The "default" rules to Roman lease contracts are addressed in this volume by Kehoe (chapter 9). Default rules provide a kind of template that cover the contingencies that would otherwise commonly lead to disputes between parties to a contract. Having clear-cut default rules relieves the parties to a contract of the necessity to reinvent the wheel by engaging in a lengthy set of negotiations to cover the types of economic relationships into which people commonly enter across society. Transparent default rules reduce the costs that people bear when entering into mutually productive contractual arrangements by defining rights and obligations precisely, specifically by outlining what rights and responsibilities each party has whenever one party is unable to fulfill his or her obligations or demonstrably breaches the contract. Default rules thus provide a broad set of expectations to guide people as they pursue an economic relationship based on a contract, with each party gaining some protection from the opportunistic behavior of the other without the need to define each and every possible defection. In a word, default rules make the outcome of contingencies that interfered with this relationship predictable.

Moreover, the people documented in the archive of the Sulpicii regularly brought lawsuits against one another. This does not mean that they wound up in court all the time, but the threat of a lawsuit provided an impetus to settle. Apparently, these people could use the possibility of a lawsuit to achieve their immediate economic goals without destroying the personal relationships that were certainly essential to long-term commercial success in Puteoli and other trading communities in the Mediterranean. They could use the threat of a lawsuit to force settlements precisely because the courts were seen as authoritative in deciding such suits in a predictable and just matter and also because one could apparently expect that the decisions of the courts would be enforced.

Using a lawsuit to settle disputes can be seen, more broadly, as a way to reduce transaction costs. Lawsuits are costly, but perhaps even more costly is the possibility that a dispute could go on without a resolution. A merchants' law system could certainly provide norms for merchants in a closed community and promote solidarity among them, but it is not clear that ad hoc rules could provide the same types of solutions to disputes that an authoritative legal system would. Legal disputes are most likely to arise when conditions develop that neither party entering into a contract had anticipated: to name a few examples, a drought might make a tenant unable to pay his rent; a ship might be delayed, leaving a merchant unable to pay back a bottomry loan; or anticipated prices for wine might not emerge, making it impossible for a wine merchant to pay back a loan in full. If merchants' laws enforced norms of honest behavior, such as those documented in the Cairo Geniza, it is not clear how enforcing such norms would help in the situations just described or in many other contingencies that led to legal disputes. The Roman courts could resolve such disputes because Roman law (or, to a lesser but still significant extent, the provincial law systems over which the Romans presided) defined the property rights and obligations of people precisely in the case of contingencies that they had no way of foreseeing. As discussed in several chapters in this volume, the possibility of going to court gave the parties to a contract a kind of "legal endowment," to use the term originally coined by Mnookin and Kornhauser (1979) in their analysis of American divorce law. This legal endowment, representing what the parties could expect to receive if they actually went to court, would establish a baseline for negotiations.

From this perspective, the value of a legal system to the economy could be measured by the extent to which default rules actually represent rules that typical parties would have chosen had they had the time and capacity to do so (untailored default rules) or that the specific parties to a contract would have chosen under the same conditions (tailored default rules). When default rules do not answer the needs of people entering into contracts, we should expect that, over time, the legal system would change so as to accommodate them. We can trace such a responsiveness in Roman law in an area of the law that played an important role in the agrarian economy, namely, contracts to purchase wine. As Éva Jakab (2009: 123–86) argues in her authoritative analysis of the management of risk in sales of wine in the Roman world, sales in advance of the vintage played a crucial role in making the production of wine a profitable enterprise. A number of such advance contracts are preserved on papyri from late Roman Egypt, but they were almost certainly common in other periods in Egypt and in other parts of the Roman Empire. For example, the Roman senator Pliny the Younger sold the vintage on his Tuscan estates to wine merchants in advance of the vintage (*Ep.* 8.2). Advance sales were advantageous because they provided the producer with much needed funds to finance the production of wine, while the merchants buying the wine would secure for themselves a supply of wine at a favorable and predictable price and would so avoid the necessity of bidding against one another after the vintage. Probably, however, the most compelling reason for such contracts centered on the need of producers, especially ones operating on a relatively modest scale, to secure funds in advance to make it possible to produce a vintage. From the perspective of classical Roman law, however, such contracts posed a problem.

As Jakab shows, in many Egyptian contracts, the sales took place as many as sixth months before delivery. In the meantime, the vineyard owner would take in the vintage, press the grapes, and allow the wine to ferment for a period of months, at which time it would become usable. This arrangement made sense because the wine merchant was acquiring a crop that the vineyard owner was in the process of producing, and it would hardly be feasible for the merchant to remove the wine from the producer before it fermented. In classical Roman law, however, if the buyer did not take immediate delivery once the sale was complete, the seller would only be responsible for *custodia*, the safekeeping of the object sold. In the case of wine sales, the producer would have little incentive to take steps to assure the quality of the wine, since the producer would only be responsible for losses arising from his or her fault. The merchant would simply have to trust the producer, which is hardly a satisfactory solution. Wine merchants and producers in Egypt found a way to bargain around this inconvenient set of default rules, according the right of the purchaser to approve the quality of the wine when taking delivery. This was a sensible arrangement because the producer of the wine was the person in the best position to monitor the quality of the wine and to make sure that the eventual product was wine of the quality that the merchant had contracted to purchase.[34] Wine merchants in Egypt had the right to approve or reject the wine at the time of delivery. In effect, wine producers and merchants found a way to create a new allocation of risk that imposed on the producer the responsibility for the quality of the wine. The jurist Gaius (*Dig.* 18.6.16) recognized that such contracts could be enforceable under Roman law. Arguably, the papyrological evidence for sales of wine represents an arrangement widespread throughout the Mediterranean, one

---

34. See Posner and Rosenfield 1977 for the efficiency gained by imposing risk on the best insurer.

that the Roman legal authorities incorporated into Roman law to make the law respond better to society's needs.

The preceding survey suggests the complex role that formal law might play in affecting the TC surrounding contractual arrangements. Certainly, the administrative policies of ancient states affected the capacity of people to invest in various enterprises and to enter into potentially beneficial contractual arrangements. Within the overall institutional setting provided by an ancient state, the law could play a crucial role in reducing TC by defining and protecting property rights: the law could reduce the incentives for opportunistic behavior as well as the likelihood of disputes, by creating clear-cut, consistent, and (in the best-case scenario) transparent rules to define any number of economic relationships. Certainly, private individuals or groups of people such as the trading groups studied by Terpstra might devise rules of their own to ease or enforce transactions. But the case of contracts to purchase wine ahead of the vintage suggests that one response of formal law to private initiatives that proved to be advantageous was to recognize and enforce them as valid legal agreements.

Contents of This Volume

The essays in this volume address basic issues concerning the role that TC played in ancient economies. Some of the essays focus on how administrative policies might serve to reduce TC, through the development of authoritative legal institutions to resolve disputes or through maintaining access to these legal institutions for a broad population. Other essays address more directly the role that law might play in TC, either by focusing on the types of negotiations that individual actors might undertake to do this or by examining how general rules for contracting could affect TC. In the case of Ptolemaic Egypt, the issue is a bit different, since the monarchy effectively raised TC in specific ways as a means of securing revenues for itself and other key groups. The underlying assumption in all of the essays is that ancient states had the capacity to influence transaction costs significantly. From this perspective, it is legitimate to consider the possibility that ancient states could formulate legal and administrative policies to influence economic life. This is to say not that ancient states had economic policies as we would understand them in the modern world but, rather, that they were conscious of the effects of their policies on the ability of people to invest their wealth and to enter into contractual relationships.

We have grouped the essays roughly by culture and chronology. We begin in classical Greece (chapters 1–2), then move to Egypt from the New Kingdom to the Roman period (chapters 3–8), before finally turning to the Roman world outside of Egypt and a last discussion based in late antiquity (chapters 9–10). The coda to the volume is an essay by Giuseppe Dari-Mattiacci (chapter 11), who draws together the themes he finds in the preceding chapters and comments on them from his perspective as an economist.

The seeming pride of place that Egypt occupies at the center of this volume is almost entirely the result of the sort of evidence preserved there, and Egypt is something of an accidental category in this sense. Manning's essay (chapter 4) is concerned with the limitations and consequences of Ptolemaic governance strategies on TC within Egypt, while Bresson's essay (chapter 5) considers much the same question while looking in the opposite direction, at merchants coming from the outside the Ptolemaic currency zone and contending with its intentionally (as Bresson argues) frustrating currency controls. In fact, in pointed contrast to Manning's chapter, there is nothing at all "Egyptian" in Bresson's discussion. Both of these essays, then, are studies of Hellenistic institutions and strategies from a TC perspective based on papyrological evidence, together representing the two faces of the Hellenistic imperial project. One would therefore be justified in seeing the essays of Thür, Ober, Manning, and Bresson (chapters 1, 2, 4, and 5) as forming a group of case studies on the Greek experience with TC and institutions in the classical and Hellenistic periods.

The same may be said for chapters 6–8, as each investigates an institution established by the Roman order. Yiftach (chapter 6) investigates the notarial fees in a system of *grapheia* that was revamped in the Roman period. Lerouxel (chapter 7) studies the effects that the establishment of a Roman office of property registration had on credit markets. Ratzan (chapter 8) studies a set of contracts for transaction types only known from the Roman period. It is not difficult to see the first two chapters as studies in Romanization (to use a controversial but convenient word): record keeping for fiscal reasons was an imperial project, not one limited to the province of Egypt. This is true in the case of Ratzan's chapter as well: wet-nursing obviously predated the Romans, but wet-nursing contracts are an entirely Roman phenomenon.[35]

---

35. Cf. Bagnall 1995: 22–24 on the change in the typology of documents during the Roman period.

It may be that for some interested in Greek and Roman history, Egypt is still too far afield. The arguments against Egypt's exceptionalism are too well worn to be worth rehearsing here; and, in any case, the entire direction of this old polemic is, by this point, misguided. After the classical period, the "Greek" and "Roman" experience was, for the majority of the Mediterranean basin, one of imperialism and cultural negotiation. The evidence from Egypt allows us to recover what this meant in practice, both from the perspective of cultural and political elites and from that of those who worked within the regimes they ruled. If we are after the lived reality of the ancient experience and the ancient problems their institutions were meant to address, Egypt becomes one of our most important historical laboratories, at least for the questions TC analysis raises.

Gerhard Thür begins his essay (chapter 1) with a discussion of the legal costs generally associated with litigation and contracting in classical Athens and of their impact on legal and commercial activity. He thus begins in the tradition of those who measure concrete transaction fees. He ends his chapter, however, with an investigation into three particular areas in which the law helped to optimize economic equilibrium between contracting partners: public auctions, the use of escrow in legal suits, and the leasing of property administered by guardians of minors.

Chapter 2, by Josiah Ober, explains several distinctive and initially puzzling features of Nikophon's law on silver coinage, in light of the Athenian state's attempt to drive down TC in order to maintain Athenian public revenues and private profits in the postimperial era. He suggests that the law was intended to even the playing field of trade by ensuring noncitizens access to an impartial system of mechanisms for coin verification and dispute resolution. For Ober, Nikophon's law is an example of the Athenian state's concern for adjusting established institutions in a way that lowered the TC associated with trading in the Athenian market, by reducing information and legal asymmetries.

With chapter 3, by Brian Muhs, we move to Egypt. Muhs deftly traces the development of documentation and enforcement practices over the course of a millennium, from the New Kingdom to the Saite Period. His study, fascinating in its own right, examines the relationship between religious, legal, and political institutions and strategies (if we may so divide them) and the pursuit by individuals to perfect and enforce their property rights. His chapter also serves to set the stage for the chapters that follow, by giving a sense of the social, economic, and legal landscape that the Ptolemies and Romans inherited. Some of what Muhs discusses may seem familiar and redolent of the *longue durée*: for example, the difficulty parties had in achieving definitive closure on their disputes through the courts. Other elements highlight the institutional changes to come: oaths and oracles had a distinctly different, more marginalized role in economic transactions in the Ptolemaic and Roman periods.

The chapter by Joseph Manning (chapter 4) meditates on the theme of continuity and change by focusing on the broad changes that Ptolemaic rule brought to Egypt. The Ptolemies did not create entirely new structures for property rights and contracts but built on existing institutions. One aspect of this policy was to allow traditional elites to maintain their privileges, since they could exact revenues from land that they controlled, notably land in the hands of temples. But important innovations under the Ptolemies included public auctions of state contracts, which became a new source of income for the people able to secure these. In addition, the Ptolemies introduced Greek legal norms into Egypt, but they had to fuse these with a long tradition of local law, the key players in which were Demotic scribes. Manning examines both how the Demotic system of contracting affected TC and also the long-term changes that the Ptolemies fostered in this type of law, such as the tendency for contracts to be witnessed and registered.

In chapter 5, Alain Bresson offers a rereading of *Pap.Cair.Zen.* I 59021. This famous letter from the Zenon archive illustrates the difficulties associated with the exchange of gold and silver in the Ptolemaic closed currency system, which include the imposition of long delays for merchants. To explain the state of affairs at the Alexandrian mint as it is communicated by the writer of the letter, who has an unusually good view of some of the mint's internal workings, Bresson appeals to medieval mints as possible comparanda. He suggests that policies similar to those found in medieval mints, which prized control above all other considerations, were established by the Ptolemies. These and other policies pushed up TC. Here, then, we have a case of a (socially) "inefficient" institution supported by a political elite willing and able to seek and extract rents on political order.

Uri Yiftach (chapter 6) studies a particular fee associated with drafting documents in Roman Egypt, which is recorded in the registries that survive from the notarial offices where the documents were drafted and recorded. The fee is variable, and the nature of the feeing pattern has constituted a scholarly crux since the publication of the registries more than seventy-five years ago. As with chapter 1, we here have an essay devoted to the first sort of TC: clearly, these were fees that helped make markets and that people were—up to a point—prepared to pay. Yiftach, however, moves beyond description and proposes a working hypothesis on the policy motives lying behind the fee, suggesting that it was a lever by which the Romans consciously attempted to manipulate and control certain markets in order to protect various interests, such as maintaining the property of the family as a cohesive economic entity.

In an important contribution stemming from his recent dissertation, François Lerouxel (chapter 7) argues that the establishment of the βιβλιοθήκη ἐγκτήσεων, an official property registry instituted in Egypt under the Romans, lowered the TC associated with mortgages and thus supported the growth of credit in Roman Egypt. All property had to be registered, and all transactions associated with property, whether mortgages or sales, had to have the approval of the registry to proceed legally. This protocol had the effect (whether intended or not) of lowering the risks of loaning on the chief asset in the ancient world, real property, since the title would be guaranteed and all encumbrances would be recorded by the office. While this may have been one of the salient effects of the establishment of the βιβλιοθήκη ἐγκτήσεων, Lerouxel doubts that this was a reason for its creation, which he instead links to the state's desire to track property that would stand as security for those undertaking liturgical obligations.

In chapter 8, David Ratzan explores how contract functioned as an economic and legal institution in Roman Egypt by examining how it operated as a "governance structure" organizing wet-nursing, apprenticeship, and labor transactions in Roman Egypt. The term *governance structure*, taken from the new institutional economics, draws attention to the way in which the form of an exchange responds to important features or dimensions of the transaction, including, for example, the nature of the goods exchanged and the envisioned length of the economic relationship. Thus we know intuitively that it makes sense to buy a couple of apples from one of the vendors in a farmer's market but to write a contract when buying a house. Thinking of these exchanges as being mediated by different governance structures, however, presses us to explain precisely why we arrange some transactions as market exchanges and others as contracts. The transactions Ratzan discusses all required the parties to negotiate a property right that parents, guardians, or owners had in their dependent minors. Legally responsible adults had the right to remove their dependents at will from the care or power of others, to whom temporary control had been assigned. This was a right that posed an obvious risk to anyone who sought to exploit such minors economically, like a master craftsman taking an apprentice. Ratzan's focused study recovers some of the social and legal complexities involved in understanding how people in an ancient society might use and enforce contracts to pursue economic goals.

In chapter 9, Dennis Kehoe considers broader issues surrounding contracts, by examining the degree to which agency contracts in Roman law could be considered economically efficient. The issue is whether the legal rules surrounding contracts established useful incentives for people to enter into productive business relationships and enforced property rights in a clear and predictable manner. This was an important question in relation to agency, since it is often observed that Roman law did not develop adequate governance structures to support increasingly integrated commercial markets in the Mediterranean world. Theoretical models drawn from the new institutional economics provide an important perspective on understanding the incentives created by contracts in Roman law, but these incentives also have to be understood against the background of social institutions and even ideology.

In chapter 10, Rudolf Haensch addresses in a late Roman context the fundamental issue that Thür examines for classical Athens: the degree to which an ancient state made its legal institutions available to the broad population. In any society, courts and other legal institutions are costly, and at issue is whether these costs are imposed on the litigants alone or are absorbed more broadly by society. The Roman Empire seems to be a society that imposed some but certainly not all of the costs of litigation on the litigants themselves. Focusing on a fee schedule from late antiquity that is preserved on an inscription from Caesarea, Haensch seeks to correct the common assumptions among scholars that the Roman state under the principate (during the first three centuries C.E.), exacted few, if any, fees from litigants and that the fees soared in late antiquity. Rather, as Haensch shows, there was likely to have been a great deal of continuity in fees from the principate to late antiquity. His conclusion that fees for litigating were substantial has important implications for understanding the strength of Roman legal institutions and the degree to which they were available to broad segments of the empire's population.

In chapter 11, Giuseppe Dari-Mattiacci, an economist with scholarly interests in the ancient world, offers his perspectives on the essays in the volume. One of the major issues he addresses concerns the complementary roles that states and individuals acting privately might play in efforts to control TC.

Bibliography

Allen, D. W. 1991. "What Are Transaction Costs?" *Research in Law and Economics* 14: 1–18.

Bagnall, R. S. 1995. *Reading Papyri, Writing Ancient History.* London.

Bang, P. 2008. *The Roman Bazaar: A Comparative Study of Trade and Markets in a Tributary Empire.* Cambridge.

Bang, P. 2009. "The Ancient Economy and New Institutional Economics." *JRS* 99: 194–206.

Barzel, Y. 2002. *A Theory of the State: Economic Rights, Legal Rights, and the Scope of the State.* Cambridge.

Boldizzoni, F. 2011. *The Poverty of Clio: Resurrecting Economic History.* Cambridge.

Calvert, R. "The Rational Choice Theory of Institutions: Cooperation, Coordination, and Communication." In J. S. Banks and E. A. Hanushek, eds., *Modern Political Economy: Old Topics, New Directions,* 216–67. Cambridge.

Camodeca, G. 1999. *Tabulae Pompeianae Sulpiciorum, edizione critica dell'archivio dei Sulpicii.* 2 vols. Vetera: Ricerche di storia epigrafia e antichità 12. Rome.

Carroll, G. R., and D. J. Teece, eds. 1999. *Firms, Markets, and Hierarchies: The Transaction Cost Economics Perspective.* New York.

Coase, R. 1937. "The Nature of the Firm." *Economica* 4: 386–405.

Coase, R. 1960. "The Problem of Social Cost." *Journal of Law and Economics* 3: 1–44.

Connolly, S. 2010. *Lives behind the Laws: The World of the "Codex Hermogenianus."* Bloomington, IN.

Coriat, J.-P. 1997. *Le prince législateur: La technique législative des Sévères et les methods de création du droit imperial à la fin du principat.* BEFAR 224. Rome.

Dixit, A. 2004. *Lawlessness and Economics: Alternative Modes of Governance.* Princeton.

Eggertson, T. 1990. *Economic Behavior and Institutions.* Cambridge.

Ellickson, R. C. 1989. "The Case for Coase and against Coaseanism." *Yale Law Journal* 99: 611–30.

Ellickson, R. C. 1991. *Order without Law: How Neighbors Settle Disputes.* Cambridge, MA.

Fischer, D. H. 1970. *Historians' Fallacies: Towards a Logic of Historical Thought.* New York.

Frier, B. W., and D. Kehoe. 2007. "Law and Economic Institutions." In Scheidel, Morris, and Saller 2007a: 113–43.

Greif, A. 2006. *Institutions and the Path to the Modern Economy: Lessons from Medieval Trade.* Political Economy of Institutions and Decisions. Cambridge.

Harris, E. 2013. "The Plaint in Athenian Law and Legal Procedure." In M. Faraguna, ed., *Archives and Archival Documents in Ancient Societies*, 143–62 Legal Documents in Ancient Societies IV. Trieste.

Harriss, J., J. Hunter, and C. M. Lewis, eds. 1995. *New Institutional Economics and Third World Development*. London.

Hawkins, C. 2012. "Manufacturing." In W. Scheidel, ed., *The Cambridge Companion to the Roman Economy*, 175–94. Cambridge.

Hirsch, P. M., and M. D. Lounsbury. 1996. "Rediscovering Volition: The Institutional Economics of Douglass C. North." *Academy of Management Review* 21: 872–84.

Howgego, C. 1990. "Why Did Ancient States Strike Coins?" *Numismatic Chronicle* 150: 1–25.

Jakab, É. 2009. *Risikomanagement beim Weinkauf: Periculum und Praxis im Imperium Romanum*. Münchener Beiträge zur Papyrusforschung und antiken Rechtsgeschichte 99. Munich.

Johnstone, S. 2011. *A History of Trust in Ancient Greece*. Chicago.

Keenan, J. G., J. G. Manning, and U. Yiftach-Firanko, eds. 2014. *Law and Legal Practice in Egypt from Alexander to the Arab Conquest*. Cambridge.

Kehoe, D. 2007. *Law and the Rural Economy in the Roman Empire*. Ann Arbor.

Kelly, B. 2011. *Petitions, Litigation, and Social Control in Roman Egypt*. Oxford.

Klaes, M. 2000a. "The Birth of the Concept of Transaction Costs: Issues and Controversies." *Industrial and Corporate Change* 9: 567–93.

Klaes, M. 2000b. "The History of the Concept of Transaction Costs: Neglected Aspects." *Journal of the History of Economic Thought* 22: 191–216.

Kreps, David. 1999. "Markets and Hierarchies and (Mathematical) Economic Theory." In Carroll and Teece 1999: 121–55.

Lanni, A. 2006. *Law and Justice in the Courts of Classical Athens*. Cambridge.

Liu J. 2009. *Collegia Centonariorum: The Guilds of Textile Dealers in the Roman West*. Leiden.

Manning, J. G. 2010. *The Last Pharaohs: Egypt under the Ptolemies, 305–30 BC*. Princeton.

Mnookin, R. H., and L. Kornhauser. 1979. "Bargaining in the Shadow of the Law: The Case of Divorce." *Yale Law Journal* 88: 950–97.

Monson, A. 2012. *From the Ptolemies to the Romans: Political and Economic Change in Egypt*. Cambridge.

North, D. C. 1981. *Structure and Change in Economic History*. New York.

North, D. C. 1990. *Institutions, Institutional Change, and Economic Performance*. Cambridge.

North, D. C., J. J. Wallis, and B. R. Weingast 2009. *Violence and Social Orders: A Conceptual Framework for Interpreting Recorded Human History*. Cambridge.

Ober, J. 2008. *Democracy and Knowledge: Innovation and Learning in Classical Athens*. Princeton.

Ober, J. 2010. "The Instrumental Value of Others and Institutional Change: An Athenian Case Study." In R. Rosen and I. Sluiter, eds., *Valuing Others in Classical Antiquity*, 155–78. Leiden.

Ogilvie, S. 2007. "'Whatever Is, Is Right'? Economic Institutions in Pre-industrial Europe." *Economic History Review* 60, no. 4: 649–84.

Posner, R. A. 1993. "Law and Economics Meets the New Institutional Economics." *Journal of Institutional and Theoretical Economics* 149: 73–87.

Posner, R. A., and A. M. Rosenfield. 1977. "Impossibility and Related Doctrines in Contract Law: An Economic Analysis." *Journal of Legal Studies* 6: 83–118.

Saller, R. P. 2002. "Framing the Debate over Growth in the Ancient Economy." In W. Scheidel and S. von Reden, eds., *The Ancient Economy*, 251–69. Edinburgh.

Scheidel, W., I. Morris, and R. P. Saller, eds. 2007a. *The Cambridge Economic History of the Greco-Roman World*. Cambridge.

Scheidel, W., I. Morris, and R. P. Saller, eds. 2007b. "Introduction." In Scheidel, Morris, and Saller 2007a: 1–12.

Schiavone, A. 2012. *The Invention of Law in the West*. Translated by Jeremy Carden and Antony Shugaar. Cambridge, MA.

Simon, H. A. 1983. *Reason in Human Affairs*. Stanford.

Smith, A. [1776] 2000. *The Wealth of Nations*. Modern Library Edition. New York.

Stigler, G. J. 1972. "The Law and Economics of Public Policy: A Plea to the Scholars." *Journal of Legal Studies* 1: 1–12.

Terpstra, T. T. 2013. *Trading Communities in the Roman World: A Micro-Economic and Institutional Perspective*. Leiden.

van Alfen, P. 2012. "Problems in the Political Economy of Archaic Greek Coinage." *Notae Numismaticae* 7: 13–32.

van Nijf. O. 1997. *The Civic World of Professional Associations in the Roman East*. Leiden.

Venticinque, P. 2010. "Family Affairs: Guild Regulations and Family Relationships in Roman Egypt." *GRBS* 50: 273–94.

Wallis, J. J., and D. C. North. 1986. "Measuring the Transaction Sector in the American Economy, 1870–1970." In S. L. Engerman and R. E. Gallman, eds., *Long-Term Factors in American Economic Growth*, 95–162. Chicago.

Wang, N. 2007. " Measuring Transaction Costs: Diverging Approaches, Contending Practices." *Division of Labor and Transaction Costs* 2: 111–46.

Williamson, O. 1971. "The Vertical Integration of Production: Market Failure Considerations." *American Economic Review* 6: 112–23.

Wolf, J. G. 2001. "Der neue pompejanische Urkundenfund: Zu Camodecas 'Edizione critica dell'archivio puteolano dei Sulpicii.'" *ZRG* 118: 73–132.

CHAPTER 1

Transaction Costs in Athenian Law

Gerhard Thür

One of the major issues in an analysis of the role that transaction costs played in the ancient economy is to examine the extent to which a legal system might control the costs of the most important legal acts that individuals could undertake. Doing so would have helped to make the legal system more authoritative in protecting property rights, since parties to transactions would have had a greater incentive to protect their interests through the legal system rather than through extralegal means. The costs of using legal protections are the specific topic of three other essays in this collection, those of Uri Yiftach (chapter 6), François Lerouxel (chapter 7), and Rudolf Haensch (chapter 10). The legal system of classical Athens provides an appropriate place to begin such a study, since the costs of court procedures there, in contrast to other places in the ancient world, are well documented. In this essay, I will focus on three topics important for understanding the role of transaction costs in a legal system: first, court fees, second, fees on and the costs associated with contracts, and, finally, the social mechanisms within a legal system that are designed to balance the interests of parties to lawsuits or contracts.

Court Fees

In Athens, there was a complex system of fees for public and private lawsuits.[1] In this essay, in the interests of space, I will concentrate on trials con-

---

1. No comprehensive work exists on the fees in public and private lawsuits. For Athens, see the sources and literature quoted in nn. 4 and 9–11 below.

cerning private transactions. These trials took place before different tribu-
nals. Suits between citizens usually came before the Forty. The parties had to
submit their cases to a so-called official arbitrator chosen by lot, or a διαιτητής.
This man held a preliminary hearing exactly as a magistrate vested with jurisdiction might. The task of the διαιτητής was to prepare the case for the
main hearing before the court, or δικαστήριον, or—when possible—to recon-
cile the litigants. The parties were always free to agree with the settlement
proposed by the διαιτητής, in which case no trial took place.[2] This was an
extremely efficient procedure, saving costs for both the state and the parties.
The δικαστήριον was called to hear the case only if one of the litigants was
unsatisfied with the mediation of the διαιτητής; then the matter was decided
expeditiously in one session, with no possibility of appeal. For his work, the
διαιτητής received one drachma from each litigant, and he could exact an
additional drachma for each day that the hearing was prolonged (in all likelihood from the party that had requested a delay).[3]

Court fees, or πρυτανεῖα, were to be paid when a member of the Forty
brought the case before the δικαστήριον.[4] In commercial cases, noncitizens
were permitted to bring their claims before one of the six θεσμοθέται drawn
from the board of the nine supreme magistrates, the ἄρχοντες. Citizens and
foreigners had to pay the same court fees: for an amount in dispute under
one hundred drachmas, there were no fees; when the amount was between
one hundred and one thousand drachmas, each of the litigants had to pay
three drachmas; for disputes worth more than one thousand drachmas, the
fee was set at thirty drachmas for each litigant. The state thus collected six or
sixty drachmas for every major trial. The litigant who lost had to reimburse
the winner for his πρυτανεῖα charges.

The treaty between Stymphalos and Demetrias ca. 303–300 B.C.E. envisioned an even more economically efficient process: each party had to deposit a fee equal to one-tenth of the amount in dispute. The court kept safe
the double amount, and the winner could withdraw his advance immediately.[5] The reason for this regulation was the international character of the
treaty. Since the litigants came from different poleis, such cash advances to

2. Thür 2009: 411.
3. Harpocrat., s.v. παράστασις; Poll. 8.39, 127; Harrison 1968–71: 2:67.
4. For the following paragraph, see Poll. 8.38; Harrison 1968–71: 2:93; Scafuro 2011: 172 n. 115.
5. Thür and Taeuber 1994 (hereinafter *IPArk*): no. 17.57–58. and pp. 230–32 (see discussion there also about other poleis).

the court were the safest way for the winner to get his fee reimbursed. In Athens, no judicial magistrate was allowed to accept court fees on deposit. Instead, he charged and exacted only the amount due to the polis and immediately forwarded this amount to the treasury. It therefore fell to the winner to recover his money, even against a foreigner. To offset the risk for the losing party's not paying, however, foreigners had to secure Athenian guarantors. Athens thus saved on administrative costs and took the burden off the magistrates, while leaving the risk and trouble of collection and reimbursement to the victorious party in a suit.

In Athens, private trials were surprisingly inexpensive. For disputes up to one thousand drachmas (categories 1 and 2), the state took either nothing or only six drachmas. In those cases, a δικαστήριον of 201 judges was impaneled. They were chosen by lot from the entire pool of citizens who had sworn the dikastic oath and were present the morning of the court date. At the end of the day, each juror received three obols (half a drachma);[6] the total cost of adjudication was therefore 100.5 drachmas. If one δικαστήριον could hear and decide four trials a day—this is a conservative estimate: in my own opinion, it was likely to have been closer to eight[7]—the state had revenues of at most forty-eight drachmas and expenses of 100.5 drachmas. In other words, although the fees the state collected obviously depended on the number of trials and their respective valuations (i.e., under or over one hundred drachmas), we may surmise that it had net expenses of at least 52.5 drachmas a day. One can estimate more precisely the costs of trials of the third category, those disputes for amounts over one thousand drachmas. For these cases, a court of 401 judges was impaneled. Since such cases required longer arguments, these courts probably conducted only two or three trials in one sitting. The state thus took in 120 or 180 drachmas, against a cost of 200.5 drachmas for the judges. The cost to the state for the sitting of the larger δικαστήριον was therefore either 20.5 or 80.5 drachmas, depending solely on the number of trials it was able to conduct. Given the preceding calculations, it would seem that the court fees never covered the whole expenses for the δικαστήρια. Mogens Herman Hansen has recently calculated the overall annual cost to the state for all δικαστήρια, private and public, as between twenty-two and thirty-seven talents.[8] Since he did not take into account the fees paid by the parties in private cases and the

6.   *Ath. Pol.* 62.2.
7.   Thür 2000: 43 with n. 12.
8.   Hansen 1995: 195.

fines in public ones, the actual cost was substantially lower; there are too many unknowns to estimate it more exactly.

The state tried, by various means, to prevent citizens and foreigners from abusing the legal system. I will not deal extensively here with the most well-known methods. These include the fine of one thousand drachmas on a citizen who brought a public charge and then dropped the prosecution (before a δικαστήριον of five hundred judges) or failed to secure one-fifth of the votes,[9] as well as the παρακαταβολή, the required deposit for claimants in probate cases equal to one-tenth of the value of the estate and likely forfeited to the estate if the claim was rejected.[10]

In connection with the costs of litigation, the ἐπωβελία is of interest. This was a penalty of one-sixth of the value of the claim at issue—that is, one obol for every drachma—and was assessed in various types of cases when the plaintiff lost or when he failed to secure one-fifth of the votes. It was applied, for example, in guardianship cases. Important for commercial matters was the ἐπωβελία in παραγραφή trials. When a plaintiff filed suit in a δίκη ἐμπορική, the defendant was allowed to enter a special plea—written "beside" the plaintiff's claim, hence *para-graphein*—that the action was barred on certain technical grounds. The magistrate had to bring this plea before a court, and the defendant, now a de facto plaintiff, spoke first. Whichever party lost the παραγραφή trial had to pay the penalty for frivolous suit. The payment was probably made to the opposing litigant.[11] In this case, then, the economic interests of the state were protected only indirectly, but the deterrent effect was the same as in the other penalties previously mentioned.

Today, advocacy costs are an essential part of legal costs. In Athens, every litigant had to speak his case in propria persona. Only one's closest relatives or friends were allowed to act as supporters (συνήγοροι), and they were not allowed to accept money.[12] So we do not find advocates in Athens. Theoretically, the idea of easy and equal access to the law seems to have been achieved: both citizens and foreign merchants could take advantage of the low costs of litigation and the prohibition of paid advocacy. In practice, however, matters were not so simple: litigants often spent on "speechwriters" (λογογράφοι) what they saved on advocacy costs.

---

9. Dem. 58.6; Harrison 1968–71: 2:83.
10. Harrison 1968–71: 2:181–83; Scafuro 2011: 23–25.
11. Isocr. 18.35, 37; Harrison 1968–71: 2:185. Whitehead (2002: 86–88) understands the payment as made to the treasury.
12. Dem. 46.26; Wolff 1968: 12 (= 2007: 101); Harrison 1968–71: 2:159; Rubinstein 2000: 52f–53.

At various points in their careers, most of the ten well-known Attic orators plied this trade. Pointedly, Wolff speaks of a "trade" (*Gewerbe*) in order to separate unlicensed speechwriters whose competence lay in rhetoric from the standards and controls associated with the modern profession of a lawyer.[13] The lawyer is bound to the ethical standards of the juristic profession—at least in Europe (and at least in theory). The speechwriter, unlike a lawyer, did not appear in public. Like a tailor, the speechwriter wrote a made-to-measure speech for his client and, if necessary, the συνήγορος. Like actors, the litigants then had to memorize their speeches and rehearse their appearances at court. We do not know how much the speechwriters were paid for their efforts[14] or how frequently Athenians made use of their services.

Sometimes the speechwriters had good knowledge of the law and used this to guide their clients' tactical steps. They formulated the witness depositions and formal questions and challenges (προκλήσεις), which the parties would ask or direct to each other during the preliminary hearing. All documents and statutes on the basis of which a case was to be argued had to be disclosed beforehand to the opponent, in the sessions before the διαιτήτης or the magistrate.[15] With this information, the speechwriter used his rhetorical powers to create a court speech with emotional appeal that would engage and persuade the lay judges. Since the λογογράφος—like a ghostwriter—was working out of the public eye, the winner could not prevail on the loser to reimburse him for the costs. Each party therefore bore this financial risk personally, which represented a considerable obstacle to access to the law. Only litigants well versed in the specialized art of performing court speeches had a realistic chance of winning over the enormous numbers of laymen governed by mass psychology when sitting in the δικαστήρια.

The lay judges, δικασταί, were not the only persons ruled by emotions, since the litigants themselves often pursued other interests besides rationally calculated financial ones when bringing cases. Every lawsuit was a merciless struggle, an ἀγών, for social position, reputation, and honor.[16] In ancient litigation, slandering the opponent was normal. Disputes involving simple economic matters were commonly settled before friends or in the preliminary

13. Wolff 1968: 10 (= 2007: 100).
14. Dem. 35.42 mentions one thousand drachmas in a case for three thousand; I thank Uri Yiftach for this reference.
15. Thür 2007: 142 (= 2008a: 64).
16. Cohen 1995.

hearings. Only totally irreconcilable litigants went to the court, and in doing so, they would insult each other openly in public. In fact, a topos of the court speech was to reproach an opponent with his irreconcilability: he had rejected all means of compromise out of court.[17] The social expectations not to go to court certainly reduced the costs of resolving disputes. But once the trial started, there was no more reasoning on economic considerations. With the speechwriter at his side, the party often invested more than the issue was worth financially. Nonmaterial values, which could certainly also turn into material ones, were now at stake.

Adriaan Lanni holds that trials involving overseas commerce were characterized by more rationality and less emotion.[18] If so, the costs of litigation should have been lower in such disputes. Certainly, as Lanni points out, speeches involving such cases lack the passages in which opponents personally insult one another. The reason—in her eyes—was that foreign merchants were only admitted to file suit in Athens if they had written contracts, or συγγραφαί, with the defendants. Supposedly, the use of συγγραφαί had the consequence that trials could be conducted on a more objective and fair basis when disputes arose. However, the document was only a formal prerequisite to bring a trial in Athens; its existence had nothing to do with whether or not the litigants engaged in ad hominem attacks. Rather, the explanation for the absence of such challenges lies in the fact that it made little sense to attack the reputation of a foreigner in Athens. Therefore, litigants in these cases insulted their opponents indirectly and wove their insults elaborately into the narrative part of the speech.

A good example is the speech of Demosthenes against Zenothemis (Dem. 32).[19] In Syracuse, Protos from Massalia (Marseille) had bought grain with the money belonging to the Athenian Demon, who was, incidentally, Demosthenes's uncle. The grain was loaded onto the ship of Hegestratos, also from Massalia. After being repaired in Kephallenia, the ship arrived in Athens. The grain was unloaded and stored, but Hegestratos, captain and shipowner, had lost his life on the voyage from Syracuse to Kephallenia. Before this unfortunate event, however, he had pledged the grain to his compatriot Zenothemis, who was sailing with him. In Athens, Zenothemis had to use a legal ritual to gain possession of the pledge: he formally invaded the storehouse to take

---

17. Scafuro 1997: 121–23, 393–96.
18. Lanni 2006: 149–74.
19. For full discussion, see Thür 2003: 60–76.

possession of the grain, for the sole reason of being—again formally—expelled by Demon and Protos, who were, it seems, the actual possessors. Thereafter, Zenothemis filed a δίκη ἐξούλης, a cause of action against expulsion, for the double value of the grain. He first filed against Protos, who escaped from Athens and was condemned in absentia. Then Zenothemis filed the same charge against Demon, who countered with a παραγραφή, arguing that he, Demon, had no commercial συγγραφή with the foreigner Zenothemis and therefore that Zenothemis's commercial claim (δίκη ἐμπορική) against him, the Athenian citizen, was inadmissible (§ 2). If the court had agreed with Demon's argument, Zenothemis would have lost his case completely: as a foreigner, he would not have the standing to file a citizen charge against Demon, and Protos was now beyond his reach. Additionally, Zenothemis would have been punished with the ἐπωβελία, the fine of one-sixth of the value of the grain in dispute.

To achieve his aim of barring Zenothemis's δίκη ἐξούλης against Demon, Demosthenes, as speechwriter, did his best to distort the facts and insult his opponent. First, he obscured the fact that a συγγραφή existed between Demon and Protos, who undoubtedly had contracted, in turn, with Zenothemis. Most likely, it was a bottomry loan, much like the one preserved in the speech against Lakritos.[20] Then Demon accused his opponent Zenothemis of conspiring, with Hegestratos, to commit "insurance fraud": in order to keep the money from all the bottomry loans they had made in Syracuse, Hegestratos had allegedly tried to sink his own ship. Caught in the act, he leaped into the sea and was drowned. Reading between the lines, one comes up with the following, much more likely scenario: Hegestratos went overboard when sailing the vessel, heavily damaged by storm, to Kephallenia, sometime after Zenothemis had loaned him money, probably drafted in a συγγραφή, to repair the ship, as collateral for which Hegestratos pledged the grain cargo. This explains the (sound) basis of Zenothemis's claim and why he pursued Demon in court. All this, however, was cleverly covered up by Demosthenes's fantastic and exciting story about the alleged "insurance fraud."

In addition to distorting the facts, Demon is also made to hurl the gravest of insults in the course of his narrative (§§ 4–13), a way of proceeding that takes us far from any standard of fairness in commercial trials. He even discredits his own agent Aristophon, who had managed to repair the ship in

---

20. Dem. 35.10–13: the debt is only due when the ship safely arrives in the harbor.

Kephallenia and now, in a fully correct way, was testifying as a witness on behalf of the plaintiff. In Demon's speech, Aristophon is cast as a well-known member of the "Piraeus mafia" (§ 10). Even Protos, Demon's erstwhile business partner, comes in for rough treatment (§§ 24–30). In a pointed contrast, the speech also includes a chapter in which Demon praises his own contributions to the Athenian grain imports (§§ 21–23). To sum up, we have here a commercial case with all the characteristics of an average court speech, only structured in a different way. In practice, by manipulating the facts to his own advantage, an Athenian litigant was able to bar a foreign merchant from due access to the law. For the foreigner, it was impossible to calculate this risk.

For these reasons, studying litigation costs resulting from the law of Athens cannot be confined to court fees and speechwriters' salaries. In theory, Athens had designed an efficient system to enforce commercial claims quickly and inexpensively. However, because of the mentality of the parties and the lay judges sitting in the huge courts, the carefully designed measures often did not work in practice. A further difficulty was the primitive structure of the Athenian law of contract. A debtor who did not perform his duties was not condemned simply to pay compensation. Instead, according to the principle of the δίκη βλάβης (an action for tort), he could be forced to pay double the amount. If the creditor had several codebtors defaulting on their common obligations, the punishment could also be cumulative. An example of redoubling and cumulating penalties is the case of Pantainetos (Dem. 37).

Instructed by Nikoboulos and Euergos, Antigenes, slave of the first, had privately seized from Pantainetos thirty minas of silver (half a talent). Pantainetos was going to use this to pay the state rent for a silver mine in Laurion (§ 22). Because of the delay in payment, Paintainetos was registered as a state debtor for double the amount, or one talent (§§ 22 and 24). He therefore sued Nikoboulos for two talents, double the amount again (§ 50), even though he had already received two talents from Nikoboulos's partner Euergos. Thus an unjustified securing of half a talent turned into a fine of one talent and private penalties of four talents.[21] This system is far from economic compensation. Nevertheless, like the high risks of lawsuits, the archaic rigor of contract enforcement indirectly brought it about that the parties performed their duties as far as possible voluntarily.

---

21. Thür 2006: 163.

Fees on and Costs of Contracts

On this topic, one can be very brief: as far as is known, there are no sources. From Athens, not a single private contract is preserved as an original document. The ὅροι (stone monuments recording mortgages) sometimes mention sale or encumbrance contracts on real property but never provide the full texts.[22] From a bottomry loan deed transmitted by Demosthenes (35.10–13), we see that Athenians did use extended contract forms—in this case, one that was widespread over the Mediterranean world down to the Roman period.[23] Yet we know nothing about professional scribes or their salaries. This technical knowledge doubtless belonged to the business of tradesmen and bankers.

Athens had fees for the services it provided in official auctions. The responsible officers for this matter were the "sellers" (πωληταί), assisted by a herald (κῆρυξ). The objects of these auctions were confiscated goods[24] and leases (Athens let out its silver mines, temple lands, building projects, and tax collection). *Athenaion Politeia* 47.2–3 deals with the duties of the πωληταί, but without mentioning any fees.[25] Only from the πωληταί records preserved in inscriptions do we know about a sales tax (ἐπώνιον) and herald's fees (κηρύκεια),[26] probably assessed at 2 percent of the price. The whole system of public finance, including an import tax exacted at the harbor, cannot be dealt with in this study.

Indirectly, the prices of goods were influenced by whether the seller had to guarantee title for the buyer. Buying from the state at an auction was safe.[27] A private seller had to offer guarantees against eviction, and he probably added a certain premium to the price to cover this risk. Not from Athens but from Stymphalos, we discover that buying in the marketplace, the agora, was privileged with just this sort of protection: even if one bought stolen goods at the agora, one was not compelled to return them to the owner.[28] This statute concerned first and foremost durable goods like slaves or livestock, not consumer items such as wine and grain. For real property, there was always one person who acted as a guarantor, a βεβαιωτής or πρατήρ.

22. Finley 1951: 21.
23. Thür 1987.
24. Hallof 1990.
25. See the 1981 commentary by Rhodes.
26. Longdon 1991: P 2, 3, 5, 53.
27. Pringsheim 1961: 305.
28. *IPArk* no. 17.121–24 with commentary.

Social Mechanisms

The free market, regulated by supply and demand, is a social mechanism that—in a global perspective—regulates the costs of goods. I cannot say whether and to what degree this economic mechanism was actually operative in classical Athens. In this section, I will concentrate on three legal institutions that optimized the economic balance between the parties of a contract or legal dispute: public auction, the estimation of the penalty in the law courts, and the leasing of an orphan's estate. In all these cases, law and psychology went hand in hand to create institutions significant for Athenian economic life.

A transparent and fair auction was a means for the seller to realize the best price, rent, or wage. From Athens, we know about only official auctions, not private ones.[29] Looking to the πωληταί records for the silver mines, the figures for the rents leave some reason to doubt whether an auction took place with every lease. On the one hand, the leases for some mines were sold for high, oddly specific prices (e.g., 17,750 drachmas).[30] Such examples seem to indicate productive mines let to the highest bidding entrepreneur. On the other hand, we have many smaller, stereotyped figures of 20 or 150 drachmas, which cannot be the result of auctions. The mines leased for these amounts seem to be unproductive. How did the πωληταί lease them? *Athenaion Politeia* 47.2 tells us that the πωληταί let the mines in conjunction with the βουλή, or Council. We should suppose that the five hundred members of the Council, presided over by the πωληταί when deciding such cases, were asked to decide which one among several applicants was the most suitable. The procedure was a social or political interaction between the competing applicants and the controlling organ of the state, rather than a purely economic one.

Much easier to explain is the social mechanism governing the relationship between litigants and the δικαστήριον when it came to assessing penalties. When the defendant in a commercial trial was found guilty, there remained the problem of how to assess the penalty. Normally, it was set at double the amount of the βλάβη, the "harm" or financial loss the plaintiff had suffered. Yet the smaller δικαστήριον of 201 citizens technically did not

---

29. Pringsheim 1961.
30. Langdon 1991: P 19.26–30; see Faraguna 2006: 146–47 with discussion of earlier literature.

have the legal capacity to assess any amount: a δικαστήριον of that size could only vote "yes" or "no." Here the Athenians followed the simple principle of giving both litigants the chance to suggest a penalty amount for an up-or-down vote. The plaintiff would submit his estimate, or τίμημα, in the written statement of his claim. If condemned, the defendant then also had the opportunity to submit his τίμημα. Both litigants had a short time to present orally the justifications for their estimates.[31] Then the judges decided for one of the two petitions. The litigants were thus confronted with a psychological dilemma: if the plaintiff gave too high of an estimate, he risked having the δικαστήριον agree with the defendant's lower estimate, and vice versa for the defendant. Of course, this mechanism did not always succeed in bringing about the legally correct result; but the court did thereby avoid making difficult calculations as to the real damage, while encouraging the parties, who were in a much better position to know the truth of the matter and the true value of the dispute, to submit reasonable estimates. Complicated lawsuits thus could be brought to an end within a single court day with the greatest probability of a just and economically fair outcome.

In the recently published fragment of the speech of Hyperides against Timandros, we find the mechanisms of auction and τίμησις (estimation) combined.[32] The trial concerned a guardianship dispute, or an action on a δίκη ἐπιτροπῆς. After coming of age, Akademos charged his former guardian Timandros with financial malfeasance. As in the case of young Demosthenes against Aphobos (*Dem.* 27), the argument revolved around the guardian's having to give an account of his administration of a business he held in trust. A guardian had two options when it came to managing a business in his ward's estate: either run it himself or lease it out. If he went the first route, the guardian was required, at the end of his duty, to give a full account of his administration, and all profit and loss fell to the ward. In such cases, guardianship trials followed a predictable script. By taking the second route, leasing the business (μίσθωσις οἴκου), the guardian secured a leaseholder who paid a rent to maintain the ward and promised to return the fortune when the ward reached his majority, with the same value as it had had when the leaseholder had received it.[33] On the one hand, the second option was safer for the

---

31. Harrison 1968–71: 2:80.
32. For the text, see Tchernetska et al. 2007; Horváth 2008. For discussion, see Thür 2008b and 2010.
33. Dem. 27.58.

ward, because the leaseholder took on all the risk; on the other hand, all profit exceeding the fixed rent fell to the leaseholder. Under the second option, the costs of resolving disputes were low, because a lawsuit on guardianship was forestalled by leasing the business.

Another problem involving transaction costs concerned how a ward's business, the οἶκος ὀρφανικός, was leased. Here the Hyperides fragment sheds some valuable new light. Up until now, we have known that the guardian had to register his guardianship with the ἄρχων and, at the time of registration, could also apply to lease out the οἶκος.[34] The ἄρχων then arranged to have the business auctioned before a δικαστήριον. But how was the highest bid determined? One conjecture is that the contract was awarded to the bidder who offered the highest rate of interest. According to another theory, the winner was the person who offered the best security,[35] but if so, this was not properly an auction at all. Auctions based on competing offers of rates of interest depend on bidders being able to assess the value of the capital with reasonable confidence, yet this was precisely the difficulty, as Athenian "businesses" were made up of a combination of slaves, stocks of raw materials and finished products, and credits and debts. In other words, an auction on the basis of rates of interest amounts to holding an auction on two independent variables simultaneously, the value of the capital and the potential business opportunity. While this could have been the case, I think it much more likely that the winning bid represented the highest assessment of the capital.

One finds some support for this conjecture in the beginning of the new Hyperides fragment. The fragment starts in the middle of the sentence: τοῦ μὲν εὑρίσκοντος ἐν τῷ δικαστηρίῳ μὴ ἔλαττον ἢ τοῖς παισίν ("so that [. . .] might not be less than that realized in court for the children"). From the context, it is clear that the issue concerned the leasing of an estate. But what was "realized" (or "fetched," εὑρίσκοντος) before the δικαστήριον? The first editors suggest that we should understand the phrase to refer to "profit" (λῆμμα),[36] that is, the interest (or, more correctly, the rate of interest). But in a guardianship case, the capital, not the interest, was at stake. It therefore stands to reason that it was the capital that was meant to be safeguarded by allowing the guardian to lease a business instead of administering it himself; moreover, in no source is a rate of interest ever mentioned. (We might reason-

---

34. Isai. 6.36.
35. Both are discussed in Harrison 1968–71: 1:196.
36. Tchernetska et al. 2007: 3f.

ably speculate that the interest rate was fixed by custom or statute.) There-fore, I suggest that we see the phrase as referring to a bid on the capital and that the word κεφάλαιον and not λῆμμα stood somewhere in the text that preceded: the translation that would result is "so that the capital in trust [when the guardianship ends] might not be less than that realized for the children in court."[37]

With this case, we thus have a comprehensible auction with a simple so-cial mechanism. In leasing and securing a ward's business, the problem was to assess the capital, the present value of the business itself. The Athenians left this task to the competing applicants. The person who won committed himself to repaying the highest value of the capital. Competition not only avoided underassessment but also guaranteed that the ward, until coming of age, would obtain the highest amount of interest, since, to win the bid, every applicant would naturally bundle into his assessment a premium based on his expected profits. Additionally, sufficient real security was demanded as a part of the bid. Finally, in lines 8–9, we read that not merely the ἄρχων but also the δικαστήριον had to accept the bid. After listening to the speeches of the applicants (ἀκούσαντας), the judges decided by vote (δικάζειν).

Combining the principles of τίμησις and auction, this balanced social mechanism seems well designed to protect the financial interests of the ward, put his business into knowledgeable and capable hands, release the guardian from the onerous and dangerous duty of having to render an account, and save the parties the costs of a guardianship lawsuit. We know that the young Demosthenes could win such a trial only with the help of his teacher, the speechwriter Isaeus. What we do not know is how much Demosthenes had to pay to his teacher out of the fortune recovered in court—in any case, the fee paid to Isaeus must have been a considerable transaction cost.

Conclusions

In the preceding discussion, we have seen that the legal framework of classi-cal Athens affected transaction costs in some unexpected ways. Three topics that shed light on transaction costs have been studied here. First, represent-

---

37. In Thür 2010: 8 n. 4, I suggested the following restoration: [ἐξῆν δὲ τοῖς ἐπιτρόποις μισθῶσαι τὸν οἶκον κατὰ τοὺς νόμους, ὥστε τὸ κεφάλαιον τὸ διαχειρισθὲν] τοῦ μὲν εὑρίσκοντος . . . (cf. Dem. 27.58).

ing a substantial cost in judicial proceedings were not the court fees but, rather, the fees for advocacy. However, since the (ghost)writers of the court speeches did not act openly, their wages remain in the dark. Even in simple business disputes, the parties had to resort to skillful oratory. Double penalties for breaching a contract and a harsh rigor of enforcement deterred merchants from bringing one another to trial. Second, it is difficult to calculate the costs in drawing up private contracts. Private deeds were drafted by the personnel of merchants or bankers. Sales taxes were only imposed in public auctions. Third, we must not overlook the importance of social mechanisms, where law and psychology went hand in hand. Public auctions did not always comply with the best bid, and self-assessing by legal opponents or competitors avoided complex jurisdictional measures.

Bibliography

Cohen, D. 1995. *Law, Violence, and Community in Classical Athens*. Cambridge.

Faraguna, M. 2006. "La città di Atene e l'amministrazione delle miniere del Laurion." In H.-A. Rupprecht, ed., *Symposion 2003*, 141–60. Vienna.

Finley, I. M. 1951. *Studies in Land and Credit in Ancient Athens, 500–200 B.C.* New Brunswick. 2nd ed., 1985.

Hallof, K. 1990. "Der Verkauf konfiszierten Vermögens vor den Poleten in Athen." *Klio* 72: 402–26.

Hansen, M. H. 1995. *Die Athenische Demokratie im Zeitalter des Demostenes*. Berlin.

Harrison, A. R. W. 1968–71. *The Law of Athens*. 2 vols. Oxford.

IPArk, see Thür and Taeuber 1994.

Horváth, L. 2008. "Note to Hyperides in Timandrum." *Acta Ant. Hung.* 48: 121–23.

Langdon, M. K. 1991. "Poletai Records." *Athenian Agora* 19: 53–143.

Lanni, A. 2006. *Law and Justice in the Courts of Classical Athens*. Cambridge.

Pringsheim, F. 1961. "Der griechische Versteigerungskauf." In *Gesammelte Abhandlungen*, 2:262–329. Heidelberg.

Rhodes, P. J. 1981. *A Commentary on the Aristotelian "Athenaion Politeia."* Oxford.

Rubinstein, L. 2000. *Litigation and Cooperation: Supporting Speakers in the Courts of Classical Athens*. Stuttgart.

Scafuro, A. C. 1997. *The Forensic Stage*. Cambridge.

Scafuro, A. C. 2011. *Demosthenes, Speeches 39–49*. Austin, TX.

Tchernetska, N., E. W. Handley, C. F. L. Austin, and L. Horváth. 2007. "New Readings in the Fragment of Hyperides' *Against Timandros* from the Archimedes Palimpsest." *ZPE* 162: 1–4.

Thür, G. 1987. "Hypotheken-Urkunde eines Seedarlehens für eine Reise nach Muz-

iris und Apographe für die Tetarte in Alexandreia (zu P. Vindob. G. 40.822)."
    Tyche 2: 229–45.

Thür, G. 2000. "Das Gerichtswesen Athens im 4. Jahrhundert v. Chr." In L. Burck-
    hardt and J. v. Ungern-Sternberg, eds., *Große Prozesse im antiken Athen*, 30–49
    with notes on 257–58. Munich.

Thür, G. 2003. "Sachverfolgung und Diebstahl in den griechischen Poleis (Dem. 32,
    Lys. 23, IC IV 72 I, IPArk 32 u. 17)." In G. Thür and F. J. Fernández Nieto, eds.,
    Symposion 1999, 57–96. Cologne.

Thür, G. 2006. "Antwort auf Michele Faraguna." In H.-A. Rupprecht, ed., *Symposion
    2003*, 161–65. Vienna.

Thür, G. 2008a. "Das Prinzip der Fairness im attischen Prozess: Gedanken zu Echi-
    nos und Enklema." In E. Cantarella, ed., *Symposion 2005*, 131–50. Vienna. Trans-
    lated by J. Miner as "The Principle of Fairness in Athenian Legal Procedure:
    Thoughts on the Echinos and Enklema." *Dike* 11 (2008): 51–73.

Thür, G. 2008b. "Zu *misthosis* und *phasis oikou orphanikou* in Hypereides, Gegen Ti-
    mandros." *Acta Ant. Hung.* 48: 125–37.

Thür, G. 2009. "Trial Procedure in Ancient Athens." In S. N. Katz, ed., *The Oxford
    International Encyclopedia of Legal History*, 4:411–16. Oxford.

Thür, G. 2010. "How to Lease an Orphan's Estate in Classical Athens." *Belgrade Law
    Review* 58: 7–19.

Thür, G., and H. Taeuber. 1994. *Prozeßrechtliche Inschriften der griechischen Poleis:
    Arkadien*. Vienna.

Whitehead, D. 2002. "Athenian Laws and Lawsuits in the Late Fifth Century B.C."
    MHelvet 59: 71–96.

Wolff, H. J. 1968. *Demosthenes als Advokat*. Berlin. Translated by J. Miner as "Demos-
    thenes as Advocate," in E. Carawan, ed., *Oxford Readings in the Attic Orators* (Ox-
    ford, 2007), 91–114.

CHAPTER 2

Access, Fairness, and Transaction Costs

Nikophon's Law on Silver Coinage
(Athens, 375/4 B.C.E.)[1]

Josiah Ober

Among the questions that can be asked of a state's regulatory policy is whether, over time and in comparison with rivals facing similar opportunities and constraints, it hindered or promoted the state's capacity to do well. I take doing well to include ensuring security, influencing neighbors, and promoting the welfare of residents. A policy decision (say, a new law) gains purchase on people's future behavior when it is codified as a potentially accessible and action-guiding item of public information. In classical Athens, policy was codified as laws (νόμοι) and decrees (ψηφίσματα). Fourth-century Athens arguably did very well in comparison to rival poleis (Ober 2008: chap. 2), in part because of Athenian public policies that regulated the conditions of exchange in Athenian markets.

The first section of this essay defines transaction costs and argues that certain Athenian policies served to lower those costs and thereby enabled Athens to do relatively well in the postimperial fourth century B.C.E. The next section introduces Nikophon's silver coinage law and describes the varieties of coinage circulating in Aegean markets in the fourth century. The essay's third section, which analyzes the categories into which coins were sorted by the approver (δοκιμαστής) of silver coinage under the rubrics of approval, confiscation, and certification, demonstrates that the approval sys-

---

1. This chapter is adapted and updated from Ober 2008: chap. 6.

tem was designed to lower transaction costs for traders by testing the actual provisions of the law against counterfactual alternatives. The fourth section considers how buying and selling in the Athenian market would be carried out by recourse to the approval process. The final section of the essay considers residual status inequality and offers conclusions.

Transaction Costs

The productivity of a society is, in large part, a function of how well that society captures the benefits of social cooperation (Benkler 2006). Voluntary exchanges of goods and services—that is, transactions regarded as beneficial by all parties to the exchange—are an important kind of productive cooperation. All other things being equal, the aggregate value of exchanges increases when the costs associated with transacting exchanges are lower. This means that one determinant of the effect a new policy will have on a state's productivity is whether it serves to raise or to lower the costs of transactions—that is, the *ex ante* and *ex post* costs to individuals of making potentially profitable contracts or bargains. Information is a central element in the equation between transaction costs and productivity: If both parties to an exchange share full and transparent access to all the information relevant to the exchange, their transaction costs drop accordingly, and when transaction costs are lowered, productivity is raised (at least potentially), because the increased profit from low-cost bargains increases the value and the frequency of transactions. But under conditions of incomplete information—especially conditions of asymmetrical access to important information—transaction costs increase.[2]

The basic idea behind transaction cost economics is simple: if the costs of doing business are low, more business will be done, and, all other things being equal, this will benefit the society as a whole—it will raise the society's stock of material goods by allowing society to reap more benefit from the socially cooperative activity of free exchange. Of course, whether that larger basket of goods is distributed fairly and what "fairness" in respect to distribution means to a given society are extremely important questions, but they are centered on distributive rather than procedural justice. The "fairness" I

---

2.   On transaction cost economics, see Coase 1988; Williamson 1981; Benkler 2006: 106–16. For the application of transaction cost principles to questions of state formation and international institutions, see North 1981; Keohane 1984.

am concerned with here is procedural impartiality and its role in increasing goods, not fairness in respect to distribution of the surplus goods thereby gained.[3]

How, then, might decisions made by Athens, as a state, affect the transaction costs incurred by the members of the extended Athenian community — understood as those persons doing business and making their living within Athenian territory? In the fifth and fourth centuries, Athens was extremely productive in comparison with rival poleis. For much of the fifth century, superior Athenian productivity was, at least in part, a function of coercive imperialism and violent (or at least potentially violent) resource extraction. But in the early democracy (ca. 506–478) that preceded the imperial period and in the postimperial fourth century, Athens had no substantial empire from which to extract major resources. During these preimperial and postimperial eras, Athenian economic performance depended primarily on domestic production and on exchange.[4]

Athenian material flourishing, especially in the fourth century, can be explained partly by the success of Athens in lowering transaction costs. Low transaction costs encouraged traders to do their business in Athens, which benefited both the Athenian state, by increasing tax revenue, and individual Athenians who engaged in trade. These advantages of increased trade were evident at the time: they were enumerated by the Athenian historian and essayist Xenophon in a mid-fourth-century treatise, *Poroi* (Revenues), suggesting means for increasing the state income of Athens (Ober 2010). I will argue that the Athenians recognized that if transaction costs were relatively lower in Athens than they were in other Greek states, noncitizen traders would, all other things being equal, be relatively more likely to do business in Athens than elsewhere. Of course, this assumes that Athenian policy makers had at least a rough-and-ready conception of what is now called transaction cost

---

3. The ancient Greeks understood justice both as procedural fairness and as fairness in respect to distribution in ancient Greek moral thought and law (Ober 2005). On the relationship between procedural and substantive (distributive) justice in contemporary liberal thought, see Cohen 1996.

4. It is wrong to imagine that Athens had no imperialistic ambitions or tendencies in the fourth century: see Buckler 2003 for detailed discussion. But in any event, with the exception of the control of three Aegean islands—Lemnos, Imbros, and Skyros—which were regular sources of revenue from a grain tax (Stroud 1998), Athenian imperial enterprises before and after the period of the fifth-century "high empire" neither produced net revenue gains nor promoted overall Athenian material flourishing. See, further, Griffith 1978; Oliver 2007; Moreno 2008.

economics. Xenophon's text justifies a prima facie assumption that this was so, but it remains a hypothesis to be tested against other evidence.

Transaction costs can be lowered through standardizing and publicizing rules and practices that, in turn, help to build and maintain a relatively reliable and secure exchange environment. We can test the idea that Athenians grasped the value of lowering transaction costs by, first, specifying how various instruments available to a participatory democracy should operate if the state's goal were lowering transaction costs and, second, asking how far Athens conformed to or diverged from that position (see table 2.1). We should keep in mind, however, that in light of the various nonmaterial ends sought by the democratic polis, low transaction costs must be thought of as what economists call a "satisficing condition"—a condition that is necessary for the achievement of a general goal (e.g., polis flourishing) but is not subject to maximization, because it must be limited somehow to allow for the presence of other necessary conditions (Simon 1955). Thus we should not expect Athenian institutions (or those of any other state) to do everything that might be done to minimize the costs of transactions.

Among the regulatory instruments available to participatory democracies (as well as to more hierarchical organizations) seeking to lower transaction costs are clear and accessible codes of formal rules (laws, customs, administrative protocols) designed to protect persons and their property, standardized and easy-to-use procedures for dispute resolution (mandatory or optional modes of binding or nonbinding arbitration, courts of law), and dependable state-imposed sanctions for punishing delinquents. A second set of instruments includes established standards for weights and measures (Johnstone 2011: chap. 3); standardized exchange media (government-issued and guaranteed currency, standard forms of contract); convenient facilities, such as centralized market places, and well-designed transport and communication networks; and effective policing. Finally, the state can keep transaction costs low by keeping down the rents it extracts (directly or indirectly) on exchanges or that it allows others to extract.

Each of these various instruments must manifest two general properties if it is to work effectively to lower transaction costs: it must be open, and it must be fair. By "open," I mean that the instrument is accessible in respect to entry (as opposed to restricting entry according to extraneous criteria) and clear in respect to interpretation (as opposed, e.g., to being interpretable only by insiders "in the know"). By "fair," I mean that the instrument is impartial in its effects, in that it distributes goods and bads according to criteria that are evenhanded (as opposed to criteria that are arbitrary or "loaded" in favor of insiders), and impersonal, in that it does not identify and preselect particular categories of individuals for special treatment (good or bad) on the basis of extraneous criteria. These various optimizing criteria are laid out schematically in table 2.1.

The table is meant to specify the ways that government actions in respect to a market would render bargaining in that market as close to frictionless as

Table 2.1. State-determined conditions for bargain making with low transaction costs

Instrument	Openness: Access	Fairness: Impartiality
1a. **Formal rules** (laws, decrees, customs)	Publicly posted or common knowledge, stable, archived, legible, simple, non-contradictory, comprehensive, relevant to current conditions.	Apply impartially to all parties; protect bodily integrity, property, dignity of all. *Bodily integrity and dignity of citizens favored.*
1b. **Dispute procedures** (litigation, arbitration)	Swift, reliable, easy to use, difficult to abuse, available to all. *Noncitizens without standing in some legal procedures.*	Treat similar cases and similar disputants similarly.
1c. **Sanctions** (punishments, limitations)	All delinquents are liable to punishments that are standardized, appropriate to the infraction, widely publicized.	Applied similarly to similar infractions. *Intentional murder of citizen punished more severely. Slaves liable to beating as additional or replacement penalty.*
2a. **Exchange media** (coinage, weights, measures, contracts, sureties)	Readily obtainable, comprehensive, stable, recognizable, reliable, standardized.	Impersonal, used by all. *Only citizens (with some exceptions) may own real estate.*
2b. **Facilities** (marketplaces, communications, transport, storage, security)	Centralized open-access markets, low-cost communication and transport systems, reliable and secure storage. Housing, religious apparatus readily available.	Available for use by all on similar terms.
3. **Third-party rents** (taxes, bribes, protection)	Taxes on exchanges low, simple, centralized, returned to productive system. Restraints on corruption, violence, rent seeking, misuse of government apparatus.	Applied similarly to similar cases. *Most metics pay special taxes. Athenian settlements abroad and tax farming favor citizens.*

Note: Italics indicate substantial and systematic Athenian deviations from optimal conditions.

possible—thus as close as possible to the ideal conditions of exchange imagined in what has become known as the Coase theorem. As Ronald Coase (1988) emphatically pointed out, the ideal conditions of the Coase theorem do not and could not exist in the real world—and thus, even with the best possible will, no government could eliminate transaction costs. To exist and thereby facilitate a regime of low transaction costs, a government must have some way to maintain itself, which makes it very likely that it will need to levy taxes of some sort on at least some kinds of exchange (see table 2.1, row 3). Of course, for a complex state to do well, governments must do some things other than keep transaction costs low.

Every real-world government falls short of achieving perfect access and impartiality. This shortfall occurs at least partly because governments attempt to achieve a variety of ends in legislation. The goal of lowering transaction costs is balanced against other goals of state policy. In modern governments, for example, the principle of openness, in terms of both entry and clarity, is compromised not only by security considerations but also by rules created by legislative enactment and by administrative protocols developed and administered by professional bureaucrats. These rules are intended to fulfill important public purposes; they are meant (inter alia) to protect consumers from fraud or safety risks. The net result of the complexity of modern rules and the technical legal language in which they are cast is to raise some transaction costs. Complex rules require (inter alia) that those making bargains employ legal specialists to design contracts and to defend the principals to exchanges against charges of having violated rules that are far from transparent to nonexperts lacking the necessary technical training. This, in turn, bars entry to those who cannot afford to purchase the requisite legal expertise.[5]

Athenian legislative processes produced government rules and other instruments that, in comparison to modern legislation, were publicly accessible, simple, and clear. Athenian laws and decrees, for example, were relatively brief, composed in ordinary language, posted in public places, and available for consultation in standard forms.[6] There is no reason to suppose

---

5.   Huber and Shipan (2002) offer a comparative analysis of the choice of modern legislators to draft detailed legislation or to leave the details to administrative rules to be drafted by unelected civil servants—in either case, the result is that the end users are subject to rules that require expert interpretation. See Sunstein 2013 and Thaler and Sunstein 2008, arguing for increasing welfare by a strong regulatory regime but also for simplification of regulations.

6.   See, e.g., Thomas 1989: 60–93; Harris 1994; Hedrick 1999; Hedrick 2000; Richardson 2000; Davies 2003.

that there were complex administrative protocols working in the background. Athenian government instruments were not, however, completely open and impartial. As noted on table 2.1, various Athenian instruments discriminated, in one way or another, according to the status of the individual in question. I argue here that Athenian rules sought (per Xenophon's recommendations) to enhance the value of noncitizen others to the polis. Yet that goal, which entailed greater openness in respect to access, was compromised, to some degree, by the perceived need to maintain certain legal distinctions between citizens and others. Because the relatively greater openness is the change most relevant to enhancing the status of noncitizens in Athenian institutions in the postimperial fourth century B.C.E., the open-access side of the equation is the primary focus of this essay.

Obvious candidates for "postimperial" fourth-century Athenian state policies for lowering transaction costs include two innovations from the middle to late fourth century. The first is the new legal category of "commercial cases" (δίκαι ἐμποϱικαί) instituted in the mid-fourth century (Lanni 2006: 149–74). The second is the planned operation against pirates in 325 B.C.E. (Ober 2008: chap. 4). The commercial cases were specifically designed to avoid costly delays in dispute resolution and to place foreign traders on an even footing with native Athenians in resolving contract disputes. The antipirate operations of 325 were aimed specifically at enabling both Athenian and non-Athenian traders to move their goods safely (Rhodes and Osborne 2003: no. 100). The third quarter of the fourth century may have been a particularly active period for Athenian policies aimed at lowering transaction costs.[7] Yet, as demonstrated by Nikophon's law on silver coinage, the turn to developing policy that would lower transaction costs of exchanges in the Athenian market antedated the mid-fourth century.

Nikophon's Law and Athenian Coinage

Facilitating mercantile exchange was the publicly stated goal of a well-known Athenian law on silver coinage, proposed by Nikophon in 375 B.C.E. (see the

---

7.   Brian Rutishauser (2007; 2012: chap. 6) argues that the period from 355 (the year in which the Social War ended) to 314 (the year in which the Athenians lost Delos) was one of especially vibrant economic activity in the island poleis of the central and northern Aegean, and he attributes this partly to the islands' symbiotic relationship, based on mutual economic interests, with Athens and its big and open market.

appendix to this essay for text of the law), which revised the arrangements for public scrutiny of silver coins circulating in Athens. The new approver (δοκιμαστής) in the Piraeus marketplace, mandated by the law, is established explicitly (§ 11: section numbers are per the translation in the appendix, in lieu of line numbers) for the convenience of shipowners, traders, and "others." The law's aim is that silver coinage remain a reliable exchange medium; the reliability of coinage is to be ensured by the approvers, whose responsibilities are detailed in the law. Both in the agora (as before the new law) and (after the law) in the Piraeus, an expert state official was made freely available to any party uncertain about the provenience of silver coins that appeared to be Athenian silver drachms or tetradrachms, nicknamed "owls." The law mandates that those trading in Athens accept approved Athens-produced silver coins bearing the standard "stamp" (χαρακτήρ), featuring a bust of Athena on the obverse and an owl on the reverse (§ 1). It specifically requires the acceptance of owls that have been approved by the approvers (§ 5). It provides for the tacit certification of certain "owl-like" silver foreign coins as good and for the confiscation of bad coins. Finally, it provides incentives and sanctions so that that Athenian officials involved in the approval process (the approvers and others) are motivated to fulfill their duties. The result was that all persons involved in exchange in Athenian markets were provided, in common, with an essential item of information: that the currency in circulation in Athens was trustworthy.[8]

The "owl brand" of Athenian silver coinage was well established and stood for solid quality: Athenian tetradrachms were nearly pure silver and standardized in weight (17 grams ± .15 grams for post-Persian war coins). A genuine "owl" was thus dependable as an exchange medium, a dependability that served to lower transaction costs. For traders carrying out exchanges in silver (the primary medium of exchange in the ancient eastern Mediterranean), exchanging goods for owls (or trustworthy coins minted by other states) eliminated the labor-intensive steps of assaying the purity of silver and weighing bulk silver.[9] Although Athenian owls (like all Greek silver coins) were exchanged primarily on the basis of their commodity value (the

---

8. Johnstone 2011 is now the standard work on the role of trust in market exchanges in the Greek world.
9. Johnstone (2011: chap. 2) rightly points out, however, that information asymmetry remained in respect to the quality of goods being sold. He attributes Greek (and especially Athenian) "haggling culture" partly to that residual asymmetry.

worth of the silver itself), they also possessed a "fiduciary value" in the state's guarantee of precious metal content and standard weight.

In the fourth century, Athenian owls remained among the most common coins in circulation in the eastern Mediterranean region (see table 2.2).[10] A market favoring Athenian coinage was beneficial to Athens in a number of ways: the state probably made a small profit on each coin it produced. Mining enriched many individual Athenians. It supported local deme economies, like that of Thorikos, in southern Attica. Perhaps most important, it helped attract traders and their business to Athens, where they knew that they would be contracting their bargains in a reliable exchange medium.[11]

The esteem in which owls were held in the eastern Mediterranean led to the production of "owl-like" coins outside of Athens. By the mid-370s, substantial numbers of imitation owls—that is, coins not issued by the Athenian state but bearing the "Athenian stamp" of a bust of Athena on the obverse and an owl on the reverse—were circulating in eastern Mediterranean markets,

Table 2.2. Polis coins found in coin hoards of the fifth and fourth centuries B.C.E. and percentage of total hoards from top ten polis mints

Polis	Hoards 5th		Hoards 4th		Coins 5th		Coins 4th	
	Count	%	Count	%	Count	%	Count	%
Athens	45	18.9	56	9.9	1284	3.7	7152	6.5
Syracuse	48	20.2	33	5.9	963	2.8	793	0.7
Aigina	24	10.1	25	4.4	960	2.8	535	0.5
Akragas	35	14.7	8	1.4	698	2.0	22	0.0
Taras	20	8.4	23	4.1	593	1.7	1426	1.3
Kroton	21	8.8	18	3.2	466	1.4	155	0.1
Metapon-tion	19	8.0	20	3.5	1017	3.0	226	0.2
Gela	30	12.6	9	1.6	565	1.6	72	0.1
Olbia	11	4.6	21	3.7	456	1.3	813	0.7
Corinth	10	4.2	19	3.4	197	0.6	1145	1.0
All hoards	238		564		34385		109433	
10-polis %		Mean 11.1		Mean 4.1		Total 20.9		Total 11.3

10. The wide extent of the circulation of Athenian owls, especially in the fourth century, is evident in even a superficial perusal of the evidence from coin hoards that is collected in Thompson, Mørkholm, and Kraay 1973. See, in detail, Flament 2007 (catalog of hoards that include Athenian owls). See further discussion of the hoard evidence in Ober 2008: chap. 2.
11. On the question of Athenian state profits from the production of coinage, see Kroll 2011; on silver in the southern townships of Attica, Osborne 1985. In his *Poroi*, Xenophon makes a point of the desirability of silver as a medium of trade. Cf. Aristotle, *Nicomachean Ethics* 1133a.

including Athens. The phenomenon of "pseudo-owls" has been well documented by numismatists: imitation owls, produced especially in the Syria/Palestine and Egypt, begin to appear in the fifth century but become very common only in the early fourth century. Some pseudo-owls were good coins, in that they were comparable in weight and silver content to Athenian-produced owls. Other pseudo-owls were bad coins, in that they looked like real owls but had a much lower silver content. As indicated in Nikophon's law, an important part of the approver's job was discriminating between good and bad pseudo-owls and treating them accordingly (§ 2).[12]

In economies where the value of money is fiduciary, it is natural to think of all imitation money as counterfeit—produced with the intention to deceive and thereby defraud. Yet Athenian law clearly did not treat all imitation owls as counterfeits in this sense. Peter van Alfen has brought greater terminological precision to the numismatic discussion of imitation by distinguishing among seven categories of ancient coins:[13]

1. Prototypes (state-issued originals—in this case, real silver owls: see fig. 2.1 nos. 1–2). These are coins produced by a state mint. Production of prototypes began in the Greek world in a number of city-states in the sixth century and continued through the classical period. Most major Greek states, although not all of them, produced prototype coins.

2. Artistic imitations (e.g., medallions that are clearly distinguishable from prototypes and may have had different functions). These are state-produced objects of art, with relatively little relevance to the current study.

3. Anonymous imitations (close copies, that may, at the margin, be indis-

---

12. On the imitation owl phenomenon, see Thompson, Mørkholm, and Kraay 1973: 154 (cf. 200); Stroud 1974: 175–78 with plate 25d–f; Figueira 1998: 528–35; van Alfen 2000; van Alfen 2002: 32–48. See especially van Alfen 2005. Stewart and Martin (2005) note that the jump in imitation owls ca. 400–375 B.C.E. coincides with a massive increase of imports of Athenian-made pottery into Egypt. Kroll (1993: 4–5) reports that 22 percent of the 129 Greek silver coins found in the excavations of the Athenian agora were "unofficial" (not "prototypes," in van Alfen's typology): twenty-two of these were clads ("plated"), and between five and seven were imitations with high silver content. Van Alfen (2005: 344) notes that of 791 Athenian coin types in the collection of the American Numismatic Society, some 19 percent are imitations with high silver content, and 8 percent are plated. These are noisy statistics, as van Alfen points out, especially because one expert's real owl may be another expert's imitation, but they certainly show that pseudo-owls were circulating in Athens and that the approvers would have had some work to do.

13. Van Alfen 2005, with excellent discussion of Nikophon's law in the context of the problem of imitation coinages. Athenian law specified death for producing van Alfen's category 7 counterfeits (Dem. 20.167).

tinguishable from the prototype: see fig. 2.1 no. 4). These coins are produced at mints (by states or individuals) other than the prototype mint. Anonymous imitation owls begin being produced in the Middle East by the fifth century and are very common in the eastern Mediterranean by the fourth century.

4. Marked imitations (relatively close copies of prototypes that are clearly distinguished by their producers from prototypes—e.g., by the addition of a special symbol—and are therefore unlikely to be confused with prototypes by experienced traders: see fig. 2.1 no. 5). Like category 3, these coins are produced by mints other than the prototype mint. They are common in the fourth-century eastern Aegean.

5. Perfunctory imitations (not close copies of the prototype in any sense: see fig. 2.1 no. 6). These coins are like category 3 but bear only casual resemblance to the prototype and were produced in nonprototype mints (e.g., in Babylonia).

6. Official plated and debased coins (e.g., the emergency Athenian war issues of plated bronze owls: see fig. 2.1 no. 3). Official products of a state mint, these appear in Athens in the late fifth century.

7. Counterfeit plated and debased coins (privately manufactured for the purpose of deception). Produced probably by individuals, these explicit counterfeits were known almost from the beginning of Greek coinage, in the sixth century, and continue through the classical period.

Nikophon's law (§ 1) seeks to ensure that prototypes (Athenian state-produced silver owls: van Alfen category 1) are accepted in Athens. The law then refers to two primary categories of imitations. Section 2a mentions foreign silver coins that possess the two bona fide characteristics possessed by prototypes: the public stamp (the bust of Athena on the obverse and an owl on the reverse) and (apparently—there is a lacuna in the text of the law) the right silver content. These coins, which we may call "good fakes," are to be returned by the approver to the individual who brought them forward. Van Alfen's categories 3 and 4 (anonymous and marked imitations) are presumably the primary categories involved such returns, although coins in categories 2 and 5 might also be regarded as "good fakes." These "good fake" owls are contrasted with bad coins: counterfeits of van Alfen's category 7 and perhaps still-circulating state-produced plated coins from category 6.[14] The law

---

14. The law does not mention category 6 coins explicitly, and a strict interpretation of the

Fig. 2.1. Athenian state-issued owls (left column, nos. 1–3) and imitation owls (right column, nos. 4–6), era of Nikophon's law. (Courtesy of Peter Van Alfen and ANS.)

    1. Athens, late 5th c. AR tetradrachm (bona fide owl), 17.15 g (ANS 1997.9.196)

    2. Athens, early 4th c. AR tetradrachm (bona fide owl), 17.15 g (ANS 1959.137.1)

    3. Athens, c. 405 B.C.E. AR/AE drachm (official plated issue), 3.65 g (ANS 1966.232.1)

    4. Egypt?, early 4th c. AR double shekel? (anonymous imitation, note countermarking), 16.82 g (ANS 1944.100.24208)

    5. Palestine, late 5th/early 4th c. AR double shekel? (marked imitation, note Aramaic shin on the cheek), 16.52 g (ANS 1971.196.2)

    6. Babylonia?, 4th c. AR double shekel? (perfunctory imitation, note cut on reverse, perhaps to check purity), 16.97 g (ANS 1974.274.2)

(§ 2b) mentions clads (coins with lead and bronze cores) and "fraudulent" (κίβδηλος) coins—presumably referring especially to counterfeits made from alloys of silver and base metal. These coins with low silver content were presumably being passed off as solid silver owls, with the intention of defrauding naive traders. In contrast to the good fakes, these bad coins are to be confiscated by the approver.

Approval, Confiscation, Certification

It is a notable feature of Nikophon's law that it does not lump all pseudo-owls into a single category of bad (because "nonprototype") coinage. Good fakes—that is, coins that look like owls and are presumed by the approver to have silver content similar to real owls—are to be "handed back" to the individual who presented them for approval (ἀποδιδότω τῶι προσενεγκόντι). There has been much scholarly debate over the question of whether the good fakes were handed back to their owners as "approved." Although the wording of the law is not decisive on this point, there is good reason to believe that pseudo-owls that were handed back were not "approved"—and thus their acceptance by sellers was not mandatory.[15] Yet it is clear from the law that good fakes are not being pulled out of circulation by the Athenian state, nor are their owners penalized. Indeed, by returning it to the owner, the approver may be said to have "certified" a given pseudo-owl by issuing his expert

grammar of the key sentence in section 2 of the law would mean that all plated and fraudulent coins are regarded as ξενικόν (i.e., not Athenian state produced). Yet the fact that section 1 of the law specifies Attic silver coins with the public stamp as the coins that must be accepted makes room for a category of Attic nonsilver coins with the public stamp that are not approved. In any event, any war issues still in circulation were clearly to be treated by the approver as if they were foreign frauds.

15. Stroud (1974: esp. 169 and 186) makes the argument for mandatory acceptance of good fakes—that is, that being handed back means "approved." This interpretation was vigorously challenged by (inter alios) Buttrey (1981 and 1982), who regarded it as impossible that any Greek polis would mandate the acceptance of imitations. The φάσις dispute procedure might seem to favor Stroud's interpretation: assuming that approved coins and unapproved good fakes are both handed back by the approver to the buyer, there is potential for postapproval dispute about which was which. But in Buttrey's favor is the fact that mandatory acceptance of coins not produced by the state opens a dangerous possibility for fraud: if fakes of 85 to 95 percent silver contents produced by mala fide contractors were perceptually indistinguishable from near-pure silver coins, the state could find itself in the untenable position of mandating the use of bad counterfeits. I thank Peter van Alfen for clarification of this point and other issues regarding Nikophon's law and Athenian coinage.

opinion that it was good (καλόν—on Stroud's restoration). According to the law, the bad fakes (clads and counterfeits: see § 2b) and presumably also Athenian-produced plated coins (the emergency issue of the late Peloponnesian War, now no longer regarded as legal tender: see fig. 2.1 no. 3) are not only to be confiscated by the approver; they are to be cut through (as has been fig. 2.1 no. 3) and then dedicated by the Council of Five Hundred to the Mother of the Gods. This apparently meant storing them in the Metroon.[16]

Table 2.3 lays out a schematic judgment grid for the approvers, on the dimensions of origin (Athenian or foreign) and quality (good or bad). Upon making his expert judgment regarding the "box" into which the coin should fall, the approver takes a mandatory action. That action results in the coin remaining in circulation or being removed from circulation. In the case of good coins (left column), the buyer is either legally required to accept the coin in payment for goods (if it is both certified as good and approved as Athenian) or, according to the most likely interpretation, left free to accept the coin or not (if it is certified as good but is not approved as Athenian).

Box 1 is straightforward: the law's explicit intent is to protect the value of Athenian-produced silver by guaranteeing its quality and mandating its ac-

Table 2.3. Approvers' judgment matrix

1. Athenian (Ἀττικόν)	3. Athenian (Ἀττικόν)
Good (silver)	Bad (plated bronze = withdrawn war issue)
Certify and approve (as δόκιμος)	**Cut, confiscate, dedicate**
Remains in circulation	*Removed from circulation*
Mandatory acceptance	*Unacceptable*
2. Foreign (ξενικόν)	4. Foreign (ξενικόν)
Good (silver)	Bad (plated bronze or lead, fraudulent)
Certify (as καλόν), return to owner	**Cut, confiscate, dedicate**
Remains in circulation	*Removed from circulation*
Optional acceptance	*Unacceptable*

Note: Boldface indicates mandatory actions taken; boldface italics indicates consequences for subsequent circulation and use as legal tender.

16. Stroud 1974: 177–78 discusses two plated coins found by excavators near the Metroon-Bouleuterion complex and plausibly concludes that these had been confiscated by the approver and subsequently cut through and dedicated to the Mother of the Gods, as called for in Nikophon's law. It is particularly notable that confiscated coins are deposited in a building used to house state archives; it is tempting to suppose that these bad coins were kept as a study collection that the approvers could refer to when preparing themselves to deal with potentially suspect coin series (see n. 19 below).

ceptance in trade. Box 4 is equally unproblematic, given that counterfeits posed an obvious threat to the Athenian owl brand. Box 3 is likewise unproblematic: it was essential to distinguish between the state-produced but now withdrawn emergency war series and silver owls. If coins that looked like owls and were passed off as owls but did not have the silver content of owls proliferated in the polis and were allowed to circulate freely, traders would lose faith in owls as a means of exchange and in Athens as a market. If the state ignored fraud based on the passing of counterfeits, the danger arose that, according to Gresham's law, bad money would drive out good. This would, in turn, drive up the transaction costs that had been lowered by the reputation of owls for purity, because traders would be hesitant to accept genuine owls, on the chance that they were counterfeit. The state absorbed the costs of an official no-fee approval process in order to combat that deleterious outcome.

Ordering the approver to confiscate bad fakes without reimbursement to their owners imposed a cost on their owners, who can be roughly divided into cheats (those who knew the coins were bad) and naives (those who had taken counterfeit coins from others, believing them to be good coins). Given both the sanction entailed by confiscation (at minimum the loss of the residual silver content) and the likelihood that bad coins would be identified and confiscated by the expert approver, cautious cheaters were likely to be discouraged from trading *ex ante*. Bolder cheaters would be weeded out *ex post*. In either case, their removal helped to optimize the market. For their folly, naives were penalized by the state rather than by opportunistic and better-informed traders. Given the existence of the approvers, naive traders in Athens always had recourse to the services of an expert and so had only themselves to blame if they ended up in possession of counterfeits. Any injustice associated with penalizing the innocent naïf whose coins were confiscated was apparently countered by the gains associated with quickly removing bad fakes from the system and efficiently punishing cheaters.

Box 2 of table 2.3 is initially puzzling. It is not immediately obvious why the law should have allowed coins (like fig. 2.1 nos. 4–5) that might be confused with real owls (like fig. 2.1 nos. 1–2) to remain in circulation. A "handed-back" pseudo-owl was, in effect, given expert certification as "good" (καλόν)— that is, pronounced by a state-appointed currency expert to be "neither clad, nor fraudulent." Thus the production of "sincere imitations" of Athenian coinage was not criminalized by the Athenian state, nor was possession of pseudo-owls discouraged. Indeed, the fact that the law makes a point of stating that good pseudo-owls were exempt from confiscation may be regarded as an explicit guarantee to the trading community that Athens will protect the property rights of those in possession of good fakes. All of this would be inexplicable if we were to think of pseudo-owls simply as counterfeits.

Assuming that the owl "brand" was important to the Athenian trading environment and that the gains to the Athenian community from the production of silver coins were considerable, why would the state allow "generic" owls to circulate in the city without penalty? Why would it not protect the brand by confiscating pseudo-owls as fraudulent or (on the Egyptian model— see the analysis by Bresson in chapter 5 of this volume) by charging their owners a state-mandated reminting fee? I suggest that the law's framers realized that penalizing "good fakes" would drive up transaction costs, by burdening legitimate transactions. The Athenians tacitly permitted "franchising" of their owl brand because doing so facilitated trade.[17]

A hypothetical decision tree for the law's framers (fig. 2.2) shows that the choices Nikophon's law actually makes—confiscating bad fakes and allowing good fakes to remain in circulation—optimizes the trading environment by keeping transaction costs low for well-informed and honest traders, while discouraging cheats and fools. Comparing the decision tree's actual branches (in bold and shaded) and its counterfactual branches strongly suggests that Athenian interest in protecting the state "brand" and/or reaping profits by gathering rents from traders in the form of mandatory reminting costs was trumped by a concern for keeping transaction costs low.[18]

---

17. On the likely negative impact that cutting a coin would have on its subsequence acceptance, see van Alfen 2002: 6; 2004–5: 18. A modern analogy might be generic drugs, which lack the "brand" of the original but are chemically identical. Negotiations between, on the one hand, drugmakers eager to defend their profits and their brand and, on the other, public agencies eager to provide inexpensive health care produce, in their turn, complex rules. It is very likely, based on the relatively few legible lines of an as-yet-unpublished Athenian law from 354/3 (Agora inv. no. 7495) and a recent reanalysis of fourth-century owls, that there was a general recall and reminting of owls two decades after Nikophon's law; see Kroll, 2011. The recall law is explicitly attentive to the needs of private individuals and to the necessity of accomplishing its goals quickly. I thank Molly Richardson for allowing me to consult her in-progress transcript of this important inscription.

18. Robert Keohane points out to me that maintaining currency liquidity (i.e., ready availability of coins) is another (in this case, macroeconomic) public good that is supported by the official Athenian tolerance of the pseudo-owls. Currency liquidity is especially important for trading states and difficult to maintain in currencies with a specie standard (cf. the practice of hoarding). It is implausible that the Athenians could have clearly understood the economic reasons why loss of liquidity would have deflationary effects (depressing production of goods and potentially precipitating economic depression, as in Europe in

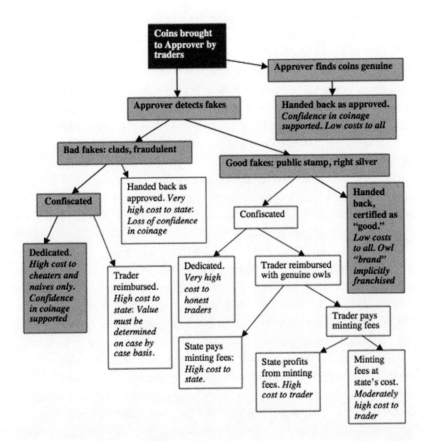

Fig. 2.2. Decision tree of Nikophon's law on silver coinage. Shaded boxes with boldface indicate actual decisions made by the law; white boxes indicate counterfactuals, possible policies rejected by the law; italics indicate costs to individuals and to the Athenian state.

Suppose, counterfactually, that the Athenians had chosen to confiscate all coins regarded as fakes, good and bad, without reimbursement. This would impose very high costs on honest traders who were in possession of good fakes and were offering their trading partners silver with value similar to that

<hr />

1873–96). But the Athenians could certainly have noted the empirical fact that markets flourished when silver currency (even if not Athens-produced) was readily available, and they must have recognized that taxing "good fakes" would discourage the import of foreign silver to the Athenian market.

of real owls. Many good fakes are indistinguishable from real owls except by experts, and even modern experts disagree on whether a given coin or coin series is Athenian prototype or sincere imitation. If honest traders, who were presumably no more expert than modern numismatists at distinguishing real owls from "good fakes," were at risk of losing good silver coins to confiscation every time they sought to make a bargain, it would be a severe damper to trade in Athens. Alternatively, suppose the state had demanded that when good fakes were presented to the approver and identified as such, they must be turned in to the state in exchange for genuine Athenian coins. In this case, the Athenians would have to decide who should pay reminting costs—that is, the labor costs associated with gathering and transporting the good fakes, melting down the silver, recasting new blank flans, and restamping the blanks with official Athenian dies.

The state could run this (counterfactual) reminting operation at a profit—as did, later, the Ptolemaic state monopoly in Hellenistic Egypt (as detailed by Bresson in chapter 5).[19] Depending on the state's profit margin, this would have imposed fairly high costs on traders. Or the state could exchange real owls for good fakes at par, thereby eliminating costs to traders but running a deficit-producing operation that could prove prohibitively costly to the state, given the large number of pseudo-owls in circulation. Finally, the state could charge just enough for exchanging good fakes for real owls to cover its reminting costs. This last option would impose moderate costs on traders. The actual law took the approach with the lowest transaction costs—the approach most likely to be favored by the trading community and thus most likely to attract trade to the Athens market. Not enjoying the Egyptian quasi-monopoly on various commodities, the Athenians could not afford to act otherwise concerning fake coinage if they wished to attract traders to Athens. The result was a relatively fair and open trading environment.

---

19. On the Egyptian monopoly on coinage, see Le Rider and Callataÿ 2006: 140–44. Von Reden 2007 provides the context. A mid-fourth-century decree of Olbia (Dubois 1996: no. 15 = Austin and Vidal-Naquet 1977: no. 103), which is modeled on the Nikophon law (a copy of which was found in Olbia), stakes out a middle ground: mandatory use of Olbian gold and silver coinage, with restrictions on rents from reminting. At about the same time, two Athenians (along with their kinsmen and slaves) were granted special traders' privileges in Olbia (Dubois 1996: no. 21), suggesting a possible relationship between the dissemination of institutions (in this case, an adapted law), on the one hand, and close trade relations, on the other.

Buying and Selling in Fourth-Century Athens

The law recognizes three distinct classes of coins: prototypes (van Alfen category 1), good fakes (van Alfen categories 2–5), and bad coins (van Alfen categories 6 and 7). The box matrix in table 2.3 indicates that each class was treated differently. But what approach was taken for coins at the margin, such as a good fake that was a bit off-color—possibly indicating a lower-than-standard silver content, although equally possibly indicating some innocent environmental condition? Or what if a coin so accurately imitated a real owl that even an expert could not quickly decide whether or not it was a state-produced prototype? Some cases could not be objectively decided without resort to laborious tests. Yet the speed and clarity of the approval process was intrinsic to its economic value: a slow and uncertain approval process would be worse than none at all. All of this suggests that the expert approver should not be regarded merely as a sort of automaton, ordered to do a technically demanding but merely mechanical job. Rather, he was an umpire, empowered to make quick and absolute judgment calls (confiscate vs. return; certify and approve vs. certify without approval) on inherently ambiguous cases. Just as a pitch in baseball is a strike if and when the umpire has called it a strike, a foreign silver pseudo-owl circulating in Athens was good if and when the approver called it good; a coin was a real owl if and when the approver declared it real. In essence, then, by adding an expert to the system of exchange, the Athenian state added a marginal fiduciary value to coins about which there was always some inherent ambiguity.[20]

---

20. On the means that a δοκιμαστής could use for quick judgment, see Bogaert 1976, citing [Arrian], *Discourses of Epictetus* 1.20.7–9, noting that a silver tester (ἀργυρογνώμων) used sight, touch, smell, and hearing to test coins. It is tempting (although completely speculative) to guess that when they were not on duty at their tables, the δοκιμασταί engaged in tests (by cupellation, a destructive method that allows for accurate determination of silver content) when examples of new series of pseudo-owls came their way. Once a few examples from a series had been tested "in the lab," the δοκιμασταί would be able to deal efficiently with all coins from that series through visual inspection in their daily practice "at the table." A concern with standardizing assaying practices is not uniquely ancient: in 1856, a British parliamentary committee found "that the laws regulating the assaying of gold and silver are in a most confused state, and that almost every office is established and regulated by Statues or Charters exclusively applicable to itself. The practice of assaying is to afford protection to the public against fraud, and the Committee believe that it ought to be maintained, and since it is a convenient mode of collecting the revenue. They suggest that several statutes should be repealed, to remove the anomalies and confusion on assaying, and the consolidation of the laws into one statute for the establishment and regulation of Assay Offices throughout the UK" (HMSO 1856, paper 190: Select Committee on Silver and Gold Wares).

For this quasi-fiduciary system to work properly, both the approver in the agora and the Piraeus approver must judge consistently on similar cases: if the two umpires did not make their calls on the basis of very similar standards, the "spread" between them might be manipulated by more sophisticated traders to the disadvantage of the less sophisticated. This would, in turn, obviate the intended goal of equalizing information among traders. These considerations point to the need for expertise on the part of the approvers and for close coordination between them. We can now begin to understand at least part of the reason why the approvers were public slaves. The choice of public slaves for this vital office meant that approvers could become true experts. Men who had engaged in the same demanding task for thousands of hours, who had looked carefully at tens of thousands of coins, could be expected to develop a high level of professionalism and consistency of judgment. That would have been impossible had the approvers been citizen amateurs chosen by lottery to hold office for only a year. Moreover, as we shall see, the fact that the approvers were slaves allowed for frightful sanctions if an approver did not properly fulfill his duties.

With these considerations in mind, we can better imagine how the system worked in practice. Suppose that a seller (S) is offered one hundred drachmas by a buyer (B) for a certain quantity of wheat. Because, if S demands an approval, any bad fakes detected by the approver among B's coins would be confiscated, B had a strong incentive not to offer S bad fakes in the first place (i.e., to be neither a dishonest nor a naive possessor of bad money). S wants to make the deal but is concerned about the quality of B's coins. Because they are trading grain in the Piraeus, B (or his agent), accompanied by S (or his agent), takes the coins to the Piraeus approver. S and B can be quite sure that they will find the approver sitting at his table in front of the stele of Poseidon, because they know he can be punished if he is not. The approver examines the coins offered by B. Prototypes are certified and approved. Pseudo-owls that turn up in the process are returned to B unapproved. B may choose to offer them to S nonetheless, at a discount. S is within his rights to demand prototypes in payment and can walk away from the deal if they are not forthcoming. So B may need to exchange his pseudo-owls for real owls at a money changer—conveniently located nearby if the transaction was in the agora and presumably not hard to find in the Piraeus. But S may not choose to exercise this legal option, because S has received a tacit guarantee that he will in any case be receiving "good coins": B and S now share symmetrical information about the quality of the coins and may be able to agree on a fair discount rate for good fakes.

Once enough coins have been reviewed to complete the sale, B proffers them to S. But suppose S now refuses to make the deal. Assuming that all the coins involved in the sale had been approved, B (in person or via a third party) can "expose" S to the relevant magistrate (§ 5a–c). Because the amount of the transaction is over ten drachmas, the magistrate refers the matter to a people's court. If the court sides with B, then S loses all the grain he offered for sale that day. The state takes half of S's grain, and B (or the third party) takes the other half of it. S therefore has a very high incentive to accept approved coins without demur. The requirement that S accept the approved coins removes any incentive on S's part to use the official apparatus of the approval process as a delaying device—to tie up B's capital while S seeks a higher price for his goods. Thus B is protected from S's use of the referral to the approver merely as a way to keep B's offer alive while seeking a better price from some other buyer. Because he understands S's incentives and because his ownership of the coins is at risk only if they are bad, B need not fear that the transaction cost involved in bringing his coins before the approver will be increased by the risk of losing either his bargain or the property he holds honestly.

The mandatory acceptance provision means that S will not challenge B's coins unless he really doubts the coins' quality while sincerely wanting to make the deal. The transaction cost incurred by the resort to the approver is not, therefore, built into every exchange. The office of approver remains a state-provided third-party guarantee that works in the background to lower the information asymmetry that exists because B might know something about the quality of his coins that S does not. It does not become a burdensome mandatory bureaucratic step that must be factored into the cost of doing business in Athens.

An incidental benefit to equalizing valuable information is the gain in common knowledge that comes with the resort to the approver: S and B (or their agents) are both present before the approver and so have common knowledge of the value of the coins and the good faith of those offering and accepting them. That common knowledge extends to any interested bystanders, because the process is carried out in a public place: B's incentive not to offer bad fakes is increased because he stands to lose his reputation for honesty if the approver confiscates his coins. Likewise, S stands to lose reputation if he seeks to back out of a deal after the approval process has been completed.

In sum, the approver system protected both sellers and buyers. If we suppose that S and B had a choice of polis markets in which to do business and if we assume that Athens was (at least initially) unique in its provision of expert approvers, we can see why, all other things being equal, S and B would choose to trade in Athens. Thus we can begin to see how the democratic legal system provided Athens with differential transaction cost advantages over its polis rivals.

The legal system of Athens provided traders with an incentive to trade in Athenian state-minted owls. By doing his business in approved prototypes in Athens, B is offered a sort of state-funded business insurance in the form of easy access to the legal apparatus of Athenian magistrates and courts. Traders' use of prototype owls is voluntary, in that there seems to be no Athenian sanction against the use of good pseudo-owls or, for that matter, the coinage of other states. Yet, given the choice, traders who knew that they might do business in Athens are likely to prefer prototype owls, which would therefore have circulated in the Greek world at a premium. The fifth-century command-and-control imperial requirement that traders employ Athenian owls (Figueira 1998) was thus replaced with an incentive that seems to have achieved very much the same end.

Table 2.2 shows that in the fourth century, as in the fifth, more Athenian coins appear in more Greek coin hoards than do coins of any other Greek polis. Athenian coins were more heavily favored, relative to coins of other poleis, by hoarders of coins in the fourth century than had been the case in the fifth century. The percentage totals suggest that the growth of nonpolis mints in the fourth century (especially under Philip of Macedon, Alexander, and the early Hellenistic dynasts) limited the "market share" of the polis mints, with the aggregate share of the ten top poleis in the total number of hoarded coins dropping from about 21 percent in the fifth century to about 11 percent in the fourth. One or more Athenian coins appear in about 10 percent of fourth-century hoards, down from 19 percent of hoards in the fifth century; all rival poleis also experienced declines in this measure. Meanwhile, however, the percentage of Athenian coins in all hoards grew from 3.7 to 6.5 percent; among rival mints, only Corinth similarly exhibits growth. These are noisy data, but the conclusion that Athenian coins remained very much in demand in the Mediterranean world long after the end of the imperial era is not in doubt.

Status Inequality and Unfairness

Among the notable aspects of Nikophon's law is the way in which it takes account of the legal status of those whose behavior it regulates, even as it creates the conditions for impersonal, "status-blind" exchanges in the Athenian market. As we have seen, the approvers were public slaves. This is made explicit in the law's provision (§ 11) for establishing a new Piraeus approver. He is either to be selected from the existing body of state-owned slaves (presumably from among those working currently in the mint or as clerks in the magistracies) or to be purchased on the open market, if there is no suitable candidate (i.e., no one with the necessary expertise) among the state's current human inventory. We have already seen that the requirement for both expertise and consistency in the office of approver made it preferable not to fill this position with citizen magistrates chosen by lottery.

Unlike free persons, the slave approvers can be whipped if they are derelict in their duties; the "parallel" legal penalty for free persons would be a monetary fine.[21] Likewise, if a slave selling merchandise is exposed as refusing approved coinage and is convicted, whipping is added to the confiscation of goods (§ 9). There is a glaring asymmetry here: the sanctions are much more severe for slaves than for free persons. Yet slaves are otherwise assumed to be full parties to transactions. The public slave approvers are, for example, to be paid a regular salary—section 14 of the law is devoted exclusively to the issue of paying the salary of the two approvers and to ensuring that the new Piraeus approver is properly compensated for the partial-year service that is anticipated. How, then, are we to explain the asymmetry in a system that seems to be so concerned with creating symmetry in the conditions of exchange?

A seller slave (§ 9) might well be using his or her own capital and acting as an independent agent—slaves who "lived apart" from their masters and

---

21. On corporal punishment of slaves at Athens, see Hunter 1994: 154–84. On the hypothesis that a drachma is regarded as the equivalent of a stroke of the whip, see Hansen 1999: 121.

paid over a portion of the earnings of their own privately owned businesses are well documented in Athens.[22] In this case, the function of the additional punishment would be expressive: whipping the slave reminds all parties of the yawning gulf between slaves and the free. In other cases, however, the seller slave might be acting as an agent for his or her owner. In this latter circumstance, in addition to maintaining the expressive purpose of enforcing status distinction, the legal threat of beating has a rational purpose.

A slave acting entirely as an agent for a master might choose to engage in fraudulent business practices, which would increase transaction costs if allowed to go unpunished. Given that the goods confiscated by the state were not his or her own, the slave's material incentive not to defect from ordinary and honest business practices depended on the unpredictable monitoring and response of his master. Recognizing this, the state adds a severe physical sanction, one that would operate irrespective of any sanction that the slave's owner might or might not choose to impose.

Alternatively, a slave owner, as an "invisible" third party thereby insulated from suffering reputation losses, having calculated the risks of losing goods to confiscation, might seek to coerce his slave into fraudulent market practices by the threat of punishment. The state matches that (potential) threat with its own coercive threat, while also (in other legislation) limiting the absoluteness of the coercive authority exercised by masters over slaves.[23] Nikophon's law thus creates a "rational choice" situation for the seller slave, who could choose between being punished by the state or by his or her masters. The obvious fact that both choices are fundamentally bad (even if not equally bad) vividly illustrates Terry Moe's argument for why rational choice theory must take structural power asymmetries into account. The Athenian system of slavery allowed choice making by slaves, but treating a slave's choice between his torturers simply as a subset of choice about economic risk would obviously obscure essential moral as well as functional features of the system.[24] Athenian fairness had strict limits.

---

22. On slaves living apart from the masters, see Cohen 2000 with literature cited there.
23. See the discussion of the law on ὕβρις in Ober 2000. Compare the establishment of the Theseion as an official slave refuge (Christensen 1984).
24. Moe 2005. Cohen 1997 offers a detailed and insightful analysis of slavery along these lines.

Appendix: Nikophon's Law, 375/4 B.C.E.
(Rhodes and Osborne 2003: no. 25)

Resolved by the νομοθέται in the archonship of Hippodamas [375/4 B.C.E.];
Nikophon made the proposal:

1. Athenian [Ἀττικόν] silver [coin] shall be accepted [by all sellers of
   goods] when
   a. it is found [by the Approver] to be [solid] silver and
   b. has the public stamp [δημόσιος χαρακτήρ].
2. The public Approver [δοκιμαστής: a public slave, see below] shall sit
   between the [banker's] tables [in the Agora] and approve [coins] on
   these terms every day except when there is a deposit of money [state
   revenue payment], in which case [he sits] in the Council-building
   [βουλευτήριον].
   a. If anyone brings forward [to the Approver] foreign [ξενικόν] silver
      [coin] having the same stamp as Attic [coin], ἐ[ὰν καλὸν]: <if it is
      good> [the Approver] shall give it back to the man who brought it
      forward [for review];
   b. but if it has a bronze core or lead core or is fraudulent [κίβδηλος],
      he [the Approver] shall cut through it immediately and it shall be
      [confiscated as] sacred property of the Mother of the Gods and he
      shall deposit it with the Council [of 500].
3. If the Approver does not sit, or does not approve in accordance with
   the law, he shall be beaten by the συλλογεῖς τοῦ δήμου with 50 lashes
   of the whip [i.e., punished as a slave].
4. If anyone does not accept the silver which the Approver approves, he
   shall be deprived of what he is selling that day.
5. Exposures [φάσεις] shall be made [by individuals, to magistrates, as
   follows]
   a. For matters in the grain-market to the σιτοφύλακες;
   b. For matters in the Agora and the rest of the city to the συλλογεῖς
      τοῦ δήμου;
   c. For matters in the import market [ἐμπόριον] and in [the rest of] the
      Piraeus to the ἐπιμεληταὶ τοῦ ἐμπορίου—except for matters in the
      grain-market, since [φάσεις about matters] in the grain market are
      [to be made] to the σιτοφύλακες [per § 5a].

6. For matters exposed [by the legal process described in § 5], those that [concern sums that] are up to 10 drachmas the relevant magistrates [listed in § 5] shall have the power to decide. Those that are beyond 10 drachmas they [the magistrates] shall introduce to the δικαστήριον.

7. The Θεσμοθέται shall provide and allot a δικαστήριον for [the magistrates named in § 5a–c] whenever they request, or shall be fined 1,000 (?) drachmas.

8. For the man who exposes [wrongdoing, per § 5], there shall be a share of a half [of the assessed penalty] if he [serving as legal prosecutor: ὁ βουλόμενος] convicts the man whom he exposes.

9. If the [exposed and convicted] seller is a slave-man or slave-woman, he/she shall be beaten with 50 lashes of the whip by the magistrates [in § 5a–c] with responsibility in the matter.

10. If any of the magistrates does not act in accordance with what is written [here], he shall be legally denounced [εἰσαγγελλέτω] to the Council of 500 by of the Athenians who have the legal right to do so [ἔξεστιν];
    a. if he [the accused magistrate] is convicted he shall be dismissed from his office
    b. and the Council of 500 may levy an additional fine up to 500 drachmas.

11. So that there shall also be in the Piraeus an Approver for the shipowners [ναύκληροι] and the traders [ἔμποροι] and all the others [involved in exchange], the Council of 500 shall [either]
    a. appoint [an Approver] from the [existing] public slaves if available
    b. or shall buy [a slave, in which case] the ἀποδέκται shall allocate funds [for his purchase].

12. The Overseers of the import market [see § 5c] shall see that he [the Approver in the Piraeus] sits in front of the stele of Poseidon, and they [the Approver in the Piraeus and responsible magistrates] shall use the law in the same way as has been stated [above] concerning the Approver in the city.

13. Write up this law on a stone stele and set it up [καταθεῖναι]
    a. in the city between the [bankers'] tables [i.e., where the city Approver sits]
    b. and [set up a copy] in the Piraeus in front of the stele of Poseidon [i.e., where the Piraeus Approver sits].

   c. The secretary of the Council of 500 shall commission the contract
from the πωληταί, and the Sellers shall introduce [the contract] into
the Council.

14. The salary payment [μισθοφορία] for the Approver in the ἐμπόριον
[in the Piraeus] shall be [in the current year, prorated] from when he is
appointed; and the Receivers shall allocate as much [salary for him] as
for the Approver in the city.

   a. [After the current year] the salary payment [of both Approvers]
shall be from the same source as for the mint-workers [i.e., a specific
budget controlled by some board of magistrates, not specified here
but presumably ascertainable by Athenians].

15. If there is any ψήφισμα written on a stele contrary to this νόμος, the
secretary of the Council of 500 shall demolish [καθελέτω] it.

       (translation Stroud 1974, slightly emended; my section numbers)

Bibliography

Austin, M., and P. Vidal-Naquet. 1977. *Economic and Social History of Ancient Greece: An Introduction*. Berkeley.

Benkler, Y. 2006. *The Wealth of Networks: How Social Production Transforms Markets and Freedom*. New Haven.

Bogaert, R. 1976. "L'essai des monnaies dans l'antiquité." *Revue Belge de Numismatique* 122:5–34.

Buckler, J. 2003. *Aegean Greece in the Fourth Century BC*. Leiden and Boston.

Buttrey, T. V. 1981. "The Athenian Currency Law of 375/4 B.C." In O. Mørkholm and N. Waggoner, eds., *Greek Numismatics and Archaeology: Essays in Honor of Margaret Thompson*, 33–45. Wetteren, Belgium.

Buttrey, T. V. 1982. "More on the Athenian Coinage Law of 375/4 B.C." *Numismatica e Antichità Classiche* 10: 71–94.

Christensen, K. A. 1984. "The Theseion: A Slave Refuge at Athens." *AJAH* 9: 23–32.

Coase, R. H. 1988. *The Firm, the Market, and the Law*. Chicago.

Cohen, E. E. 2000. *The Athenian Nation*. Princeton.

Cohen, J. 1996. "Procedure and Substance in Deliberative Democracy." In S. Benhabib, ed., *Democracy and Difference: Contesting the Boundaries of the Political*, 94–119. Princeton.

Cohen, J. 1997. "The Arc of the Moral Universe." *Philosophy and Public Affairs* 26: 91–134.

Davies, J. K. 2003. "Greek Archives: From Record to Monument." In M. Brosius, ed.,

Ancient Archives and Archival Traditions: Concepts of Record-Keeping in the Ancient World, 323–43. Oxford.

Dubois, L. 1996. *Inscriptions grecques dialectales d'Olbia du Pont*. Geneva.

Figueira, T. J. 1998. *The Power of Money: Coinage and Politics in the Athenian Empire*. Philadelphia.

Flament, C. 2007. *Le monnayage en argent d'Athènes: De l'époque archaïque à l'époque hellénistique (c. 550–c. 40 av. J.C.)*. Louvain.

Flensted-Jensen, P., T. H. Neilsen, and L. Rubinstein, eds. 2000. *Polis and Politics: Studies in Ancient Greek History*. Copenhagen.

Griffith, G. T. 1978. "Athens in the Fourth Century." In P. Garnsey and C. R. Whittaker, eds., *Imperialism in the Ancient World*, 127–44. Cambridge.

Hansen, M. H. 1999. *The Athenian Democracy in the Age of Demosthenes: Structure, Principles, and Ideology*. Norman.

Harris, D. 1994. "Freedom of Information and Accountability: The Inventory Lists of the Parthenon." In R. Osborne and Simon Hornblower, eds., *Ritual, Finance, Politics: Athenian Democratic Accounts Presented to David Lewis*, 213–26. Oxford.

Hedrick, C. W. 1999. "Democracy and the Athenian Epigraphic Habit." *Hesperia* 68: 387–439.

Hedrick, C. W. 2000. "Epigraphic Writing and the Democratic Restoration of 307." In Flensted-Jensen, Neilsen, and Rubinstein 2000, 327–35.

Huber, J. D., and C. R. Shipan. 2002. *Deliberate Discretion: The Institutional Foundations of Bureaucratic Autonomy*. Cambridge.

Hunter, V. J. 1994. *Policing Athens: Social Control in the Attic Lawsuits, 420–320 BC*. Princeton.

Johnstone, S. 2011. *A History of Trust in Ancient Greece*. Chicago.

Keohane, R. O. 1984. *After Hegemony: Cooperation and Discord in the World Political Economy*. Princeton.

Kroll, J. H. 2011. "The Reminting of Athenian Silver Coinage, 353 BC." *Hesperia* 80: 229–59.

Kroll, J. H., and A. S. Walker. 1993. *The Greek Coins*. Princeton.

Lanni, A. 2006. *Law and Justice in the Courts of Classical Athens*. Cambridge.

Le Rider, G., and F. de Callataÿ. 2006. *Les Séleucides et les Ptolémées: L'héritage monétaire et financier d'Alexandre le Grand*. Paris.

Moe, T. 2005. "Power and Political Institutions." *Perspectives on Politics* 3: 215–33.

Moreno, A. 2008. *Feeding the Democracy: The Athenian Grain Supply in the Fifth and Fourth Centuries BC*. Oxford.

North, D. C. 1981. *Structure and Change in Economic History*. New York.

Ober, J. 2000. "Quasi-rights: Participatory Citizenship and Negative Liberties in Democratic Athens." *Social Philosophy and Policy* 17: 27–61.

Ober, J. 2005. "Law and Political Theory." In M. Gagarin and D. Cohen, eds., *Cambridge Companion to Ancient Greek Law*, 394–411. Cambridge.

Ober, J. 2008. *Democracy and Knowledge: Learning and Innovation in Classical Athens*. Princeton.

Ober, J. 2010. "The Instrumental Value of Others and Institutional Change: An Athenian Case Study." In I. Sluiter and R. Rosen, eds., *Valuing Others in Classical Antiquity*, 156–78. Leiden.

Oliver, G. J. 2007. *War, Food, and Politics in Early Hellenistic Athens*. Oxford.

Osborne, R. 1985. *Demos: The Discovery of Classical Attika*. Cambridge.

Rhodes, P. J., and R. Osborne. 2003. *Greek Historical Inscriptions, 404–323 BC*. Oxford.

Richardson, M. B. 2000. "The Location of Inscribed Laws in Fourth-Century Athens: *IG* II 2 244, on Rebuilding the Walls of Piraeus (337/6 B.C.)." In Flensted-Jensen, Neilsen, and Rubinstein 2000, 601–15.

Rutishauser, B. 2007. "A Dark Wine in the Wine Dark Sea: Production, Trade, and Athenian Policy in the Northern Aegean." *REA* 109, no. 2: 465–73.

Rutishauser, B. 2012. *Athens and the Cyclades: Economic Strategies, 540–314 BC*. Oxford.

Simon, H. A. 1955. "A Behavioral Model of Rational Choice." *Quarterly Journal of Economics* 65: 99–118.

Stewart, A., and R. S. Martin. 2005. "Attic Imported Pottery at Tel Dor Israel: An Overview." *Bulletin of the American Institutes of Oriental Research* 337: 79–94.

Stroud, R. S. 1974. "An Athenian Law on Silver Coinage." *Hesperia* 43: 157–88.

Stroud, R. S. 1998. *The Athenian Grain-Tax Law of 374/3 B.C.* Princeton.

Sunstein, C. R. 2013. *Simpler: The Future of Government*. New York.

Thaler, R. H., and C. R. Sunstein. 2008. *Nudge: Improving Decisions about Health, Wealth, and Happiness*. New Haven.

Thomas, R. 1989. *Oral Tradition and Written Record in Classical Athens*. Cambridge.

Thompson, M., O. Mørkholm, and C. M. Kraay. 1973. *An Inventory of Greek Coin Hoards*. New York.

van Alfen, P. G. 2000. "The 'Owls' from the 1973 Iraq Hoard." *AJN* 12: 9–58.

van Alfen, P. G. 2002. "The 'Owls' from the 1989 Syria Hoard, with a Review of Pre-Macedonian Coinage in Egypt." *AJN* 14:1–57.

van Alfen, P. G. 2004–5. "Herodotos' 'Aryandic' Silver and Bullion Use in Persian-Period Egypt." *AJN* 16–17: 7–46.

van Alfen, P. G. 2005. "Problems in Ancient Imitative and Counterfeit Coinage." In Z. Archibald, J. Davies, and V. Gabrielsen, eds., *Making, Moving, and Managing: The New World of Ancient Economics, 323–31 B.C.*, 322–54. Oxford.

von Reden, S. 2007. *Money in Ptolemaic Egypt: From the Macedonian Conquest to the End of the Third Century BC*. Cambridge.

Williamson, O. E. 1981. "The Economics of Organization: The Transaction Cost Approach." *American Journal of Sociology* 87: 548–77.

CHAPTER 3

Transaction Costs and Institutional Change in Egypt, ca. 1070–525 B.C.E.

Brian Muhs

Transaction costs arise from uncertainties in transactions, including the risk of disputes about the terms of an agreement or the risk of failure to fulfill the terms. Reduction of such uncertainties can assist in maximizing profits; consequently, most transactions make use of institutions to reduce uncertainties, risks, and transaction costs (North 1990: 1–9, 61–69). For example, witnesses may be used to document verbal agreements to reduce the chance of disputes about the terms, and courts may be used to try either to enforce the terms or to exact penalties. It is often theoretically possible to change institutions to reduce transaction costs. For example, notaries could be introduced to produce written transcripts of verbal agreements, and courts could require such documentation to hear a dispute. In practice, however, such changes are unlikely to be implemented unless the increased institutional costs to transactors and society are justified by the potential risk reductions. In general, higher value transactions present greater potential risks and justify the use of more effective and expensive risk-reducing institutions. Similarly, more frequent transactions allow fixed institutional costs to be more widely distributed, reducing the cost per transaction.

The ancient Egyptian institutions for documenting and enforcing agreements underwent profound changes between the end of the New Kingdom (ca. 1550–1070 B.C.E.) and the end of the Saite Period (664–525 B.C.E.). These changes used to be attributed to external influences from the Aramaic or Babylonian legal traditions, but recent studies have shown that they owed more to internal developments within the Egyptian legal tradition (Ritner 2002; Botta 2009: 199–203). This essay will argue that these internal developments had the effect of reducing transaction costs. The Egyptian state introduced increasingly effective and expensive documentation and enforcement institutions between the New Kingdom and the Saite Period. These institutions were justified by an increase in volume and value of transactions. At the same time, the Egyptian state withdrew formal support for documentation and enforcement institutions that were less expensive and socially based. Nonetheless, these socially based institutions continued to be used for lower-value transactions with correspondingly lower potential risks.

The New Kingdom (ca. 1550–1070 B.C.E.)

Documentation: Verbal Agreements and Witnesses

Documentation of property transfers and exchanges in the New Kingdom usually took the form of verbal agreements before witnesses. However, the surviving evidence for such agreements depends on written transcripts, even though transcripts may have been the exception rather than the rule. In some cases, usually on papyri, the transcripts give the names of the scribe and the witnesses who authenticated the agreements. These transcripts could have functioned as public memorandums, to remind the contracting parties and the witnesses of what they had said. This can be seen in the archive of the herder Mesi, consisting of four papyri from Gurob (in the southeast corner of the Fayyum), dating to the mid-fourteenth century B.C.E. These papyri contain transcripts of several verbal agreements that Mesi made for the purchase of land or the lease of days of slave labor, as well as a court case arising from a dispute over payment (Gardiner 1906).

In many transcripts, however, particularly those written on limestone ostraca rather than papyri, no witnesses are named. These transcripts presumably served as private memorandums. The village of Deir el-Medina has preserved many such private memorandums recording what property was exchanged, lent, or borrowed and what weight of gold, silver, or copper it was worth. Presumably, the authors of these memorandums used them as reminders of what they or others had bought, sold, lent, and borrowed. They could refer to them if they testified in a dispute, but they could not use them as independent proof, because they could not be independently authenticated. This is corroborated by several trial records from Deir el-Medina and elsewhere, which usually refer to the verbal testimonies of witnesses and only rarely to written documents (Gardiner 1905, 1935).

The limited use of written documentation in the New Kingdom should probably not be seen as mere primitivism, however. In the earlier Middle Kingdom (ca. 2050–1800 B.C.E.), there is evidence for a system for notarizing and registering written transcripts of transactions (Logan 2000). The limited use of written documentation in the New Kingdom was therefore a choice, possibly motivated by the nature of the New Kingdom economy. Property transfers and exchanges in New Kingdom Egypt regularly used weights of gold, silver, and copper as measures of value, but these were rarely exchanged themselves. Instead, real property, furniture, slaves, and animals, worth a specified weight of gold, silver, or copper, were exchanged for other property worth the same weight of gold, silver, or copper (Janssen 1975a: 494–523; Janssen 1975b: 177–79; Kemp 1989: 248–55; Römer 1998: 119–42). Often, a seller lacked sufficient property or, at least, property that the buyer desired in exchange, and the seller therefore had to borrow property from family, friends, and neighbors to complete a transaction. Lists of lent objects from Deir el-Medina suggest that a system of "open credit" existed within communities, to make it easier to complete such complicated chains of transactions (Janssen 1994: 129–36). However, while "open credit" may have facilitated local transactions, it may also have greatly complicated written documention of such transactions. There may thus have been a conscious decision to use local remedies to avoid high documentation costs.

Remedies: *Kenbet Courts* and Oracular Consultations

Disputes in New Kingdom Egypt were normally heard very locally, in village *kenbet courts*, councils composed of the notables of the village. The village of Deir el-Medina, with no more than five hundred inhabitants, had its own *kenbet* court, which shows just how local these courts were. The *kenbet* courts could themselves give judgment or refer a case to the motion oracle of the local god, whose statue was carried by his priests, usually the notables of the village. Records of trials from Deir el-Medina give the impression that the *kenbet* courts often heard disputes involving the same properties or transactions on multiple occasions, sometimes handing down the same judgment repeatedly, presumably because it had previously not been enforced (Mc-Dowell 1990). One might conclude that enforcement costs were extremely high, but the surviving evidence may overrepresent exceptional disputes. One would expect the local *kenbet* courts to be effective in resolving many local disputes. They presumably had personal knowledge of many disputes and their participants, as well as direct access to witnesses, which could have been extremely useful given the general lack of written documentation of transactions. The local *kenbet* courts presumably could also exercise considerable social pressure to resolve disputes within their villages, since they were composed of the notables of the village. They may well have been partisan, but their judgments would probably have tended to confirm the established social order. Other studies of transaction costs have noted a preference for resolving local disputes locally (cf. Kowaleski 1995: 179–221).

Exceptional disputes probably occurred when the local communities were unable to create a consensus or bring social pressure to bear. The village notables who formed the local *kenbet* courts were themselves subject to social pressure and so were unlikely to be able to resolve disputes that divided both the village and themselves. They were also unlikely to be able to apply social pressure to transacting parties from outside the community in disputes about nonlocal transactions. One might expect that these were the cases that were handled by the two national courts of appeal, the great *kenbet* courts, each led by one of Egypt's two viziers, in northern and southern Egypt, respectively. Records of trials involving the great *kenbet* courts, however, give the impression that they too heard the same disputes repeatedly, sometimes repeating their decisions and sometimes reversing them. In the most extreme case, the lawsuit of Mes, the local *kenbet* court of Memphis and one of the great *kenbet* courts heard disputes about the division and inheritance of the same plot of land on five different occasions from the late fourteenth century through the mid-thirteenth century B.C.E. and reversed themselves on each occasion. The case is also noteworthy because it privileged verbal over written testimony. The courts made their decision in the fourth suit on the basis of cadastral records and then overturned that decision in the fifth suit on the basis of witnesses, concluding that the cadastral records had been falsified. Mes then had a transcript of the lawsuit inscribed on the walls of the semipublic chapel of his tomb at Saqqara, presumably in an attempt to document his title and prevent further suits (Gardiner 1905).

Perhaps because *kenbet* courts could be seen as partisan, they made considerable use of oracular consultations in the New Kingdom (McDowell 1990). Most oracular consultations occurred during processions and other appearances of divine images during festivals, as the god was otherwise inaccessible to the greater public (Černy 1962: 36). During oracular consultations, the petitioner approached the divine image and presented it with a verbal or written statement or choice of statements, which some scholars call "oracle petitions." The god then expressed its approval, disapproval, or choice, through movements transmitted by the bearers of the divine image. The entire process of petition and answer was sometimes recorded, in records that some scholars call "oracle protocols." The approved or chosen statements were sometimes recast as the speech of the god, both within oracle protocols and in independent texts sometimes called "oracle decrees" (Römer 1994: 161–66; Winand 2003: 607–12). It is generally believed, however, that there were no true voice oracles in ancient Egypt (Černy 1962: 43–45).

The Early Third Intermediate Period (ca. 1070–850 B.C.E.)

Documentation and Remedies

Documentation of property transfers and exchanges in the early Third Intermediate Period probably continued to consist primarily of verbal agreements before witnesses, as in the New Kingdom. Few written transcripts of such agreements have survived from this period, but several oracular consultations refer solely to the verbal claims of the disputing parties (see below). Furthermore, the few surviving transcripts rarely record the names of scribes or witnesses, even when the document was clearly intended to serve as a public record of a transaction. One such public record is the stela Cairo JdE 70218, found in the ruins of Fustat and dating to the early tenth century B.C.E. (Munier 1922; Jansen-Winkeln 2007a: 150–51). It records that Ity has purchased two arouras of fields from Ankhefenkhonsu for two deben and two kite of silver. Despite the lack of authentication, this simple public record of the transaction and the amount paid might have deterred disputes about payment, which were exceedingly common (Muhs 2009: 273).

Disputes arising from agreements in the early Third Intermediate Period probably continued to be resolved locally, often with the help of oracular consultions, as in the New Kingdom. There is little evidence for *kenbet* courts from this period, but the New Kingdom tradition of oracular consultations continued, as seen in the oracular consultations in the hieratic papyrus Brooklyn 16.205 (Parker 1962: 49–52), which probably comes from Thebes and, contrary to the editor, probably dates to the late eleventh or early tenth century B.C.E. (Von Beckerath 1994). The text is an oracle protocol and records the use of oracular consultations to resolve disputes over payments, namely, whether the payments had been made. In these oracular consultations, the god was probably presented with two written alternatives and did no more than indicate which of the two proposals he prefered. Nonetheless, his choice was then paraphrased as his speech (Muhs 2009: 272). Similar oracular consultations include those in the larger Dakhla stela Ashmolean 1894.107a, from the Dakhla Oasis (Spiegelberg 1899; Gardiner 1933), and those on papyri from el-Hiba and/or Nag' ed-Deir (Ryholt 1993; Fischer-Elfert 1996). The latter are oracle petitions consisting of two written alternatives that would have been presented to the god. These were apparently intended to resolve another dispute about payment (Muhs 2009: 272–73).

Oracular Property Decrees and Donation Stelae

During the early Third Intermediate Period, the First Prophets of Amun at Thebes essentially ruled southern Egypt, though they acknowledged the nominal kings at Tanis in the north. The First Prophets used their authority in the south to introduce a new form of oracular consultation, here called an "oracular property decree," to divinely guarantee recently acquired property titles against future litigation. These oracular property decrees thus reduced enforcement risks and transaction costs, at least for those few who had access to them, because their use appears to have been restricted to a privileged elite, namely, the immediate family members of the First Prophets.

The First Prophets of Amun at Thebes introduced a number of innovations alongside traditional oracular consultations. One such innovation consisted of special oracular consultations called "divine audiences" (pḥ-nṯr), held within the temple of Amun at Karnak. There, the First Prophets consulted the god Amun-Re about important political and judicial affairs and received divine sanction for their authority (Kruchten 1986: 325–36). For example, the Banishment Stela from Thebes (Louvre C. 256) records that the First Prophet Menkheperre consulted Amun-Re before recalling exiles from the oases (Von Beckerath 1968; Jansen-Winkeln 2007a: 72–74). Similarly, an inscription in the temple of Amun at Karnak records that the First Prophet Pinudjem II presided over consultations with Amun-Re in the investigation and acquital of the scribe Thotmose son of Suawyamun (Kruchten 1986; Jansen-Winkeln 2007a: 169–77).

The form of oracular property decrees closely resembles that of the special oracular consultations orchestrated by the First Prophets in the temple of Amun at Karnak, and one oracular property decree may be explicitly called a divine audience (Winand 2003: 639). However, oracular property decrees were intended to prevent title disputes from occurring, in contrast to traditional judicial oracular consultations that were intended to resolve disputes after they had arisen. There are three well-preserved examples of oracular property decrees:

1. the oracular property decree for Henettawy daughter of Istemkheb, inscribed in the temple of Amun at Karnak, dating to the early tenth century B.C.E. (Gardiner 1962: 57–64; Winand 2003: 614–72; Jansen-Winkeln 2007a: 177–82);

2. the oracular property decree for Maatkare daughter of King Psusennes, also inscribed in the temple of Amun at Karnak, dating to the late tenth century B.C.E. (Gardiner 1962: 64–69; Winand 2003: 672–90; Jansen-Winkeln 2007a: 182–83); and

3. the oracular property decree for Iuwerot and his son Khaenwase, inscribed on a red granite stela found at Karnak, dating to the early ninth century B.C.E. (Legrain 1897; Erman 1897; Menu 1989, 1998; Jansen-Winkeln 2007b: 77–80).

All the beneficiaries were immediate family members of First Prophets of Amun at Karnak (Muhs 2009: 267–68).

The use of oracular consultations in oracular property decrees to guarantee title for private property has a parallel in the use of oracular consultations in donation stelae to guarantee title for property donated to temples for funerary and other pious foundations. Donation stelae appear already in the New Kingdom, but the majority date to the Third Intermediate Period (Meeks 1979). The earliest in the Third Intermediate Period series is Cairo JdE 66285, a red granite donation stela of the future king Shoshenk I for his father, Nemrat, found at Abydos and dating to the mid-tenth century B.C.E. (Blackman 1941; Jansen-Winkeln 2007a: 159–62). The text records an oracular consultation in the form of an oracle protocol. An unnamed king, perhaps Psusennes II, puts two statements to Amun-Re, king of the gods. First, Shoshenk shall succeed his father, Nemrat; second, Amun-Re shall slay anyone who interferes with the pious foundation for a statue of Nemrat son of Mehetenweskhet. The great god assents, and the king reiterates that Shoshenk shall succeed his father, Nemrat. The king then orders that the statue be sent to Abydos and that a stela bearing the decree be erected in the temple of Osiris at Abydos (Muhs 2009: 270–71). Another donation stela that explicitly records an oracular consultation in the form of an oracle protocol is Cairo JdE 45327, a donation stela of Nimlot for Djedptahiuefankh, found at Tell el-Minia wa el-Shorafa and dating to the mid-ninth century B.C.E. (Daressy 1915: 140–43; Iversen 1941: 3–18; Jansen-Winkeln 2007b: 131–33). It begins with the date, followed by the specifications of the field being presented to Ptah. Then Nimlot son of Osorkon II states that he has donated the field for Djedptahiue-fankh and that the god Ptah shall slay anyone who interferes with the pious foundation. The great god assents very greatly (Muhs 2009: 271).

Oracular property decrees and donation stelae with oracular consultations usually contain a statement declaring that the current owner legally acquired the property. This shows that the purpose of these oracles was not to make a disputed title clear for the owner, because the title was not in dispute. Rather, the purpose of these oracles was to confirm that the title was clear (Muhs 2009: 268–69). The statement that the property was acquired legally may consist of a simple declaration that the property was acquired by purchase or by inheritance (Winand 2003: 666–68, 688–90). Alternatively, the statement may provide actual evidence that the property was acquired in a legal manner, by (a) declaring that the properties were purchased and that the sellers were satisfied, (b) specifying that the properties have been registered with the temple of Amun according to the names of the previous owners and the amount of money paid to them, and (c) explicitly listing each of the properties with the names of their previous owners and amount paid (Menu 1989: 347–52; 1998: 190–96). The donation stela of Shoshenk I for Nemrat similarly provides proofs that the property used to establish the pious foundation was acquired legally, including a list of the properties and servants assigned to the pious foundation and the amounts paid for them to the treasury of the temple of Osiris at Abydos.

Oracular property decrees and donation stelae with oracular consultations usually also contain a statement declaring that the owner will pass the property to his heir or other designate. This explains the need to confirm that the title is clear: the current owner wishes to guarantee title for the new owner to protect him from challenges to his title (Winand 2003: 668–70; Muhs 2009: 269–

70). The oracular property decree for Iuwerot and Khaenwase is more explicit and thereby reveals who was thought to be most likely to challenge the title of the new owner, namely, the new owner's brothers, sisters, and cousins. In the donation stela of Shoshenk I for Nemrat, Shoshenk cannot inherit the pious foundation, but the foundation cements his right to succeed his father.

Oracular property decrees and donation stelae with oracular consultations typically also contain one or more statements declaring that anyone who defies or challenges the preceding statements will incur a wrathful manifestation of the gods (Sottas 1913: 161–65; Menu 1989: 356–57; Menu 1998: 200–201; Muhs 2009: 270–71). This is the ostensible means by which the title is guaranteed for the owners. Oracular property decrees and donation stelae with oracular consultations may not have had to rely solely on the wrath of the gods to guarantee their titles, however. Their proofs of legal acquisition, together with their statement of intent to transfer to heirs, would have been difficult for even the most partisan *kenbet* court, local or great, to dispute. Their monumental semipublic format—on stelae standing in the courts of temples or inscribed on the walls of the temples—would have made them hard to ignore. The temple personnel who ordered, permitted, or simply witnessed these stelae and inscriptions being erected or inscribed could have authenticated them. Egyptians evidently considered stelae to be a reliable form of documentation, as seen in the later demotic petition *P.Ryl.dem.* 9 (Vittmann 1998), from el-Hiba and dating to 513 B.C.E., which provides copies of two Hieratic stelae as evidence.

The use of oracular property decrees died out rapidly in the Twenty-Second Dynasty, as did the use of oracular consultations in donation stelae. In most later donation stelae, emphasis is placed on the local prince presenting the property to the gods, with a simple statement that the gods will inflict unpleasant and obscene punishments on the person and families of anyone who interferes with the pious foundation (Sottas 1913: 145–54). A response by the gods is not given, making it unlikely that any oracular consultation took place.

The Late Third Intermediate Period (ca. 850–664 B.C.E.)

Documentation: Abnormal Hieratic Contracts

The use of oracular consultations in oracular property decrees and donation stelae disappeared in the late Third Intermediate Period and were replaced by a much more accessible means of reducing enforcement risks and transaction costs. Verbal agreements were increasingly transcribed, notarized, and registered. Because Egypt was divided into multiple principalities, agreements made in southern Egypt employed the script and contract formulary today called "abnormal hieratic," while those made in northern Egypt presumably employed the demotic script and contract formulary, though virtually no documents from northern Egypt survive from this period. Both of these new formularies required the first contracting party to give the resulting contract to the second contracting party as proof of title transfer and to guarantee clear title for the second party.

The abnormal hieratic system of witnessed and notarized contracts was based on a verbal statement made by the first contracting party to the second contracting party, usually containing an oath with a series of promises including a guarantee of clear title. A notary made a transcript of the statement of the first contracting party, and a number of literate witnesses then copied the transcript, to certify that it agreed with the verbal statement in the event that one or both contracting parties were illiterate, as well as to guarantee the identities of the contracting parties (Pestman 1981: 161; 1994: 26–27, 30–31). Occasionally, the first contracting party also signed the transcript (Depauw 2003). The second contracting party assented to the statement by accepting the transcript of it (Pestman 1981: 161–62; 1994: 21–22).

The abnormal hieratic contract formulary may have begun to develop already in the late ninth or early eighth century B.C.E. Evidence for this is provided by a group of abstracts of hieratic contracts preserved on *P.Berlin* 3048 verso, from Thebes and probably dating to that period (Payraudeau 2004: 82–85; 2009: 291–97). *P.Berlin* 3048 verso contains thirty-seven separate texts, most of which are as yet unpublished (Donker van Heel 2002). One of the few published texts (no. 36) consists of abstracts of marriage contracts (Möller 1918: 1–31; Lüddeckens 1960: 10–11), which contained an oath by a contractor swearing to fulfill his obligations, thereby guaranteeing the contract (Muhs 2009: 274). The use of oaths was not standard in the abstracts of contracts on *P.Berlin* 3048 verso, however, because another published text (no. 5) consists of a loan contract without an oath (Möller 1921).

The oldest actual abnormal hieratic contracts, as opposed to abstracts, date to the late eighth century B.C.E., as in *P.Leiden* K 128, an abnormal hieratic record of the sale of a slave, from Thebes and dating to 726 B.C.E. (Vleeming 1980). The seller first confirms that he has received payment for the slave, thereby deterring disputes over whether payment had actually been made. The seller then swears an oath that no one else has a claim to the slave, thereby guaranteeing that the title to the slave is clear. Note that the seller identifies his children and siblings as those most likely to challenge the title of the new owner. The seller should know better than anyone else who such heirs might be and whether they indeed had any unsatisfied claims; therefore it was quite logical to require the seller to guarantee that the title was clear (Muhs 2009: 274).

The need for these documents may have been generated by an increase in the volume and value of nonlocal transactions. There is some evidence that weights of gold, copper, and especially silver were increasingly used as a media of exchange, rather than just as measures of value, in the late Third Intermediate Period. Texts increasingly refer to exchanges of property for a weight of silver rather than for other property worth a weight of silver. One can never know exactly what was really exchanged, of course; but the very fact that it was no longer necessary to mention what was exchanged is surely significant. Furthermore, texts refer to silver from the treasury of Harsaphes. This may simply indicate a certain quality, but some have suggested that it indicates a form of coinage, though there is no physical evidence for this (Müller-Wollermann 2007a; 2007b: 176–78).

Remedies: The Great *Kenbet* Court and the Quitclaim

The oath in abnormal hieratic contracts has the first contractor swear that the title is clear from claims by children and siblings. In contrast to the contracts of the Ptolemaic period, the abnormal hieratic contracts never record that the children were present and consented to the transaction or ceded their claim to the property. In the event that such a claim should arise, however, responsibility for enforcement is said to lie with the courts, who are instructed not to hear the claim. In the late Third Intermediate Period, there are no references to local village *kenbet* courts and a total of five references to the great *kenbet* court of Thebes (Allam 1991: 115). The latter suggest that the two-level court system of the New Kingdom remained in use in the late Third Intermediate Period. It is best not to read too much into the absence of references to local courts, given the small number of references of any kind.

Access to the courts may have been restricted. Among the comparatively few documents surviving from the late Third Intermediate Period is an abnormal hieratic public protest (*šꜥr*), from Thebes and dating to 686 B.C.E. (Vittmann 2000: 135–50). In the demotic legal system, public protests were used to prevent others from obtaining clear title to a piece of property. If one made a public protest each year for three years, the dispute could be heard by a law court (Muhs 2002). The abnormal hieratic legal system is less well known than the demotic, but it seems likely that the abnormal hieratic public protest had a similar use.

Furthermore, one of the five references to the great *kenbet* court of Thebes occurs in the abnormal hieratic quitclaim contract *P.Louvre* E. 3228c, from Thebes and dating to 685 (Malinine 1951; Menu 1986). In it, two parties are said to have disputed before the great *kenbet* court, the judges of the court and the chief scribe of documents have ordered the first party to write for the second party that they no longer lay claim to the object of dispute, and the result is the papyrus. It is highly significant that the court has ordered the loser of the dispute to write a quitclaim, because this would have served as a proof of clear title, preventing further dispute over payment and making the decision far more decisive than the nonbinding decisions of local *kenbet* courts in earlier periods.

The Saite Period (664–525 B.C.E.)

Documentation: Demotic Contracts

The reform of the Egyptian documentation system begun in the late Third Intermediate Period appears to have been completed in the Saite Period. Verbal agreements continued to be transcribed, notarized, and registered, and the first contracting party continued to give the resulting contract to the second contracting party as proof of title transfer and to guarantee clear title for the second party. However, the demotic script and contract formulary, which developed in northern Egypt during the late Third Intermediate Period, was now imposed on southern Egypt as well, though it took nearly a century for both to be fully adopted (Donker van Heel 1994). The change from the abnormal hieratic script and contract formulary to the demotic was subtle, because, in southern Egypt, both contract formularies were written by the same families of contract notaries, usually attached to temples in major regional towns (Pestman 1994: 155–63; Donker van Heel 1994). Literate witnesses, often members of the families of contract notaries, now usually only signed the contract, rather than fully recopying it (Pestman 1994: 165).

The oldest examples of the demotic formulary from the early seventh century B.C.E. begin with the date and the statement "The first contracting party has said to the second contracting party." This statement was followed by a first-person transcript of the statements of the first party, consisting of a series of promises, including both a guarantee that the title was clear and a guarantee to clear the title if it was not clear, concluded by an oath confirming the promises. By the sixth century B.C.E., however, the oath was omitted, presumably because the remedies offered by the state were considered sufficient without invoking the gods.

The costs of these documents were considerable. Two abnormal hieratic contracts from Thebes, *P.Choix* 9 and 10 (635 and 620 B.C.E.; Malinine 1953: 56–71, 72–84), and two demotic contracts from Thebes, *P.BM Reich* 10117 (ca. 524 B.C.E.; Reich 1914: 9–25) and *P.Tsenhor* 10 (510 B.C.E.; Pestman 1994: 71–73), suggest that there was a transfer tax of 10 percent of the cost of the property involved (Vleeming 1992). However, the cost of these documents may have been justified because they made nonlocal transactions more enforceable, thereby increasing the market for and presumably the value of the properties involved. Furthermore, the increasing use of gold, copper, and especially silver as both a store of credit and a medium of exchange in the Saite Period facilitated both the purchase of properties and the payment of the transfer tax. This increased use can be seen in the large numbers and sizes of silver hoards found in the Egyptian Delta that are composed of archaic Greek silver coins. Egypt was rich in native gold but poor in native silver; therefore many of the coins in these hoards must be imports, presumably in exchange for Egyptian papyrus and linen, though probably not for grain at this date (Muhs 2005: 2–6). The increasing use of imported Greek silver coins or imitations thereof is reflected in references to Greek staters in demotic texts in the fifth century B.C.E. (Chauveau 2000: 134–43).

Remedies: The Houses of Judgment and Private Associations.

The demotic contract formulary has the first contractor promise that the title is clear from claims by children and siblings, much like the oath in abnormal hieratic contracts. However, demotic contracts also make the first contractor explicitly liable for clearing the title of any such claim that should arise, as in *P.Ryl.* 1, from el-Hiba and dating to 644 B.C.E. (Griffith 1909: 44–47, 201–6).

Responsibility for enforcement of demotic contracts was therefore shared between the contractors and the courts.

Perhaps for this reason, the two levels of courts in use since the New Kingdom were probably abolished in the Saite Period in favor of a single level of courts. The evidence for this reform consists of the disappearance of the paired terms "*kenbet* court" and "great *kenbet* court" and their replacement by a single term, "houses of judgment" ($^c.wy.w$ n *wpy*). These houses of judgment were composed of boards of judges (*wp.w* or *wpty.w*) and were associated with temples in major regional towns, perhaps the same temples with which contract notaries were associated (Allam 1991: 116–19). Unsuccessful litigants continued to be required to cede all further claims to disputed property.

This disappearance of local *kenbet* courts might be associated with the appearance of local private associations in Egypt from the Saite Period onward. Elsewhere in the Near East, private associations known as *marzēaḥ* date back to the third millenium B.C.E. (McLaughlin 2001), but the earliest evidence for formal private associations in Egypt dates from the sixth century B.C.E. (De Cenival 1986); the earliest preserved association rules date from the early fourth century B.C.E. (De Cenival 1988). Better preserved association rules from the Ptolemaic period show similarities to contemporary Greek association rules, with provisions for regular social gathering and drinking, funds for the collective care and burial of association members and their families, and fines for antisocial behavior between association members, including instigating formal legal proceedings against other members of the association before first attempting to resolve the dispute within the association (Muhs 2001).

The comparatively late appearance of private associations in Egypt compared to the rest of the Near East may thus be due to the existence of local *kenbet* courts, which filled many of the roles of local private associations elsewhere. The disappearance of local *kenbet* courts in the Saite Period may, in turn, have created a social and judicial void, which was then filled by private associations. The private associations re-created a local forum where social networks could attempt to negotiate, mediate, arbitrate, or otherwise resolve local disputes, without resorting to regional authorities, such as the houses of judgment. As noted earlier, this could reflect a preference for resolving some local disputes locally (Kowaleski 1995: 179–221).

Conclusion

During the New Kingdom, agreements were primarily verbal. They were usually witnessed by local village courts, sometimes transcribed, but rarely notarized, and there were no explicit title guarantees. The first tier of litigation began in the same local village courts that witnessed the agreements, and decisions were often not binding. Reading between the lines, it appears that local social networks played an important role in preventing and resolving disputes and in enforcing remedies. Such local networks can provide considerable protection to transacting parties, as long as the parties are and remain part of the same network and as long as disputes do not divide the network. Numerous examples of long-running disputes suggest that such divisions were not uncommon. Nonetheless, this system of documentation and enforcement sufficed, because most transactions involved barter and were local.

During the first half of the second millenium B.C.E., there was a series of reforms to the ancient Egyptian legal system that seem intended to provide additional protection to transacting parties external to local social networks. During the early Third Intermediate Period, the First Prophets of Amun at Thebes became the effective rulers of much of southern Egypt, and their position allowed them to use oracular consultations with the gods to divinely guarantee property titles against litigation for a priviledged elite. This reform was abandoned after the rule of the First Prophets came to an end.

A more profound transformation of the ancient Egyptian legal system occurred during the late Third Intermediate Period and the Saite Period, when the state transferred much of the responsibility for protecting property rights from local social networks to regional authorities. Notaries associated with regional temples increasingly transcribed and registered verbal agreements in the abnormal hieratic or demotic scripts. New formularies required the first contracting party to guarantee property titles for the second party against litigation. The first tier of litigation moved to courts associated with the regional temples. Access to the courts was restricted, and unsuccessful litigants were required to cede all further claims to disputed property. This new system of documentation and enforcement was undoubtedly more expensive, but it was probably also more effective at reducing the risks and costs of unsuccessful enforcement, especially for nonlocal transactions. Its introduction was probably justified by the increasing volume and value of nonlocal transactions, reflected in the increased use of silver as a medium of exchange rather than a measure of value.

Bibliography

Allam, S. 1991. "Egyptian Law Courts in Pharaonic and Hellenistic Times." *JEA* 77: 115–26.

Blackman, A. M. 1941. "The Stela of Shoshenk, Great Chief of the Meshwesh." *JEA* 27: 83–95 and pls. 10–12.

Botta, A. F. 2009. *The Aramaic and Egyptian Legal Traditions at Elephantine, an Egyptological Approach.* Library of Second Temple Studies 64. London.

Broekman, G. P. F., R. F. Demarée, and O. E. Kaper, eds. 2009. *The Libyan Period in Egypt: Historical and Cultural Studies into the 21st–24th Dynasties: Proceedings of a Conference at Leiden University, 25–27 October 2007.* Egyptologische Uitgaven 23. Louvain.

Černy, J. 1962. "Egyptian Oracles." In Parker 1962: 35–48.

Chauveau, M. 2000. "La première mention du statère d'argent en Égypte." *Transeuphratène* 20: 137–43.

Daressy, G. 1915. "Trois stèles de la période Bubastite." *Annales du Service des Antiquités de l'Égypte* 15: 140–47.

De Cenival, F. 1986. "Comptes d'une association religieuse thébaine datant des années 29 à 33 du roi Amasis." *Revue d'Égyptologie* 37: 13–29.

De Cenival, F. 1988. "Papyrus Seymour de Ricci: Le plus ancien des règlements d'association religieuse (4ème siècle av. J.-C.) (*Pap.Bibl.Nationale* E 241)." *Revue d'Égyptologie* 39: 37–46.

Depauw, M. 2003. "Autograph Confirmation in Demotic Contracts." *CE* 78: 66–88.

Donker van Heel, K. 1994. "The Lost Battle of Peteamonip Son of Petehorresbe." *Egitto e vicino oriente* 17: 115–24.

Donker van Heel, K. 2002. "The Scribbling-Pad of Djedmontefankh Son of Aafenmut, Priest of Amonrasonter and Overseer of the King's Treasury (*P. Berlin* 3048 verso)." In Ryholt 2002: 139–47.

Erman, A. 1897. "Zu den Legrain'schen Inschriften," Part I. "Das Testament eines Hohenpriesters." *Zeitschrift für Ägyptische Sprache und Altertumskunde* 35: 19–24.

Fischer-Elfert, H.-W. 1996. "Two Oracle Petitions Addressed to Horus-khau with Some Notes on the Oracular Amuletic Decrees (*P. Berlin* P 8525 and P 8526)." *JEA* 82: 129–44.

Gardiner, A. H. 1905. *The Inscription of Mes: A Contribution to the Study of Egyptian Judicial Procedure.* Leipzig.

Gardiner, A. H. 1906. "Four Papyri of the 18th Dynasty from Kahun." *ZÄS* 43: 27–47.

Gardiner, A. H. 1933. "The Dakhleh Stela." *JEA* 19: 19–30 and pls. 5–7.

Gardiner, A. H. 1935. "A Lawsuit Arising from the Purchase of Two Slaves." *JEA* 21: 140–46.

Gardiner, A. H. 1962. "The Gods of Thebes as Guarantors of Personal Property." *JEA* 48: 57–69.

Griffith, F. L. 1909. *Catalogue of the Demotic Papyri in the John Rylands Library.* Vol. 3, *Key-List, Translations, Commentaries, and Indices.* Manchester.

Iversen, E. 1941. *Two Inscriptions concerning Private Donations to Temples.* Det Kgl. Danske Videnskabernes Selskab. Historisk-filologiske Meddeleelser. 27, no. 5. Copenhagen.

Jansen-Winkeln, K. 2007a. *Inschriften der Spätzeit.* Vol. 1, *Die 21. Dynastie.* Wiesbaden.

Jansen-Winkeln, K. 2007b. *Inschriften der Spätzeit.* Vol. 2, *Die 22.–24. Dynastie.* Wiesbaden.

Janssen, J. J. 1975a. *Commodity Prices from the Ramessid Period: An Economic Study of the Village of Necropolis Workmen at Thebes.* Leiden.

Janssen, J. J. 1975b. "Economic History during the New Kingdom." *Studien zur altägyptischen Kultur* 3: 127–85.

Janssen, J. J. 1994. "Debts and Credit in the New Kingdom." *JEA* 80: 129–36.

Kemp, B. 1989. *Ancient Egypt: Anatomy of a Civilization.* London.

Kowaleski, M. 1995. *Local Markets and Regional Trade in Medieval Exeter.* Cambridge.

Kruchten, J.-M. 1986. *Le grand texte oraculaire de Djéhoutymose: Intendent du domaine d'Amon sous le pontificat de Pinedjem II.* Monographies Reine Élisabeth 5. Brussels.

Legrain, G. 1897. "Deux stèles trouvées à Karnak en février 1897," Part I. "Stèle de l'apanage." *Zeitschrift für Ägyptische Sprache und Altertumskunde* 35: 13–16.

Logan, T. 2000. "The *Jmyt-pr* Document: Form, Function, and Significance." *JARCE* 37: 49–73.

Lüddeckens, E. 1960. *Ägyptische Eheverträge.* Ägyptologische Abhandlungen 1. Wiesbaden.

Malinine, M. 1951. "Un judgement rendu à Thèbes sous la XXVe dynastie (*Pap. Louvre* E. 3228 c)." *Revue d'Égyptologie* 6: 157–78.

Malinine, M. 1953. *Choix de textes juridiques en hiératique "anormale" et en démotique (XXVe–XXVIIe dynasties), première partie.* Bibliothèque de l'École des Hautes Études 300. Paris.

McDowell, A. G. 1990. *Jurisdiction in the Workmen's Community of Deir el-Medina.* Egyptologische Uitgaven 5. Leiden.

McLaughlin, J. J. 2001. *The Marzēaḥ in the Prophetic Literature: References and Allusions in Light of the Extra-Biblical Evidence.* Supplements to Vetus Testamentum 86. Leiden.

Meeks, D. 1979. "Les donations aux temples dans l'Égypte du Ier millénaire avant J.-C." In C. Lipiński, ed., *State and Temple Economy in the Ancient Near East,* 2: 605–87. Orientalia Lovaniensia Analecta 6. Louvain.

Menu, B. 1986. "Cessions de services et engagements pour dette sous les rois kouchites et saïtes." *Revue d'Égyptologie* 36: 73–87. Reprinted in Menu 1998: 369–83.

Menu, B. 1989. "La stèle dite de l'Apanage." In M.-M. Mactoux and E. Geny, eds., *Mélanges P. Lévêque*, vol. 2, *Anthropologie et société*, 337–57. Centre de Recherches d'Histoire Ancienne 82. Besançon. Reprinted in Menu 1998: 183–203.

Menu, B. 1998. *Recherches sur l'histoire juridique, économique et sociale de l'ancienne Égypte.* Vol. 2. Bibliothèque d'étude 122. Cairo.

Möller, G. 1918. *Zwei ägyptische Eheverträge aus vorsaitischer Zeit.* Abhandlungen der preussischen Akademie der Wissenschaften, phil.-hist. Klasse, no. 3. Berlin.

Möller, G. 1921. "Ein ägyptischer Schuldschein der zweiundzwanzigsten Dynastie." *Sitzungsberichte der preussischen Akademie der Wissenschaften* 1921: 298–304.

Muhs, B. 2001. "Membership in Private Associations in Ptolemaic Tebtunis." *JESHO* 44: 1–21.

Muhs, B. 2002. "Clear Title, Public Protests, and *P. Brux. dem.* 4." In Ryholt 2002: 259–72.

Muhs, B. 2005. *Tax Receipts, Taxpayers, and Taxes in Early Ptolemaic Thebes.* Oriental Institute Publications 126. Chicago.

Muhs, B. 2009. "Oracular Property Decrees in Their Historical and Chronological Context." In Broekman, Demarée, and Kaper 2009: 265–75.

Müller-Wollermann, R. 2007a. "Ägypten auf dem Weg zur Geldwirtschaft." In J.-C. Goyon and C. Cardin, eds., *Proceedings of the Ninth International Congress of Egyptologists / Actes du Neuvième Congrès International des Égyptologues*, 2: 1351–59. Orientalia Lovaniensia Analecta 150. Louvain.

Müller-Wollermann, R. 2007b. "Die ökonomische Bedeutung von Tempelschatzhäusern." In M. Fitzenreiter, ed., *Das Heilige und die Ware, Zum Spannungsfeld von Religion und Ökonomie, Workshop vom 26.05 bis 28.05.2006*, 171–78. Internet-Beiträge zur Ägyptologie und Sudanarchäologie 7. London.

Munier, H. 1922. "Un achat de terrains au temps du roi Si-Amon." In *Recueil d'études égyptologiques dédiées à la mémoire de Jean-François Champollion*, 361–66. Bibliothèque de l'École de Hautes Études 234. Paris.

North, D. C. 1990. *Institutions, Institutional Change, and Economic Performance.* Cambridge.

Parker, R. A., ed. 1962. *A Saite Oracle Papyrus from Thebes in the Brooklyn Museum (Papyrus Brooklyn 47.218.3).* Brown Egyptological Studies 4. Providence.

Payraudeau, F. 2004. "Le règne de Takélot III et les débuts de la domination koushite à Thèbes." *Göttinger Miszellen* 198: 79–90.

Payraudeau, F. 2009. "Takeloth III: Considerations on Old and New Documents." In Broekman, Demarée, and Kaper 2009: 291–302.

Pestman, P. W. 1981. *L'archivo di Amenothes figlio di Horos (P. Tor. Amenothes).* Milan.

Pestman, P. W. 1994. *Les papyrus démotiques de Tsenhor (P. Tsenhor).* Vol. 1, *Textes.* Studia Demotica 4. Louvain.

Reich, N. 1914. *Papyri juristischen Inhalts in hieratischer und demotischer Schrift aus dem British Museum*. Denkschriften der Kaiserlichen Akademie der Wissenschaften in Wien, Philosophisch-historische Klasse 55.3. Vienna.

Ritner, R. K. 2002. "Third Intermediate Period Antecedents of Demotic Legal Terminology." In Ryholt 2002: 343–59.

Römer, M. 1994. *Gottes- und Priesterherrschaft in Ägypten am Ende des Neuen Reiches: Ein religionsgechichtliches Phänomen und seine sozialen Grundlagen*. Ägypten und Altes Testament 21. Wiesbaden.

Römer, M. 1998. "Gold/Silber/Kupfer—Geld oder nicht? Die Bedeutung der drei Metalle als allgemeine Äquivalente im Neuen Reich, mit einem Anhang zu den Geldtheorien der Volkswirtschaftslehre." *Studien zur altägyptischen Kultur* 26: 119–42.

Ryholt, K. 1993. "A Pair of Oracle Petitions Addressed to Horus-of-the-Camp." *JEA* 79: 189–98.

Ryholt, K., ed. 2002. *Acts of the Seventh International Conference of Demotic Studies, Copenhagen 23–27 August 1999*. Carsten Niebuhr Publications 27. Copenhagen.

Sottas, H. 1913. *La préservation de la propriété funéraire dans l'ancienne Égypte avec le recueil des formules d'imprécation*. Bibliothèque de l'École des Hautes Études 205. Paris.

Spiegelberg, W. 1899. "Eine Stele aus der Oase Dachel." *Recueil de Travaux* 21: 12–21.

Vittmann, G. 1998. *Der demotische Papyrus Rylands 9*. Vol. 1, *Text und Übersetzung*; vol. 2, *Kommentare und Indizes*. Ägypten und Altes Testament 38. Wiesbaden.

Vittmann, G. 2000. "Zwei kursivhieratische Urkunden in Kairo." *Enchoria* 26: 125–50.

Vleeming, S. P. 1980. "The Sale of a Slave in the Time of Pharaoh Py." *Oudheidkundige Mededelingen uit het Rijksmuseum van Oudheden* 61: 1–17.

Vleeming, S. P. 1992. "The Tithe of the Scribes (and) Representatives." In J. H. Johnson, ed., *Life in a Multi-Cultural Society: Egypt from Cambyses to Constantine and Beyond*, 343–50. Studies in Ancient Oriental Civilization 51. Chicago.

Von Beckerath, J. 1968. "Die 'Stele der Verbannten' im Museum des Louvre." *Revue d'Égyptologie* 20: 7–36 and pl. 1.

Von Beckerath, J. 1994. "Zur Datierung des Papyrus Brooklyn 16.205." *Göttinger Miszellen* 140: 15–17.

Winand, J. 2003. "Les décrets oraculaires pris en l'honneur d'Henouttaouy et de Maâtkarê (Xe et VIIe Pylônes)." *Cahiers de Karnak* 11: 603–710.

CHAPTER 4

Ptolemaic Governance and Transaction Costs

J. G. Manning

I discuss in this essay the relationship between Ptolemaic governance and transaction costs with respect to private contracts written in demotic Egyptian. I examine the nexus between governance and the cost of transacting by highlighting one new institution, the acquisition of property via the public auction, and two key features of Ptolemaic Egyptian contracts: witnessing and registration.[1] Although the Ptolemaic and Roman papyri provide legal historians with comparative riches, a small percentage of what was written survives, the documents come from only a few places in Egypt, and the number of both Greek and demotic Egyptian contracts fall off considerably in the first century B.C.E.[2] Any general model for structure and change over time, while worthwhile proposing, must therefore remain tentative. In that spirit, while acknowledging the independent developments of the demotic Egyptian scribal tradition, I suggest that the written forms of demotic contract in the Ptolemaic period underwent significant changes under the pressure of what I have called elsewhere (Manning 2003a) the "Ptolemaicizing" of the Egyptian economy.

This process of reform, however, did not entirely displace the ancient organizational and institutional structures or social networks that were tradi-

---

1. For an overview, see Yiftach-Firanko 2014 and chap. 6 in the present volume.
2. One issue that I explore elsewhere (Manning 2003b) is the paucity of contracts for animal sale in the Ptolemaic period and their relative abundance in the Roman period. On the survival of papyrus texts, see Cuvigny 2009.

tionally centered around the temples and their ancient scribal traditions of contract making. To be sure, the shift from hieratic to the demotic script in the middle of the seventh century B.C.E. was important. In chapter 3 of this volume, Brian Muhs provides a general sketch of the history and the developments of Egyptian written contracts from the New Kingdom to the Saite Period.[3] The early Ptolemaic kings reshaped state institutions in accordance with the formation of what North, Wallis, and Weingast (2009) have called the "dominant coalition" that supported the foundation of the new state. That coalition was comprised of two main groups, Egyptians who were associated with temples, including scribal families, and Greeks, primarily bureaucrats and soldiers, who came to Egypt from throughout the Greek world. These groups were the main beneficiaries of the rents created by the new state, a "Ptolemaicized" Egypt. The results of this new coalition formation are clear in the documentation. Temples were built and/or improved, soldiers and reservists were settled on the land, and parties to Greek and Egyptian language contracts overwhelmingly bore status titles that tied them to a local temple or to state service.[4] Greek became an increasingly important language of governance and of private contracts.

The introduction and the distribution of new political and economic power across the dominant ruling coalition, though hardly stable throughout the period, fundamentally shaped the private contracting environment. At the same time, the influence of Greek—primarily Athenian—institutions such as banking, as well as an emphasis on market transactions, brought fundamental changes. Gradually the demotic Egyptian contracting tradition was incorporated into the new Ptolemaic administrative structure. We can observe this in the registration of demotic legal instruments and in changes in recording the witnesses to contracts. It is clear that Ptolemaic governance altered certain features of Egyptian contracting, but at the same time, the preservation of ancient institutional structures such as landholding and conveyance within temple estates probably limited the state's ability to improve efficiencies and reduce costs further.

---

3. See also the fundamental analysis of Menu 1988.
4. In my own view, I do not think it is fair to term this "corruption," although it often is called so. The point is that the system, as it was in ancient Egypt, was set up this way. Complaints of official behavior are legion in the papyri. One nice example is *P.Mich.Zen.* 43.5–6 (253 B.C.E.): "the nomarchs have not been acting correctly in the measuring of sesame and grain."

Transaction Cost Economics

The problem of how to use the concepts developed in transaction cost economics in economic analysis is not straightforward even in a modern context.[5] Most scholars trace the origins of the term *transaction cost* to Coase's pioneering 1937 article that aimed to study the real world of firms and why they emerged, in which Coase suggested that neoclassical theory's assumption of an environment with zero transaction cost was wrong. The issue was explicitly explained by Coase (1960: 15).

> In order to carry out a market transaction it is necessary to discover who it is that one wishes to deal with, to inform people that one wishes to deal and on what terms, to conduct negotiations leading up to a bargain, to draw up the contract, to undertake the inspection needed to make sure that the terms of the contract are being observed, and so on. These operations are often extremely costly, sufficiently costly at any rate to prevent many transactions that would be carried out in a world in which the pricing system worked without cost.

This straightforward definition belies the fact that the subsequent use of the term *transaction cost* in economic analysis is highly contentious. Despite Coase's early work, the idea was "only dimly perceived and/or lacked operationalization" until recently (Williamson 2008: 41).

There are now two large literatures in economics that operationalize the concept of transaction cost. In neoclassical analysis, transaction costs are the "costs establishing and maintaining property rights." In literature from the field of law and economics and from the new institutional economics, transaction cost is defined as "the cost of negotiating, securing, and completing transactions in a market economy" (Nee 2005: 50). Underlying both uses of the terminology is the problem of the cost of information, particularly emphasized by the new institutional economics.[6] For my purposes, I shall use the term *transaction costs* to mean the "total amount" (*ex ante* and *ex post*) of the costs to parties

---

5. Summaries of the use of the term are given in Allen 1999 and Nee 2005. The overview in Williamson 2008 is superb.
6. An introduction to the new institutional economics may be found in Ménard and Shirley 2008.

in coming to terms in a contract. It must be stressed again that not all private transactions in Ptolemaic Egypt were "market" transactions.

Beyond the different uses of the term lies another, more important issue for ancient historians. How can transaction cost economics be removed from its usual context of the modern analysis of corporate governance and contract or incentive theory and applied to an (ancient) historical context in which market activity was considerably different (and far less) and in which no firms existed? A scholar of early modern Chinese contracts (Ocko 2004) has recently raised similar concerns about the use of terms such as *transaction cost* and *economic development*, because they are a distinctive feature of Western economic thought.

We are at risk of finding what we set out to seek if we simply transfer modern categories to ancient texts without considering how ancient contracting worked. The modern analysis of transaction costs is even more problematic in the context of Ptolemaic Egypt, where Greek institutions and concepts came together with very ancient and quite distinctive social norms and customs of exchange and bargaining, a tradition, like early Chinese contracting, about which there is much we do not yet understand. Ocko (2004: 179) concludes the following about early Chinese contracts:

> Thus, those of us who are studying contract and property in this (early modern China) period are wont to look to the West, especially to economic and legal theory, for analytical categories to help us make sense out of the mountains of materials that we are lately discovering. But, in doing so, it is easy to fall prey to the problems that face a society that looks to another for tools of social analysis. We tend to forget that economic and legal theories develop within the context of the particularistic concerns of their creators and the political and cultural environments in which they have lived. We also forget that debates about the nature of contract, the role of non-legal norms, the creation and character of property rights, the relationship between law and custom, and the meaning, effect, and significance of transaction costs reflect larger political debates within the societies that produce them.

Ocko's emphasis on the particular historical and institutional framework is an important place to begin.

Ptolemaic Institutions, Old and New

Ptolemaic economic institutions were a combination of old and new. An ancient system of agricultural production, landholding and conveyance, political legitimacy and economic extraction by the state through the maintenance of close ties with temples remained in place and was indeed supported by the new political regime. The Greek population brought new economic habits, including banking, public auctions, and more market exchange. In between old and new institutions stood a bureaucratic hierarchy that demanded written documentation in Greek. While this Ptolemaic "system" (a term that emphasizes the effectiveness of the bureaucracy at managing extraction) has often been described as "efficient," some caution is required. Rather than seeing an institution as efficient because it survived over time and was therefore solving a particular problem, a historical approach to how institutions actually function within an economy suggests that "institutions affect not just the efficiency of an economy but also how its resources are distributed" (Ogilvie 2007: 662). Ogilvie's study of merchant guilds in medieval Europe suggests that rather than viewing them as efficiently solving problems that led to a "commercial revolution," guilds sought out rents and distorted markets (Ogilvie 2011: 2–3).

Similar issues existed in Ptolemaic Egypt. The introduction of Greek (Athenian) fiscal institutions (coinage, banking, the use of auctions) caused institutional friction: new state aims (revenue extraction) met with ancient economic structures, and Greek ideas encountered ancient social norms and institutions. Jean Bingen (1984) famously termed this the "structural tension" of Ptolemaic society. Beneath the new state structure, both Egyptian law (now guaranteed under Ptolemaic authority) and the continuing importance of Egyptian temples continued to facilitate the making of Egyptian language contracts. Temples were the location of notary scribes who drew up legal instruments, and they were also where the swearing of oaths to confirm agreements and the adjudication of disputes occurred. Egyptian temples were economic powers in their own right, controlling landed estates that remained, in the case of the major temples, quite large. The notary scribes attached to the temples occupied hereditary offices and preserved their own local and even, at times, personal scribal peculiarities, a product of regional traditions in education.[7] The continuation of this ancient legal structure as part of the Ptolemies' ruling coalition represents a good example of Ogilvie's observation that some institutions are preserved because they serve the interests of key constituencies, rather than because they promote efficiency.

At the same time, the Ptolemies reshaped the bureaucratic hierarchy by establishing Greek as the administrative language and introducing fiscal and legal reforms. The two languages of contract, Egyptian and Greek, were used with two court jurisdictions, one for Greeks and another for hearing disputes based on Egyptian law. This suggests a relatively high cost of the enforcement of what Cheung (1998: 515) calls "commands from higher authority." The use of written rules and regulations were very much a central feature of the Ptolemaic economy, and the Ptolemaic system generated new kinds of documentation, including the issuance by the state of licenses for the selling of certain commodities (e.g., beer). Ptolemaic banks generated an enormous amount of documentation in the form of banker's archives, receipts, payment orders, reports, and accounts.[8]

Ptolemaic governance also fostered more market activity, caused partly by the more widespread use of coinage.[9] The introduction of the public auction is an interesting case study in itself of the Ptolemaic impact on transactions.[10] Written rules and publicity were key parts of the process. The rules of public auction are recorded in a text from Edfu dated to the third century B.C.E.:

1. A public announcement was posted.
2. The auction was presided over by a "herald." The bidding process could occur over several days. After a high bid was accepted, new overbidding could occur before the knockdown price was established by the payment of taxes and the first installment of the purchase price.
3. Possession was established with an order of the royal bank to accept the price.
4. New bids were accepted until the first installment was paid, but the minimum bid had to exceed 10 percent above the knockdown price.

---

7. Zauzich 1968; Arlt 2008, 2009.
8. See the brief survey of Geens 2008.
9. See, e.g., Gabrielsen 2011 on the Hellenistic increase in market activity driven by state actors interacting with private ones.
10. See Pringsheim 1949; Morcillo 2008. On the demotic evidence, see Manning 1999.

5. Within a certain time frame, the original owner could repurchase, or redeem, their property at the auction price.[11]

The public auction was primarily used for the letting out of state contracts and for the sale of land that had been confiscated by the state. Importantly, it appears "efficient" on paper, but we know from the outcome of this particular auction event at Edfu that the winner was not the highest bidder and was very likely an acquaintance of the state official in charge (Manning 2010). This case is a fine example of the conflict between mechanism design and rent-seeking human behavior.[12] The public auction (normally called the "auction of Pharaoh" in demotic texts) is referred to in demotic texts as a mode of land acquisition. But as far as I am aware, the documentation of the public auction was limited to the state sale of confiscated land in the Thebaid region in the second century B.C.E., in the wake of the massive revolts there. A papyrus from the collection at Berkeley gives the impression of a market in real property (i.e., beyond intrafamily transfers) created partly by the use of public auctions, but it was probably quite a limited market.[13]

Traditional Contract: Demotic Egyptian Land Contracts

Property rights in land were traditionally accorded to those who served the state. The most prominent groups were soldiers and those who worked within temple estates. Such rights to holding land were conveyable. The institution is well documented in private land conveyances from Upper Egypt in particular.[14] Demotic Egyptian "contracts" were, in the vast majority of cases, a record of a settled transaction. Such instruments were concerned with the "sanctioning" of the legal relationship of the two parties rather than

---

11. Preisigke 1949: 288–89. This procedure is essentially that laid out in the auction announcement *P.Eleph.* 14 (= *Select Papyri* 2.233, Edfu), part of the Milon archive, for which see Clarysse 2003.
12. I have found the approach of Ogilvie 2007 to economic institutions illuminating. I am grateful to Richard Saller for first drawing my attention to this article.
13. A demotic document of property transfer formerly in Boston (*P.BMFA* 38.2063b) and now in Berkeley (*P.Hearst* 7), dating to 175 B.C.E., shows that a considerable amount of land had been purchased (mainly jointly with others) and specifically refers to the public auctions as the means by which a man acquired land before subsequently transferring it to his son. For the text, see Parker 1964.
14. Manning 2003a. Monson (2008, 2012) developed a demographic density model to explain property rights in Upper Egypt.

with the determination of that relationship.[15] The legal instrument, to paraphrase Pierce (1972), was an *ex post* memorialization of an oral agreement, concerned more with documenting clear title, the enforcement of the agreement, and potential litigation than with the legal relationship established between the parties.[16] All previous "contracts" were required to be conveyed to the new owner at the time of the sale. The demotic sale "contract," then, functioned as a warranty of clear title, guaranteed by the seller, which could be asserted by the purchaser.[17]

Demotic instruments of real sale in the Ptolemaic and Roman period were composed of two documents. In the Ptolemaic period, the demotic text was often written to the left of the sale at the same time as the date of sale and on the same sheet of papyrus as the Greek text. This form was standard in the demotic sales in the Roman period. The legal clauses of the sale and the cession instruments overlap considerably, but they were originally two separate acts developed in early demotic during the seventh century B.C.E. In origin, the cession instrument was a quitclaim, documenting the renunciation of rights. Such instruments could be drawn up after a lawsuit or after the repayment of a debt, to indicate the resolution over disputed property claims. The losing party was required to draw up the cession to renounce any further claim to the property in question. The ceding of any future claim to property became a standard part of sales in the Ptolemaic period, it seems, to forestall any potential litigation. Scribal practice was conservative. Thus the real demotic sale contract, conveying property rights from one party to another, preserves this older conception of sale, with heavily redundant formulas, as two transactions (acknowledgment of receipt of price, cession of rights). It surely used up considerably more papyrus and scribal time, even more so with the "witness-copy texts" that I will describe below.

The surviving demotic instruments from the Ptolemaic period, certainly a much bigger corpus than exists from previous periods, preserve only a very tiny fraction of all transactions. We have not just a large number of actual contracts but an even greater number of contracts documented in secondary ways, that is, in archival registers of contracts summarized by local records offices (e.g., *P.Tebt.* III/1 815; *CPR* XVIII).[18] Many of the contracts involved

---

15. Pierce 1972: 83–93 remains the classic account.
16. See Muhs' analysis in chapter 3 in this volume.
17. On the process of disputing title, see Muhs 2002.
18. Bagnall 2011: 36. For a demotic register, see de Cenival 1987.

both parties to the transaction who had the same or similar status titles and were tied to a temple estate in whose estate the land was located. Typically, no purchase price is mentioned in the document, and we do not have associated tax receipts from which we can infer the value of the land. In most cases, the plot of land was quite small, a fraction of an acre. The monumental character of some demotic legal instruments is noteworthy: one example measured 4.3 meters in length, with five copies of both the sale and cession.[19] In other ways, this immensely sized text is a standard example of an Upper Egyptian sale of land, with the vendor guaranteeing clear title to the land by conveying any previous documents made concerning the land and by promising by oath that he would defend the title against all claims.

The majority of such sales were relational contracts, that is, nonmarket transactions. They were embedded in local "homophilic" relationships and thereby relied on trust networks outside of any institutional arrangement including markets (Granovetter 1985).[20] Some of the written conveyances may have been intrafamily conveyances, as part of marriage, while other conveyances may reflect unusual family circumstances, such as a lack of direct heirs. In any case, recorded transactions were mainly local agreements between persons generally living in the same village or town.[21]

Innovation in Contract Forms

As Kehoe stresses in chapter 9 in this volume, the relationship between law and the economy is a complex topic. In the case of Egypt, it is made more so by the bilingual environment of Ptolemaic "law." Greek became the dominant administrative language, and new forms of contract recorded in Greek existed side by side with older Egyptian forms. Egyptian scribes certainly occasionally borrowed new language from Greek contracts. For example, one of the final clauses at the end of a cession instrument, "Yours is the approach to the property, *both coming and going*" (*P.BM* 10616, Fayyum, 244/243 B.C.E.; Glanville 1932: 160), translated into demotic Egyptian the Greek phrase εἴσοδος καὶ ἔξοδος. This phrase was doubtless borrowed from standard

---

19. *P.Hausw.* 10.
20. On homophily, see Lazarsfeld and Merton 1954.
21. The sociology of land conveyances is explored in Rowlandson 1981 for the Roman period and in Manning 2003a for the Ptolemaic period.

phraseology in Greek contracts of property sale, but it was not, apparently, used widely. The introduction of the phrase into this demotic text may be merely scribal preference under the influence of Greek practice. The mention of a "trustee" (demotic ʿrbt), a third party who kept a contract in his possession to ensure its enforcement, while specifically only documented in a few instances, was a feature of most contracting. Official contracts like agreements of tax farming were kept by a third party, the *sungraphophylax* or *sumbolophylax* (Burkhalter 1996). Third-party securitization was a standard feature in certain types of labor contract and in agreements to make payments to the state (de Cenival 1973).

A good example of contract innovation can be seen in a group of four demotic documents written in 109 and 108 B.C.E. that are part of the archive of Harmachis son of Herienoupis, a merchant living in the environs of the ancient Egyptian capital of Memphis. These texts have been interpreted in various ways; some scholars argue that they are loans, others that they are grain sales with deferred delivery.[22] The former type of agreement is well documented in both demotic and Greek, the latter much more so in Greek. These contracts were written in demotic and drawn up by scribes attached to a temple of Anubis at Memphis, but they shared many similarities with Greek contracts. One Greek feature of these contracts was the insertion of a clause of "mulct," that is, burnt offerings paid to the king in the case of nonperformance. This was clearly a source of revenue introduced by the new Ptolemaic system (Pierce 1972: 159–78). The introduction of this clause by Egyptian scribes, as Pierce argues, served to equalize legal conceptions of contract enforcement between Greek and demotic legal instruments. To be sure, such new forms of contract were the result of the monetized environment of the Ptolemaic economy, and they perhaps reflect a growing market in credit. Whether this facilitated contracting between Greeks and non-Greeks is an open question.

Alongside innovation and the borrowing of clauses and forms from Greek into demotic contracts was the issue of personal choice in the use of Greek or demotic instruments. Clearly, even in regions of Egypt with a strong Greek presence, Greek and demotic instruments could be written side by side. Such appears to be the case, for example, in the famous Dryton archive, where Dryton, a Greek cavalry officer and citizen of the Greek city of Ptolemais, and his Egyptian wife seem to have preferred Greek language contracts

---

22. See Pierce 1972; Pestman 1977.

as a marker of their social status. Their children had a preference for Egyptian language contracts.[23] But that practice cut against the larger trend of Greek notarial practice that, like the spread of demotic in Upper Egypt in the sixth century B.C.E., put increasing pressure against using older demotic forms. The use of Greek in contracts may have initially represented a "superficial" change (Vandorpe and Waebens 2009: 47), merely a switch in language, but there were longer-term consequences. The Ptolemaic introduction of Greek notary scribes, the *agoranomoi*, in southern Egypt during the second century B.C.E. altered not only the language but also the structure of contract and, arguably, eliminated the costs of registering and witnessing an agreement.[24]

It is unclear to what extent Ptolemaic governance and/or political events altered the costs of drawing up a demotic legal instrument. Many of these costs were traditional, although certain aspects of contracting costs were increased in the Ptolemaic period. The sale tax collected by the state, for example, increased from 5 to 10 percent of the value by 171 B.C.E.,[25] and mandatory registration was required after 145 B.C.E. (see below). Whether or not such costs deterred parties from bargaining "in the shadow of the law" (Mnookin and Kornhauser 1979), the free exchange of land probably remained limited despite the introduction of public auctions.[26]

Registration

Developments in the archiving of private agreements in the Ptolemaic period are noteworthy, although the overall picture is still far from clear.[27] These developments can be traced in the archival dockets recorded on contracts.[28] Some scribal practices in a given region might have borrowed from elsewhere; other practices doubtless continued local record-keeping traditions. There can be little doubt that the keeping of registers was an ancient practice in Egypt. But the Ptolemaic practice of docketing private demotic contracts

---

23. Vandorpe and Waebens 2009: 108; Clarysse 2010: 68–69.
24. Witnesses, a part of the ancient system, were no longer required.
25. Depauw 2000: 63.
26. This is one of the major points of Ellickson 1991. There are also, of course, costs associated with unwritten agreements within "trust networks" inside of villages. I am unsure of how we can get at the issue, but the coming of large numbers of Greeks to Egypt, particularly the settling of soldiers in Egyptian villages, must have greatly impacted these trust networks and may have shaped the legal landscape in new ways.
27. See the summaries in Wolff 1978 and Yiftach-Firanko 2014.
28. Pierce 1972: 179–88.

(in Greek) was adapted from a practice in the Greek world in the fourth century.[29] Taken as a whole, the evidence from the Hellenistic Mediterranean suggests that the fourth and third centuries B.C.E. saw an increase in impersonal (i.e., market) exchange that required a written record and state supervision.[30] While registration of private documents in the pre-Ptolemaic period is well known, the Ptolemaic state showed great interest in registering private agreements. Beginning in the reign of Ptolemy II, demotic contracts begin to show a form of the Greek notation, initially written with a reed brush (a habit of Egyptian scribes), that "the agreement has been deposited into the public archive."[31] It is not altogether clear whether an official copy of the entire contract was kept in a state archive or whether merely the basic details of the contract were simply noted.[32] *P.Tebt.* III/1 815 (228–221 B.C.E., Tebtunis), an important register of contracts from the third century B.C.E., reveals some variability here. Sometimes the scribe would note only the barest details of the contract; in other cases, the contract was copied into the register almost verbatim. The bank tax receipt of the sale tax was recorded on the demotic instrument itself or on a separate sheet of papyrus.[33] During the second century B.C.E., a special office was developed, the *grapheion*, which recorded private agreements. In 145 B.C.E., the Ptolemaic state required the registration of demotic instruments (*P.Par.* 65; Pestman 1985) in order for them to be valid. While we cannot track in detail the relationship between demotic and Greek legal instruments in the period, the introduction at the end of the third century B.C.E. of a new kind of Greek language notary scribe known as the *agoranomos* may have played an important role in diminishing the role of older forms of registering and witnessing private agreements.

Witnessing Private Agreements

A crucial aspect of the enforcement of property rights was the act of witnessing demotic contracts. By the Ptolemaic period, it had become standard in

---

29. Pierce 1972: 188.
30. See, e.g., the summary in Posner 1972. For the registration of documents, cf. Aristot., *Pol.* 8.1321b.
31. Pierce 1972: 180.
32. Such is the case in *P.Lille* I 20 (Ghoran, early Ptolemaic period), an official register that records the number of agreement types (sale contract, marriage agreement, etc.) that reached the records office each day.
33. Clarysse 2010: 71.

demotic sales to list the names of sixteen persons who were presumably present at the agreement or who at least knew the parties in question and could attest to the agreement between the parties. This high number of witnesses served as a means of publicizing the transaction and presumably also facilitated both clearing the title and enforcing the agreement. The Greek tradition required six witnesses. We do not know if the witnesses to demotic contracts were paid. Given that literacy rates were low, we might suppose that that they were. Even if there were no formal costs associated with the process of witnessing private agreements, the list of names of those parties who in some way witnessed the agreement reflected informal social costs that came with local trust networks.

Some of the witnesses to an agreement occasionally copied out verbatim the text of the agreement written by the professional scribe. These texts are known as "witness-copy texts" and were an old form of demotic legal document, the first such example dating to 644 B.C.E.[34] The careful copying out of the text written by a professional scribe by a number of persons served, perhaps, as a means to train document scribes. In some cases, it reinforced the exact wording of the agreement and also served to notarize the agreement publicly.[35] All but four of the thirty-five examples of this form of contract come from Upper Egypt.[36] The last example of this type of contract, however, comes from the Fayyum (Philadelphia) in northern Egypt and is dated to 213 B.C.E.

It is tempting to associate the decline in this form of Egyptian contract with the state's attempts to increase the use of Greek notary contracts, but the loss of witness-copy texts may only reflect a change in scribal practice. At the very least, we can say that the decline was systematic throughout Egypt, a process that must reflect a global change in the scribal tradition. In my view,

---

34. The history of this type of legal document is discussed in Depauw 1999.

35. Pestman 1978: 203. Proof that the witnesses in these cases merely copied out what was written by the professional scribe is shown by a document (*P.BM Andrews* 1) in which all three witnesses to a house sale followed the professional scribe in recording the neighbors of the house according to the nonstandard directional order of south, north, east, and west.

36. A good example of the demotic witness-copy text is *P.Hausw.* 10, which forms part of an important family archive from Edfu dated to the mid-third century B.C.E. Many of the texts preserved in the archive concern the transfer of small plots of land. The text is dated to 264 B.C.E. and records the conveyance of land and dôm palm trees, in the standard bipartite demotic form of a sale text and a cession text, with a list of sixteen witnesses on the verso of each document. Four of the witnesses who appear on the witness list on the verso wrote out a copy of the sale and cession in full on the recto. Next to these witnesses' names on the verso is a small demotic sign that can be read "receipt" (although it could simply be a check mark), and I have speculated elsewhere that this sign might be evidence that the makers of witness-copy texts were paid for their efforts.

the obsolescence of witness-copy contracts reflects the state's attempt to standardize contract making by involving Greek notary scribes, whose contracts did not require any witnesses. These documents by *agoranomoi* represented a new form of contract that was guaranteed not by the community represented by the witness list but by the state itself.

Conclusions

An analysis of transaction costs with respect to demotic contracts from the Ptolemaic period tells a mixed story. In all premodern societies, exchange was constrained by the high costs of transaction, the high costs of obtaining information, and limited market exchange. Ptolemaic Egypt was no exception. The Ptolemaic state played an important role in improving conditions for contracting between individuals. More market-based exchange was introduced, including the public auctioning of state licenses and, at least in certain cases, of land. The introduction of coinage and the demand for taxes paid in coinage may have led to more market-based private exchange (see, further, Bresson's analysis in chapter 5 in this volume). The registration of transactions, the introduction of Greek notary scribes (though we do not know how widespread they were), and the use of public auctions (again perhaps limited) served to increase the predictability and security of title. Despite all of these changes, however, the maintenance of an ancient institutional structure centered on temple estates and Egyptian legal traditions created a complicated institutional environment that would have constrained attempts at creating more open, market-based transactions.

Bibliography

Allam, S. 1985. "Bemerkungen zur Abstandschrift." *Enchoria* 13: 1–5.

Allen, D. W. 1999. "Transaction Costs." In Bouckaert and De Geest 2000: 1: 893–926.

Aperghis, G. G. 2004. *The Seleukid Royal Economy: The Finances and Financial Administration of the Seleukid Empire*. Cambridge.

Arlt, C. 2008. "The Egyptian Notary Offices in the Ptolemaic Fayyum." In Lippert and Schentuleit 2008: 15–26.

Arlt, C. 2009. "Die thebanischen Notare." In G. Widmer and D. Devauchelle, eds., *Actes du IXe congrès international des études démotiques, Paris, 31 août–3 septembre 2005*, 29–50. Bibliothèque d'études 147. Cairo.

Austin, M. M. 2006. *The Hellenistic World from Alexander to the Roman Conquest: A Selection of Ancient Sources in Translation.* 2nd ed. Cambridge.

Bagnall, R. S. 1993. *Egypt in Late Antiquity.* Princeton.

Bagnall, R. S. 2011. *Everyday Writing in the Graeco-Roman East.* Berkeley.

Bagnall, R., and P. Derow, eds. 2004. *The Hellenistic Period: Historical Sources in Translation.* 2nd ed. Oxford.

Berger, M., T. Abel, and C. Page, eds. 1954. *Freedom and Control in Modern Society.* New York.

Bingen, J. 1952. *Papyrus Revenue Laws.* New ed. Sammelbuch griechischer Urkunden aus Ägypten 1. Göttingen.

Bingen, J. 1984. "Les tensions structurelles de la société ptolémaïque." In *Atti del XVII Congresso Internazionale di Papirologia*, 3: 921–37. Naples. Translated as *Hellenistic Egypt: Monarchy, Society, Economy, Culture*, ed. R. S. Bagnall (Berkeley, 2007), 189–205.

Bogaert, R. 1994. *Trapezitica Aegyptiaca: Recueil de recherches sur la banque en Égypte gréco-romaine.* Papyrologica Florentina 25. Florence.

Bogaert, R. 1998–99. "Les operations des banques de l'Égypte ptolémaïque." *Ancient Society* 29: 49–145.

Bogaert, R. 2001. "Les Documents bancaires de l'égypte gréco-romaine et byzantine." *Ancient Society* 31: 173–288.

Bouckaert, B., and G. De Geest, eds. 2000. *Encyclopedia of Law and Economics.* 5 vols. Cheltenham. Online 1999 edition available at http://encyclo.findlaw.com/tablebib.html.

Bresson, A. 2000. *La cité marchande.* Bordeaux.

Burkhalter, F. 1996. "Symbolophulax." In M.-F. Boussac and A. Invernizzi, eds., *Arhives et sceaux du monde héllenistique.* BCH suppl. 29, 293–301. Athens.

Cheung, S. N. S. 1998. "The Transaction Costs Paradigm." *Economic Inquiry* 36 (October): 514–21.

Clarysse, W. 2003. "The Archive of the Praktor Milon." In K. Vandorpe and W. Clarysse, eds., *Edfu, an Egyptian Provincial Capital in the Ptolemaic Period*, 17–27. Brussels.

Clarysse, W. 2010. "Bilingual Papyrological Archives." In A. Papaconstantinou, ed., *The Multilingual Experience in Egypt, from the Ptolemies to the 'Abbasids*, 47–72. Farnham.

Clarysse, W., and D. J. Thompson. 2006. *Counting the People in Hellenistic Egypt.* 2 vols. Cambridge.

Coase, R. H. 1937. "The Nature of the Firm." *Economica* 4: 386–405.

Coase, R. H. 1960. "The Problem of Social Cost." *Journal of Law and Economics* 3: 1–44. Reprinted in *The Firm, the Market, and the Law* (Chicago, 1990), 95–156.

Cuvigny, H. 2009. "The Finds of Papyri: The Archaeology of Papyri." In R. S. Bagnall, ed., *The Oxford Handbook of Papyrology*, 30–58. Oxford.

de Cenival, F. 1973. *Cautionnements démotiques du début de l'époque ptolémaïque (P. Dem. Lille 34 à 96)*. Paris.

de Cenival, F. 1987. "Répertoire journalier d'un bureau de notaire de l'époque ptolémaïque en démotique (P. dém. Lille 120)." *Enchoria* 15: 1–9.

Depauw, M. 1999. "Demotic Witness-Copy-Contracts." *Revue d'Égyptologie* 50: 67–105.

Depauw, M. 2000. *The Archive of Teos and Thabis from Early Ptolemaic Thebes*. Turnhout.

Eisenstadt, S. N. [1963] 1993. *The Political Systems of Empires*. New Brunswick.

Ellickson, R. C. 1991. *Order without Law: How Neighbors Settle Disputes*. Cambridge, MA.

Frier, B. W., and D. P. Kehoe 2007. "Law and Economic Institutions." In Scheidel, Morris, and Saller 2007: 113–43.

Gabrielsen, V. 2011. "Profitable Partnerships: Monopolies, Traders, Kings, and Cities." In Z. Archibald, J. K. Davies, and V. Gabrielsen, eds., *The Economies of Hellenistic Societies, Third to First Centuries BC*, 216–50. Oxford.

Geens, Karolien. 2008. "Financial Archives of Graeco-Roman Egypt." In Verboven, Vandorpe, and Chankowski 2008: 133–51.

Glanville, S. R. K. 1932. "A Demotic Contract of the Third Century from the Fayyum (Dem. P. Brit. Mus. 10616)." In S. R .K. Glanville, ed., *Studies Presented to F. Ll. Griffith*. London, 152–60.

Glanville, S. R. K. 1939. *A Theban Archive of the Reign of Ptolemy I Soter*. Vol. 1 of *Catalogue of Demotic Papyri in the British Museum*. London.

Granovetter, Mark 1985. "Economic Action and Social Structure: The Problem of Embeddedness." *American Journal of Sociology* 91: 481–510.

Lazarsfeld, P. F., and R. K. Merton. 1954. "Friendship as Social Process: A Substantive and Methodological Analysis." In Berger, Abel, and Page 1954: 18–66.

Lewis, N. 1993. "The Demise of the Demotic Document: When and Why." *JEA* 79: 276–81.

Lippert, S., and M. Schentuleit, eds. 2008. *Graeco-Roman Fayyum-Texts and Archaeology*. Wiesbaden.

Manning, J. G. 1996. "Demotic Egyptian Instruments of Transfer as Evidence for Ownership of Real Property." *Chicago Kent Law Review* 71, no. 1 (Spring): 237–68.

Manning, J. G. 1997. *The Hauswaldt Papyri: A Third Century B.C. Dossier from Edfu, Upper Egypt*. Würzburg.

Manning, J. G. 1999. "The Auction of Pharaoh." In J. Larsen and E. Teeter, eds., *Gold of Praise: Studies in Honor of Edward F. Wente*, 277–84. Chicago.

Manning, J. G. 2003a. *Land and Power in Ptolemaic Egypt: The Structure of Land Tenure*. Cambridge.

Manning, J. G. 2003b. "A Ptolemaic Agreement concerning a Donkey with an Unusual Warranty Clause: The Strange Case of P. dem. Princ. 1 (inv. 7524)." *Enchoria* 28: 46–61.

Manning, J. G. 2004. "Property Rights and Contracting in Ptolemaic Egypt (332 BC–30 BC)." *Journal of Institutional and Theoretical Economics* 160: 758–64.

Manning, J. G. 2010. *The Last Pharaohs: Egypt under the Ptolemies, 305–30 BC.* Princeton.

Martin, C. J. 1996. "Demotic Texts." In B. Porten, ed., *The Elephantine Papyri in English: Three Millennia of Cross-Cultural Continuity and Change*, 277–385. Leiden.

Ménard, C., and M. M. Shirley, eds. 2008. *Handbook of New Institutional Economics.* Berlin.

Menu, B. 1988. "Les Actes de Vente en Égypte ancienne, particulièrement sous les Rois kouchites et saïtes." *Journal of Egyptian Archaeology* 74: 165–81. Reprinted in *Recherches sur l'Histoire juridique, économique et sociale de l'ancienne Égypte* 2: 305–23. Cairo.

Monson, A. 2008. "Communal Agriculture in the Ptolemaic and Roman Fayyum." In Lippert and Schentuleit 2008: 173–86.

Monson, A. 2012. *From the Ptolemies to the Romans: Political and Economic Change in Egypt.* Cambridge.

Mnookin, R. H., and L Kornhauser. 1979. "Bargaining in the Shadow of the Law: The Case of Divorce." *Yale Law Journal* 88: 950–97.

Morcillo, M. G. 2008. "Auctions, Bankers, and Public Finances in the Roman World." In Verboven, Vandorpe, and Chankowski 2008: 257–75.

Moyer, I. 2011. *Egypt and the Limits of Hellenism.* Cambridge.

Muhs, B. P. 2002. "Clear Title, Public Protests, and P. Brux. Dem. 4." In K. Ryholt, ed., *Acts of the Seventh International Conference of Demotic Studies, Copenhagen, 23–27 August 1999*, 259–72. Copenhagen.

Muhs, B. P. 2005a. "The *Grapheion* and the Disappearance of Demotic Contracts in Early Roman Tebtynis and Soknopaiou Nesos." In S. Lippert and M. Schentuleit, eds., *Tebtynis und Soknopaiou Nesos: Leben im römerzeitlichen Fajum*, 93–104. Wiesbaden.

Muhs, B. P. 2005b. *Tax Receipts, Taxpayers, and Taxes in Early Ptolemaic Thebes.* Oriental Institute Publications 126. Chicago.

Nee, V. 2005. "The New Institutionalisms in Economics and Sociology." In N. J. Smelser and R. Swedberg, eds., *The Handbook of Economic Sociology*, 49–74. Princeton.

North, D. C., J. J. Wallis, and B. R. Weingast 2009. *Violence and Social Orders: A Conceptual Framework for Interpreting Recorded Human History.* Cambridge.

Ocko, J. 2004. "The Missing Metaphor: Applying Western Legal Scholarship to the Study of Contract and Property in Early Modern China." In M. Zelin, J. K. Ocko, and R. Gardella, eds., *Contract and Property in Early Modern China*, 178–205. Stanford.

Ogilvie, S. 2007. "'Whatever Is, Is Right'? Economic Institutions in Pre-industrial Europe." *Economic History Review* 60, no.4: 649–84.

Ogilvie, S. 2011. *Institutions and European Trade: Merchant Guilds, 1000–1800.* Cambridge.

Parker, R. 1964. "A Demotic Property Settlement from Deir el-Ballas." *JARCE* 3: 89–103.

Pestman, P. W. 1977. *Recueil de textes démotiques et bilingues.* 3 vols. Leiden.

Pestman, P. W. 1978. "L'agoranomie: Un avant-poste de l'administration grecque enlevé par les Égyptiens." In H. Maehler and V. M. Strocka, eds., *Das ptolemäische Ägypten*, 203–10. Mainz.

Pestman, P. W. 1985. "Registration of Demotic Contracts in Egypt: P. Par. 65; 2nd Cent. B.C." In J. Ankum, J. E. Spruit, and F. B. J. Wubbe, eds., *Satura Roberto Feenstra sexagesimum quintum annum aetatis complenti ab alumnis collegis amicis oblata*, 17–25. Fribourg.

Pierce, R. H. 1972. *Three Demotic Papyri in the Brooklyn Museum: A Contribution to the Study of Contracts and Their Instruments in Ptolemaic Egypt.* Symbolae Osloenses Supplement 24. Oslo.

Posner, E. 1972. *Archives in the Ancient World.* Cambridge, MA.

Pringsheim, F. 1949. "The Greek Sale by Auction." In *Scritti in Onore di Contardo Ferrini. Pubblicati in occasione della sua beatificazione* 4: 284–343. Milan.

Ray, J. 1994a. "How Demotic Is Demotic?" In *Acta Demotica: Acts of the Fifth International Conference for Demotists, Pisa, 4th–8th September 1993*, 251–64. Pisa.

Ray, J. 1994b. "Literacy and Language in Egypt in the Late and Persian Periods." In A. K. Bowman and G. Woolf, eds., *Literacy and Power in the Ancient World*, 51–66. Cambridge.

Rowlandson, J. 1981. "Sales of Land in Their Social Context." In R. S. Bagnall, G. Browne, A. E. Hanson, and L. Koenen, eds., *Proceedings of the Sixteenth International Congress of Papyrology, New York, 24–31 July 1980*, 371–78. Chico.

Samuel, A. E. 1983. *From Athens to Alexandria: Hellenism and Social Goals in Ptolemaic Egypt.* Studia Hellenistica 26. Louvain.

Scheidel, W., I. Morris, and R. Saller, eds. 2007. *The Cambridge Economic History of the Greco-Roman World.* Cambridge.

Sethe, K., and J. Partsch. 1920. *Demotische Urkunden zum ägyptischen Bürgschaftsrechte vorzüglich der Ptolemäerzeit.* Leipzig.

Tait, W. J. 1994. "Some Notes on Demotic Scribal Training in the Roman Period." In A. Bülow-Jacobsen, ed., *Proceedings of the 20th International Congress of Papyrologists, Copenhagen, 23–29 August, 1992*, 188–92. Copenhagen.

Terpstra, T. 2008. "Roman Law, Transaction Costs, and the Roman Economy: Evidence from the Sulpicii Archive." In Verboven, Vandorpe, and Chankowski 2008: 345–69.

Vandorpe, K., and S. Wabens. 2009. *Reconstructing Pathyris' Archives: A Multicultural Community in Hellenistic Egypt.* Brussels.

Verboven, K., K. Vandorpe, and V. Chankowski, eds. 2008. *Pistoi dia tèn technèn: Bankers, Loans, and Archives in the Ancient World; Studies in Honour of Raymond Bogaert.* Louvain.

Vleeming, S. P. 1994. *Ostraka Varia: Tax Receipts and Legal Documents on Demotic, Greek, and Greek-Demotic Ostraka, Chiefly of the Early Ptolemaic Period, from Various Collections.* Papyrologica Lugduno-Batava 26. Leiden.

Williamson, O. E. 2008. "Transaction Cost Economics." In Ménard and Shirley 2008: 41–65.

Wolff, H. J. 1978. *Das Recht der Griechischen Papyri Ägyptens in der Zeit der Ptolemaeer und des Prinzipats,* vol. 2 HdA x.5.2. Munich.

Yiftach-Firanko, U. 2014. "State Registration of Sales: The Katagraphê." In J. G. Keenan, J. G. Manning, and U. Yiftach-Firanko, eds., *Law and Legal Practice in Egypt from Alexander to the Arab Conquest: A Selection of Papyrological Sources in Translation, with Introductions and Commentary,* 314–25. Cambridge.

Zauzich, K.-T. 1968. *Die Ägyptische Schreibertradition in Aufbau, Sprache und Schrift der demotischen Kaufverträge aus ptolemäischer Zeit.* 2 vols. Ägyptologische Abhandlungen 19. Wiesbaden.

CHAPTER 5

The Cost of Getting Money in Early Ptolemaic Egypt

The Case of *P.Cair.Zen.* 1 59021 (258 B.C.E.)[1]

Alain Bresson

What was the cost of transacting business for merchants coming to Ptolemaic Egypt in the third century B.C.E.? There is certainly a debate over whether taxes or customs duties should be included in transaction costs. Taxes and customs duties are not linked to the direct interaction between partners of a transaction, which is at the core of the theory of transaction costs. But they inevitably must be considered transaction costs in a market economy insofar as "usually, the existence of this market requires a third party or outside force with the power to enforce the law" and insofar as any ruler "with the power to make laws and guarantee the functioning of market institutions is also powerful enough to abuse those who need such protection."[2] This essay takes the stand that taxes and customs duties should be included in transaction costs.

Coming to Egypt, a foreign trader faced the usual uncertainties linked to a transaction: reliability of the trading partner, quality of the traded goods, and so on. But the very fact of coming to Egypt to trade implied paying heavy taxes to the state. These took the form of customs duties for goods entering

---

1. I would like to express my gratitude to A. Meadows, T. Faucher, and K. Donahue, as well as to the editors of this volume, for their help in the preparation of this study.
2. Nye 2008: 70.

the country, which could reach fifty percent of value for luxury items, as is well known from a papyrus of the year 259 B.C.E. relating to the activity of the Pelousion customhouse.[3] There was also the high cost of getting local money, linked to the existence of a closed currency system in the Ptolemaic possessions. To be able to trade, all traders coming to a Ptolemaic port (at least in Egypt, Cyprus, and Syria and perhaps also in the other Ptolemaic territories) had to exchange their foreign gold and silver coins, mostly on the Attic standard, into local Ptolemaic coinage on a lower standard. With the process of exchange, the traders had to pay a significant tax. But this was not the only transaction cost that could affect the traders coming to Egypt. Other difficulties, linked to the very nature of the "commodity money" that gold and silver coins represented, could affect their business, in an even more unpredictable way.[4] Their activities could be hampered by the very difficulty of getting Ptolemaic coins even when they themselves came to a Ptolemaic port with gold coins on the Attic standard or with old Ptolemaic gold coins that had to be reminted.

Indeed, in a system of commodity money that takes the form of coinage, not only does transacting have a cost, but obtaining the instrument of transaction itself—that is, coins—has a specific cost. The important book *The Big Problem of Small Change*, by T. J. Sargent and F. R. Velde, shows that in the medieval or early modern period, getting small change was often a real challenge, because the mints did not produce small change in sufficient quantities to meet the needs of the public.[5] Similar shortages existed in the ancient world, for instance, in Ptolemaic Egypt.[6] The basic explanation is that, for various reasons, the states simply did not produce enough small change. But there could also be shortages—at least temporary ones—for high-value coins. This was true not only in medieval and early modern times but also in the ancient world. In a letter to Apollonios, the *dioikētēs* (finance minister) of King Ptolemy II, a certain Demetrios reported difficulties at the mint of Alexandria in 258 B.C.E. Either foreign merchants coming to Alexandria or their local partners wanted to get cash to trade in the country but could not obtain it and thus lost time and money. Although several explanations have been pro-

---

3. *P.Cair.Zen.* 1 59012 (259 B.C.E.) proves that the customs duties at import were in a range of 20 to 50 percent (see the detailed analysis in Bresson 2012).
4. A commodity money is a money whose value is at least initially based on the commodity of which it is made.
5. Sargent and Velde 2002: e.g., 131–38 (for England and France).
6. Reekmans 1993: 206 n. 31; Le Rider and de Callataÿ 2006: 143.

posed for the incapacity of the mint of Alexandria to produce the required supply of coins, the causes need to be reinvestigated. Parallels between the ancient world and the medieval and early modern periods help to illuminate what was at stake at the mint of Alexandria and enable us to make some more general conclusions on the costs of using commodity money for commercial transactions.

The Letter of Demetrios

Editions: Edgar 1918: 168–71, no. 5; *P.Cair.Zen.* (Edgar 1925) 1 59021; SB 3 6707; Hunt and Edgar 1934: 548–51, no. 409.

Translations and introductions: Hunt and Edgar 1934: 548–51, no. 409; Bagnall and Derow 2004: 163–65, no. 102 (based on Hunt and Edgar); Austin 2006: 535–36, no. 299.

Comments: Reinach 1928: 192–93; Préaux 1939: 271 n. 2, 267–80; Rostovtseff 1941: 1:402, 3:1417 n. 201; Bagnall 1976: 176; Will 1979: 1:175–79; Pestman 1981: 6, 544; Mørkholm, Grierson, and Westermark 1991: 104; Davesne 1998: 432–33; Le Rider 1998a: 796–97 (= 1999: 1120–21); Le Rider 1998b; von Reden 2007: 46–47 (with reproduction of Bagnall and Derow's translation); Burkhalter 2007: 46–80 (*non vidi*; referred to in Olivier and Lorber 2013); Cavagna 2008: 165–67; Olivier and Lorber 2013: 53–55 (apropos of the date of the introduction of the *mnaieia*), 87, 127.

Photos: Website of the Centre for the Study of Ancient Documents, Oxford.

1 Ἀπολ[λων]ίωι χαίρειν Δημήτριος.
2 καλῶς ἔχει εἰ αὐτός τε ἔρρωσαι καὶ
3 τὰ ἄλλα σοι κατὰ γνώμην ἐστίν.
4 καὶ ἐγὼ δὲ καθάπερ μοι ἔγραψας
5 προσέχειν ποιῶ αὐτὸ καὶ δέδεγμαι
6 ἐκ χρ(υσίου) μ(υριάδας) εζ΄ καὶ κατεργασάμενος
7 ἀπέδωκα. ἐδεξάμεθα δ᾽ ἂν καὶ
8 πολλαπλάσιον, ἀλλὰ καθά σοι καὶ
9 πρότερον ἔγραψα ὅτι οἵ τε ξένοι
10 οἱ εἰσπλέοντες καὶ οἱ ἔμποροι καὶ οἱ
11 ἐγδοχεῖς καὶ ἄλλοι φέρουσιν τό τε

12 ἐπιχώριο[ν] νόμισμα τὸ ἀκριβὲς καὶ
13 τὰ τρίχρυσα, ἵνα καινὸν αὐτοῖς γέ-
14 ηται, κατὰ τὸ πρόσταγμα ὃ κε-
15 λεύει ἡμᾶς λαμβάνειν καὶ κ[ατερ]-
16 γάζεσ[θα]ι, Φιλαρέτου (?) με οὐκ ἐ-
17 ῶντος δέχεσθαι, οὐκ ἔχον[τ]ες ἐ[πὶ]
18 τίνα τὴν ἀναφορὰν ποιησώ[με]θα
19 περὶ τούτων, ἀναγκαζ[όμεθ]ά τ[ε]
20 [τ]αῦτα μὴ δέχεσθαι, οἱ δὲ ἄν-
21 θ[ρω]ποι ἀγανακτοῦσιν οὔ[τε] ἐπ[ὶ]
22 τραπεζῶν οὔτε εἰς τὰ τ[.]λ[--?--]-
23 τα (?) ἡμῶν δεχομ[ένω]ν οὔτε δυνά-
24 μενοι εἰς τὴν χώραν ἀποστέλλειν
25 ἐπὶ τὰ φορτία, ἀλλὰ ἀργὸν φάσκουσιν
26 ἔχειν τὸ χρυσίον καὶ βλάπτεσθαι οὐ-
27 κ ὀλίγα ἔξοθεν μεταπεπεμμένοι
28 καὶ οὐδ᾿ ἄλλοις ἔχοντες ἐλάσσονος τιμῆς διαθέσθαι εὐχερῶς.
29 καὶ οἱ κατὰ πόλιν δὲ πάντες τῶι ἀπο-
30 τετριμμένωι χρυσίωι δυσχερῶς χρῶνται.
31 οὐδεὶς γὰρ τούτων ἔχει οὗ τὴν ἀναφο-
32 ρὰν ποιησάμενος καὶ προσθείς τι κο-
33 μιεῖται ἢ καλὸν χρυσίον ἢ ἀργύριον
34 ἀντ᾿ αὐτοῦ. νῦν μὲν γὰρ τούτων τοι-
35 ούτων ὄντων ὁρῶ καὶ τὰς τοῦ βασι-
36 λέως προσόδους βλαπτομένας οὐ-
37 κ ὀλίγα. γέγραφα οὖν σοι ταῦτα ἵ-
38 να εἰδῆις καὶ ἐάν σοι φαίνηται ⟦ἢ⟧ τῶι
39 βασιλεῖ γράψηις περὶ τούτων \καὶ/ ⟦.⟧ ἐμοὶ
40 ἐπὶ τίνα τὴν ἀναφορὰν περὶ τούτων
41 ποιῶμαι. συμφέρειν γὰρ ὑπολαμβάνω
42 ἐὰ[ν] καὶ ἐκ τῆς ἔξοθεν χώρας χρυσίον
43 ὅτι πλεῖστον εἰσάγηται καὶ τὸ νό-
44 μισμα τ[ὸ] τ[ο]ῦ [β]ασιλέως καλὸν καὶ
45 καινὸν ἦι διὰ παντός, ἀνηλώματ[ος]
46 μηθενὸς γινομένου αὐτῶι. περὶ μὲν
47 γὰρ τινων ὡς ἡμῖν χρῶνται οὐ καλῶς
48 εἶχεν γράφειν, ἀλλ᾿ ὡς ἂν παραγένηι ἀ-

49 κούσει[ς --?--] γρά-
50 ψον μοι περὶ τούτων ἵνα οὕτω ποιῶ.
51 ἔρρωσο.
52 (ἔτους) κη, Γορπιαίου ιε.
v
53 Δημητρίου. Ἀπολλωνίωι.

(Line 28 is longer than the others. Written in smaller characters, it is
obviously an addition.)

[Demetrios to Apollonios, greetings. It is well if you are in good health and everything else is as you wish. As for me I am devoting myself to what you wrote
me to do: I have received 57,000 [units] in gold, which I processed and returned.
We would have received many times as much, but, as I have written to you before, the foreigners who come here by sea, the merchants, wholesale buyers, and
others, bring their own fine local coins and the *trichrysa* to get them back as new
coins, in accordance with the ordinance that instructs us to take and process
them, but as Philaretos [?] does not allow me to accept them, we have no one to
refer to on this matter, and we are compelled not to accept them. The men are
furious since we refuse the coins at the banks and for the [--?--] and they cannot
send their agents into the country to purchase merchandise, but they say their
gold coins lie idle and that they are suffering great loss, since they brought it
from abroad and cannot easily dispose of it to others even at a lower price. As
for the people in the city (*i.e.* Alexandria) they are all reluctant to make use of the
worn gold coins. For none of them knows to whom he can refer and, after adding a little, get back fine gold or silver coins in exchange. In the present circumstances, I see that the king's revenues are suffering no small loss. I have therefore written to inform you, and, if you think fit, please write to the king about it
and tell me to whom I can report on these matters. For I believe it is advantageous that as many gold coins as possible should be imported from abroad and
that the royal coinage should always be fine and new, at no expense to the king.
It is not proper for me to say in writing how some people are treating me, but as
soon as you will hear [---]. Write to me on these matters that I may follow your
instructions. Farewell. Year 28, Gorpiaios 15. [Address] To Apollonios. [Docket]
From Demetrios.[7]

7.   The translation is Austin's but is modified on some points (e.g., at lines 6 and 15–16,

Discussions

Since the first publication by Edgar, discussions on the establishment of the text have focused on two passages, lines 16–17 and 22–23.

- Lines 16–17: φιάλας τοῦδε με οὐκ ἐ/ῶντος δέχεσθαι Edgar; i.e., Demetrios would not have been allowed to accept the gold cups. Φιλαρέτου (?) με οὐκ ἐ/ῶντος δέχεσθαι Reinach; i.e., a certain Philaretos would not have allowed Demetrios to accept the coins brought to the mint. Even though the reading "Philaretos" remains quite uncertain, Reinach's proposal makes better sense: cups are not mentioned before, and the problem at the mint stems not from the nature of the gold input but from a ban on producing more coins. Reinach's text has been accepted by Edgar in Hunt and Edgar 1934, 548, no. 409. Richter's attempt (1992) to revive the *phialai* restoration cannot be followed (see Bagnall and Derow 2004: 164–65).

- Lines 21–23: οὔ[τε] ἐπ[ὶ] / τραπεζῶν οὔτε εἰς τὰ τ[ά]λ[αν]/τα ἡμῶν δεχομ[ένω]ν Edgar. "Scales" could make perfect sense in this context, but τάλαντα designates scales in poetic usage only. A single mention in a sixth-century B.C.E. inscription from Cyzicus seems to allude to a "tax on the use of public scales," but this text does not provide a clear parallel.[8] For now, since it cannot be proved that τάλαντα had a special meaning as "mint scales," this restoration cannot be adopted. Reinach proposed to read οὔ[τε] ἐπ[ὶ] / τραπεζῶν οὔτε εἰς τὰ τ[έ]λ[η αὖ]/τα ἡμῶν δεχομ[ένω]ν. A parallel between the banks and the payment of taxes could also make sense, but τὰ τ[έ]λ[η αὖ]/τα is poor Greek. In line 7, with ἐδεξάμεθα, the implicit ἡμεῖς designates the gold-minting authority. However, in lines 22–23, ἡμεῖς may have a broader sense, as is suggested by the reference to the banks, and might allude to the king's administration in general. One might suggest restoring τ[έ]λ[εσμα]/τα, a word that had the meaning of "payments," especially by or to the treasury of a city or a king. But that word is attested in inscriptions only from the end of the third century or second century B.C.E. on and in papyri and in literary prose from the first century B.C.E.[9] Thus this restoration

κατεργάζεσθαι is rendered by "to process" instead of "to mint").

8. *Syll.*3 4B, line 7 (Van Effenterre and Ruzé 1994–95: 1:138–39, no. 32), trans. Dillon and Garland 1994: 346, no. 10.25. Cyzicus was famous for its electrum coins, and there must have been an active trade in precious metals. It is unfortunate that we do not know more about the τάλαντον in that city.

9. Cf. C. B. Welles 1934: 369: "The noun is a Hellenistic formation, the equivalent of the com-

cannot be valid. Hunt and Edgar, Austin, Bagnall, and Derow, and von Reden have preferred to leave a vacuum, and for the time being, this is still the best solution.

The Difficulty at the Mint of Alexandria

General Context and Proposed Explanations

Under Ptolemy I, the Ptolemaic kingdom had introduced a new currency. Most of the rest of the Greek world used the international Attic standard, with a drachma weighing ca. 4.33 grams in the fourth century B.C.E. After several reductions, Ptolemy I had finally stabilized the Ptolemaic drachma at ca. 3.58 grams.[10] This means that foreign merchants coming to Egypt with their gold or silver coins on the Attic standard had to exchange them and pay an exchange rate to get the Ptolemaic coins that were required to trade in the country.

The Ptolemaic drachma was (like coins everywhere else) both a weight unit and the standard of silver coins. Ptolemaic gold was not struck on a simple pattern, as opposed to the gold currency on the Attic standard, which consisted of one-drachma coins or, more commonly, two-drachma staters. Under Ptolemy II, at the beginning of his reign, the main gold coin was the *trichryson*, which, at ca. 17.90 grams, corresponded exactly in weight to five drachmas, each at 3.58 grams; the reason for the coin's weight, however, was

---

mon τέλος." In the inscriptions, the earliest mentions seem to be the decree *IG* XII.3, 30, lines 5 and 10, from Telos and probably from the end of the third or the early second centuries B.C.E. (for the date of the Rhodian priest Aglokritos [line 5] as the last quarter of the second century, see Habicht 2003: 550–51; the inscription itself is to be dated a few years later), and a contemporary treaty between Rhodes and Hierapytna, *IC* III iii, 3, line 100 (201/200 B.C.E.). For payments to the Attalid treasure under Eumenes II, see the discussion in Welles 1934: no. 51, line 26 [τελέ]σματα εἰς τὸ βασιλικόν]; 54, line 13. The word τέλεσματα has been wrongly restored in *C.Ord.Ptol.* 20, line 10 (260 B.C.E.); see the commentary of M.-L. Lenger. Diodorus is the first literary author to use the word.

10. Variations for the weight of the Ptolemaic drachma include 3.55 grams (Bagnall 2009b: 190), 3.56 grams (Le Rider and de Callataÿ 2006: 138), 3.5675 grams (Lorber 2012: 213, implicitly), and 3.57 grams (von Reden 2007: 40). Yenisoğancı and Davesne (1992) calculate that the standard weight of a *trichryson* (which weighed five drachmas) was 17.90 grams, which means that the weight of the drachma must have been 3.58 grams. On Ptolemaic coinage in general, see Lorber 2012.

its easy correspondence with silver.[11] In August 272 B.C.E. at the latest (the precise date being unknown for now), Ptolemaic authorities introduced a new gold coinage, the full denomination of which was the *mnaieion*, of ca. 27.80 grams, which, as implied by its name, was worth one hundred silver drachms (with a new ratio of one gram of gold to 12.8 grams of silver).[12] However, there was a certain delay before the *mnaieion* was introduced. The new coinage began with a half-*mnaieion*, the *pentekontadrachmon*, which was struck in large quantities (fifty-two obverse dies). When the *mnaieion* was introduced, it was also produced in large quantities (twenty-one obverse dies). *Mnaieia* and *pentekontadrachma* were supplemented by small series of quarters (two obverse dies) and eighths (one obverse die).[13] The *pentekontadrachma*, initial *mnaieia*, and fractions bore (most of the time) the jugate busts of Ptolemy II and Arsinoe II and were started before August 272. They were apparently replaced in 261/0 by the new Arsinoe *mnaieia* series, which was produced in smaller quantities (seventeen obverse dies) and with an irregular production pattern.[14]

At this time, not only did people from abroad have to exchange their Attic standard coins into local Ptolemaic coinage as usual, but to obtain the new coins, foreigners and locals in possession of old *trichrysa* had to go to the mint or to banks acting as agents for the mint (this is why, at lines 21–22 of his letter, Demetrios underscores that the banks could not perform their normal role: as they were not supplied by the mint, they could not exchange the foreign coins or the old *trichrysa* for the new coinage). Chemical analysis of western Seleukid and Ptolemaic gold coins proves that their composition was quite similar, which probably reflects the restriking of (among others) Seleukid coins by the Ptolemaic authorities.[15]

The fifteenth of Gorpiaios of the year 28 of Ptolemy II, to which the document by Demetrios is dated (line 52), corresponds to 24 October 258 B.C.E.[16] This was the end of the season of navigation for merchants who came from abroad—for example, from Greece, Asia Minor, or further away—and

---

11. According to Le Rider and de Callataÿ (2006: 137–38), one *trichryson* was worth sixty silver drachmas or fifteen tetradrachms, with a ratio of one gram of gold to twelve grams of silver.

12. Le Rider and de Callataÿ 2006: 148–54. For the date, see von Reden 2007: 51; Cavagna 2007: 181; Lorber 2012: 215; above all, Olivier and Lorber 2013: 55, 117.

13. Oliver and Lorber 2013: 65–78.

14. Olivier and Lorber 2013: 64, 83.

15. Duyrat and Olivier 2010: 86, fig. 5; Olivier and Lorber 2013: 119–22.

16. Pestman 1981: 1:281. Both Apollonios and Zenon were in the Fayum at this time.

wanted to return home with, among other commodities, Egyptian grain (harvested in the spring of the same year) or other goods produced in the country. Those merchants who desired to return to their homeland had all the more reason to be anxious, as they knew they would soon face much more difficult weather on their way back. Demetrios's letter reveals a paradoxical situation. While foreign and local merchants wanted to see the gold they brought converted into official Ptolemaic currency, the mint was unable to provide coins in adequate quantities. Everyone complained of the commercial loss they suffered. Two main explanations for this problem have been proposed.

According to Bagnall and Derow, there was no problem with the old gold Ptolemaic coinage; the difficulty came from the coins brought from abroad, the majority of which could apparently not be reminted: "Demetrios repeatedly speaks of the absence of anyone authorized to accept the money, suggesting that the issue was a lack of means for assaying foreign money or badly worn currency, which could not be accepted at face value."[17] Thus the difficulty would be linked to the (massive) presence of foreign coins, the metal of which had to be scrutinized with special care before being reminted. A similar but even more refined explanation is proposed by R. Bogaert, who suggests that no dokimastēs (assayer or approver) had yet been appointed at the mint in 258.[18] G. Le Rider and F. de Callataÿ propose another scenario. For them, the delay in receiving the coins was not at all exceptional. The Ptolemaic administration probably routinely waited for the protest of the merchants to launch the production of a new series of coins. The risk for the state, of course, was the temporary harm to commercial operations and the resulting losses caused by this. But the real demand for coins could be better gauged by waiting, and the danger of circulating a quantity of coins too large for the local needs was thus avoided.[19]

The first explanation is of a technical nature: it attributes the delay to the lack of competent staff at the mint. However, the text nowhere alludes to a dokimastēs (and thus to a lack of a dokimastēs), which would have been ex-

---

17. Bagnall and Derow 2004: 163. The fineness of the Ptolemaic gold coins minted at Alexandria was excellent and regular, between 98.2 and 98.75 percent, but the Seleukid gold was also of excellent quality, even if its fineness varied a little more (Duyrat and Olivier 2010: 75–76). This supposes a new refining process at the Alexandria mint, but this was not the job of a dokimastēs anyway.

18. Bogaert 1998–99, 123.

19. Le Rider and de Callataÿ 2006: 142–43.

pected in the context. Besides, R. Bogaert's radical view that there was no *dokimastēs* at all at the mint in 258 cannot be accepted, as Demetrios explicitly states that he has already reminted a large quantity of coins. The second explanation is financial and economic; the Ptolemaic state made a deliberate decision to adjust the quantity of coins it wanted to circulate, *post eventum* and on the basis of perceived economic needs. But if this was the case, why was the state unable to respond more quickly to the needs of the merchants, since any delay in doing so could seriously compromise the king's income?

One should also observe that at the end of 258, the Second Syrian War against the Seleukids had been going on for at least one year.[20] One may wonder whether this affected coin production. Was the mint mobilized to produce coins for the needs of the king and his armies? Certainly with the Arsinoe *mnaieia*, the opposite can be observed, since, at least for gold, the beginning of the Second Syrian War was a period of low coinage production.[21] Besides, whatever the impact of the war may have been, we would still need an explanation for the specific difficulty at the mint. Whether there was a technical obstacle or a deliberate strategy of delaying the production, it is vitally important to analyze the process of coin production in order to make sense of the letter of Demetrios.

Who Was Demetrios?

The first question that must be raised, which can be solved only by investigating ancient evidence, is the role of Demetrios. Some view him not as the person in charge of the mint but as a banker or changer.[22] For F. Burkhalter, the verb κατεργάζομαι in line 6 refers to completing a conversion from one standard to another.[23] But κατεργάζομαι (see *LSJ*, s.v., II) commonly has the meaning of "to process" or "to produce." This is the case in literary texts, among others, for metals (cf. Dem. 27.10, where σίδηρον, ὃν κατηργάζοντο

20. On the beginning of the war in 260, see Hölbl 2001: 43–44; "at the latest in 259," Huss 2001: 282.
21. Olivier and Lorber 2013: 86–87, with the caveat that one must assume that gold was continuously struck at Alexandria at the beginning of the 250s, even if in smaller quantities than in the previous decade. The evidence from *P.Cair.Zen.* I 59021 suggests not that the mint of Alexandria had stopped minting but that it minted in smaller quantities than before and in smaller quantities than it could have.
22. Davesne 1998: 435. Seeing him as a simple accountant in charge of receiving foreign money at the *emporion* would not provide a better solution.
23. Burkhalter 2007, quoted in Olivier and Duyrat 2013: 87 n. 84.

is used for iron processed in the workshop of Demosthenes's father).[24] In the papyri, the verb also appears directly in production contexts.[25] If κατεργάζομαι refers not to an actual production process but to a pure accounting operation, one should suppose that Ptolemaic authorities kept large quantities of cash ready to be exchanged, which seems very unlikely. Above all, in this hypothesis, it is impossible to make sense of Demetrios's statement that the interests of the king are harmed by the delays because the mint's coinage cannot be "fine and fresh" as expected (lines 43–45: καλὸν καὶ καινόν).[26] In Demetrios's letter, there is thus no doubt that processing the metal meant minting it.

Scholars generally see Demetrios as the "mint master."[27] But if one considers the concerns of Demetrios, this is unlikely. The reason he had to write this letter to the dioikētēs is clear: he was not able to perform his job the way he would have liked to and so had to go over the head of his superior to explain his views (lines 7–8: "We would have received many times as much"). The document also refers to a certain "Philaretos" (as previously mentioned, the name is uncertain) who evidently had authority over Demetrios; "Philaretos" ordered Demetrios not to accept any more coins (lines 16–17: "but as Philaretos [?] does not allow me to accept"). Therefore Demetrios was definitely not the head of the mint. His task was obviously only to receive and mint gold (lines 6 [where the crucial point is that he receives gold], 13, 30, 33). Silver is mentioned only in line 33, in parallel with gold for the merchants who cannot get the coinage they want, even when paying a little more. This interesting illustration of the difficulties encountered by the merchants has

---

24. See also Theophrastus, CP 5.17.2, for worked wood.
25. For use of the verb in reference to exploitation or tilling of land, see P.Lond. 7 1954 (257 B.C.E.), lines 2 and 5 (to till land); P.Lond. 7 1954 (257 B.C.E.), lines 2 and 5 (to till land); P.Mich. 1 45 (252 B.C.E.), line 14 (to till an orchard); P.Tebt. 3 1 769 (237–236 or 212–211 B.C.E.), line 50 (to till land); CPR 18 7 (from Samaria, 231 or 206 B.C.E.), lines 13–14 (to exploit a vineyard); PSI 8 976 (248 B.C.E.), lines 10 and 15 (to exploit a vineyard); P.Enteux. 61 (246–40 B.C.E.), line 9 (to exploit an estate); P.Tebt. 1 105 (103–102 B.C.E.), lines 32 and 38 (to till land). For use of the verb in reference to production of various items, see P.Rev.Laws (259–258 B.C.E.), line 45.3 (for oil that has been produced by the oil producers, the ἐλαιουργοί); P.Cair.Zen. 4 59779 (mid-third century B.C.E.), line 3 (for worked fine flax); P.Col. 4 113 (mid-third century B.C.E.), line 27 (for wool dye produced from flowers); P.Tebt. 3 1 769 (237–236 or 212–211 B.C.E.), line 70 (for producing fine flax); P.Tebt. 3 1 703 (ca. 210 B.C.E.), line 147 (for the processing of raw product in oil factories).
26. For the meaning of καινόν in the context of Demetrios's letter as "fresh" and not "new" or "of new standard," as opposed to παλαιόν, "of old standard," see Cavagna 2008.
27. Hunt and Edgar 1934, 548; Le Rider 1998b: 403; Bagnall and Derow 2004: 163; Austin 2006: 536.; Mørkholm, Grierson, and Westermark (1991: 104) speak simply of "an official of the mint at Alexandria."

no direct connection with Demetrios's activity, which concerned only the processing of gold.

Was Demetrios the only one in charge of minting gold? This is a possibility, but it is not certain. Indeed, Demetrios had a specific task to perform, named in lines 4–7: "As for me I am devoting myself to what you wrote me to do: I have received 57,000 [units] in gold, which I processed and returned." But immediately after specifying his task, Demetrios switches to the plural, in line 7: "We would have received many times as much." The "we" probably alludes to Demetrios and his staff, with Demetrios as head of the office. It is a less likely solution that Demetrios was one of several officials in charge of minting gold, since the text makes no reference to colleagues.

Thus Demetrios was in charge of minting gold and only gold. As a consequence, it seems logical to consider that other officials were in charge of minting silver and bronze.[28] The mint of Alexandria must have been organized on a tripartite basis, with a top manager at the head of the three departments. This manager may have been "Philaretos," whom Demetrios had to bypass to alert Apollonios. Such an interpretation supposes that Demetrios was Apollonios's right-hand man, whom the *dioikētēs* had probably set in this function at the mint to get the information he needed on its management or mismanagement: this reading gives nuanced meaning to Demetrios's statement "As for me I am devoting myself to what you wrote me to do" (lines 4–5).

"57,000 in gold"

Demetrios received two types of gold coins from the merchants. First, he accepted good-quality (*akribes*) gold "local coins." As explained by G. Le Rider, we should understand these as mostly gold Alexanders, Lysimachi, or Seleukid coins on the Attic standard or other coins on the same standard. The diversity of these coins explains the lack of precision in their designation. The descriptor *akribes* has been interpreted, with good reason, as meaning "of good alloy" (Bagnall and Derow 2004) or "of good quality" (Le Rider 1998b). This implies that controllers had to detect and reject the fakes and other *fourrée* coins. Second, Demetrios had to process the Ptolemaic *trichrysa* with an official weight of ca. 17.90 grams that had to be reminted in accordance with

---

28. Davesne 1998.

the recent *prostagma* of the king. The new coinage, with its full denomination the *mnaieion* of ca. 27.80 grams, replaced the *trichryson* and its fractions.[29]

The figure of fifty-seven thousand—indicating, without further qualification, a ceiling that Demetrios was not authorized to break—has puzzled commentators. Although she does not have an answer, S. von Reden has rightfully asked whether the figure refers to "pieces" or "drachmas." Austin (hesitantly) speaks of "drachms (?)." Bagnall and Derow have understood "pieces," while Le Rider speaks of "57 000 pièces d'or."[30] Burkhalter has considered that the figure "57,000 gold" referred to the nominal value in silver drachmas.[31] These hypotheses must be examined in detail.

Can a reference to a specific number of coins make sense? First, the figure of fifty-seven thousand refers to Demetrios's receiving an amount "in gold" (lines 5–6: δέδεγμαι / ἐκ χρ(υσίου) μ(υριάδας) εζ´), which means, in the context, a certain quantity of gold in the form of coins, not a number of coins. Second, the text states that these coins were not of a homogeneous standard. Ptolemaic *trichrysa* could figure alongside Attic standard coins. The denominations could also vary. Coins on the Attic standard could be either didrachm staters (at ca. 8.50 grams) or drachmas (at ca. 4.25 grams); for *trichrysa*, they could be the full-weight coins at 17.90 grams (for the full standard of fresh coins) or the fractions at 1.78 grams.[32] Because of this diversity of standards and denominations and certainly also because of the inevitable wear, the size of the deposit of the individual merchants, which provided the basis for what Demetrios was to provide in new Ptolemaic coinage (with the deduction of the profit of the mint), can only have been reckoned in terms of weight, that is, in Ptolemaic drachmas.

But were these drachmas units of account in silver, or were they weight units? Indeed, χρυσίου (δραχμαί), ἀργυρίου, and χαλκοῦ (δραχμαί) all refer to the same unit of account, the silver drachma.[33] Only the metal of the coins that were used to pay the sum differed. But in the letter of Demetrios, we have not χρυσίου but ἐκ χρυσίου—actually ἐκ χρ(υσίου), but the expan-

---

29. On the reform, see already the discussion above; Le Rider 1998a: 796–97 (= 1999: 1120–21); Le Rider 1998b; Le Rider and de Callataÿ 2006: 149–53; von Reden 2007: 47; Olivier and Lorber 2013.
30. Le Rider 1998b: 404.
31. Burkhalter 2007: 49–51 (*non vidi*; quoted in Olivier and Lorber 2013: 87 n. 84).
32. See Le Rider and de Callataÿ 2006: 138, for the two series of *trichrysa*.
33. See, e.g., *P.Hib.* 1 110, lines 19–20 (August 272 at the latest); *P.Lond.* 7 1934 (258 B.C.E.); *P.Cair.Zen.* 3 59351 (244 B.C.E.).

sion is certainly the right one. When the word appears in the literary sources, it refers to the material from which an object is made. To cite one example, Chares of Mytilene, who participated in Alexander's expedition and was one of the king's historiographers, mentions that among the Persians, the Medes, and the people of Asia in general, pearls were considered more valuable than objects made of gold, τῶν ἐκ χρυσίου γεγενημένων.[34] In the Septuagint, ἐκ χρυσίου also regularly refers to objects made of gold.[35] Thus χρυσίου and ἐκ χρυσίου are not equivalent. The first designation refers to the metal of a coin in an account in silver. The second usually refers explicitly to the material from which an object is made. It seems explicit that the drachmas in question in Demetrios's letter are actual gold drachmas, not units of account.

Adopting the hypothesis of units of account in silver fits better with the idea that the operation at the mint of Alexandria consisted only in a conversion from one system to another, not in an actual reminting. But as already observed, the verb κατεργάζομαι, as well as the whole logic of the text, refers to a process of reminting. Besides, it was common to weigh gold objects with weight units in this metal (e.g., in drachmas). Among other parallels, the Delian documentation is clear on this point.[36] At a mint and in a process of reminting, the quantity of metal that was manipulated was at stake; it is thus obvious that Demetrios is referring to units of gold, that is, of gold drachmas. By simple arithmetic, he could easily determine at what moment a certain weight was reached. Insofar as it was the actual weight of metal that mattered at a mint, the figure of fifty-seven thousand must correspond to the value in terms of gold drachmas of the total quantity of coins received and minted by Demetrios and the staff of the gold section of the Alexandria mint.

A comparison with the *apousia* accounts of Delphi for the minting of the new Amphictionic coinage is very telling. At Delphi in 336–335 B.C.E., there had been a deficit between the official standard of the coins coming to the mint and their weight.[37] A similar case is provided by the Roman demand from the Seleukids after the peace of Apameia. Rome exacted the payment of the Seleukid indemnity in ἀργύριον Ἀττικὸν ἄριστον, which clearly meant

---

34. Chares of Mytilene *FGrHist* II B, 125 fr. 3 (from Athenaeus 3 45 93cd). See also Theophrastus, *HP* 9.19.3; Lucian, *Gallus* 24. Note that, with the same meaning, ἐκ χρυσοῦ would be significantly more frequent.

35. Septuagint of Exodus 25.31, 38; 28.8, 13–15, 22; 36.9, 12, 15, 22, 24; 38.5, 9; Paralipomenon 28.18.

36. Bresson 2000: 228–35.

37. Kinns 1983; Picard 1988; *CID* II.75–78.

full Attic standard and weighed silver coins, rather than simply a total number of coins, whatever their actual weight.[38] It is thus impossible to imagine that the mint at Alexandria would have only counted the coins and not weighed them, as this would have a negative impact on the profit of the mint. Scales, we should note, are routinely figured on representations of medieval mints, as they were present in the very similar representation of the workshop of a jeweler on a fresco of the House of the Vettii at Pompei.[39]

The Mints of Medieval Venice and of Ptolemaic Alexandria

We would like to know more from written sources about the management of a mint in a classical or Hellenistic Greek city or kingdom, but given the present state of our documentation, this information is out of reach. For now, our information is mainly based on that provided by the coins themselves.[40] We have much more information, through archives, on medieval mints. Indeed, they provide a striking parallel for the situation of the Alexandria mint in 258. This anachronistic comparison may seem to be a bold jump, but it is less daring if one considers that the technical conditions of minting remained almost unchanged from ancient times to the sixteenth century C.E., the period that saw the first introduction of mechanization into the process of minting, although this did not immediately eliminate the old technology of hand-hammered coins.[41] In fact, there are illuminating parallels in the medieval world for the little we do know about ancient mints, and these will help us to make reasonable hypotheses on the management of the Alexandria mint.

In the medieval world, a mint could be either directly managed by the state or leased out. The same diversity probably prevailed in antiquity. In Venice, as was certainly the case in Ptolemaic Alexandria (or Demetrios would not have written to the *dioikētēs* Apollonios), the mint was a state-organized institution. It is also significant to underscore that, in most cases, medieval mints carefully separated the minting of gold, silver, and bronze. At

---

38. On the stipulations of the treaty of Apamea, see Plb. 21.17.1–8, 21.43.19–21; Liv. 37.45.4–21, 37.55.1–3, 38.38.1–18; App., *Syr.* 38–39.
39. Ulrich 2008: 44–45.
40. See de Callataÿ 2012.
41. For many examples from the medieval or early modern period illustrating the continuity in minting technology from the ancient world, see Caspar 1974, 46–78, figs. 1–39; Travaini 2007b. See Sargent and Velde 2002: 53–61 for the innovations; Travaini 2007a: 48–49 for the long coexistence of the old and new technologies in the mints of early modern Europe.

the Venetian mint (the *zecca*), after the gold ducat was introduced, silver and gold were minted in the same building. However, although there is no detailed description of the rooms, it seems clear that a strict separation was observed between the minting operations of gold and silver: there were two mint masters and one weigher exclusively for gold, and there were obviously separate rooms with special keys, albeit in the same complex.[42] The intention was strict control over the several mint operations, which were specific to the two precious metals.[43] As the segregation of the various metals is exactly the organization that has been independently hinted at for the mint of Alexandria, this parallel between the two mints is quite striking.

Indeed, a mint was a source of revenue, in antiquity as well as in the medieval world. There was motivation to minimize costs and maximize benefits: this is what Demetrios's letter alludes to when he mentions that the king should get his coinage at no cost and make a profit (lines 43–46, 35–37). Severe control of productivity and exact measurement of cost and loss during the operations were crucial to this maximization. Embezzlement was always possible among the officials or staff in charge at the mint. Although the controls were very strict, the Venetian *zecca* experienced several cases of embezzlement, and the culprits were severely punished.[44] Again, similar situations can be observed in antiquity. At Sinope, probably before 370 B.C.E., the public banker Hikesias, who was in charge of the mint and was the father of the future Cynic philosopher Diogenes, was accused—alone or with his son (unless the crime was only that of the son, as the story is rather obscure)—of *paracharaxis*, mismanagement of the mint. Diogenes was exiled. The much later account of Diogenes Laertius says that Diogenes's own staff persuaded him to go astray. It is difficult to assess the truth of this story, but coins signed by a Hikesias have been discovered. As for his son, the story might be simply an invention to justify his future philosophical inspiration, which consisted in flouting established customs.[45] Whatever the case, the possibility of mismanagement was a constant problem, and authorities in ancient and medieval times had to exert a persistent control over the officials in charge of the mint and their staff, carefully examining the workshop's accounts and activ-

---

42. Stahl 2000: 33.
43. Stahl 2000: 138–39: thus the touchstone could be used to test the fineness of gold, which was not the case with silver.
44. Stahl 2000: 39–40, 73, 88, 263, 269–73.
45. DL 6.20–21, with 6.1; *Suda*, s.v. "Diogenes" δ 1143. On the philosophical inspiration, see Seltman 1938; Figueira 1993: 366; Branham 1996.

ity (weight of the incoming metal, number of coins, weight of the coin output). The Ptolemaic mint was not exempt from such fraud. The Meydancıkkale hoard (buried ca. 235 B.C.E.) contained four *fourrée* coins that seem to have been struck with official dies. This suggests some form of embezzlement from within the mint, despite the likely efforts to monitor it.[46]

It is clear not only that ancient and medieval mints operated under similar technical constraints but also that these constraints led to similar administrative solutions. In this respect, the parallel of the Venetian *zecca* becomes even more crucial to explaining the difficulty at the mint of Alexandria in 258 B.C.E. Indeed, it helps to illuminate the underlying causes of the situation described by Demetrios. At medieval Venice, one of the main systems of control at the mint was the so-called *quindena*, a period of time during which a mint master was in charge. Originally, the *quindena* probably corresponded to a fortnight; later, it was certainly a longer period, probably two months.[47] Basically, the system consisted in fixing a quota of production per day to be accomplished by each member of the staff, which meant also a quota of production per *quindena*.[48] The aim was to make sure that the quality of the production would be maintained and that no precious metal would be subverted. The system provided a good method of control, but if the quantity of precious metal brought by the foreign merchants exceeded the number of the coins to be minted as determined by the authorities, a bottleneck occurred. The merchants complained of the situation, and reforms were introduced that allowed more flexibility in accepting the bullion into the mint. But this did not solve the difficulties on the production side. Thus the Venetian Senate required that mint masters pay for the gold in the sequence in which they received it, or pay all the accounts of a *quindena* within a week of the start of the next one. Privileges could be granted to some categories of merchants, as when German traders in 1338 obtained the privilege to receive their coins within four days when they brought their gold to the mint. Of course, it was strictly forbidden for other traders to use Germans as middlemen. However, it was considered a normal situation for the merchants to wait between two and three weeks to receive their silver at the Venetian mint, as is mentioned in the merchant manual of Pegolotti. In 1368, Venetians complained that they had to wait four months to get ducats for their gold. At the beginning of the

46. Davesne 1998: 433.
47. Stahl 2000: 246–49.
48. Stahl 2000: 246–47.

Quattrocento, "a provision to punish masters who did not make full settlement within two months was defeated in the Senate"; thus it was clearly not uncommon to wait more than two months to get back the whole of one's gold.[49]

What was the situation at the mint of Alexandria? The starting point of our analysis should be the mention in lines 14–16 of an "ordinance that instructs us to take and process" foreign coins. The normal situation was thus to accept the foreign coins and mint the new Ptolemaic coinage. Nothing allows us to suppose that there was any Ptolemaic policy of deliberately waiting for the protests of the merchants before launching a new production. There is also no trace of an intention to avoid an excess of coins on the market, as has been hypothesized.[50] Given that the ordinance (*prostagma*) of the king was very clear and that Demetrios was supposed to receive and remint the coins brought by the traders, how is it that he was not allowed to do so? There must have been some sort of backlog, whereby Demetrios's immediate superior could invoke a priority rule that allowed him to block the production temporarily. The hypothesis proposed here is that at the mint of Alexandria, as at the medieval Venetian *zecca*, there was a maximum of production defined by rule for a certain period of time (what this period was remains unknown). At Venice, the point was to maintain the quality of the production and to prevent embezzlement. The same motivations must have been present at Alexandria. Thus, for the first point, the letter of Demetrios (lines 44–45) refers to the expectation that the coinage of the king "should always be fine and new." However, in the context of the beginning of the 250s, a period of low production of gold coinage at Alexandria, there were certainly also other and specific reasons for the low ceiling, although we cannot determine what they were.[51] As he explains, Demetrios could easily have minted many more coins, and only a bureaucratic decision coming from an upper level prevented him to do so.

Thus the hypothesis offered here is that the difficulty encountered by Demetrios was a consequence of a bureaucratic decision by the mint authorities concerning the quotas of production they set for the mint. This decision, however, contradicted the general principal that all the coins had to be ac-

49. Stahl 2000: 254–55.
50. See Le Rider and de Callataÿ 2006: 142–43.
51. For the output drop at the mint at the beginning of the Arsinoe *mnaieia*, see Olivier and Lorber 2013: 80–88.

cepted and reminted. The head of the mint could always hide behind the facts that, in principle, he did not refuse the coins and that the merchants only had to wait for a while. In practice, this meant that a bureaucratic constraint on the coin production was incompatible with the unpredictable quantity of gold that would be brought by the merchants. A difference between the Venetian situation and that of Ptolemaic Alexandria, however, is that the gold brought by the merchants was not even accepted to be processed at the mint of Alexandria, whereas there was a delay in delivering the ducats after the gold had been received by the Venetian *zecca*.

One can also try to make sense of the figure of the quota. Fifty-seven thousand Ptolemaic drachmas corresponded to nine talents and three thousand drachmas of gold. Why would Demetrios not use the rounded figure of ten talents? Strangely enough, the figure of fifty-seven thousand Ptolemaic drachmas finds a direct equivalent on the Attic standard. With a Ptolemaic drachma weighing ca. 3.58 grams, Demetrios had weighed 204.060 kilograms of gold. If we suppose that this weight was the equivalent of forty-eight thousand Attic drachmas, or eight Attic talents, we would have an Attic drachma weighing a little over 4.25 grams. This is only a fraction below what can be observed for the actual weight of Attic standard gold coins in this period, as can be verified from the Seleukid gold coins minted at this time.[52] The weight that was actually measured at the mint allowed an easy calculation of the inevitable weight loss (*apousia*) compared to the full Attic standard for gold (4.31 grams). One may consider that the authorities of the mint had set the level of fifty-seven thousand (Ptolemaic) drachmas to simplify their work. Based on round figures of talents, the figure must have provided a convenient way to calculate both the cost of minting and the profit expected on the difference between the Attic standard, which was the international standard, and the Ptolemaic one. This supposition also provides a logical explanation for the strange figure of fifty-seven thousand drachmas and supports the hypothesis that the figure of fifty-seven thousand corresponded to a quantity of drachmas, not of coins.

The 204.060 kilograms weighed by Demetrios were the equivalent of 7,340 *mnaieia* at 27.80 grams. It is commonly admitted that a die could strike around twenty thousand silver coins. On the one hand, gold is softer than

---

52. See Olivier and Duyrat 2010 for the Seleukid gold staters under Seleukos I and Antiochos I.

silver, which normally contributes to the longevity of a die. On the other hand, we know that gold was struck with greater care than silver, which means that as soon as a die was no longer in perfect condition, it had a good chance of being discarded. Besides, other reasons (e.g., the lack of metal) may have affected the productivity of a die. Thus, for gold, dies may not have been used to the limits of their lifetimes, and ten thousand coins per die has seemed a reasonable assumption of typical productivity.[53] If the estimate is correct, the processing of 204.060 kilograms of gold, over an unknown period of time, probably could have been accomplished using one obverse die. But this would mean that the mint of Alexandria was still minting gold in October 258, which might imply some slight revision (by one year) of the chronology of the first Arsinoe *mnaieia*.[54]

A regulation setting an upper limit to the production of every section of the mint for a defined period of time certainly had many advantages in terms of control and accounting. But if the demand for coins was higher than the volume of production specified by the authorities, a bottleneck occurred. The impact was immediately felt: the merchants could not get the coins they expected to receive in exchange of the precious metal they had brought with them. Should we consider that the reminting (and the king's *prostagma*) concerned only gold coins?[55] Demetrios's allusion to silver (line 33) does not prove that similar difficulties occurred for silver minting (silver may have been used as "small change" in the process of gold exchange), although the possibility is not excluded either. In any case, as already observed, Demetrios was obviously not in charge of minting silver. Even with gold, Demetrios could deplore the system of minting, but he was not himself in the position to modify the rule. His letter was the second one he wrote to inform Apollonios of the current situation at the mint (lines 8–9: "but as I have written to you before"). It is possible that Apollonios had anticipated this difficulty and that Demetrios's letter only brought him confirmation of it. It is more likely that the problem had emerged one or several times before, which would be consistent with a difficulty inherent to the system of minting. Interestingly, this proves that although Apollonios was the *dioikētēs*, he did not exercise full authority over the mint, even if he had there an insider who could inform him of its current activity. The case suggests some of the rivalries existing at

---

53. See the detailed discussion in Olivier and Lorber 2013: 101.
54. See Olivier and Lorber 2013: 80–83.
55. Le Rider 1998b: 404–5.

the top level of Ptolemaic administration, as alluded to in Demetrios's conclusion: "It is not proper for me to say in writing how some people are treating me, but as soon as you will hear [---]."

The Cost of Getting Money at Alexandria: Some Provisional Conclusions

The foreign or local traders at Alexandria found themselves in an uneasy situation, as they had to use local coinage in their business. Coins of Attic and other non-Ptolemaic standards were not legal tender in Egypt. As for the Ptolemaic coins, the *trichrysa* were not demonetized.[56] Obviously, people preferred to receive the new coins, and there was some reluctance at accepting the old standard coins, a situation that also affected Alexandrian merchants (lines 29–34: "As for the people in the city [*i.e.* Alexandria] they are all reluctant to make use of the worn gold coins. For none of them knows to whom he can refer and, after adding a little, get back fine gold or silver coins in exchange"). A fortunate few could get the money they needed in due time. Others were less fortunate, and Demetrios's letter to Apollonios shows that the waiting periods harmed their commercial activity. There was thus a strong disparity among traders, in terms of access to the market; foreigners coming to Egypt had no way of knowing whether they could get their gold coins quickly or would be forced to wait for weeks or months to obtain them. It is likely that pure chance determined the level of transaction costs of the individual traders most of the time.

Large sums of money were at stake: on a ratio of one gram of gold to 12.8 grams of silver, the proposed fifty-seven thousand gold drachmas were the equivalent of 729,600 silver drachmas, or 121 talents and thirty-six hundred drachmas, a large sum for the time. That Demetrios boasted that he could have minted several times more proves how significant the issue was and suggests that much more gold waited to be minted. The text deals with substantial money transfers, but they are perfectly compatible with what we know of the volumes of transactions of large ports in the Hellenistic period. The figure can be compared with that of the volume of activity of the port of

---

56. See, e.g., *P.Cair.Zen.* 1 59022, of probably 258–256 B.C.E., where *trichrysa, mnaieia,* and *pentekontadrachma* appear in the same account.

Rhodes before 166. According to Polybius (30.31.12), the tax customs represented an amount of one million drachms, or 166 talents. As the rate of customs duties (the revenue of which was sold at auction) was one-fiftieth, the volume of activity of the port of Rhodes (import and export) was thus over eighty-three hundred talents. The amount of 121 talents and thirty-six hundred drachmas (in silver equivalent) in local gold coins obtained by the foreign merchants at Alexandria was thus perfectly in the range of what we know of the volume of activity of first-rank harbors in the Hellenistic period (and, as expected, also far below the global volume of activity of such a port).

To estimate the level of the transaction costs involved in the very operation of getting money, one should first separate the customs duties on gold or silver imports from the proper fees for converting money from one kind into another. Indeed, the text makes a clear distinction between the case of the foreign merchants and that of the local people of Alexandria. Of the latter, it is said that by "adding a little" (line 32: προσθείς τι), they would be able to swap their old *trichrysa* into the new *mnaieia*. A minimal fee would be exacted. The gold that was imported, however, may well have been subject to heavy duties. It seems to have been common to distinguish between import (or export) duties and proper exchange fees. This distinction is basic to making sense of the law of Olbia of ca. 370 B.C.E.[57] The law advertised that all commercial operations should be performed in local Olbiopolitan silver or bronze coinage, that import and export of coined "gold" (in fact, certainly electrum) and silver money would be free (which implies that import and export of uncoined precious metal would not be), and that the fees for money exchange would be set by mutual agreement. The exemption from customs duties on imported or exported precious metal coins was certainly exceptional and was advertised as one of the privileges granted by Olbia to attract foreign traders. Ptolemaic Egypt also famously required the use of its local coins by foreign merchants. Unfortunately, no document informs us of the possible customs duties on the import of foreign precious metal coins, although it seems reasonable to imagine that they were significantly high, given the high level of customs duties on a whole range of imported goods.[58]

G. Le Rider has argued that the exchange rate between the silver Attic drachma and the Ptolemaic drachma was one to one.[59] If this was the case, the

---

57. *Syll.*3 218.
58. See n. 1 above.
59. Le Rider 1986; Le Rider and de Callataÿ 2006: 143.

rate of exchange, according to the respective values of the Attic and Ptolemaic drachma mentioned above, would have been between 16 and 17 percent—that is, about one-sixth of drachma, or one obol per drachma. For gold, however, Le Rider and de Callataÿ admit that since prices were denominated in silver drachmas, foreign traders would have received their local gold coins at little or no cost.[60] One could also envisage—unfortunately, with no better evidence—that, as for silver, the duties for gold were established on the basis of the equivalence of one Ptolemaic drachma for one Attic drachma, which would mean a tax of ca. 16–17 percent. Of course, if this solution is correct, this tax was not all profit for the mint, as the cost of minting (*brassage*) was to be deducted from this amount. Given the high value of the metal and the minimal cost of minting in proportion to the value of the coin, the cost of minting gold must have been very low, certainly well below 1 percent of the value of heavy-weight coins like the *trichrysa* or *mnaieia*. The parallel with the medieval evidence should leave no doubt on this point.[61] To consider the state's profit, the comparative margin at the Venetian *zecca* for silver in 1278 was only ca. 2.3 percent, with the cost of *brassage* at 1.6 percent and the seigniorage (profit) of the mint at ca. 0.7 percent.[62] For now, it seems perfectly possible to envisage that, just as they probably did with silver, the Ptolemies made a profit of ca. 16–17 percent on gold coins brought to Egypt by foreign merchants.

While there is certainly a similarity between ancient Ptolemaic Alexandria and medieval Venice in terms of the possible delays in getting gold or silver coinage from a mint, there remain differences between the two states for the cost of access to cash. The Venetian authorities deliberately maintained a minimal seigniorage to attract gold and silver bullion. They knew that if they did not, German traders would go to other mints with the gold or silver that they brought from the kingdom of Hungary (as bullion, but sometimes also as coins). Competition between mints kept exchange rates low. A different situation prevailed at Alexandria in 258. Traders coming from abroad did not come to this port to acquire coins that they would be able to

---

60. Le Rider and de Callataÿ 2006: 143–44.
61. In medieval Europe, although the coins were much lighter than the Ptolemaic *trichrysa* or *mnaieia*, the *brassage* in percentage of the value of the gold coin was always under 1 percent, and it was down to 0.14 percent for the Florentine *fiorino* in 1347 (out of eight examples, the only exception is the Flemish *noble* of 1389, with a *brassage* at 1.58 percent); see Sargent and Velde 2002: 51.
62. Stahl 2000: 173

trade everywhere, since the gold or silver they brought with them was already in coins. They had to obtain local coins to be able to trade in Egypt and within the Ptolemaic empire. Demetrios's letter nowhere refers to bullion, which was the main input at the Venetian *zecca*. Foreign merchants came to Egypt to buy grain, textiles, alum, or papyrus that they would resell overseas for a high profit. Egypt apparently benefited by having large supplies of these products, which were in constant demand. This could explain why foreign merchants might have accepted high import duties and other costs that were imposed on them to get local cash. But again, for now, evidence on this point is still lacking.

As for the delays necessary to obtain local coins, the situation observed at Alexandria may not have been exceptional in the Greek world. It may have been especially frequent in closed currency systems requiring a nonstandard coinage for which local authorities were sometimes unable to meet demand. However, this cannot be considered to have been the norm. In the *Poroi* (3.2), written in 355/4 B.C.E., Xenophon stressed that one could easily get good silver coins at Athens and that merchants could export them without difficulty if they were not able to purchase a cargo to export. In classical Athens, the metal production was local, and the mine entrepreneurs brought the metal to the mint under the form of bullion.[63] In this city, as in many others, it was certainly through money changers that foreign traders could obtain the cash they needed, as discussed in the essay by Ober in this volume (chapter 2). The exchange was apparently around 5 percent.[64] As for Egypt, it had its own gold mines.[65] Yet foreign traders brought into Egypt the gold from which the coins that they would use in the country were produced. This affected trade, but the state knew that the merchants were prepared to pay the high price to gain access to their market and to the goods that they would resell at a high profit in Greece. Demetrios could complain that the king's revenues suffered, which was partly true in the short term. But it is hard to believe that many merchants decided, in the end, to leave Egypt or other Ptolemaic possessions empty-handed. A monopolist can develop a rentier mentality and does not really care if transaction costs are high, as long as it is

63. Flament 2007a, 2007b.
64. On money exchange, see Bogaert 1962: 42–50, 308–31, 397–98.
65. Diod. 3.12–14, with Le Rider and de Callataÿ 2006: 23–24. See other recent bibliography in Olivier and Lorber: 122 n. 143. On gold mines in the Ptolemaic period, marked by the introduction of technologies that had previously been developed in the Laurion, see Klemm and Klemm 2013: 12–15, 294–340.

only or mainly the consumer who is affected. This was the situation in Ptolemaic Egypt.

Bibliography

Austin, M. 2006. *The Hellenistic World from Alexander to Roman Conquest: A Selection of Ancient Sources in Translation*. 2nd ed. Cambridge.

Bagnall, R. S., ed. 1976. *The Administration of the Ptolemaic Possessions outside Egypt*. Leiden.

Bagnall, R. S. 2009a. *The Oxford Handbook of Papyrology*. Oxford.

Bagnall, R. S. 2009b. "Practical Help: Chronology, Geography, Measures, Currency, Names, Prosopography, and Technical Vocabulary." In Bagnall 2009a: 179–96.

Bagnall, R., and P. Derow. 2004. *Historical Sources in Translation: The Hellenistic Period*. Oxford.

Bogaert, R. 1962. *Banques et banquiers dans les cités grecques*. Leiden.

Bogaert, R. 1998–99. "Les opérations des banques de l'Égypte ptolémaïque." *AS* 29: 49–145.

Branham, R. B. 1996. "Defacing the Currency: Diogenes' Rhetoric and the Invention of Cynicism." In Branham and Goulet-Cazé 1996: 81–104.

Branham, R. B., and M.-O. Goulet-Cazé, eds. 1996. *The Cynics: The Cynic Movement in Antiquity and Its Legacy*. Berkeley.

Bresson, A. 2000. *La cité marchande*. Bordeaux.

Bresson, A. 2012. "Wine, Oil, and Delicacies at the Pelousion Customs." In Günther and Grieb 2012: 69–88.

Brousseau, E., and J.-M. Glachant, eds. 2008. *New Institutional Economics: A Guidebook*. Cambridge.

Burkhalter, F. 2007. "Comptes et monnaies en Égypte ptolémaïque d'après les papyrus." PhD diss., Université Paris–Sorbonne.

Caspar, H. 1974. *In meiner Müntz schlag ich Gericht* . . . . Berlin. Illustrations from pp. 46–98 reprinted in Travaini and Bolis 2007: 426–78.

Cavagna, A. 2008. "L'oro dei theoi adelphoi." In Zanetto, Martinelli Tempesta, and Ornaghi 2008: 161–82.

Davesne, A. 1998. "L'atelier monétaire d'Alexandrie au IIIe siècle av. J.-C." In Empereur 1998: 429–42.

de Callataÿ, F. 2012. "Control Marks on Hellenistic Royal Coinages: Use, and Evolution Toward Simplification?" *RBN* 158: 39–62.

Dillon, M., and L. Garland. 1994. *Ancient Greece: Social and Historical Documents from Archaic Times to the Death of Socrates (c. 800– 399 BC)*. London.

Duyrat, F., and J. Olivier. 2010. "Deux politiques de l'or: Séleucides et Lagides au IIIe et IIe siècle avant J.-C." *RN* 166: 71–93.

Edgar, C. C. 1918. "Selected Papyri from the Zenon Archives." *ASAE* 18, no. 5: 168–71.

Edgar, C. C. 1925. *Zenon Papyri*. Vol. 1 of *Catalogue Général des Antiquités Égyptiennes du Musée du Caire*. Cairo.

Empereur, J.-Y., ed. 1998. *Commerce et artisanat dans l'Alexandrie hellénistique et romaine: Actes du Colloque d'Athènes, 11–12 décembre 1988*. Bulletin de Correspondance Hellénique Supplement 33. Athens.

Figueira, T. 1993. *Excursions in Epichoric History: Aiginetan Essays*. Lanham, MD.

Flament, C. 2007a. *Le monnayage en argent d'Athènes: De l'époque archaïque à l'époque hellénistique (c. 550–c. 40 av. J.-C.)*. Louvain-la-Neuve.

Flament, C. 2007b. *Une économie monétarisée: Athènes à l'époque classique (440–338): Contribution à l'étude du phénomène monétaire en Grèce ancienne*. Louvain-la-Neuve.

Günther, L.-M., and V. Grieb, eds. 2012. *Das imperiale Rom und der hellenistische Osten: Festschrift für Jürgen Deininger zum 75. Geburtstag*. Wiesbaden.

Habicht, C. 2003. "Rhodian Amphora Stamps and Rhodian Eponyms." *REA* 105: 541–78.

Hölbl, G. 2001. *History of the Ptolemaic Empire*. London.

Hunt, A. S., and C. C. Edgar. 1934. *Select Papyri*. Vol. 2. Loeb Classical Library. Cambridge, MA.

Huss, W. 2001. *Ägypten in hellenistischer Zeit 332–30 v. Chr.* Munich.

Kinns, P. 1983. "The Amphictionic Coinage Reconsidered." *NC* 143: 1–22.

Klemm, R., and D. D. Klemm. 2013. *Gold and Gold Mining in Ancient Egypt and Nubia: Geoarchaeology of the Ancient Gold Mining Sites in the Egyptian and Sudanese Eastern Deserts*. Berlin.

Knoepfler, D., ed. 1988. *Comptes et inventaires dans la cité grecque*. Neuchâtel.

Le Rider, G. 1986. "Les alexandres d'argent en Asie Mineure et dans l'Orient séleucide au IIIe siècle av. J.-C. (c. 275–225)." *JS*, 3–51. Reprinted in Le Rider 1999: 3: 1183–237.

Le Rider, G. 1998a. "Histoire économique et monétaire de l'Orient hellénistique." *Annuaire du Collège de France 1997–1998* 98: 783–809. Reprinted in Le Rider 1999: 3: 1107–33.

Le Rider, G. 1998b. "Sur un passage du papyrus de Zénon 59021." In Empereur 1998: 403–7.

Le Rider, G. 1999. *Études d'histoire monétaire et financière du monde grec: Écrits 1958–1998*. Edited by E. Papaefthymiou, F. de Callataÿ, and F. Queyrel. Société hellénique de numismatique. Athens.

Le Rider, G., and F. de Callataÿ. 2006. *Les Séleucides et les Ptolémées: L'héritage monétaire et financier d'Alexandre le Grand*. Paris.

Lorber, C. C. 2012. "The Coinage of the Ptolemies." In Metcalf 2012: 211–34.

Metcalf, W. E., ed. 2012. *The Oxford Handbook of Greek and Roman Coinage*. Oxford.

Mørkholm, O., P. Grierson, and U. Westermark. 1991. *Early Hellenistic Coinage*. Cambridge.

Nye. J. "Institutions and the Institutional." In Brousseau and Glachant 2008: 67–80.

Oleson, J. P., ed. 2008. *The Oxford Handbook of Engineering and Technology in the Classical World*. Oxford.

Olivier, J., and C. Lorber. 2013. "Three Gold Coinages of Third-Century Ptolemaic Egypt." *RBN* 159: 49–150.

Pestman, P. W. 1981. *A Guide to the Zenon Archive*. 2 vols. Leiden.

Picard, O. 1988. "Les monnaies des comptes de Delphes à 'apousia.'" In Knoepfler 1988: 91–101.

Préaux, C. 1939. *L'économie royale des Lagides*. Brussels.

Reekmans, T. 1993. "Allocation, prêt à usage et don de biens de consommation dans les archives de Zénon." *CE* 68: 202–11.

Reinach, T. 1928. "Du rapport de valeur des métaux monétaires dans l'Égypte au temps des Ptolémées." *REG* 41: 121–96.

Richter, H. D. 1992. "Ein Verwaltungswiderstand gegen ein Prostagma Ptolemaios' II. Philadelphos? (*P.Cairo Zen.* 59021)." *Tyche* 7: 177–86.

Rostovtseff, M. I. 1941. *The Social and Economic History of the Hellenistic World*. 3 vols. Oxford.

Sargent, T. J., and F. R. Velde. 2002. *The Big Problem of Small Change*. Princeton.

Seltman, C. T. 1938. "Diogenes of Sinope, Son of the Banker Hikesias." In *Transactions of the International Numismatic Congress, June 30–July 3, 1936*, 121. London.

Stahl, A. M. 2000. *Zecca: The Mint of Venice in the Middle Ages*. Baltimore.

Travaini, L. 2007a. "I conii e le zecche." In Travaini and Bolis 2007: 27–66.

Travaini, L. 2007b. "Le zecche illustrate: Iconografia e interpretazione." In Travaini and Bolis 2007: 259–99.

Travaini, L., and A. Bolis, eds. 2007, *Conii e scene di coniazione*. Monete 2. Rome.

Ulrich, R. 2008. "Representations of Technical Processes." In Oleson 2008: 35–61.

Van Effenterre, H., and F. Ruzé. 1994–95. *Nomima*. 2 vols. Paris.

von Reden, S. 2007. *Money in Ptolemaic Egypt from the Macedonian Conquest to the End of the Third Century BC*. Cambridge.

Welles, C. B. 1934. *Royal Correspondence in the Hellenistic Period*. New Haven.

Will, É. 1979–82. *Histoire politique du monde hellénistique*. 2nd ed. 2 vols. Nancy.

Yenisoğancı, V., and A. Davesne. 1992. "Les Ptolémées en Séleucide: Le trésor d'Hüseyinli." *RN*, 23–36.

Zanetto, G., S. Martinelli Tempesta, and M. Ornaghi, eds. 2008. *Nova vestigia antiquitatis*. Milan.

CHAPTER 6

The *Grammatikon*

Some Considerations on the Feeing Policies of Legal Documents in the Ptolemaic and Roman Periods

Uri Yiftach

One of the themes studied in this volume is state policy with respect to economic activity generally and contractual activity specifically. It has been acknowledged throughout this book that the ancient "state" was interested, for different reasons, in monitoring, promoting, or discouraging certain economic activities and was able to employ a wide range of means to pursue its policies. It is also clear that the ancient state was interested in increasing its wealth: one need only read Xenophon's *Poroi* to establish both this interest and some of the means, at times quite sophisticated, by which this goal could be attained. The question remains, however, to what extent promoting economic activity was a goal set above others.

The answer to this question is by no means necessarily positive, certainly not when one is considering the ancient world. After all, the very notion of private property—that is, property of which one can freely dispose, regardless of the interests and wishes of others—was very slow to develop. Even in the case of the so-called "law of the papyri" (i.e., legal practice in Greco-Roman Egypt evident from papyrological sources), one finds restrictions on private property. Consider, for example, the πρωτοπραξία, or the right of the *fiscus* (the imperial treasury), as well as of the wife, to exact debts prior to any other creditor, which is best documented in the widely cited edict of Tiberius Julius Alexander from 68 C.E. (*OGIS* II 669.18–26); or the κατοχή (*katochê*), the right of children to acquire the property of their parents after their death; or the right of family members who own the same object in partnership to make void the alienation of some of the assets by one of their partners.[1] Now, the origin of most of these rights is not always evident: the *katochê*, for example, is mentioned in the edict of Mettius Rufus—the most important source of information on this institution—as originating from "some local practice" or "some local law," and there is no evidence that it was introduced by the Roman administration.[2] But how did the Romans deal with such institutions?

Over the last couple of years, several studies have been dedicated to the institution of the "archive of acquisitions," the βιβλιοθήκη ἐγκτήσεων (see Lerouxel's analysis in chapter 7). The creation of this archive, providing reliable information on the legal status of landed property, was meant, it is claimed, to enhance the certainty of the law and thus to promote economic activity. While I share the view that promoting contractual activity formed a key incentive for the foundation of the archive of acquisitions (Yiftach-Firanko 2009), I remain doubtful whether the same general policy lies behind other early Roman measures relating to the institution of the contract.

One of the key means of promoting economic and contractual activity is to secure the autonomy of the contracting party to dispose of his or her property freely. To achieve this goal, one would aim at rescinding or at least curtailing the ability of other persons to encroach on one's freedom to transact. But complete freedom of transacting was never achieved in early Roman Egypt. If anything, provincial legislation tended in the other direction, aiming at protecting the rights of family members at the expense of the individual's capacity to dispose freely of his or her property. One remarkable example of this state of affairs is found in the documentation of land sales at Tebtynis in the first century C.E.: to purchase land, one needed to gain the consent not only of the prospective vendor but also of family members, who would have had to express their approval in writing on the document of sale. One can only guess at the impact this requirement had on the immediate costs of the transaction (i.e., what it cost to gain consent), as well as on the future costs, that is, those incurred in the protection of one's title in court

---

1. Cf. nn. 51–53.
2. *P.Oxy.* II 237.viii.34: κατά τινα ἐπιχώριον νόμον (89 C.E.).

against the challenges of third parties if the acknowledgment of consent was not incorporated in the document of sale. My current view, then, is that while some institutions created or developed by the Roman administration indeed reduced transaction costs and thus perhaps promoted economic activity, promoting contractual activity was not the only incentive that motivated Roman contractual policy in general.[3] In this essay, I illustrate this conclusion by discussing the γραμματικόν, a fee charged by scribes drafting legal (and other) documents at a scribal office called a γραφεῖον. This fee is especially well documented in the source material surviving from the Fayyum.[4]

The expense of drafting a written document was one of the most important recurring costs involved in the conclusion of contracts in ancient times. Quite frequently, the parties turned to a professional scribe, who charged money for recording the contract in writing, storing a copy of the document in his files, and performing whatever formalities were required for warranting the document's status as an authoritative legal instrument.[5] The Ptolemaic and Roman states, for their part, both exhibited an ongoing effort to render professional scribes available to potential contracting parties.

One of the manifestations of this effort was the development, at the beginning of the Roman period, of a network of scribal offices, or *grapheia*, in every large village (at least in some parts of Egypt). The care taken by the *grapheia* with respect to preserving evidence of contracts is manifested in the system of multiple documentation they employed. Several copies of a contract were produced, one to be kept in the *grapheion*'s files, others (termed ἐκδόσιμα) to be handed over to the two (or more) interested parties. The office's scribes also prepared summaries of the contracts, called εἰρόμενα, and created lists, called ἀναγραφαί, of all the documents composed at the *grapheion*, ordered chronologically, with a record of the transaction, the parties, and the value of

---

3. I reached similar conclusions in a recent paper focusing on the Roman policy relating to the taxation of the conveyance of catoecic land. The paper was delivered at the fifth meeting of the research group Legal Documents in Ancient Societies (Budapest, October 2012). In this context, cf., in particular, *P.Iand.* VII 137 (2nd C.E., Arsinoitês).
4. The γραμματικόν is the subject of a forthcoming publication by M. Choat. I thank Dr. Choat for sharing with me the manuscript of his forthcoming study.
5. A survey of the adjective ἄκυρος in literary and documentary sources yields numerous provisions invalidating the applicability of a legal document in the absence of some required features. The provision in the Gnomon of the Idios Logos (an office in the Roman provincial administration charged with certain fiscal responsibilities) on the invalidity of wills not drawn up κατὰ δημοσίους χρηματισμούς is a relatively well-known example (*BGU* V 1210 § 7, after 149 C.E., Theadelphia).

the transaction.[6] Some of these lists, dating to the early first century (42–47 C.E.), also report the γραμματικόν, a term used in early Roman Egypt[7] to designate the fee charged by the scribe for his services.[8]

One such list records 1,030 documents drafted in the *grapheion* of Tebtynis (a rather large village in the Arsinoite nome, the modern Fayyum) over the course of sixteen months, from the beginning of Claudius's sixth year (September 45) to the fourth month of his seventh (December 46).[9] For more than nine hundred documents, this list also records the amount of the *grammatikon*, which varies. These documents, the Claudian *anagraphai*, now in the papyrus collection of the University of Michigan, were published more than half a century ago, yet they have failed to gain the attention they merit as a key source for the study of ancient law and economy, particularly with respect to what they tell us about transaction costs in the Roman world and the policy such fees were meant to serve. Analyzing the data provided by these documents allows us to reach a conclusion that accords with the characterization advanced above concerning Roman contractual policy and its goals. Before embarking on this analysis, however, it is necessary to study the Ptolemaic background, as manifested in the source material from the third and early second centuries B.C.E.

The Ptolemaic Feeing Policy

P.Ryl. IV 572 (2nd cent. B.C.E., Arsinoitês?) is probably the most important piece of evidence on feeing policies of scribes in Ptolemaic Egypt. It preserves a letter sent in the early second century B.C.E., likely issued by a high-ranking official named Prôtarchos to Ptolemaios, a *stratêgos* in the Arsinoite nome.[10]

---

6. Wolff 1978: 18–25.
7. Use of the term γραμματικόν to denote a fee paid to a scribe is not frequently attested outside the lists from Tebtynis. Cf. *P.Mich.* II, pp. 89–90; most recently, *P.Col.* X 254.12–13 (129 C.E., Oxrhynchos?); *P.NYU* II 26.4 (103 C.E., provenance unknown), with further sources quoted in the commentary (p. 65). *LSJ* 9, s.v. (p. 359), records no literary attestation of the term.
8. Cf., e.g., *P.Mich.* II 123 recto 2.6: [ὁμολογία] Πτολεμαίο(υ) καὶ τῆ(ς) γυ(ναικὸς) πρὸ(ς) Ἡρωδίωνα παρα(θήκης) (δραχμῶν) σμη). (δραχμαὶ) ϛ.
9. Cf. *P.Mich.* II, pp. 88–94; *P.Mich.* V, pp. 53–57.
10. The surviving text of *P.Ryl.* IV 572 does not reveal the identity of its author or addressee, but the original editors plausibly suggested on the basis of the letter's contents that we may infer that the author was the Prôtarchos mentioned in *BGU* VI 1214.8-9 (see *P.Ryl.* IV, p. 19). This latter text is a letter by Ptolemaios, in which the *stratêgos* discusses matters substan-

Prôtarchos addresses two issues: the nomination procedure of Egyptian scribes[11] and the fee (μισθός) they charge their clients. The latter provision also discloses the objective of the new regulations (discussed below) concerning such fees: "In order that men may not be required to pay more than the proper sum, it is necessary to fix the proper fee for each document."[12] This formulation is interesting for three reasons. First, it proves the existence, in the eyes of the author of the regulation, of a "proper" (μέτριος) fee for legal documents. Second, it implies that scribes frequently overcharged for their work. Finally, it reveals that the scribes were not expected to charge a flat rate for all their documents: there were several fees, each "within measure" (μέτριος) with respect to the type of document drafted. The importance of this issue in the eyes of the author of the letter is stressed even more by the following provisions: scribes should take an oath that they will neither, on any pretext, overcharge for documents they draft nor have anyone do so on their behalf. Any contravention should not merely be registered with the *stratêgos*; it should also be reported to the letter's author himself.[13] In a second document, we then find the *stratêgos* Ptolemaios following these instructions. *BGU* VI 1214 (185–165 B.C.E., Arsinoitês) preserves a subsequent letter that Ptolemaios issues to the *epistatai* of the villages in the Hêrakleidês *meris* of the Arsinoite nome, in which he reports the

---

tively identical to the order issued in *P.Ryl.* IV 572 and which I will discuss shortly. I see no reason not to accept this suggestion as a working hypothesis.

11. *P.Ryl.* IV 572.30–35 (2nd B.C.E., Arsinoitês?): [ἵνα ἐπιτή]δειοι προχ ῾ε᾽ ιρισθῶσειν καὶ I 31 [συγκριθῶσ]ι γράφειν τὰ συναλλάγματα I 32 [ταῦτα κατὰ τὸν] τῆς χώρας νόμον, γενέσθαι I 33 [δὲ τὸν προχει]ρισμ[ὸ]ν αὐτῶν διὰ τῶν ἐπισI34[τατῶν τῶν] ἱερῶν (vac) I col. 2 I I 35 καὶ τῶν ἀρχιερείων καὶ τῶν [λαοκριτῶν].

12. Lines 36–38: ἵνα δὲ μὴ πλῆον πράτ᾽τ῾ων[ται οἱ ἄν]I 37θρωποι τοῦ καθήκοντος στ[ῆσαι δεῖ] τὸν I 38 μέτριον μισθὸν ἑκάστης [συγγρα]φῆς.

13. Lines 39–66: καλῶς οὖν π[ο]ι[ήσ]εις συνεδρ[εύ]σας μετὰ I 40 {τα} τοῦ ἐπισ[τά]του καὶ τ[οῦ] ἐπιστάτου I 41 τῶν φυλακι[τῶ]ν καὶ οἰκον[όμ]ου καὶ τοῦ I 42 βασιλικ[ο]ῦ γρα[μμα]τέως καὶ [με]ταπεμ I 43 ψάμ[ε]νος τοὺς [ἐ]ν [τ]οῖς κάτ[ω]{ι} τόποις I 44 ἐπιστάτας τῶν ἱερῶν κα[ὶ ἀρχι]ερεῖς καὶ I 45 λαοκρ[ίτ]ας καὶ ἐπιλαβὼν [παρ'] αὐτῶν I 46 γρ[α]φὴν τῶν ἐπιτ[η]δείων [γράφ]ειν καὶ I 47 ὅσ[ο]ν ἱκανὸν ἴσω[ς κα]θ᾽ ἕκασ[τον . . . .] ον I 48 [±7–8] τα πε[. . τ]οὺς ἀνθρώπους I 49 [±13–15] . . αφει [τ]ών ἐν I 50 [τού] τοῖς ἀδικημάτων. [ἵνα] τοίνυν I 51 μὴ πλεῖον πράτ᾽τ῾ωσ[ι τοὺς ἰδ]ιώτας I 52 τῶν ὑποτεταγμένω[ν γραφείων ἑκά]σ I 53 του συναλλάγματος καὶ [±10]υ I 54 ἐ[π]ιμελέστερον λαβὲ πα[ρ' αὐτῶν] χειρ[ο] I 55 γραφίαν ὅρκου βασιλικοῦ μὴ [πρά]ξειν I 56 παρευρέσει ἡ ῾ι᾽τινιοῦν μηδ᾽ ἑτέρωι I 57 ἐπιτρέπειν ἀπὸ τοῦ εἴδους τ[ο]υ῾ του῾ παρα I 58 λογεῖν ῾. . . . ᾽ μήτε εἰς τὸ βασιλικὸν μήτε I 59 κατ᾽ ἄλλον μηθένα τρόπον. οἷς ἂν συν I 60 ιστορήσει (read συνιστορήσῃ) τοιούτοις (read τοιοῦτο) ῾τι᾽ πεπραχόσι παρα I 61 χρῆμα διασαφήσειν ἡμI̯ε̯Iῖν καὶ ὅσ᾽ ἂν I 62 οἰκονομήσῃ ῾ι᾽ς γράψον ἡμᾶς, εὐθέως I 63 δὲ καὶ τὰ ὀνόματα τῶν προχ῾ε᾽ιρισθησο I 64 μένων κατὰ τὸν νόμον ὑπόταξον. I 65 ζ(ήτησον) ἵνα δὲ καὶ οἱ ἰδιῶται σσυσ῾τι᾽αντας μὴ I 66 πλῆον τάσσονται (read τάσσωνται) τοῦ ὁρισμένου (read ὡρισμένου).

instructions from the letter he received (i.e., *P.Ryl.* IV 572) and also specifies how much should be charged for each type of document. The system Ptolemaios implements is quite simple: the scribes should apply two rates, twenty drachmas for documents recording sales and deeds of cession and ten drachmas for all the others. Ptolemaios also notes that this system is not new: he mentions, almost en passant, that this same pricing regime is in force in the Delta nome of Bousiritês.[14]

No similar regulation has come down to us relating to Greek scribes. Yet the existence of one is very likely. Greek legal documents frequently take, in the early Ptolemaic period, the shape of a double document. The contract is written twice, in two identical versions, on the same papyrus sheet. The upper text is sealed by the parties and the six witnesses who attended the act, while the lower text remains unsealed. The document is then handed over to one of the witnesses, the *syngraphophylax*, who becomes responsible for the document's safekeeping.[15]

In the late third century, key details of transactions recorded in double documents were also registered in periodical accounts, compiled by village in which the documents were composed.[16] These accounts also report the *misthos*, the fee charged by the scribe for the documents he composed, as well as how much it cost the scribe to produce the documents and his net profit.[17]

---

14. *BGU* VI 1214 (185–165 B.C.E., Arsinoitês): Πτολεμαῖος στρατηγὸς τοῖς ἐπιστά[ταις] | 2 τῶν ἐν τῆι Ἡρακλείδου μερίδι κομων (read κωμῶν) [χαίρειν]. | 3 ἀπὸ τῶν ὑπαρχόντων παρ᾽ ὑμῖν Α[ἰ]γυπτίων | 4 γραμματοδιδασκάλων τῶν εἰωθότων γράφειν | 5 τὰ συναλλάγματα κατὰ τὸν τῆς χώρας νόμον συν | 6 κεκριμένοι{ς} εἰσὶν οἱ ὑπογεγραμμένοι ὑπὸ | 7 Πάσιτος τοῦ ἐπιστάτου τῶν ἐν τῶι νομῶι | 8 ἱερῶν καὶ τῶν ἄλλων κατὰ τὰ ὑπὸ Πρωτάρχου | 9 τῶν φίλων δι[α]σαφηθέντα ἡμῖν ἐπιτήδειοι εἶναι | 10 γίνεσθαι πρὸς τῆ ι' κειμένη χρείαι, παρ᾽ ὧν καὶ λαβόντες | 11 χειρογ[ρ]αφίαν ὅρκου βασιλικοῦ διεστάλμεθα [ποτει] ὅτι | 12 οὐ πλ[ε]ῖον πράξονται τῶν διακειμένων γραφ(ε)ίων | 13 παρ[ευ]ρέσει ἡτ[ι]νιοῦν [οὐδὲ] ἑτέροις ἐπιτρέψουσιν | 14 ἀπ[ὸ] τ[ο]ῦ εἴδους τού[του παραλο]γεύειν (?) [οὔ]τε εἰς τὸ | 15 βασιλικὸν ο[ὔ]τε [κατ᾽ ἄλλον οὐδ]έν[ατρόπ]ον. | 16 οἷς δ᾽ ἂν συνισορή[σητε τοιοῦτό τι] πεπρά | 17 κοσι παραχρῆμα [. . . . .] δια [.]ημ[.]τ[. . . μηνύ]ειν | 18 τῶι Πρωτά[ρ]χωι, ε[ἶ]ναι δὲ τὸ συνκεκριμέν[ο]ν | 19 καθότι καὶ τοὺς [ἐ]ν τ[ώ]ι Βουσιρίτηι γράφοντας | 20 εστ[ε]ικεναι (read ἑστηκέναι) τῆ[ς] μὲν πράσεως καὶ ἀπο | 21 στασ[ίου] συνγρ[α]φῆς [επιδισαι] γράφοντα (δραχμῶν) κ | 22 τῶν δ᾽ [ἄ]λλων (δραχμῶν) ι. ὅπως δὲ καὶ οἱ ἰδιῶται | 23 παρακολουθήσαντες περὶ τούτων τασ | 24 σονται (read τάσσωνται) τὸ διασεσαφημένον πλῆθος, | 25 ἔκθετε πρόγραμμα πρὸ τῶν ἐπιφανεσ | 26 τάτων ἐν ταῖς κώ{ι}μαις ἱερῶν [ὁμοίως], | 27 ὁμοίως δὲ καὶ ἐπὶ τῶν τόπων ἐν οἷς ἂν [- -].

15. Cf., most recently, Yiftach-Firanko 2008. For an updated list of hitherto published double documents, see http://artlid.net/ArtLogon.aspx?project=GLRT&username=u_Double Document-2&password=CMHHGJFQJINFOOFQXUHU.

16. Cf. Kramer, *CPR* XVIII, pp. 10–34; Rupprecht 1995: 37–39.

17. *CPR* XVIII, lines 457–60 (231 or 206 B.C.E., Theogonis): τοῦ Φαρμοῦ[θ(ι)] συναλ(λάγματα)· Θεογε(νίδος) ς, | [Σ]αμα(ρείας) ε, Ὀξυ(ρύγχων) ε, Καλλιφά(νους) β, Δικα(ίου) γ, τὰ

The author of one of these accounts, *P.Tebt.* III.1 815 (223–222 B.C.E., Tebtynis), also reports how much he charged for each particular document.[18] Such an account is best explained in light of *P.Ryl.* IV 572: the state was interested in monitoring not only the fees charged for the composition of Egyptian documents but also those relating to Greek double documents, and an account of the *misthoi* in the lists of contract abstracts was recorded in order to serve this purpose.

But what feeing policy is reflected by these documents? Was it similar or even identical to that enjoined for Egyptian documents in *P.Ryl.* IV 572 and *BGU* VI 1214? I believe that the answer is yes. As we saw above, in the Egyptian sphere, the policy aimed at introducing two flat rates: one for deeds of sale and conveyance, the other for all other documents. In the Greek sphere, private scribes were discouraged from drawing up documents recording land sales or land conveyances of any kind. In the *chora*, this was the exclusive capacity of the *agoranomos*.[19] As for all other contracts, scribes are reported charging different fees for different documents. In *P.Tebt.* III.1 815, most fees range between one drachma and one drachma plus four obols;[20] a little more than one drachma is also the fee per document charged according to synoptic accounts of the scribe's periodical revenues.[21] Scribes were apparently not free, then, to charge any fee they wanted. They were allowed one flat rate, perhaps of one drachma and two obols, from which they could depart by no more than 50 percent in either direction. I wonder if this was not the actual practice in the demotic sphere as well.

How did the existence of a flat rate affect the shape of a document and the

---

πάν[τα] κα (δραχμῶν) κα . . Ι προσωφελῆ [.] . .[.] . . . [- -]; *P.Tebt.* III.1 815, fr. 2, verso, col. II, lines 39–45 (223/232 B.C.E., Tebtynis): ι. συγ(γραφαὶ) ιβ, Ι μισ(θὸς) (δραχμαὶ) ιδ̲ (τριώβολον), Ι ἀνη(λώματος) (δραχμαὶ) η (τριώβολον), Ι ἐλαίου (δραχμὴ) α, Ι λ(οιπαὶ) (δραχμαὶ) ε . .

18. Cf., e.g., *P.Tebt.* III.1 815, fr. 2, recto, col. II, lines 1–8 (223/232 B.C.E., Tebtynis): ἐμίσθωσεν Ἀριστίων Κυρηναῖος δεκανικὸς τῶν Μενελάου̲ (?) Ι 2 Πετεμούτι Ἁρμιύσιος Ἄραβι γεωργῶι καὶ Ταύρωι Ι 3 Πτολεμαίου Θρᾳ‹α›ικὶ τῆς ἐπιγονῆς τὸν αὑτοῦ κλ(ῆρον) Ι 4 ὃν ἔχει ἐκ βασιλικοῦ περὶ κ(ώμην (?))᾿ Ἀρσιν[ό]ην γῆς (ἀρουρῶν) λς ἐκφορ[ί[ου] Ι 5 ἑκάστην (ἄρουραν) η ἄνευ σπέρματος, Ι 6 τούτου τὸ ἥμισυ, καὶ καταστῆι μηνὶ Δύστρω̲ι̲ τὰ ἐκφόρια. Ι 7 ----- μισ(θὸς) (δραχμὴ) α. συγγραφοφύλαξ Ι 8 Κλεώνυμος.

19. I discuss this phenomenon in detail in Yiftach-Firanko 2014.

20. Cf., e.g., *P.Tebt.* III.1 815, fr. 4, recto, col. I, lines 18–22 (loan): one drachma and four obols; fr. 4, recto, col. I, lines 23–29 (loan): at least one drachma; fr. 4, recto, col. I, lines 30–37 (lease): four and a half obols; fr. 4, recto, col. I, lines 38–45: four and a half obols; fr. 4, recto, col. I, lines 46–55: one drachma and four and a half obols; fr. 5, recto, col. I, lines 2–9: one drachma; fr. 5, recto, col. I, lines 10–27: one drachma and one (?) obol; fr. 5, recto, col. I, lines 28–34: five obols.

21. Cf. n. 17.

value of the transaction involved? If a scribe is instructed to charge the same fee for any document he composes, it stands to reason that he will also invest the same amount of work on each document and will therefore produce a fairly uniform format, regardless of the type of contract and the value of the transaction recorded. This assumption seems to be corroborated by our sources. In Thôlthis, virtually the only locality that provides enough material for a systematic survey of the format of double documents, the documents seem to be equally wide (about twenty to twenty-five centimeters), long, and detailed, regardless of the contract type or value of the transaction.[22] Inasmuch as the remaining Ptolemaic source material at hand allows us to gauge, structural uniformity remains a distinctive feature of double documents throughout the Ptolemaic period.[23]

The relationship of the fee to the value of transactions recorded as contracts is difficult to ascertain. Double documents from the third century B.C.E. usually record transactions of substantial value, most between 150 and 1,000 drachmas.[24] Some documents record transactions of smaller amounts, but they are rare.[25] In the third century B.C.E., parties to a contract valued at only twenty drachmas were inclined to record it in a letter format (a cheirograph) or in a *diptychon symbolon*, both narrow formats and both very short.[26] Does the scribal fee account for this pattern of recording? For a transaction of 150 drachmas, a scribal fee of one drachma and two obols would represent less than 1 percent of the value of the contract: this is a very low price. The

---

22. This is exemplified by a record of the number of letters per line in these documents: *BGU* X 1943 (lease, 215/214 B.C.E.), 110–20 letters per line; 1944 (lease, 214/213 B.C.E.), 80–90; 1946 (lease, 213/212 B.C.E.), 90; 1947 (lease, 213/212 B.C.E.), 70–100; 1964 (loan, 221 or 205 B.C.E.), 85–95; 1969 (loan, 215/214 B.C.E.), 80–95; XIV 2383 (lease, 215/214 B.C.E.), 70–80; 2396 (loan, 213/212 B.C.E.), 70–90; 2398 (213/212 B.C.E.), 70–85. As to the length of the contract, the lease contract *BGU* XIV 2390 (160/159 B.C.E., Hêrakleopolitês) contains thirty-one lines of text, while *BGU* XIV 2398 (213/212 B.C.E., Thôlthis), a contract recording a payments in anticipation of land conveyance, contains twenty-eight.
23. The only archive of double documents that allows a comparative study, similar to that of the Thôlthis documentation, is that stemming from Philadelphia in 179/178 B.C.E.: cf., e.g., *P.Freib.* III 24 (lease contract, ca. one hundred letters per line); 26 (marriage document, ca. ninety letters per line). The texts of this archive are heavily damaged.
24. E.g., *CPR* XVIII 4 (*parachôrêsis*): 500 drachmas; 5 (wine sale): 680; 6 (dowry receipt): 400; 7 (lease and labor): 400; 8 (dowry): 630–90; 9 (dowry): more than 500; 11 (rent in lease): 400 (?); 12 (dowry): 400; 14 (loan): 930.
25. Cf., e.g., *P.Tebt.* III.1: 815 frag. 4 recto col. I, lines 23–29: 48 drachmas.
26. Cf., e.g., the *dyptichon symbolon P.Zen.Pest.* 7 (257 B.C.E., Arsinoitês), lines 8–14, a record of a loan of fourteen drachmas with twenty to twenty-five letters per line; the letter format of *P.Eleph.* 30 (223 B.C.E., Apollonopolitês), a receipt of twenty drachmas with fifteen to twenty letters per line. Cf. Vandorpe 2012; Wolff 1978: 75–77, 108–9.

cost of the document would still be quite low even when set in relation to the interest alone: starting out from an interest rate of 2 percent a month, a loan of 150 drachmas would yield for the lender a return of thirty-six drachmas a year. A fee of one drachma and two obols would reduce the expected return on investment by just 3 percent. But what if the amount loaned is merely fifty drachmas? The annual interest would be twelve drachmas, and so the fee would represent 11 percent of the expected return. If the loan is for just six months (i.e., with expected interest of six drachmas), one would spend more than 20 percent of the expected return on the written document.[27] This reckoning may provide at least a partial explanation for the tendency in the third century B.C.E. to record low-value transactions in formats other than the double document.

The Ptolemaic Agoranomeia and the Roman Grapheia

As already mentioned, double documents were not used in the Ptolemaic period for the recording of land conveyances. This act could only be executed at an office called the *agoranomeion* and could only be recorded in a special certificate, the *katagraphê*, issued by the *agoranomos* in person.[28] I am not familiar with any direct evidence on the costs associated with the *katagraphê*, but its format suggests that they were comparatively high, perhaps much higher than those connected to the double document. The *katagraphê* is characterized by an extensive, oblong shape, consisting of three columns: a short account of the particulars of the transaction as recorded in the *agoranomeion*'s files; a solemn attestation of the performance of the act before the *agoranomos*; and a confirmation, by the public bank, of the payment of the conveyance tax, the *enkyklion*. The production of copies of this document is also documented.[29] At

---

27. This is roughly the case in *P.Cair.Zen.* I 59001 = *Sel.Pap.* I 66 (274/273 B.C.E., Pitôs): the amount of the loan is thirty-four drachmas, the interest rate is 2 percent a month, and the duration of the contract is three months (from Peritios through Artemisios of year 12 of Ptolemy II). The expected return for the entire period would be about two drachmas, that is, roughly the cost of the composition of the document.

28. Wolff 1948: 23, 1978: 87–88. For a relatively recent publication of a roll of documents drafted by an *agoranomos*, cf. Vandorpe 2004.

29. *P.Adler* 7 and *P.Ryl.* IV 581 = *P.Mil.* I 2 (104 B.C.E., Pathyris). Cf. Nielsen 2000: 199 no. 160. Multiple copies are produced in upper Egyptian *agoranomeia*, also in the case of *donationes mortis causa* (*BGU* III 993, 127 B.C.E., Hermônthis; Nielsen 2000: 189 no. 13) and wills (*P.Dryton* 3 and 4, 126 B.C.E., Pathyris; Nielsen 2000: 195 no. 89).

a certain stage, the *agoranomoi* started to record other types of contracts. When they did, they did not record them in the same format as the *katagraphê* but used in a much narrower format, which presumably was also much cheaper to produce. For example, in the *katagraphê P.Adler* 13 (100, Crocodilopolis), the scribes used a papyrus 52.6 centimeters wide, whereas in *P.Adler* 6 (106, Pathyris), which records a seed loan, the width is just 8.6 centimeters.[30] This, I suggest, is an important development. For the first time, Greek scribes in Egypt employ different formats for different types of contract: a wide, relatively expensive format for land sales; a narrow, cheaper one for others. The same strategy is also evident in the early Roman *grapheia*.

In the Ptolemaic period, double documents were composed privately, that is, by private scribes, not acting in any official capacity. This continued to be the case throughout the Ptolemaic period, but the state's interest in the contents of the documents, which was already evident, as we have seen, in the production of summary reports in the third century B.C.E., eventually resulted, around 125 B.C.E., in the *anagraphê*, the obligatory registration of every double document at the *grapheion*.[31] At first, the double document retained its original features. Thus, even in the late Ptolemaic period, double documents still have an inner script (albeit in a vestigial form) and a list of witnesses who attended the act. Yet these features were eventually abandoned: toward the end of the Augustan period, the *grapheion* was transformed from an office that merely registered documents composed elsewhere into a true scribal office that produced legal documents in its own right. At that juncture, the office assumed the double document as its default format but introduced some major changes. The new *grapheion* document contains no inner script or account of witnesses and features new information, such as the age and physical traits of the parties, which were not recorded in double documents of earlier times.[32] One of the most significant changes, however, relates to the feeing policy.

As we saw earlier, the currently available evidence indicates that scribes composing double documents in the third century B.C.E. charged around one drachma and two obols for their work, with relatively small deviations of

---

30. Cf. picture of *P.Adler* 13, plate IV; Wolff 1978: 26–27.
31. Yiftach-Firanko 2008: 209-12.
32. One of the earliest samples of the new type of document is *P.Corn.* 6 (17 C.E., Oxyrhyncha). The new scheme was introduced around 14 C.E. Cf. Wolff 1978: 88–89.

up to 50 percent in either direction. The picture provided by the *anagraphê* lists from Claudian Tebtynis is starkly different. The lists record 1,154 documents and note the amount of the *grammatikon* for 924 of them. Among these 924 cases, we find fees ranging from half an obol to fifty drachmas.[33] How did the scribe decide how much to charge for each document? In 471 cases, we are given or can calculate the monetary value of the transaction. In 448 of these instances, we are also given the amount of the *grammatikon*. We are therefore in a position to test whether the scribe set the fee in proportion to the value of the transaction recorded. The answer is no. Take, for example, the sixteen entries recording a transaction whose value is two hundred drachmas: in four cases, the fee is eight drachmas or more (i.e., 4 percent); in five cases, it is four drachmas or less; and in six cases, it is less than two drachmas (i.e., 1 percent).[34]

The entries usually report the type of transaction. Accordingly, we may take a different approach and examine the relationship between the transaction type and the amount of the *grammatikon*. Here we seem to find a correlation. A survey of the *grammatikon* data by transaction reveals that there was no fixed rate for any transaction and that, on average, one paid less for some transactions than for others. For some types of contracts—*meriteiai* (the local form of a will),[35] *diaireseis* (division of family estate), land sales, and *parachôrêseis* (conveyances of title for catoecic land, formally distinct from sale, but functionally equivalent in the Roman period)—the parties pay a median of eight drachmas per document;[36] for others, loans and dowries and prodomatic leases (i.e., leases with the rent paid in advance), the fee gravitates around four drachmas;[37] for a third group of documents—regular leases,

---

33. Cf., e.g., *P.Mich.* II 123r col. 5 32 (two obols); *P.Mich.* II 123r col. 21 18 (fifty drachmas).
34. For eight drachmas or more, see *P.Mich.* II 123r col. 2 33; col. 5 22; col. 7 13; col 18 38 (eight drachmas and six obols). For six drachmas, see *P.Mich.* V 238 219. For four drachmas, see *P.Mich.* II 123 col. 12 28; col. 12 29; *P.Mich.* V 238 12; 116; 182. For two drachmas or less, see *P.Mich.* II 123 col. 3 7 (1.931 drachmas); col. 8 1 (1.931 drachmas); col. 15 36 (two drachmas); *P.Mich.* 126 2 (1.3793 drachmas); *P.Mich.* V 238 13 (two drachmas); 171 (two drachmas).
35. Cf. Yiftach 2002: 150–51.
36. Sale of landed property: number of cases: 15, average: 10.4, median: 8 drachmas. *Parachôrêsis*: number of cases: 10, average: 7.2, median: 8. Hereditary Settlement (*meriteia*): number of cases: 13, average: 10.77, median: 8 drachmas. *Diairesis*: number of cases: 9, average: 9.7, median: 8 drachmas.
37. *Daneion* (loan): number of cases: 111, average: 3.64, median: 4 drachmas. Dowry receipt (*phernê*): number of cases: 55, average: 4.84, median: 4 drachmas. Prodomatic lease: number of cases: 25, average: 4.2, median: 4 drachmas.

animal and loom sales, and receipts—the parties usually pay 1.5 drachmas or less,[38] a quarter or less of what they would usually pay for a contract recording the conveyance of landed property.

The variation in fees can be easily explained. The source material from Egypt contains quite a few documents issued at village *grapheia* in the early Roman period. The first century C.E. alone yields 330 legal documents composed in the Arsinoite *grapheia*—inter alia (including the types of documents just mentioned) land sales, animal sales, leases, marriage documents, loans, and *meriteiai*. An examination of these contracts accounts for the differential pricing of the *grammatikon*. Contracts for land sales, the most common of the "expensive" contracts, were drafted in an extremely wide format, frequently measuring fifty by thirty centimeters. Contracts for land sales in the early first century C.E. were also expected to be bilingual, with a demotic text followed by a Greek subscription (*hypographê*).[39] Therefore, the composition of the contract required the work of two scribes, Greek and demotic, or of a scribe skilled in writing documents in both languages. Documents recording land sales were also regularly issued in multiple copies.[40]

At least some of these features appear in other "expensive" types of documents: *diaireseis* and *meriteiai* from the first century show just as wide a format as land sales and were also issued in multiple copies.[41] Some *diaireseis* are also bilingual.[42] In the case of contracts for which the scribe charges just a few obols, by contrast, the documents tend to be monolingual (usually Greek), and the format is much narrower, occasionally very narrow: in contracts recording animal sales, for example, the default size seems to be around twelve

38. *Parathêkê* (deposit): number of cases: 75, average: 3.59, median: 2.83 drachmas = 20 obols. *Apochê* (quitclaim): number of cases: 80, average: 2.4, median: 2 drachmas. *Enoikêsis*: number of cases: 61, average: 2.75, median: 2 drachmas. *Cheirographia* (declarations of oath): number of cases: 22, average: 3.16, median: 1.93 drachmas = 14 obols. *Misthôsis*: number of cases: 169, average: 2.28, median: 1.66 drachmas = 12 obols. *Paramonê*: number of cases: 25, average: 1.5, median: 1.38 drachmas = 10 obols. Animal sale: number of cases: 17, average: 1.4, median: 0.97 drachmas = 7 obols. Loom sale: number of cases: 13, average: 1.25, median: 0.83 = 6 obols. *Hypomnêma*: number of cases: 36, average: 0.7, median: 0.2579 drachmas = 2 obols.
39. Cf. Depauw 2003; Muhs 2005.
40. The data bank Synallagma: Greek Contracts in Context records nineteen documents of land sale for which more than one copy was prepared or was in the process of being prepared: http://artlid.net/ArtLogon.aspx?project=GLRT&username=u_duplicate+grapheion+documents-2&password=OARFAFCDSFCWUINUCGNG.. Cf., e.g., *P.Mich.* V 282; *PSI* VIII 917 (1st cent. C.E., Arsinoitês); discussion in *P.Mich.* V, pp. 4–11; Wolff 1978: 41–42.
41. Cf., e.g., *P.Mich.* IX 555, 556 (107 C.E., Karanis). Cf. also Choat, forthcoming, text to n. 44, on *P.Mich.* V 322a (46 C.E., Tebtynis).
42. Lippert 2008: 139.

by twenty-eight centimeters. Needless to say, the text is also much shorter in the "low-cost" category than in the "expensive" one.[43] As to the number of copies issued, Bruce Nielsen's catalog of duplicate papyri records just two *grapheion* documents, both from Tebtynis, which are not in wide format.[44] Accordingly, the dichotomy manifested in the source material from the late Ptolemaic *agoranomeia* recurs in connection with the early Roman *grapheia*: the effort invested in the composition of one group of documents is spared when other types of documents are involved.

Why did the scribe decide on different formats for different transactions? Parties to a contract reduce the terms of the agreement to writing in order to make it possible to refer to them. As the value of the transaction rises, so does the parties' interest in incorporating into their document additional elements that would help them to secure their claims. Since these additions (e.g., the preparation of additional copies) cost money, parties are willing to pay more for the composition of a document recording a high-cost transaction than for a document recording a low-cost one. Perhaps, then, the differentiated format system was meant to allow everyone to benefit from just the amount of security he or she needed and to pay for the document accordingly, with less security and a lower fee for low-cost transactions (e.g., animal sales, leases) and with more security and a higher fee for high-cost ones (e.g., land sales).[45]

This explanation is not backed up by our sources. Contracts recording animal sales, distinctly narrow in format, sometimes document a transaction whose value is just sixty drachmas, but some donkeys are sold for as much as 340 drachmas.[46] In the case of camels, the price rises to as much as one thousand drachmas apiece.[47] These transactions are by no means "low-value." The same obtains for land leases: in the lease *P.Athen.* 14 (22 C.E., Theadel-

---

43. Cf., e.g., *P.Mich.* IX 551 (103 C.E., Kerkesoucha), recording a sale of a donkey (dimensions: 7.9 × 23.7 cm; letters per line: 10–20; 34 lines; picture at http://quod.lib.umich.edu/cgi/i/image/getimage-idx?cc=apis&entryid=X-2197&viewid=4389R.TIF&quality=large).

44. *P.Mich.* V 333, 334 (52 C.E., Tebtynis, *daneion*, Nielsen: 2000: 199 no. 149); *P.Mich.* IX 633 (30 C.E., Tebtynis, Nielsen 2000: 199 no. 156). However, as duplicates of narrow-format documents are a widespread phenomenon outside the *grapheia* in the early Roman period (cf., e.g., *P.Col.* X, p. 159, lease *hypomnêmata*), one should avoid drawing conclusions from this relative paucity.

45. The distinction between transactions of short and long duration has recently been discussed in Jacquet 2013.

46. See, e.g., *P.Lond.* II 313 (148 C.E., Kerkesoucha): 64 drachmas; *P.Louvre* I 15 (139 C.E., Psintanou): 290; *P.Meyer* 13 (141 C.E., Apias): 340.

47. Cf., e.g., *BGU* I 88 (146 C.E., Soknopaiou Nêsos): 800 drachmas; *P.Lond.* II 320 (157/158 C.E., Soknopaiou Nêsos): 800; *SPP* XXII 30 (158 C.E., Arsinoitês): 820.

phia), the lessee pledges himself to pay, over a period of three years, a rent of 121 artabas of wheat, which, reckoned at a price of six drachmas per artaba comes to total of more than seven hundred drachmas for the value of the lease.[48] According to *SB* XX 14315 (32/33 C.E., Tebtynis), a document of extremely narrow format, the lessee is to pay not less than 412 artabas of wheat and 160 artabas of fodder in the course of three years.[49] In contracts of land sales from the first century C.E., comprising among the most distinctively wide-format and high-cost contracts, the value ranges between twenty and nine hundred drachmas, a range similar to that we witnessed for animal sales and land leases.[50] I do not believe, therefore, that the format applied had anything to do with the value of the transaction it recorded.

I here propose a different working hypothesis, based on the fact that edicts and court rulings from early Roman Egypt show a continuous tendency to restrict the alienability of landed property, especially if the property is alienated without the approval of the vendor's family members. This tendency has several manifestations. For example, through the type of lien called *katochê*, children and wives could prevent the alienation of landed property by fathers and husbands, even to the extent of rendering alienations void retroactively.[51] A person's ability to bequeath his property by will to strangers was also severely limited, as long as he had living family members.[52] Finally, papyri from the second century C.E. document a restriction of one's ability to alienate a piece of property held in community with others, particularly if they are his or her next of kin.[53] This tendency to restrict alienability of landed property, if it indeed dated back to the first century, may also explain the feeing policy presented and discussed in this essay.

In the Tebtynis *grapheion*, four types of instrument stand out for their high cost: land sales, *parachôrêseis*, *meriteiai*, and *diairêseis*. In all four cases, the in-

---

48. Rathbone 1997: 191–92.
49. Cf. also *BGU* XI 2032 (113 C.E., Ptolemais Euergetis): 1300 drachmas (rent); *P.Amh.* II 85 (78 C.E., Hermopolis): 600; *P.Phil.* 12 (150/151 or 173/174 C.E., Philadelphia): 1700 (and other commodities). A further copy of the last was published as *PSI* I 33.
50. Cf., e.g., *P.Louvre* I 10 (late 1st cent. C.E., Soknopaiou Nêsos): 20 drachmas ; *P.Louvre* II 109 (123/124 or 136/137 C.E., Arsinoitês): 1600. See further data at http://hudd.huji.ac.il/ArtLogon. aspx?project=GLRT&username=u_Roman+Land+Sales%2C+Considerations-2&password=QFXTJ ACOKYUREXGRBKLU.
51. Kreller 1919: 188–200.
52. Cf., e.g., *P.Oxy.* XLII 3015.20–28 (after 117 C.E., Oxyrhnchos); *SPP* XX 4.15–20 = *CPR* I 18 = *MChr* 84 = *Jur.Pap.* 89 (124 C.E., Ptolemais Euergetis [?]); Yiftach-Firanko 2009: 550–52.
53. Cf., in particular, *SB* XIV 12139.2.17–3.3 (18.2.146 C.E., Oxyrhnchitês); 12139.5.11. In the second century (the period from which the bulk of the evidence stems), the rule could be applied even if the partners were not relatives. On the origin, application, and date of introduction of the rule, cf., in particular, Rupprecht 1979.

strument records a change in title of landed property: in the case of land sales and *parachôrêseis*, the land is alienated outright; in *meriteiai*, it is bequeathed to beneficiaries; and in *diairêseis*, a joint asset is divided between the parties to whom it had already been bequeathed. The high price charged for these types of documents is, according to the hypothesis proposed here, not coincidental: the state, wishing to check the circulation of landed property, did so not only by direct means (i.e., through edicts and court rulings) but also indirectly, by raising the costs involved in the transaction. One way to raise these costs was to tax the circulation of landed property: the tax on land conveyance, the *enkyklion*, amounted to 5 percent of the value of the land itself. A special fee was also introduced in the case of catoecic land, which depended on the gender of the purchaser, his or her personal status, and the nature of the alienated land. Another tax, the *vicesima hereditatum*, was imposed on bequests by Roman citizens.[54] Yet a different, indirect method was to raise the costs of written documentation. One would be less inclined to draw up a document if doing so cost ten drachmas rather than five obols. Still, the state did not simply introduce a higher tariff for an identical product. The drafting of a contract for land sale really was more costly than the recording of an animal sale, since the document for the former was longer and more complex. But the high cost of producing these documents was not the natural reflection of the complexity of the underlying transaction. Instead, it resulted from markedly different conventions on how each type of contract should be committed to writing, conventions that, in turn, resulted from or were at least influenced by the state's policy of promoting or discouraging the use of different types of contract.

Conclusion

In this essay, I have discussed the feeing policy at three successive stages of documentary practice in Ptolemaic and Roman Egypt: the Ptolemaic drafting of double documents, the drafting and registration of agoranomic documents in the late Ptolemaic period, and the drafting and registration of documents by the Roman *grapheia* in the first century C.E. I claimed that the feeing policy of each scribe was closely linked with the variety of formats he used. Ptolemaic scribes drafting double documents charged what seems close to a flat

---

54. Wallace 1938: 234; Yiftach 2002: 160–61; *P.Iand.* VI 137 (2nd cent. C.E., Arsinoitês).

rate (at least in comparison to what we observe in the Roman *grapheion*). In what seems to be a connected phenomenon, the formats used were also quite uniform. In the Greek sphere, a policy of differential fees leading to the application of different formats is evident for the first time in the Ptolemaic *agoranomeia*: the *agoranomoi* used entirely different formats for the documentation of land conveyances and for other transactions, and we may assume that they did not charge the same fee for the two (or more) basic formats they used. The instrument commonly used in the Roman *grapheia* was created through a reform that simplified the scheme of the double document. Unlike the composers of double documents in the early Ptolemaic period but like the Ptolemaic *agoranomoi*, the *grapheion* scribes employed a multiformat system. They were not instructed to charge a flat rate or even a schedule of flat rates for their work, but, as we conclude from the *anagraphê* lists, they charged fees more or less proportional to the work they invested and the documents they produced. As in the earlier *agoranomeia*, the choice of the format was dictated by the nature of the transaction: wide format for land sales, *meriteiai, diairêseis*, and *parachôrêseis*; narrow format for animal sales, leases, receipts, and other sundry transactions.

The recourse to a wide or narrow format cannot be accounted for by the value of the transaction per se: the value of a land sale is not always higher than that of animal sale or lease. According to the hypothesis I have put forward here, costly formats were made (or allowed to remain) costly, in order to raise the transaction costs and to discourage the execution—or at least the frequent execution— of certain types of transactions, particularly land conveyances.

Bibliography

Choat, M. Forthcoming. "Stichometry and Scribal Practice in Documentary Texts from Roman Egypt." *Proceedings of the Twenty-Seventh International Congress of Papyrology*, Warsaw, 29 July–3 August 2013.

Depauw, M. 2003. "Autograph Confirmation in Demotic Private Contracts." *CE* 78: 66–111.

Jacquet, A. 2013. "Family Archives in Mesopotamia during the Old Babylonian Period." In M. Faraguna, ed., *Archives and Archival Documents in Ancient Societies*, 63–86. Legal Documents in Ancient Societies IV. Trieste.

Kreller, H. 1919. *Erbrechtliche Untersuchungen auf Grund der graeco-aegyptischen Papyrusurkunden.* Leipzig.

Lippert, S. 2008. *Einführung in die altägyptische Rechtsgeschichte.* Münster.

Muhs, B. 2005. "The Grapheion and the Disappearance of Demotic Contracts in Early Roman Tebtynis and Soknopaiou Nesos." In S. Lippert and M. Schentuleit, eds., *Tebtynis und Soknopaiou Nesos: Leben im römerzeitlichen Fajum; Akten des Internationalen Symposions vom 11. bis 13. Dezember 2003 in Sommerhausen bei Würzburg,* 93–104. Wiesbaden.

Nielsen, B. E. 2000. "A Catalog of Duplicate Papyri." *ZPE* 129: 187–214.

Rathbone, D. 1997. "Prices and Price Formation in Roman Egypt." In J. Andreau, P. Briant, and R. Descat, eds., *Économie antique: Prix et formation des prix dans les économies antiques,* 183–244. Saint-Bertrand-de-Comminges.

Rupprecht, H.-A. 1995. "Sechs-Zeugenurkunde und Registrierung." *Aegyptus* 75: 37–53.

Rupprecht, H.-A. "Zu Voraussetzungen, Umfang und Herkunft des Vorkaufsrechts der Gemeinschaflter nach den Papyri." *Symposion 1979: Vorträge zur griechischen und hellenistischen Rechtsgeschichte (Ägina, 3.–7. September 1979),* 287–301. Cologne.

Vandorpe, K. 2004. "A Greek Register from Pathyris' Notarial Office: Loans and Sales from the Pathyrite and Latopolite Nomes." *ZPE* 150: 161–86.

Vandorpe, K. 2012. "Greek and Demotic Loan Agreements in Epistolary Style: Formalisation and Registration in the Later Ptolemaic Period." In U. Yiftach-Firanko, ed., *The Letter: Law, State, Society, and the Epistolary Format in the Ancient World; Proceedings of a Colloquium Held at the American Academy in Rome (28–30.9.2008),* 171–85. Philippika: Marburger altertumskundliche Abhandlungen 55.1. Marburg.

Wallace, S. L. 1938. *Taxation in Egypt from Augustus to Diocletian.* Princeton University Studies in Papyrology 2. Princeton.

Wolff, H. J. 1948. "Registration of Conveyances in Ptolemaic Egypt." *Aegyptus* 28: 17–96.

Wolff, H. J. 1978. *Das Recht der griechischen Papyri Ägyptens in der Zeit der Ptolemaeer und des Prinzipats.* Vol. 2, *Organisation und Kontrolle des privaten Rechtsverkehrs.* Handbuch der Altertumswissenschaft 10.5.2. Munich.

Yiftach, U. 2002. "Deeds of Last Will in Graeco-Roman Egypt: A Case Study in Regionalism." *BASP* 39: 149–64.

Yiftach-Firanko, U. 2008. "Who Killed the Double Document in Ptolemaic Egypt?" *APF* 54: 203-18.

Yiftach-Firanko, U. 2009. "Law in Graeco-Roman Egypt: Hellenization, Fusion, Romanization." In R. S. Bagnall, ed., *The Oxford Handbook of Papyrology,* 541–60. Oxford.

Yiftach-Firanko, U. 2014. "State Registration of Sales: The *katagraphê.*" In J. G. Manning, J. G. Keenan, and U. Yiftach-Firanko, eds., *Law and Society in Egypt from Alexander to the Arab Conquest, 332 BC–AD 640,* 314–25. Cambridge.

CHAPTER 7

The βιβλιοθήκη ἐγκτήσεων and Transaction Costs in the Credit Market of Roman Egypt (30 B.C.E.–ca. 170 C.E.)[1]

F. Lerouxel

The object of this essay is to illuminate the role played by the "archive of acquisitions" (βιβλιοθήκη ἐγκτήσεων) in reducing transaction costs in the private credit market of Roman Egypt between 30 B.C.E., the date of the Roman conquest of Egypt, and approximately 170 C.E. The body of evidence for this study comprises some 280 documents—principally loan contracts and receipts, but also petitions and the rare private letter pertaining to credit—originating from five different locations: two villages, Tebtynis and Soknopaiou Nesos in the Fayyum, and the three *metropoleis*, or nome capitals, Ptolemais Euergetis, Oxyrhynchus, and Hermopolis. These represent all the places in Roman Egypt for which we have a consistent financial documentation during that period. To this evidence of daily practice, we may add several edicts of the Roman prefects that regulated the drafting of contracts in the province.[2] Two features distinguish these documents from any other source relating to Roman economic and financial history.[3] First, their date of

---

1. My warmest thanks go to the editors of this volume for their comments and for the English translation of my article.
2. For the administration of the province of Egypt, see Jördens 2009.
3. The papyrological documentation of Roman Egypt is still rarely exploited by historians of the Roman economy, as today's historians tend to privilege the study of the banking profession and the financial affairs of the Roman elite from the evidence of the literature, inscriptions, and legal sources. For the Roman West, see Andreau 1987; 2001; Ioannatou 2006. For the Roman East, excluding Egypt, see Bogaert 1968, treating both the Hellenistic and imperial periods. Raymond Bogaert has also dedicated several articles to banks and bank-

composition is commonly stated in the document itself—often to the very day—which allows us to establish a relatively precise chronological evolution of the institutions to which they attest. Second, many of the documents record loans in cash (the others are transactions in kind, mostly in cereals). Since the value of cash remained relatively stable in Roman Egypt between 30 B.C.E. and 170 C.E., the value of transactions can easily be compared across the entire period (i.e., there was very little inflation), which explains the chronological boundaries chosen for this study.[4] It would be much more difficult to compare, for example, the price of slaves, since the quality and hence the value of a slave varied according to several parameters, most of which are unknown to us. Despite these two remarkable and complementary features, chronological precision and comparability, the financial transactions attested on papyrus in Egypt have not yet been the object of proper historical analysis. Such an analysis demands, at the very least, that we see these documents as the product of the specific institutional and financial history that produced them and that we understand significant changes in the documents as reflecting significant changes in the underlying historical conditions or institutions.[5] As will be shown below, the establishment of the βιβλιοθήκη ἐγκτήσεων between 68 and 72 C.E. constituted one such change that has left an impression in the documents, a true turning point in the history of the private credit market of Roman Egypt.[6]

Lending money was one of the most widespread and common economic activities in Roman Egypt. Every inhabitant of the province, at any given moment, was likely to be both a creditor and a debtor, regardless of status, residence, wealth, age, or gender.[7] Private banks were very active in Egypt, leaving numerous traces in the papyrological record, but they were not engaged in lending money. This often comes as a surprise to modern scholars, since it runs counter to our experience, but it seems to be an inescapable conclusion.[8] Instead, the essential functions that banks in Roman Egypt provided to ac-

---

ing in the Egyptian papyri: see Bogaert 2001 (with bibliography of earlier scholarship on pp. 279–80).

4. Rathbone 1997. I leave to the side the problem of the precise date in the Julio-Claudian period at which the value of the Alexandrian tetradrachm was pegged to the Roman denarius and the ultimate consequences of this arrangement for price levels in Roman Egypt.
5. On debt in Roman Egypt, see Tenger 1993. For the different types of loan contract, see Kühnert 1965. For rates of interest, see Finckh 1962; Foraboschi and Gara 1981, 1982.
6. For the date of the institution of the βιβλιοθήκη ἐγκτήσεων, see Burkhalter 1990.
7. Lerouxel 2006.
8. Lerouxel 2008.

count holders were the safekeeping of deposits and the payment of cash on demand. This is not to say that such banks played no role in the credit markets, since it is very likely that they acted as passive financial intermediaries; but this does not change the fact that they did not act as lenders. Lending was therefore essentially nonprofessional, meaning that both parties, lender and borrower alike, were private individuals. The nature of banking and credit in Roman Egypt raises the fundamental questions of how creditors and debtors found one other and on what criteria they decided to do business. To put the matter in terms of the new institutional economics, we can ask what sort of formal and informal institutions governed the processes of the credit market in Roman Egypt.

For our purposes here, I adopt the following definition of a "market":

> Every collectively organized mechanism of exchange, hierarchical or decentralized, formal or informal, which allocates resources on the basis of price, information, or some combination of the two. Whatever its degree of imperfection, a market is correspondingly more imperfect as transaction costs grow (i.e., as the difference grows between what buyers pay and sellers receive) . . . The list of transaction costs is in fact quite long: in the case of credit, they include the costs of legal acts, the taxes imposed on contracts, the remuneration of the efforts of intermediaries, and any losses realized, whether they arise from a creditor's demand for payment at an inopportune time or from the inability of a debtor to pay.[9]

Over the last decade or so, some ancient economic historians have made use of new institutional economic theory,[10] particularly the notion of transaction costs.[11] However, this methodology has met with skepticism in some quarters.[12] One must admit that this theory has, on occasion, been applied in a general manner, insufficiently contextualized in a concrete historical or geographical setting. To show that this theory is useful for the study of the ancient world, one should apply it in a precise historical context and not make do with general assertions that "transaction costs were high" or "markets

9.   Hoffman, Postel-Vinay, and Rosenthal 2001: 25–26.
10. See, e.g., Manning 2003; Lo Cascio 2005; Lerouxel 2006; Kehoe 2007; Bresson 2007, 2008; Bang 2008; Terpstra 2008.
11. D. C. North (1985) probably pushes the analysis of the nature of transactions cost the furthest.
12. See, e.g., Andreau and Maucourant 1999.

were imperfect" in the Roman Empire. The concept of transaction costs enables the historian to measure the degree of imperfection in particular markets at particular times. The best use of this concept, then, is in a comparative
setting, not an absolute one: this would be the case, for example, if we compare the level of transaction costs in a single market at two given periods. In
the case of the credit market in Roman Egypt, it is possible to document a
significant drop in transaction costs from one period to another.

In this market, it is possible to distinguish three transaction costs (TC) of
varying importance:

- Type 1: the costs of recording and registering legal documents and the taxes
  levied on loan contracts.
- Type 2: the cost of intermediation, or "market making"—that is, the search
  costs associated with creditors and debtors finding each other.
- Type 3: the costs associated with a debtor's default.

Intermediation probably did take place in Roman Egypt, and one can hypothesize that the bankers played a passive role in arranging market
transactions;[13] however, it is difficult to know if they were remunerated in
some way for this service. I will therefore concentrate on the first and third
types of TC and the role they played in shaping the credit market.

The TC of type 1, those associated with recording, registration, and taxation, are incurred by the parties when the contract is executed. The simple
drafting of a loan contract, whether in public or private forms (to be discussed below), therefore involved expenses that some inhabitants of Egypt
could have regarded as too high. Indeed, in any sort of inquiry into the history of credit, it is prudent to assume that some fraction of financial transactions, presumably those for small amounts of money, are almost entirely invisible because the parties preferred not to commit the transaction to writing
because of the costs involved in doing so.[14] The degree to which our surviving evidence is representative of the historical market is therefore partly affected by TC of type 1.

Once a person decided to document a transaction in writing, he could

---

13. Lerouxel 2008.
14. Occasionally, a rare surviving letter or private account allows us to catch a glimpse of the
world of the pawnbroker, otherwise largely invisible in our written contracts: see, e.g.,
P.Oxy. III 530.

choose between a public and a private document.[15] The former drew its public nature from the fact that it was drafted and, more important, registered by an institution officially authorized to do so. The notarized contract is the public document to which parties in a credit transaction made the most frequent recourse in their affairs. A private document (in the context of the present study, predominantly the *cheirographon*, an informal note of hand typically written in the form of a letter) was not automatically registered the day it was drafted. Theoretically, it could therefore be written up by anyone familiar with the contractual formulas in use in that particular nome. We may hence conclude that these costs (type 1) were lower for those parties that opted for *cheirographa* than for those who chose notarized contracts.

In a notarized loan contract, the costs associated with drafting and registration changed, at least up to a certain point, in accordance with the value of the loan and the complexity of the terms. For a simple, unsecured loan, TC of type 1 consist in the cost of drafting and registration only.[16] If the creditor and the debitor went to the γραφεῖον, or village notary, for example, one or both of them had to pay for the scribe who drafted and registered the document.[17] The registers of the Tebtynis γραφεῖον reveal the amount of the γραμματικόν paid for each of the contracts drawn up by that office.[18] So far as I know, in the case of loans, it is not possible to determine who paid the amount indicated in the register, the creditor or the debtor. Since each of the parties likely received a copy of the contract, it is reasonable to suppose that the fee listed in the register was split and paid jointly by both parties. As we shall see in a moment, it is necessary to make a hypothesis on this point if we are to attempt to quantify the creditor's real return on the loan. For the sake of modeling, I will impute 50 percent of these costs to the creditor, assuming that the fee was equally split between the two parties.[19]

P.Oxy. XLIX 3485 represents a good example of this type of loan docu-

---

15. For the systems of drafting and registration private contracts in Roman Egypt, see, in general, Wolff 1978; Burkhalter 1990. See also chapter 8 (Ratzan) in the present volume for a discussion of how transaction costs may have affected the choice of which form to use, public or private.

16. By "unsecured," I mean a loan that is not backed by any specified piece of real property, as defined by the terms of the contract. Personal sureties are practically never attested in the loan documents of Roman Egypt, contrary to what one observes in the tablets that have survived from Campania (e.g., *T. Sulpicii*), in which one finds both types of guarantees.

17. The most well-known γραφεῖον of the Roman period is that of Tebtynis during the 40s, by virtue of the registers that survived and are edited in *P.Mich.* II and V. See Husselman 1970.

18. See, e.g., *P.Mich.* V 238. See also chapter 6 (Yiftach) in the present volume for a discussion of the γραμματικόν.

19. It may not necessarily be the case generally.

ment. At Sinary, a village in the Oxyrhynchite nome, in 38 C.E., a certain Is-chyrion lent 108 drachmas to two men. The contract made no explicit provi-sion for interest, but it did include penalties and the payment of default interest if the principal was not repaid by the end of the stipulated term of four months.[20] The two debtors acted as mutual sureties, and the creditor disposed of the right of execution (*praxis*) against them. No specific piece of property (e.g., a plot of land or a house) was placed as security for the debt. For the composition of the legal document, the parties went to the γραφεῖον of Sinary, and a scribe (ὁ πρὸς τὸ γραφεῖον) called Achilleus drafted and registered the instrument, presumably after receiving the fee, the γραμματικόν.

In the case of a loan secured by landed property, TC of type 1 were consid-erably higher: in addition to the costs of drafting and registering the document itself, the creditor had to pay a conveyance tax (ἐγκύκλιον) at the moment of execution.[21] This tax could, according to *P.Oxy.* II 243, amount to 2 percent of the value of the loan.[22] In contrast to the γραμματικόν, it is certain that the creditor alone paid this tax. If the loan was given for a period longer than one year (the majority of loans in Roman Egypt were for a year or less), the creditor was obliged to renew his mortgage and again pay the pertinent charges.[23]

P.Brem. 68.1–15 belongs to this category of more complex loan contracts. In the village of Thallou, of the Hermopolite nome, in 99 C.E., an inhabitant of the city of Hermopolis loaned thirteen hundred drachmas to a woman from Thallou, at an interest rate of 12 percent, payable over two years. The loan was secured by a specific piece of property, six arouras of catoecic land (a category of land inherited from the Ptolemaic regime, which, in the Roman period, was essentially another form of private property). The creditor made over the funds to the debtor via the bank of Hermaios in Thallou,[24] and the contract was recorded in the notary office of the same village by the γραμματεύς Hephaistion.[25]

---

20. See Lerouxel 2012.
21. See n. 22.
22. To my knowledge, *P.Oxy.* II 243 is the only text in which we may calculate the rate of the ἐγκύκλιον for mortgages. For sales, the buyer paid the ἐγκύκλιον, and the general consen-sus is that the rate was 10 percent (Wallace 1938: 228). However, in his study of the slave market in Roman Egypt, Jean Straus, who suggests that this is a rather hasty conclusion, believes that it is difficult to arrive at any certainty on the rate (Straus 2004: 71–77).
23. Wallace 1938: 229–30, citing *P.Oxy.* II 274.20–22.
24. On this bank, see Bogaert 1995: 160.
25. The titles of public notaries varied according to the nome, but this did not affect their legal powers or competencies.

To calculate the type 1 TC for the contract preserved in *P.Brem.* 68.1–15, we must add the costs of drafting (γραμματικόν) to the mortgage tax (ἐγκύκλιον). The γραμματικόν paid by the creditor is not specifically mentioned in this document, but it is reasonable to estimate its amount on the basis of the Tebtynis γραφεῖον registers. The largest mortgage attested in those accounts was for 832 drachmas (*P.Mich.*V238.i.17–18),[26] and the γραμματικόν paid in that instance was 12 drachmas. If, as above, we assume that the creditor paid half of the γραμματικόν indicated in the registers, the creditor in this instance paid only 6 drachmas. Since the amount loaned in the case of *P.Brem.* 68.1–15 was higher—1,300 drachmas as opposed to 832—we may assume that the creditor paid, at the minimum, the same amount. The ἐγκύκλιον paid by the creditor was 26 drachmas, or 2 percent of 1,300 drachmas. In total, one may therefore estimate that the type 1 TC borne by the creditor for this contract was at least around 32 drachmas for the first year of the loan (ca. 6 dr. for his half of the γραμματικόν plus 26 for the ἐγκύκλιον) and around 26 drachmas for the second year (no γραμματικόν plus 26 dr. for the ἐγκύκλιον). Now, the loan gave the creditor a nominal rate of return on his capital of 12 percent, or 156 drachmas (12 percent of 1,300 dr.) each year, that is, 312 drachmas for the total duration of the loan. To calculate the real return, we must subtract from the interest the TC of type 1, which gives us a total of 254 drachmas (= 312 – [32 + 26]). If we suppose that there was little or no inflation over the two years (which is reasonable for this period), we see that the actual rate of return drops from 24 to 19.5 percent; in other words, the type 1 TC consumed approximately 18.75 percent of the nominal return on this loan.

In the case of such complex or longer-term loans in which the capital was secured by real property, we thus see that the type 1 TC were relatively high, as the creditor had to pay both his half of the γραμματικόν and the ἐγκύκλιον. Whenever the loans were not guaranteed with a specific security, as we saw in *P.Oxy.* XLIX 3485, the creditor paid only the γραμματικόν, and the type 1 TC remained relatively low.

From the wider perspective, however, type 1 TC were not the most important costs shaping the credit market. Loans are, in effect, peculiar transactions insofar as they are not simultaneous transactions: the creditor exchanges his money against a simple promise of repayment (usually with interest). If

---

26. The loan is guaranteed by a μεσιτεία, a type of mortgage agreement. See below and n. 27.

the debtor fails to repay, the creditor stands to lose the entire capital amount he advanced. Of course, this is the most extreme scenario, but the risk is always there. Therefore, while TC of type 1 are certain and incurred as soon as the creditor decides to reduce the contract to writing, TC of type 3 are merely potential. Yet type 3 TC play a much more important role in the credit market, because they could be catastrophically high. In the case of *P.Brem.* 68.1–15, for example, the creditor pays fifty-eight drachmas over two years for the type 1 TC, precisely in order to reduce type 3 TC to the lowest possible level, that is, the potential cost of losing his capital of thirteen hundred drachmas and the attendant interest.

As we just saw in the case of *P.Brem.* 68.1–15, real security for loans in Roman Egypt commonly took the form of a mortgage (there were several common types: ὑποθήκη, ὑπάλλαγμα, and μεσιτεία).[27] Scholars also frequently refer to an additional form of real security, the so-called ὠνὴ ἐν πίστει (sale on faith),[28] or a fiduciary sale. This last is a double act, combining a contract for sale with one for loan wherein the debtor is simultaneously the seller and the creditor is the buyer. The property sold, usually a house, serves as a guarantee for the loan and will be kept by the creditor/buyer in the case of default. If the loan is repaid as stipulated, the conveyance is made void, and the debtor regains legal ownership of the property. The historical median amount loaned in such contracts is one hundred drachmas.[29]

---

27. In this context, there is no need to enter into the juristic debate over the possible legal differences between these forms of mortgage, as they all achieve the same economic end and as there is no relative difference between the types and levels of TC associated with each form.

28. Pestman 1985; Hermann 1989. Yet more extreme, but more rare, are the fiduciary sales of neonates. Here we also see a double legal act, combining a wet-nursing contract executed by a woman, accompanied by her husband, and a third party (cf. Ratzan's analysis in chapter 8) and a contract for loan. In the nursing contract, the third party entrusts an infant to the couple. In the loan contract, the third party appears as the couple's creditor. Manca Masciadri and Montevecchi (1982) have interpreted this as a double act: a contract for loan in which the infant, who is the child of the debtor couple but is represented as the creditor's slave in the nursing contract, serves as the guarantee for repayment.

29. I count thirteen documentary ὠναὶ ἐν πίστει from the Roman period (excluding entries in the Tebtynis γραφεῖον registers): *BGU* III 910 (Soknopaiou Nesos, 100 dr.); *BGU* XIII 2337 (Niloupolis, 100 dr.); *P.Lond.* II 277 (p. 217) (Soknopaiou Nesos, 64 dr. and 4 ob.); *P.Mich.* V 328 (Tebtynis, 420 dr.); *P.Mich.* V 329–30 (Tebtynis, 72 dr.); *P.Mich.* V 332 (Tebtynis, 132 dr.); *P.Mich.* V 335 (Tebtynis, 448 dr.); *P.Ryl.* II 160c (Soknopaiou Nesos, 100 dr.); *P.Ryl.* II 310 descr. (Soknopaiou Nesos, amount unknown); *PSI* VIII 908 (Tebtynis, 100 dr.); *P.Vindob. Tandem* 24 (Soknopaiou Nesos, amount unknown); *SB* I 5109–10 = *P.Ryl.* II 160d + *P.dem. Ryl.* 45 (Soknopaiou Nesos, 34 dr.); *SB* V 8952 (Soknopaiou Nesos, 220 dr.). I count seven ὠναὶ ἐν πίστει in the Tebtynis γραφεῖον registers, where the median is comparable (112 dr.).

This type of secured loan is severely restricted both geographically and chronologically, attested only in three villages of the Fayyum—Tebtynis, Soknopaiou Nesos, and Nilopolis—from 7 B.C.E. to 76 C.E.;[30] after that, it disappears from the record. This distribution becomes more significant when one considers that the total number of papyri for the years 70–170 C.E. is 3.4 times larger than that for the span between 30 B.C.E. and 69 C.E.[31] In Ptolemaic documentation, the ὠνὴ ἐν πίστει is only attested from Upper Egypt, particularly from Pathyris, a region of strong Egyptian tradition.[32] The Roman ὠναὶ ἐν πίστει from Soknopaiou Nesos are frequently bilingual, containing both a Greek and demotic text. The Greek is, however, frequently of a poor quality.[33] It is worth noting, in this connection, that Soknopaiou Nesos was a village dominated by an Egyptian temple with a largely Egyptian population adhering to a variety of Egyptian institutions (particularly in the legal sphere).[34] This type of contract therefore appears to have had an Egyptian origin, since it is attested during the Ptolemaic period only in Upper Egypt and during the Roman period only in those villages that clung to Egyptian customs, particularly in the legal realm. By contrast, at Oxyrhynchus, a strongly hellenized metropolis, the ὠνὴ ἐν πίστει is never attested.[35]

From a legal point of view, these contracts present a fundamental difference from ὑποθῆκαι as seen in *P.Brem.* 68.1–15: the conveyance of title, an obligation imposed on the debtor in the case of the ὠνὴ ἐν πίστει, is not required in the case of the ὑποθήκη. However, three ὠναὶ ἐν πίστει are characterized as ὑποθῆκαι in the documents themselves, in *P.Mich.* V 332 and 335 and *P.Lond.* II 277 (p. 217). I suggest that the notaries of Tebtynis and Soknopaiou Nesos used the term as a gloss in order to communicate to a Greek or

---

30. Nilopolis is much more poorly attested in the documentary record than either Tebtynis or Soknoupaiou Nesos. Soknopaiou Nesos and Nilopolis are geographically close to each other, and the two villages even shared a common γραφεῖον in 145 C.E. (*SPP* XXII 36).

31. The *Heidelberger Gesamtverzeichnis der griechischen Papyrusurkunden Ägyptens* (HGV, now accessible through papyri.info; as of 7 April 2011) counts 2,773 texts published for the period 30 B.C.E.–69 C.E. and 9,536 for the period 70–170 C.E. Since the βιβλιοθήκη ἐγκτήσεων was created between 68 and 72 C.E., I have here adopted the year 69 as the historically significant boundary for economic periodization.

32. Depauw 1997: 141–42; Pestman 1985.

33. Depauw 2003: 110–11.

34. Lippert and Schentuleit 2005, 2006a, 2006b, 2010. Lippert (2010) emphasized the importance of the demotic documentation for the study of Roman Soknoupaiou Nesos.

35. Manca Masciadri and Montevecchi 1982: 158 n. 22 gives a list of all known ὠναὶ ἐν πίστει. That list contains *P.Oxy.* VI 980 descr. (Oxyrhynchus, 3rd century C.E.). It is, however, highly unlikely that *P.Oxy.* VI 980 descr. is an ὠνὴ ἐν πίστει, as such transactions are attested neither after 76 nor for Oxyrhynchus.

Greco-Roman public the basic nature of this Egyptian contract. We also encounter this practice in the γραφεῖον registers from Tebtynis, dated to the reign of Claudius, in which seven contracts are recorded as ὑποθῆκαι.[36] To my mind, one should see these contracts as ὠναὶ ἐν πίστει and not ὑποθῆκαι of the sort discussed above with respect to P.Brem. 68.1–15, since these Tebtynis contracts present two common, essential attributes of the former: (1) the object securing the loan is nearly always a house; and (2) the median of the amount loaned, 112 drachmas, is comparable to that of ὠναὶ ἐν πίστει generally (100 dr.). By way of comparison, we may note that loans executed as μεσιτεῖαι, the form of mortgage most widely attested in the period during which we find ὠναὶ ἐν πίστει (7 B.C.E.–76 C.E.), always use land as security and are for higher sums of money.[37] Before 69 C.E., the word ὑποθήκη is therefore (in my opinion) not attested in the papyrological corpus except as an approximation to describe an ὠνὴ ἐν πίστει.

To my knowledge, the sharply delineated chronological, geographical, and cultural setting in which the ὠνὴ ἐν πίστει was applied in Roman Egypt has never been noted, so no one has asked, much less answered, why this form of security disappeared at the end of the first century C.E. It is perhaps fair to say that, unlike legal scholars,[38] economic historians of the ancient world have generally taken little interest in security, despite the fact that it represents an absolutely crucial element in the functioning of credit markets. Indeed, one might even say that credit markets are analytically incomprehensible without a working understanding of the historical modes of security.

The analysis of the financial documents collected from the five locations considered in this study shows that secured loans via the various forms of mortgage (ὑποθήκη, ὑπάλλαγμα, and μεσιτεία) were rare in the first century of Roman rule, or from 30 B.C.E. to approximately 68–72 C.E., the date at which the βιβλιοθήκη ἐγκτήσεων was created. Instead, the form of security most frequently attested during this first period is the ὠνὴ ἐν πίστει. This is exclusively the case in Nilopolis, Soknopaiou Nesos, and Tebtynis, the

---

36. P.Mich. II 123.viii.27 (100 dr.), ix.32 (unknown amount), ix.36 (124 dr.), x.26 (140 dr.), xv.20 (140 dr.); P.Mich. V 238.i.30–31 (100 dr.), i.8–9 (100 dr.). The median amount loaned was 112 drachmas (n = 6).

37. These include all known μεσιτεῖαι for Tebtynis between 30 B.C.E. and 69 C.E. (P.Mich. V 333–34 [1,000 dr.], 232 [13,200 dr.]) and those recorded in the γραφεῖον registers (P.Mich. II 123.ii.39 [500 dr.], v.24 [400 dr.], xvii.43 [220 dr.]; P.Mich. V 238.i.17–18 [832 dr.]; 238R.i.3–4 (308 dr.). The median amount loaned was five hundred drachmas, and the security in all cases was land of significant area, unlike in any instance of ὠνὴ ἐν πίστει.

38. See, e.g., Rupprecht 1995, 1997.

three Arsinoite villages mentioned above. In contrast, the ὠνὴ ἐν πίστει is completely absent from the documents of the cities of Oxyrhynchus, Hermopolis, and Ptolemais Euergetis in this period. The century following the foundation of the βιβλιοθήκη ἐγκτήσεων—from 68–72 to ca. 170 C.E.— witnesses two fundamental changes in the credit market. First, whereas the ὑποθήκη, ὑπάλλαγμα, and μεσιτεία are absent from the source material before 72 C.E., they are widely attested in the following century, as nearly half of all loan contracts dating to the period 68–72 to ca. 170 C.E. are recorded in one of the above means of security. Second, the credit market enjoyed spectacular growth: the median principal in loans rose threefold after the creation of the βιβλιοθήκη ἐγκτήσεων in 68–72, from 107 drachmas (n = 55) to 360 (n = 155).

At this point, the fundamental question we must ask ourselves is, why did creditors appear to have asked so infrequently for real security before 69, unless in the form of an ὠνὴ ἐν πίστει in the Fayyum villages?[39] The answer, suggested by the periodization above, lies in the creation in 68–72 of a new institution, the βιβλιοθήκη ἐγκτήσεων. This "archive of acquisitions" has been known to scholars since the end of the nineteenth century, principally through the publication of *P.Oxy.* II 237, known as the "Petition of Dionysia," dated to 186 C.E. In this long and complicated text, a woman named Dionysia cites, in support of her legal claims against her father, several prefectural edicts concerning the rights of women over real property. One of these edicts is particularly informative about the βιβλιοθήκη ἐγκτήσεων. While the βιβλιοθήκη ἐγκτήσεων has been extensively studied by juristic papyrologists for more than a century,[40] it has been all but ignored by social and economic historians of the Roman world[41] and particularly by those interested in finance, both because it seems to belong to the particular provincial history of Roman Egypt and because of the questions with which ancient economic historians have traditionally approached financial documents. When one's interest lies, as it has, in distinguishing between "loans for consumption" and

---

39. The work of Uri Yiftach-Firanko (e.g., 2006) demonstrates the necessity of taking into account the geographic origin of documents when studying contractual forms and phraseology. Kühnert 1965, typical of German juristic papyrology of the 1960s, and Tenger 1993 do not do so sufficiently, which limits the value of those analyses considerably.

40. Von Woess 1924; Wolff 1978; Burkhalter 1990.

41. Egypt is now considered by most scholars as an integral and integrated part of the Roman Empire: Rathbone 1991 and Bagnall 1993 were decisive on that matter.

"loans for production"[42] or in the role of the ancient bank or interest rates—an intellectual agenda imported from work based on sources materially different than what one finds in the papyrological evidence—it is only natural that the βιβλιοθήκη ἐγκτήσεων, seeming to belong to administrative history, will be of scant interest. If, however, one begins with the recognition of the centrality of security to finance and the abundant evidence of guarantees in the papyri, the βιβλιοθήκη ἐγκτήσεων assumes a new importance.

The contribution that some of the concepts developed in connection with the new institutional economics can offer this type of research should be emphasized. Thinking in such terms excites interest in an institution like the βιβλιοθήκη ἐγκτήσεων, which considerably increases the information we have about the property rights of contracting parties, especially in real property. For example, the new institutional economics stresses that clearly defined individual property rights are necessary to good economic performance. More generally, it encourages economic historians to take account of the legal environment in which parties transact. Ancient economic historians whose research is based in the study of documents, or the evidence of practice, thus find in new institutional economics a powerful and productive theoretical framework for studying the relationship between law and economy.

To begin to understand how the βιβλιοθήκη ἐγκτήσεων was able to support and stimulate the credit market of Roman Egypt, we need to study it in operation. The most conducive source in this regard is the fundamental text cited above, the Petition of Dionysia. In column VIII.27–43, Dionysia's legal team cites an edict of the Prefect M. Mettius Rufus, dating to 89, nearly a century before Dionyia's petition was authored.

Μάρκος ΜέττιΙος Ῥοῦφος ἔπαρχος Αἰγύπτου λέγει· Κλαύδιος Ἄρειος ὁ τοῦ Ὀξυρυγχείτου στρατηγὸς [ἐ]δήλωσέν μοι μήτε τὰ ἰ[δι]ωτικὰ μ[ή]τε τὰ δημ]όσια Ι πράγματα τὴν καθήκουσαν λαμβάνειν διοίκησιν διὰ τὸ ἐκ πολλῶν χρόνων μὴ καθ' ὃν ἔδει τρόπον ᾠκονομῆσθαι τὰ ἐν τῇ τῶν ἐνΙκτήσεων βιβλιοθήκῃ δια[σ]τρώματα, καίτοι πολλάκις κριθὲν ὑπὸ τῶν πρὸ ἐμοῦ ἐπάρχων τῆς δεούσης αὐτὰ τυχεῖν ἐπανορθώΙσεως· ὅπερ οὐ καλῶς ἐνδέχεται, εἰ μὴ ἄνωθεν γένοιτο ἀντίγραφα. κελεύω οὖν πάντας τοὺς κτήτορας ἐντὸς μηνῶν ἓξ ἀπογράΙψασθαι τὴν ἰδίαν κτῆσιν εἰς τὴν τῶν ἐνκτήσεων βιβλιοθήκην καὶ τοὺς δανειστὰς ἃς ἐὰν ἔχωσι ὑποθήκας καὶ

---

42. Finley 1999; Millett 1991; Cohen 1992; Andreau 2001.

τούς ἄλλους | ὅσα ἐὰν ἔχωσι δίκαια· τὴν δὲ ἀπογραφὴν ποιείσθωσαν δηλοῦντες πόθεν ἕκαστος τῶν ὑπαρχόντων καταβέβηκεν εἰς αὐτοὺς | ἡ κτῆσεις. παρατιθέτωσαν δὲ καὶ αἱ γυναῖκες ταῖς ὑποστάσεσι τῶν ἀνδρῶν, ἐὰν κατά τινα ἐπιχώριον νόμον κρατεῖται τὰ ὑπάρ | χοντα, ὁμοίως δὲ καὶ τὰ τέκνα ταῖς τῶν γονέων, οἷς ἡ μὲν χρῆσεις διὰ δημοσίων τετήρηται χρηματισμῶν, ἡ δὲ κτῆ | σις μετὰ θάνατον τοῖς τέκνοις κεκράτηται, ἵνα οἱ συναλλάσσοντες μὴ κατ' ἄγνοιαν ἐνεδρεύονται. παραγγέλλω δὲ καὶ τοῖς συναλλα | γματογράφοις καὶ τοῖς μνήμοσι μηδὲν δίχα ἐπιστάλματος τοῦ βιβλιοφυλακ[ίου τελειῶσαι, γνοῦσιν ὡς οὐκ ὄφελος τὸ] τοιοῦτο, ἀλλα καὶ | αὐτοὶ ὡς παρὰ τὰ προστεταγμένα ποιήσοντες δίκην ὑπομενοῦσι τὴν προσήκουσαν. ἐὰν δ' εἰσὶν ἐν τῇ βιβλιοθήκῃ τῶν ἐπά | νω χρόνων ἀπογραφαί, μετὰ πάσης ἀκρειβείας φυλασσέσθωσαν, ὁμοίως δὲ καὶ τὰ διαστρώματα, ἵν' εἴ τις γένοιτο ζήτησις εἰς | ὕστερον περὶ τῶν μὴ δεόντως ἀπογραψαμένων ἐξ ἐκείνων ἐλεγχθῶσι. [ἵνα] δ' [ο]ὖν β[εβ]αία τε καὶ εἰς ἅπαν διαμένῃ τῶν διασ | τρωμάτων ἡ χρῆσ{ε}ις πρὸς τὸ μὴ πάλιν ἀπογραφῆς δεηθῆναι, παραγγέλλω τοῖς βιβλιοφύλαξι διὰ πενταετίας ἐπανανεοῦσθαι | τὰ διαστρώματα μεταφερομένης εἰς τὰ καινοποιούμενα τῆς τελευταίας ἑκάστου ὀνόματος ὑποστάσεως κατὰ κώμην καὶ κα | τ' εἶδος. (ἔτους) θ' Δομειτιανο[ῦ], μηνὸς Δομιτ{τ}ιανοῦ δ'.

Proclamation of Marcus Mettius Rufus, Prefect of Egypt:

Claudius Arius the strategus of the Oxyrhynchite nome has informed me that neither private nor public business is receiving proper treatment owing to the fact that for many years the abstracts in the βιβλιοθήκη ἐγκτήσεων have not been kept in the manner required, athough the prefects before me have often ordered that they should undergo the necessary revision, which is not really practicable unless copies are made from the beginning. Therefore I command all owners to register their property at the βιβλιοθήκη ἐγκτήσεων within six months, and all lenders the mortgages which they hold, and all other persons the claims which they possess. In making the return they shall declare the source from which in each case the possession of the property devolved upon them. Wives also, if on the strength of some local law they have a lien on the property, shall add an annotation to the property-statements of their husbands, and likewise children to those of their parents, if the enjoyment of the property has been secured to the latter by public instruments and the possession of it after their death has been settled on their children, in order that those who make agreements with them may not be defrauded through ignorance. I also command the drafters and keepers of contracts not [to execute] any deed without authorization of the βιβλιοθήκη ἐγκτήσεων, [being warned that such a transaction has no validity] and that they themselves will suffer the due penalty for disregarding orders. If the βιβλιοθήκη ἐγκτήσεων contains any property-returns of earlier date, let them be preserved with the utmost care, and likewise the abstracts of them, in order that if afterwards an inquiry should be held concerning persons who have made false returns, they may be convicted thereby. In order then that the use of the abstracts may become secure and permanent, so that another registration shall not be required, I command the keepers of the βιβλιοθήκη ἐγκτήσεων to revise the abstracts every five years, transferring to the new list the last statement of property of each person arranged under villages and category. The 9th year of Domitian, the fourth day of the month of Domitianus.[43]

The prefect M. Mettius Rufus promulgated this edict in 89 following the discovery of grave problems in the βιβλιοθήκη ἐγκτήσεων of the Oxyrhynchite nome. The Roman administration was not directly in charge of this institution, since the office of *bibliophylax* was a liturgy whose full financial weight was supported by the richest individuals in each nome. Nevertheless, the Prefect clearly kept a close watch on the institution. To help put its affairs back in order, he issued two commands (among other actions), each of which had a distinct object and audience.

The first intended audience of the edict was comprised of those people who had rights over specific property. Such people were obliged to declare those rights to the βιβλιοθήκη ἐγκτήσεων within six months. This group may be divided into two categories: (1) those with direct, evident rights, like owners and secured creditors; and (2) those with what one may call latent, indirect, or derivative rights, such as dowered women and children of property holders. Wives had to report in their husbands' declarations those rights they had over his property, if they had any. Children likewise had to report in their parents' declarations any rights they had over assets that their parents currently enjoyed but that subsequently reverted to them after their parents' death. The instructions given to women and children with such claims aimed at rendering the head of household's declaration as complete as possible with respect to the full array of property claims, actual and eventual, on each piece of property.

The βιβλιοθήκη ἐγκτήσεων held records of real property, principally

---

43. Trans. Hunt and Edgar, *Sel.Pap.* II 219 (pp. 105–9), slightly adapted.

land and houses. Since land represented the most significant element in the estates of almost all individuals, it is in this capacity that the βιβλιοθήκη ἐγκτήσεων played a vital role in credit markets. Slaves, whose value was often of the same magnitude as some houses in Roman Egypt, also fell within the purview of this institution.[44] With competence over these two broad categories, real estate and slaves, the βιβλιοθήκη ἐγκτήσεων effectively held a record of the two types of property accounting for the vast majority of individual wealth in Roman Egypt.

The second audience of the edict was "the drafters and keepers of contracts" (συναλλαγματογράφοι καὶ μνήμονες), or the scribes officially authorized to record and register private contracts—that is, the notaries of the γραφεῖα and ἀγορανομεῖα, to whom parties wishing to record their contracts in public instruments went and paid a γραμματικόν for drafting and registration. Two such notaries we have met already are Achilleus, from the γραφεῖον at Sinary, a village in the Oxyrhynchite nome (P.Oxy. XLIX 3485), and Hephaistion, from Thallou in the Hermopolite nome (P.Brem. 68.1–15). Without them and their colleagues, the system for which the βιβλιοθήκη ἐγκτήσεων was the sophisticated keystone would have fallen apart. The edict of M. Mettius Rufus forbade these scribes from drafting public documents without having received the prior authorization (the ἐπίσταλμα, or "command") from the officials in charge of the βιβλιοθήκη ἐγκτήσεων. This document, the ἐπίσταλμα, was requested by the party selling or mortgaging a piece of property, in order to demonstrate that he had title to the property in question. Thanks to another important document, the so-called Gnomon of the Idios Logos, we know that scribes were subject to a fine of fifty drachmas if they ignored Mettius's order and issued a public instrument without the express prior authorization of the βιβλιοθήκη ἐγκτήσεων (BGU V 1210 § 101, lines 227–28). Theoretically, this rule applied only to those contracts that concerned the types of property monitored by the βιβλιοθήκη ἐγκτήσεων; in practice, however, it covered, for reasons discussed above, transactions related to a majority of personal wealth in the Roman Egyptian economy. So, whenever a loan was to be drafted by public instrument and guaranteed by land, a house, or a slave, the debtor was obliged to present the scribe with an ἐπίσταλμα from the βιβλιοθήκη ἐγκτήσεων confirming not only his title to the property but also the sufficiency of the equity in the property that was to

---

44. Straus 2004: 58–60.

serve as the security for the loan. *P.Oxy.* III 483 (Oxyrhynchus, 108 C.E.) is a
good example of this step in the process. Achillas, who wished to mortgage
six arouras of land, wrote to the βιβλιοθήκη ἐγκτήσεων requesting an
ἐπίσταλμα so as to proceed with the loan.⁴⁵ After he verified the property in
his registers, Sarapion, one of the two βιβλιοφύλακες, or "archive keepers"
in charge of the βιβλιοθήκη ἐγκτήσεων, issued an order to the ἀγορανόμοι
of Oxyrhynchus that they execute the contract in accordance with Achillas's
wishes.⁴⁶ In the Hermopolite nome, the formula used in the text of the public
mortgage instruments made explicit reference to the required consultation of
the βιβλιοθήκη ἐγκτήσεων by the debtor.⁴⁷

The βιβλιοθήκη ἐγκτήσεων was therefore a general register of individuals' property rights over real property and slaves. From the declarations submitted by individual owners or claimants, the βιβλιοφύλακες compiled a
synthetic account (called an ὄνομα, or "name") for each property holder, in
which was listed all the land and slaves he owned and all declared claims
against that property. After the creation of the βιβλιοθήκη ἐγκτήσεων,
therefore, a debtor would have found it nearly impossible to offer up a piece
of property of the type recorded by the βιβλιοθήκη ἐγκτήσεων (e.g., a parcel
of land) that did not belong to him or had already been fully mortgaged to
another lender: in either case, he would not receive the requiste ἐπίσταλμα,
and without this order, the scribe would be (under most circumstances) unwilling to draft and register the contract.

The βιβλιοθήκη ἐγκτήσεων thus helped to define individual property
rights over the most important forms of personal wealth in a much more
definite fashion than had been possible hitherto in Ptolemaic or Roman
Egypt.⁴⁸ The existence of the new archive not only assured the creditor of the

45. *P.Oxy.* III 483.18–21: ἐπιδίδ[ο]μι [τ]ὸ ὑπόμν[η]μα ὅπως σὺ ἐπισ[τείλης] | τοῖς τῆς
μητροπόλεως ἀγορανόμο[ις οὖσι] | καὶ μνήμοσι τελειῶσαι τὸν χρημα[τισμὸν] | ὡς
καθήκει (I submit this memorandum in order that you will command the *agoranomoi* and
recorders of the metropolis to execute the public document accordingly).
46. *P.Oxy.* III 483.32–34: Σαραπίων ὁ σὺν Θέωνι βυβλιοφύλ(αξ) ἀγορανό(μοις) | μητ(ρο)-
πόλ(εως) χα(ίρειν). ἔχει Ἀχιλλᾶς ἐν ἀπογραφῆ τὰς ἀρού|ρας ἕξ, διὸ ἐπιτελεῖτε ὡς
καθήκ(ει) (Sarapion, archive keeper along with Theon, to the *agoranomoi* of the metropolis,
greetings. Achillas has in his [property] declaration six *arourai*; therefore execute [the public document] accordingly).
47. *P.Flor.* I 1.11 (Hermopolis, 153 C.E.): καὶ συνεχρηματίσθη ἡ δεδαν<ε>ισμένη
ἐπιστειλάντων τῶν τῆς ἐγκτήσεως βιβλιοφυλάκων (and the debtor executed a public
document on the order of the keepers of the archive of acquisitions). The same formula is
found in *P.Stras.* I 52.12 (Hermopolis, 151 C.E.).
48. Land conveyances were recorded in the Ptolemaic period (e.g., agoranomic records of sale
or the *katalochismos* of cleruchic land; see Wolff 1978). Whether or not those records were

title of the property he agreed to accept as security from the debtor but also allowed him to assess the equity in the property by indicating whether it had already been mortgaged or if there were any other encumbrances on the property. These were, without a doubt, the most important factors that controlled the credit market of Roman Egypt. Although it was not too difficult to verify that an individual was actually the owner of a parcel of land, it was nearly impossible to discover the latent property claims of creditors, wives, or children with succession rights. This was particularly important to potential creditors because the claims of wives and such children were preferred — that is, they were made whole first — in the event of default or insolvency. Before the creation of the βιβλιοθήκη ἐγκτήσεων between 68 and 72, it therefore made less sense for creditors to loan on the basis of a ὑποθήκη, which, unlike the ὠνὴ ἐν πίστει, left debtors as owners of the property. In other words, the uncertainty surrounding title and equity before the establishment of the βιβλιοθήκη ἐγκτήσεων was so high that creditors — when they decided to loan at all — often resorted to a form of loan, i.e., the ὠνὴ ἐν πίστει, that put them in the strongest legal position possible in the case of default, effectively making them legal owners of the collateral posted against the loan. The work of the βιβλιοθήκη ἐγκτήσεων, however, reduced this uncertainty: it created an accurate and open registry of potentially collaterizable property, with the result that the Roman provincial administration essentially put itself in the position of verifying the quality of private guarantees. It thus stands to reason that we should see the tremendous growth in mortgages and an increase in the sums loaned out by individuals as the twin consequences of the establishment of the βιβλιοθήκη ἐγκτήσεων. In the history of the private credit market of Roman Egypt, the date of its creation thus constitutes a pivotal moment.

The disappearance of the ὠνὴ ἐν πίστει should also be interpreted as a happy casualty of this historic turning point. This was a particularly onerous form of real guarantee, because it demanded the transfer of ownership of the security as a condition of the loan. This, however, became unnecessary and obsolete once the βιβλιοθήκη ἐγκτήσεων was available to provide creditors with a superior level of information about property offered as security. The inhabitants of the three Fayyum villages quickly realized the advantages of the

---

available to the public remains unknown.

new system, since the last ὠνὴ ἐν πίστει attested thus far is from 76, less than eight years (at the most) from the archive's inauguration. In other words, when presented with a more effective and efficient form of security, contract parties quickly abandoned a customary form of transaction with a long history. Far from showing the inhabitants of Roman Egypt as passive subjects or hide-bound traditionalists impervious to change, this history reveals them as capable of adapting to and manipulating the sophisticated and evolving Roman administrative and legal system in which they conducted their economic lives.

For the creditor, opting for a public instrument over a cheirograph meant that he bore higher type 1 TC, particularly in the case of large loans backed by mortgages, as he had to pay both the γραμματικόν and the ἐγκύκλιον. But these certain and easily discoverable costs, which indeed lowered his real rate of return, minimized the potentially catastrophic and otherwise unknowable risk of default. Theoretically, if the debtor breached his loan contract, the creditor's degree of certainty that the security pledged in a public document would cover his exposure should have been greater than if he had drafted the loan as an unregistered, if cheaper, cheirograph.[49] Whenever a creditor decided to put out a significant sum for loan, he thus arbitraged between the costs of public drafting and registration and the probability of losing his capital. The documents studied here reveal that in the case of mortgages, creditors showed an overwhelming preference for public instruments over private ones. Creditors preferred, on average, to pay TC of type 1 from the outset in order to offset or mitigate the risk of default, or the potential of being exposed to TC of type 3 later on, when the loan came due.

The creation of the βιβλιοθήκη ἐγκτήσεων by the Roman administration was a success from the point of view of the credit market in Roman Egypt, and it supported a rise in the number of mortgages that were written (i.e., the credit market grew), regardless of the particular type of legal security in which they were drafted (i.e., ὑποθήκη, ὑπάλλαγμα, and μεσιτεία). It also raised TC of type 1—that is, the costs of drafting and registering a loan, as well as the taxes associated with mortgages. The raises in type 1 TC, however, worked precisely to reduce significantly the far more important TC of type 3—that is, the costs associated with default. One can therefore conclude that the βιβλιοθήκη ἐγκτήσεων massively reduced the aggregate TC associated

---

49. I say "theoretically" because the judicial system did not always work as it was intended.

with securing loans and that its activities after 68–72 radically transformed the private credit market of Roman Egypt.

The Roman administration was probably aware of these potential beneficial effects on the private credit market when it created the βιβλιοθήκη ἐγκτήσεων, even if it was not its primary goal.[50] The historical analysis of the contractual forms[51] and the study of several edicts from the Roman governors of the province (e.g., the edicts of Tiberius Iulius Alexander, Marcus Mettius Rufus, and Servius Sulpicius Similis) show that at least some governors had a great concern for the drafting and registration of private contracts in general.[52] They understood that a lack of clarity in individual property rights might lead to a decrease in the number of private transactions and an increase in the number of legal disputes they would have had to settle. They certainly were not neoinstitutionalists, and they probably cared less about economic growth than some current historians of ancient economies, but they probably knew, on some level, that clarifying property rights was good for the general prosperity of the province, which did increase in the second century C.E.[53] Clarifying property rights to facilitate transactions was not necessarily always the only or even the primary concern of the Roman administration. As Uri Yiftach shows in chapter 6, the Roman administration was eager to protect the rights of family members on property owned by individuals and, more broadly, to monitor the circulation of landed property. But this concern to protect the interests of family members and the state in private property does not mean that the administration sought to restrict transactions involving private property.

Bibliography

Andreau, J. 1987. *La vie financière dans le monde romain: Les métiers de manieurs d'argent, IVe siècle av. J.C.–IIIe siècle ap. J.-C.* Rome.

Andreau, J. 2001. *Banque et affaires dans le monde romain, IVe siècle av. J.-C.–IIIe siècle ap. J.-C.* Paris.

Andreau, J., P. Briant, and R. Descat, eds. 1997. *Economie antique: Prix et formation des*

---

50. The much-debated question of the motives of the Roman administration is too complex to be treated here. See Von Woess 1924; Wolff 1978; Maresch 2002; Jördens 2010a, 2010b; Yiftach-Firanko 2010.
51. On the expression of interest in loan contracts, see Lerouxel 2012: esp. 170.
52. On the edict of Tiberius Iulius Alexander, see Chalon 1964. On the edict of Ser. Sulpicius Similis, see *P.Oxy.* II 237, col. viii.21–27.
53. On growth in ancient economies, see Scheidel, Morris, and Saller 2007.

prix dans les économies antiques. Entretiens d'archéologie et d'histoire 3. Saint-Bertrand-de-Comminges.

Andreau, J., and J. Maucourant. 1999. "A propos de la 'rationalité économique' dans l'Antiquité gréco-romaine: Une interprétation des thèses de D. Rathbone." *Topoi Orient-Occident* 9: 48–102.

Bagnall, R. 1993. *Egypt in Late Antiquity.* Princeton.

Bang, P. 2008. *The Roman Bazaar: A Comparative Study of Trade and Markets in a Tributary Empire.* Cambridge.

Bogaert, R. 1968. *Banques et banquiers dans les cités grecques.* Leiden.

Bogaert, R. 1995. "Liste géographique des banques et des banquiers de l'Egypte romaine." *ZPE* 109: 133–73.

Bogaert, R. 2001. "Les documents bancaires de l'Egypte gréco-romaine et byzantine." *Ancient Society* 31: 173–288.

Bresson, A. 2007. *L'économie de la Grèce des cités (fin VIe–Ier siècle avant J.-C.).* Vol. 1, *Les structures de la production.* Paris.

Bresson, A. 2008. *L'économie de la Grèce des cités (fin VIe–Ier avant J.-C.).* Vol. 2, *Les espaces de l'échange.* Paris.

Burkhalter, F. 1990. "Archives locales et archives centrales en Egypte romaine." *Chiron* 20: 191–216.

Chalon, G. 1964. *L'édit du préfet Tiberius Iulius Alexander: Étude historique et exégétique.* Olten.

Cohen, E. 1992. *Athenian Economy and Society: A Banking Perspective.* Princeton.

Depauw, M. 1997. *A Companion to Demotic Studies.* Brussels.

Depauw, M. 2003. "Autographic Confirmation in Demotic Private Contracts." *CE* 78: 66–111.

Finckh, H. 1962. *Das Zinsrecht der gräko-ägyptischen Papyri.* Nuremberg.

Finley, M. 1999. *The Ancient Economy.* Updated edition, with a foreword by I. Morris. Berkeley.

Foraboschi, D., and A. Gara. 1981. "Sulla differenza tra tassi d'interesse in natura e in moneta nell'Egitto greco-romano." In R. Bagnall, G. Browne, and E. Hanson, eds., *Proceedings of the XVI International Congress of Papyrology,* 335–43. Chico.

Foraboschi, D. and A. Gara. 1982. "L'economia dei crediti in natura (Egitto)." *Athenaeum* 60: 69–83.

Girard, P. F., and F. Senn. 1977. *Les lois des Romains,* 7ème *édition par un groupe de romanistes des "Textes de droit romain,"Vol.* 2. Naples.

Herrmann, J. 1989. "Zur ὠνὴ ἐν πίστει des hellenistichen Rechts." In G. Thür, ed., *Symposion 1985,* 317–24. Cologne. Reprinted in G. Schiemann, ed. *Kleine Schriften zur Rechtsgeschichte,* Münchener Beiträge zur Papyrusforschung und antiken Rechtsgeschichte 83 (Munich, 1990), 305–14.

Hoffman, P. T., G. Postel-Vinay, and J.-L. Rosenthal, eds. 2001. *Des marchés sans prix: Une économie politique du crédit à Paris, 1660–1870.* Paris.

Husselman, E. 1970. "Procedures of the Record Office of Tebtunis in the First Century A.D." In D. H. Samuel, ed., *Proceedings of the 12th International Congress of Papyrology*, 223–38. Toronto.

Ioannatou, M. 2006. *Affaires d'argent dans la correspondance de Cicéron: L'aristocratie sénatoriale face à ses dettes*. Paris.

Jördens, A. 2009. *Statthalterliche Verwaltung in der römischen Kaiserzeit: Studien zum praefectus Aegypti*. Stuttgart.

Jördens, A. 2010a. "Nochmals zur Bibliotheke Enkteseon." In G. Thür, ed., *Symposion 2009*, 277–90. Vienna.

Jördens, A. 2010b. "Öffentliche archive und römische Rechtspolitik." In Lembke, Minas-Nerpel, and Pfeiffer 2010: 159–79.

Kehoe, D. 2007. *Law and Rural Economy in the Roman Empire*. Ann Arbor.

Kühnert, H. 1965. *Zum Kreditgeschäft in den hellenistischen Papyri Ägyptens bis Diokletian*. Fribourg.

Lembke, K., M. Minas-Nerpel, and S. Pfeiffer, eds. 2010. *Tradition and Transformation: Egypt under Roman Rule*. Leiden.

Lerouxel, F. 2006. "Les femmes sur le marché du crédit en Égypte romaine (30 avant J.-C.–284 après J.-C.): Une approche néo-institutionnaliste." *Cahiers du Centre de Recherches Historiques* 36: 121–36.

Lerouxel, F. 2008. "La banque privée romaine et le marché du crédit dans les tablettes de Murecine et les papyrus d'Égypte romaine." In Verboven, Vandorpe, and Chankowski 2008: 169–98.

Lerouxel, F. 2012. "Des prêts sans intérêt? Le taux d'intérêt dans le nome oxyrhynchite avant 79 après J.-C." *ZPE* 181: 161–72.

Lo Cascio, E. 2005. "La 'New Institutional Economics' e l'economia imperiale romana." In M. Pani, ed., *Storia romana e storia moderna: Fasi in prospettiva*, 69–83. Bari.

Lippert, S. 2010. "Seeing the Whole Picture: Why Reading Greek Texts from Soknopiaou Nesos Is Not Enough." In T. Gagos, ed., *Proceedings of the XXV International Congress of Papyrology*, 427–34. Ann Arbor.

Lippert, S., and M. Schentuleit, eds. 2005. *Tebtynis und Soknopaiu Nesos: Leben im römerzeitlichen Fajum*. Wiesbaden.

Lippert, S., and M. Schentuleit. 2006a. *Ostraka*. Demotische Dokumente aus Dime 1. Wiesbaden.

Lippert, S., and M. Schentuleit. 2006b. *Quittungen*. Demotische Dokumente aus Dime 2. Wiesbaden.

Lippert, S., and M. Schentuleit. 2010. *Urkunden*. Demotische Dokumente aus Dime 3. Wiesbaden.

Manca Masciadri, M. A., and O. Montevecchi. 1982. "Contratti di baliatico e vendite fiduciarie a Tebtynis." *Aegyptus* 62: 148–62.

Manning, J. 2003. *Land and Power in Ptolemaic Egypt: The Structure of Land Tenure*. Cambridge.

Maresch, K. 2002. "Die Bibliotheke Enkteseon im römischen Ägypten: Überlegungen zur Funktion zentraler Besitzarchive." *AFP* 48: 233–46.

Millett, P. 1991. *Lending and Borrowing in Ancient Athens.* Cambridge.

Muhs, B. 2005. "The Grapheion and the Disappearance of Demotic Contracts in Early Roman Tebtynis and Soknopaiu Nesos." In Lippert and Schentuleit 2005: 93–104.

North, D. 1985. "Transaction Costs in History." *Journal of European Economic History* 14: 557–76.

Pestman, P. W. 1985. "Ventes provisoires de biens pour sûreté pour dettes: *Ônai en pistei* à Pathyris et Krokodilopolis." In *Textes et études de papyrologie*, 45–59. Leiden.

Rathbone, D. 1991. "The Ancient Economy and Greco-Roman Egypt." In L. Criscuolo, and G. Geraci, eds., *Egitto e storia antica dall'ellenismo all'età araba: Bilancio di un confronto*, 159–76. Bologna.

Rathbone, D. 1997. "Prices and Price Formation in Roman Egypt." In Andreau, Briant, and Descat 1997: 183–244.

Rupprecht, H. A. 1995. "Die dinglichen Sicherungsrechte nach der Praxis der Papyri: Eine Übersicht über den urkundlichen Befund." In R. Feenstra, A. S. Hartkamp, J. E. Spruit, P. J. Sijpesteijn, , and L. C. Winkel, eds., *Collatio iuris Romani: Études dédiées à Hans Ankum à l'occasion de son 65e anniversaire*, 425–36. Amsterdam.

Rupprecht, H. A. 1997. "Zwangsvollstreckung und dingliche Sicherung in den Papyri der ptolemäischen und römischen Zeit." In G. Thür and J. Vélissaropoulos, eds., *Symposion 1995: Vorträge zur griechischen und hellenistischen Rechtsgeschichte*, 291–302. Cologne.

Scheidel, W., I. Morris, and R. Saller, eds. 2007. *The Cambridge Economic History of the Greco-Roman World.* Cambridge.

Straus, J. 2004. *L'achat et la vente d'esclaves dans l'Egypte romaine: Contribution papyrologique à l'étude de l'esclavage dans une province orientale de l'Empire romain.* Munich.

Tenger, B. 1993. *Die Verschuldung im römischen Ägypten (1.–2. Jh. n. Chr.).* St. Katharinen.

Terpstra, T. 2008. "Roman Law, Transaction Costs, and the Roman Economy: Evidence from the Sulpicii Archive." In Verboven, Vandorpe, and Chankowski 2008: 345–69.

Verboven, K., K. Vandorpe, and V. Chankowski, eds. 2008. *Pistoi dia tèn technèn: Bankers, Loans, and Archives in the Ancient World; Studies in Honour of Raymond Bogaert.* Louvain.

Von Woess, F. 1924. *Untersuchungen über das Urkundenwesen und den Publizitätsschutz im römischen.* Münchener Beiträge zur Papyrusforschung und antiken Rechtsgeschichte 6. Munich.

Wallace, L. 1938. *Taxation in Egypt from August to Diocletian*. Princeton.

Wolff, H.-J. 1978. *Das Recht der griechischen Papyri Ägyptens in der Zeit der Ptolemaeer und des Prinzipats: Organisation und Kontrolle des privaten Rechtsverkehrs*. Handbuch der Altertumswissenschaft 10.5.2. Munich.

Yiftach-Firanko, U. 2006. "Regionalism and Legal Documents: The Case of Oxyrhynchos." In H.-A. Rupprecht, ed., *Symposion 2003*, 347–65. Vienna.

Yiftach-Firanko, U. 2010. "Comments on Andrea Jördens." In G. Thür, ed., *Symposion 2009*, 291–99. Vienna.

CHAPTER 8

Transaction Costs and Contract in Roman Egypt

A Case Study in Negotiating the Right of Repossession[1]

David M. Ratzan

There is no question that transaction costs (TC) existed in antiquity; the conceptualization may be modern, but the costs themselves are as old as the first exchange. The question is how best to apply the conceptual and theoretical framework of the new institutional economics (NIE) to problems in ancient history. As Dennis Kehoe and Bruce Frier have recently noted, we lack the statistical basis from which to test the relationship between institutions and economic performance in antiquity, one of the chief goals of NIE; they therefore reasonably suggest that NIE is most productive historically when used "indirectly," that is, "to help formulate the questions, provide analytical tools with which to analyze the ancient evidence, and develop theories that advance the debate" (2007: 142). It is in this spirit that I hope to show how adopting an NIE lens can help to reshape and advance our thinking about contract in the Roman world. Through the case study below, I aim to demonstrate that (a) contract as an ancient "governance structure," or a set of rules organizing certain kinds of economic transactions, is a historical object still in need of analysis and (b) how an institutional perspective on contract chal-

1. I thank my coeditors, Uri Yiftach and Dennis Kehoe, for their suggestions on this essay, as well as W. Bentley MacLeod, Kevin Crotty, Susan Jacobs, Adam Kosto, and Taco Terpstra for their insightful comments.

lenges many widely held generalizations about the Roman world, particularly those concerning individual agency and the relationship between the individual and the state.

1. The Argument

As the geography, legal concepts, and transactions discussed in this essay are likely unfamiliar to many, I give here an outline of the argument. Most historians will find sections 5 and 6 to be of the greatest interest.

In section 2, I review the status of contract in Roman Egypt, arguing that one finds there something of an enigma, a society that routinely employed contracts and had a concept of contractual obligation (albeit an implicit one) yet lacked a formal definition, much less a robust legal theory, of contract. The historian is thus confronted with the particular problem of how to study "contract" per se. I suggest that thinking in terms of TC allows us to take full advantage of the best evidence for economic and legal practice in the Roman world, namely the papyri from Roman Egypt, since this perspective encourages us to think of contract not merely as a legal institution but also (and in the first instance) as an economic institution or "governance structure," a specific mode of transacting, distinct from, say, selling commodities in a marketplace.

In section 3, I identify an object for study that allows us to isolate contract as a governance structure over and above the particularities of stereotyped contractual transactions, formal contract types, and local scribal traditions. In other words, I identify a general economic problem, for a range of possible transactions, that was routinely solved by using contracts as the organizational framework. This object is a clause, which I will call the "ἀποσπάω clause," that penalized a parent or slave owner for unilaterally repossessing a dependent he or she had put at the disposal of the other party, usually a wet nurse, employer, or master craftsman taking on an apprentice. The analysis of clauses is, of course, a tried-and-true method of the ancient legal historian, but I employ it here to recover the landscape of historical TC that ancient individuals navigated when attempting to organize transactions involving two parties and a third-party dependent. The section ends with some hypotheses about the likely distribution of this clause given what we know of the typical socioeconomic positions of the parties when they entered into contracts with each other.

Section 4 describes the actual distribution of the clause. Here we see that although it is indeed found in all regions and contract types (i.e., the clause was deployed to solve a general rights problem over dependents), it displays significant variation by region, transaction, and contract type, "private" or "public."

Section 5 goes on to explore two specific patterns within this distribution. Section 5.1 looks at a case in which one of the hypotheses presented in section 3 is confirmed, namely, that of wet-nursing contracts, which were typically drafted by socioeconomically superior slave owners contracting with lower-status nurses. Since the clause served to protect the nurse's interests by penalizing the owner's exercise of his residual right to repossess his infant slave, we would predict that the relatively more powerful owners would seek to exclude the clause and be successful in doing so. This is indeed what we find. I argue, however, that although these contracts therefore seem "exploitative," insofar as they are tilted against the nurse, they in fact represent comparatively high TC for the more powerful owner. I then advance a theory as to why owners would write such contracts. In section 5.2, I investigate a contrary case in which one of the hypotheses presented in section 3 is confounded. Even though we have every reason to believe that master craftsmen in both the Arsinoite and Oxyrhynchite nomes had more or less the same economic interests and legal tools to pursue them, we nevertheless find that apprenticeship contracts in the Arsinoite omit the clause while those from the Oxyrhynchite include it. I argue that this difference reflects crucial differences in social conditions for weavers in the two nomes, which, in turn, produced distinctive TC calculi for the contracting parties.

Finally, section 6 turns briefly to the necessary question of enforcement. For this clause and the contracts in which it appeared to have been economically and legally salient, both the fundamental right to repossess and the ability to penalize its exercise (i.e., the ἀποσπάω clause) had to have been credible, and credibility turns on enforcement. I show (i) how the right to repossess a dependent was a self-help right in the first instance, (ii) how the Roman state in Egypt policed this right, and (iii) how individuals operated in the complex enforcement regime in which this right was negotiated and defended. I end with a famous case in which a wet nurse represents herself pro se against her erstwhile employer in a dispute over repossession, demonstrating how the arguments at court fit the system of contracts and enforcement regime I describe and how the court's decision supports the institution of contract with respect to the transations discussed.

2. Contracts without Contract: The Puzzle of Contract in the Roman East

As is well known, the Romans developed a sophisticated law of contract over the late republican and early imperial periods.[2] Massively influential in the subsequent legal history of the West, this achievement was largely irrelevant to legal practice in Roman Egypt: the Romans imposed their rule but not their law.[3] Instead, the *ius civile* remained the privilege of a small minority until the promulgation of the *Constitutio Antoniniana* of 212, when virtually the entire free population of the Roman Empire became citizens by fiat.[4] The relationship of Roman law to provincial law (and vice versa) is a complicated one that cannot be addressed here. Suffice it to say that in the realm of contract, the influence was minimal, indirect, and quite late, Caracalla's edict notwithstanding.[5] Changes or additions that the Romans did make aimed predominantly at maximizing fiscal control and revenue extraction or at clarifying the scope of the freedom of contract when it threatened to impinge on other values and institutions. This laissez-faire legal policy, moreover, ran in both directions: the Roman administration neither required nor expected citizens in Egypt to use Roman law instruments unless it suited them. Indeed, before the third century we routinely find individuals entitled to use Roman law conducting business according to "Greek" or Hellenistic legal instruments. Although the Romans had developed a refined law of contracts and sat in judgment of provincial contract disputes across the empire, Roman law neither informed nor controlled the vast majority of those contracts, nor did it represent the obvious law of choice in Egypt.[6]

What, then, were "contract" and "contract law" in Roman Egypt? The question seems simple enough but is, in fact, difficult to answer, at least in these terms. As we see from the number and distribution of contracts and the full lexicon of contract vocabulary in the documentary record, contracts were clearly part of everyday life in Roman Egypt.[7] Strikingly, however, amid this

---

2. Cf. the introduction and chapter 9 of this volume.
3. On the legal situation in Roman Egypt, see Mélèze-Modrzejewski 1970; Wolff 2002, Cf. Maehler 2005.
4. Woolf 2002: 122–30 and passim.
5. Generally, Wolff 2002; cf. Beauchamp 2007. For the late influence of Roman law on provincial contracting, see Wolff 1956.
6. Contrast this situation with the role of Roman law in the Sulpicii archive (see the text accompanying n. 33 in this book's introduction).
7. See Wolff 1978. Cf. Mitteis 1912: 72–77; Taubenschlag 1955: 292–303 (which one should use with caution). An impressive demonstration of the place written contracts had in Roman

welter of contracts and terminology, there is no Greek or Egyptian word for "legal obligation" or "liability"[8] nor any regular legal word for "contract" as such, until late antiquity.[9] Nor does there appear to have been much in the way of "contract law," if by that term we mean a systematic body of rules guided by a coherent doctrine defining and governing the formation, execution, and enforcement of promises recognized by the state.[10] We might be tempted to explain the paradox of a society intimately familiar with contracts yet seemingly without a law or even the abstract notion of contract, by noting that our documentary sources are the stuff of daily practice, not philosophical theorizing. This is fair enough; but it also seems to be the case that "contract" in Roman Egypt was radically untheorized and unsystematized in fact, and to this extent, the linguistic remains appear to be an accurate reflection of the rudimentary state of the institution's legal development.

Egypt may be found in the Tebtynis γραφεῖον registers (e.g., *P.Mich.* II 123 recto [45/46]); cf. chaps. 6 [Yiftach] and 7 [Lerouxel] in the present volume.

8. The Greek of the Ptolemaic and Roman periods regularly recognized only the active notion of execution (πρᾶξις), not the passive notion of obligation (cf. Wolff 1946; 1957: 61–62). There was, however, a notion of moral obligation, which one can find attached to contracts. For instance, while the word ἔνοχος (liable) does appear in Roman contracts (e.g., *P.Oxy.* II 275.32 [Oxyrhynchus, 66]), it is primarily associated with moral liability, hence its use in oaths (cf. Seidl 1933: 119–26). The word ἐνοχή only came to mean legal liability as such in the 5th century (cf. Wenger 1906: 262).

9. The words συνάλλαγμα and συμβόλαιον were most commonly used to refer to "contracts" in a generic sense before the fourth century, though usually with respect to a particular document or agreement, not to contract in the abstract (i.e., as distinct from a noncontractual obligation). Συγγραφή only came to mean a contract as such (i.e., regardless of form) quite late, likely influenced by usage elsewhere in the Roman East and by the Romans themselves (Wolff 1978: 139 n. 11; cf. Kunkel 1932: 1384–87). Συνάλλαγμα acquired a technical, legal significance only under the influence of Roman legal theory and education (Seidl 1932; Kaser 1959: 267 n. 34; Kaser 1971: 529–30; Zimmerman 1996: 537 n. 185). It is worth pointing out that the Romans themselves never legally defined *contractus* (Zimmermann 1996: 562).

10. This last statement holds true for the Romans as well: there was no Roman "contract law" but, rather, a Roman "law of contracts" that recognized several different types of contract (*stipulatio, mandatum,* etc.), without an overarching legal definition of contract. See Watson 1991: 122–38; cf. Nicholas 1969: 165–67. The situation was more acute in the case of the received Hellenistic law of Roman Egypt: (1) there were no legal authorities knitting contract law together conceptually, as one sees the jurists doing for Roman contracts with the notions of *obligatio* and *consensus*; (2) no identifiable body of legal specialists was granted authority over the law in Egypt in the manner in which the emperor granted certain jurists the *ius respondendi* in Roman law (although there were local legal authorities of some sort [νομικοί], which we see Roman officials drawing on in trial transcripts); and (3) the theory and decisions of the jurists were applied more or less consistently by virtue of the centralization of legal and political authority in the emperor (i.e., it helped to forge a link between theory and practice), whereas imperial responses to questions generated by the multifarious Hellenistic and local legal practices of the empire were necessarily more ad hoc and marked by explicit concessions to local custom (see, e.g., *CJ* 4.65.19, 293; cf. Kehoe 2007: 119–23).

If there was no contract law per se, there were still, of course, rules governing contracting, some of which were articulated by law. For example, a rule apparently laid down during the Augustan reorganization of the Alexandrian καταλογεῖον or recording office regulated contract penalties in συγχωρήσεις, a contract type descended from a court settlement document and issued only by the καταλογεῖον.[11] Much murkier is our evidence for a "law (νόμος) of deposits," often cited in our contracts, which called for a double penalty for failure to return a deposit. The status of this νόμος has been debated for decades, but we should perhaps see its sudden appearance in the reign of Gaius or Claudius as connected to some official recognition of an older, customary norm.[12] It has also been suggested that changes in the βεβαίωσις clause (the "confirmation clause," or guarantee of enjoyment) protecting lessees in contracts from the Roman era should be connected to a new legal dispensation making such guarantees implicit.[13] More certain are the raft of regulations pertaining directly or indirectly to contracts in the so-called Gnomon of the Idios Logos (*BGU* V 1210), a miscellaneous second-century epitome of administrative rules (many of which go back to the reign of Augustus) controlling the operations of the Idios Logos, the provincial administrative department concerned with confiscations and other fiscal matters.[14] It will come as no surprise to learn that these rules do not speak in terms of contract as such (e.g., offer and acceptance) but instead regulate it more obliquely by controlling specific contractual provisions (e.g., penalties), contract types (e.g., συγχωρήσεις), classes of transactions (e.g., deposits), or property rights (e.g., the alienability of certain types of land).[15]

In Roman Egypt, then, we have contracts without contract, contract rules without contract law. Where does this leave us? The practical effect has been

---

11. On συγχωρήσεις, see Wolff 1978: 91–95. For the law, see Berger 1911: 38–46; cf. Wolff 1978: 28.
12. Kastner 1962. See, most recently, Scheibelreiter 2010. Here the precise juridical nature of the "law" is of less concern than the fact that it clearly acquired some new importance in the Roman era (cf. Scheibelreiter's tentative suggestions on pp. 353 and 373); cf. Jakab 2009: 82–89.
13. Wolff 1946: 63 n. 24; cf. Hermann 1958a: 154–60; Rupprecht 1983: 625.
14. E.g., §§ 1–2 (concerning the alienability of tombs), 65–67 (penalties connected to the improper sale or export of slaves), 70 (restrictions on dealings between public officials and the state; cf. 109–11), 73 (prohibition on second mortgages from temple funds), 78 (priestly offices alienable only by sale, not auction), 100–101 (registration requirements for contracts), 103 (outlawing loans on "liquids"), 104 (prohibition on future sales), 105 (statutory limit on interest rates). On the Idios Logos, see Swarney 1970.
15. Cf. Jakab 2009: 89: "Gesetzliche Regelungen über handelsspezifische Rechtsinstitute bzw. über Haftungsprobleme im Vertragsrecht sind aus der Antike ohnedies kaum bekannt."

to encourage legal positivism, channeling the study of documentary contracts into one of two streams. The widest branch is represented by the study of contracts along ancient definitions, via distinct types (e.g., the ὁμολογία; von Soden 1973) or transactional types (e.g., loans; Rupprecht 1967). Such an approach effectively forecloses the possibility of studying contract as an economic institution in itself by disaggregating it into its various manifestations. Yet the argument for seeing contract whole is implicit in the narrower branch, which contains a few brave attempts, above all by Wolff and Seidl, to reconstruct some foundational principle of contractual liability.[16] Although their theories differ on important points, both scholars concluded that it is essentially anachronistic to speak of contract per se in Ptolemaic and Roman Egypt: these non-Roman law contracts ordered rights based in property, not personal obligation.[17] This conclusion thus paradoxically points to the existence of some general legal concept of contract underpinning practice, even as it ultimately justifies the positivist method and agenda of fragmentation. The scholarship has therefore reified the divide between contracts and contract, in such a way as to make it all but impossible to speak in terms of the latter.

The juristic scholarship on contract is of the highest intellectual rigor and tremendously useful with respect to understanding contract types and typical transactions. Also, if Wolff and Seidl and their followers are correct in seeing property and not personal obligation as the basis of ancient contract, this is an important and profound contribution to ancient history. No economic or legal historian will dispute the importance of the modern legal institution of contract: without a legal theory of personal obligation, promises cannot be made a species of property, which, in turn, forecloses a number of potential transactions.[18] That said, traditional juristic scholarship on ancient contract is also frustrating, in that it does not adequately address the following important questions:

- Why did ancient parties choose to organize certain transactions as contracts and not others?
- How and why did they decide with whom to enter into a contract?

---

16. E.g., Wolff 1957; Seidl 1956: 40–45; Seidl 1962: 113–16. Cf. Rupprecht 1967: 39–63.
17. An "obligation" arose at the moment one party transferred property to the other, not, as in most modern contractual systems, when a promise meeting certain requirements has been made.
18. Cf. Shavell 2004; Posner 2011.

- How did they enforce their contracts, and what did they expect the state to do?

- What pressures and considerations controlled the decision to go to court and seek a ruling versus settling out of court?

Also, while we may concede that there was no sustained legal discourse of contract as such, what about the social discourse of contract? While notaries, officials, and νομικοί (legal experts) might have thought in terms of specific contract types,[19] it seems most unlikely that most parties did, unless the type was legally required or carried with it specific rights or advantages. Instead, the evidence suggests that they thought in terms of transactions ("I want to make a loan"; cf. Wolff 1978: 142); "documents" ("I have the contract right here"); or "contract" in the abstract, whenever the transaction was not a stereotyped one ("We should make this deal into a contract.").[20] If we want to understand why and how parties organized and enforced transactions via contracts in the first place, this nonlegal discourse is significant.

Given the nature of our evidence and the state of the scholarship, our picture of a Roman Egypt of contracts without contract cries out for a new perspective, one able to conceptualize contract as a unified practice, at least to the extent that the parties did, without depending entirely on legal definitions and processes. NIE offers us precisely this perspective, since it asks us to model the complex and dynamic rules and forces embodied in economic institutions by starting from the evidence of actual transactions—to move from economic phenomena to theory, rather than from legal doctrine or

---

19. A telling lack of linguistic stability, which a technical vocabulary of contract would have afforded, is to be found even in official contexts, as in the edict preserved in *P.Oxy.* I 34 verso, col. i.8–11 (Oxyrhynchus, 127): γραμματεῖς . . . κατὰ τὸ π   αλαι[ὸν] ἔθος ἐγλογιζέσ- | θωσαν <u>τὰ συναλλάγματα</u> περιλαμβάνοντ[ες] τά τε τῶν νομογράφων | καὶ τὰ τῶν σ[υνα]λλασσόντων ὀνόματα καὶ τὸν ἀριθμὸν <u>τῶν οἰκονο|μιῶν</u> καὶ [τὰ εἴ]δη <u>τῶν συνβ[ο]λαίων</u> (The scribes shall count up the <u>agreements</u> according to the old custom, including the names of the *nomographoi* and the parties, the number of the <u>documents</u>, and the types of <u>contracts</u>).

20. E.g., *P.Gen.* I² 42 (Philadelphia, 224), an agreement by a group of liturgists to share the financial burden, that is, an idiosyncratic contractual transaction: συνέ|[θε]ντο πρ[ὸ]ς ἑαυτοὺς [πρὸς] σὺν ἀλλήλοις οἱ προγεγρ[α]μμένοι δημόσιοι γεωργοὶ (*sic*) | . . . εἰς τὸ συνμέ|[νειν] πάντ[ε]ς (*l.* πάντας) [καὶ] συνκατάθεσιν πάντες | π[ε]ποιῆσθα[ι ἐ]πὶ . . . (The aforementioned public farmers . . . have come to terms among themselves to the end that all will abide (by the following terms) and make an agreement to . . .). Consider also the charge in *P.Ryl.* II 128 (Euhemeria, post-30) that a party acted wrongly for someone "under contract" (ὑποσύνγραφος). On this term and petition, see Ratzan, forthcoming a.

large-scale sociological models of power to practice. It is, above all, a phenomenological approach to contract, particularly well suited to the opportunity for "thick economic description" presented by papyrological evidence.

One way to conceive of contract as an economic institution is to see it as a "governance structure" (Williamson 1985, 1997), a transactional mode through which certain types of exchanges are organized.[21] Governance structures evolve or are created to deal with the TC associated with exchange. To think in terms of governance structures is to recognize the basic relationship between (i) a specific transactional mode (e.g., the vertically hierarchical structure of a firm; the flat, open, competitive structure of a physical market; or the nexus structure of a contract); (ii) the significant economic properties of the assets being exchanged; and (iii) the specific relationship between the parties. From this perspective, there are two basic, interrelated decisions confronting all potential parties:

a. Shall I transact?
b. If so, what is the best way to structure the transaction?

These questions may be rewritten in terms of TC as follows:

a. Are the TC low enough for me to transact?
b. If so, what are the relative TC associated with proceeding via one governance structure over another?

One immediately appreciates how these questions make the transaction the basic unit of analysis and, thus, prior to a consideration of the law: the law and state enforcement enter the equation only insofar as they affect TC. NIE thus sees the law as vitally important (since it is a major determinant of TC) but relegates it to an instrumental role in supporting exchanges. This shift in focus also encourages us to consider other salient instrumentalities, other rules backed by other powers, which help to control the formation and enforcement of contracts. In this economic perspective, contract thus appears as an integrated set of formal and informal rules, articulated and enforced by

---

21. For a general account of the NIE approach to contract, see Furubotn and Richter 2005: chap. 4; on governance structures, see pp. 180–86.

the parties themselves and various third parties (organizations, the community, and the state), with the aim of organizing sequential (i.e., nonsimultaneous) transactions.

At this point, some readers may object that it was precisely the "decisions" presented above (i.e., to transact or not and, if so, how) that most parties in the Roman world were not "free" to make in any meaningful sense: surely most ancient "contracts" were the product of social power, not negotiation. Moses Finley, for example, believed that most, if not all, contracts simply reinscribed customary power relations as legal relations.[22] Yet how are we to explain centuries of investment in contract by the jurists, the Roman state, and the thousands upon thousands of middling people across the empire? Moreover, what are we to make of the obviously negotiated character of many of the surviving documentary contracts? Dennis Kehoe's recent work (2007 and chapter 9 in the present volume) demonstrates the extent to which Roman law was not merely epiphenomenal to social relations but represented a credible set of rules affecting the Roman economy. Clearly, the law mattered; but just as clearly (as the papyri demonstrate), it was not the only set of rules that did.

We have space here for one example. In *P.Ross.Georg.* III 1 (Alexandria, ca. 270), a certain Markos advises his mother about a forthcoming offer from a certain Apollonios.

> And Apollonios the Blind came to me, saying, "Serapiakos has released the arouras back to your mother." If he has released (them) and you know the character (γνώμη) of this Apollonios the Blind, that he is honorable (εὐγνώμων), (then) lease them to him; if he has not been [εὐγνώμων], try giving him the grain.[23]

Markos tells his mother to consult Apollonios's reputation, in effect suggesting that she do her "due diligence" to find out whether he is εὐγνώμων, or

---

22. Finley [1985] 1999: 95; cf. also Finley's frequent and telling collocation of law and custom (52, 55, 66, 69). His only mentions of private law (40, 92) are to point up, respectively, the oppressive nature of Roman debt law and the socioeconomic insignificance of the disappearance of Roman law leases in the fourth century.

23. Lines 19–23: καὶ ὁ Ἀπολλώνιος ὁ τυφλὸς ἦλθεν πρὸς ἐμαὶ (*l.* ἐμὲ) | λέ[γων μοι ὅ]τι ἐπαφίωκεν (*l.* ἐπαφέωκεν) Σεραπιακὸς τῇ μητρί σου τὰς | ἀλούρ(ας) (*l.* ἀρούρ(ας)). ἐὰ[ν οὖν ἦν(?)] ἐπα[φ]εὶς καὶ εἰδῇς τὴν τοῦ Ἀπολλω[νίου] τούτου τοῦ τυ | φλοῦ γνώμην ὅτι εὐγνώμων ἐστίν, μ[ίσ]θωσον αὐτῷ | αὐτάς, ἐὰν μή σοι ἦν ἐκεῖνος, πειρῇς (presumably for πειρᾶς [present subjunctive]) δοῦσα [τὸ]ν σεῖτον.

the sort of man to abide by a contract or not (Markos clearly had his doubts).[24] The alternatives depending on Apollonios's γνώμη are revealing. If the mother determines that Apollonios is not εὐγνώμων, she should attempt to "give" him the grain instead of leasing him the land. We should take this to mean that she should try to sell him the crop.[25] A sale might be less lucrative than a lease, but it was also less risky: a long-term contract of tenancy (like all sequential, noninstantaneous transactions) presents multiple sources of risk stemming from opportunism and unforeseen circumstances, such as lessee abandonment, late payment, lessee insolvency, poor management and consequent degradation of the land or irrigation canals, poor inundation, and crop failure (cf. Kehoe's discussion in chapter 9). In other words, Markos and his mother can here be seen engaging in a rough cost-benefit analysis of two transactions with different risk profiles, each accommodated by a different governance structure, a lease covered by contract versus what amounts to a cash sale (i.e., a market transaction).[26] Significantly, their analysis at this preliminary stage hinges not on an assessment of the law but, rather, on the "informal" rules of reputation (εὐγνωμωσύνη). These informal rules governing contracting, essentially the institution of reputation, served to lower the search costs imposed by the need to discover reliable information about Apollonios's capacity and willingness to perform, directly analogous to the effect the formal rules of the βιβλιοθήκη ἐγκτήσεων had on credit markets (see Lerouxel's analysis in chapter 7).

To sum up this section, NIE offers a methodological perspective to match both our problem and our evidence, allowing us to escape the analytical tyranny of both ancient and modern categories and to move beyond the search for quasi-essentialist legal "principles" of contract and toward a properly economic analysis of the institution as we find it used by individuals and organizations in the Roman world. Our task now is to find a way of studying contract in Roman Egypt as a governance structure, independent of transaction or contract type. In other words, we need to structure our inquiry so as to isolate contract as a general economic form distinct from the particularities of individual contracts. I believe I have found a useful lens in what I will call

---

24. I explore εὐγνωμωσύνη as a business term in a forthcoming essay.
25. Kiessling, *Wörterbuch*, s.v. δίδωμι (4); cf. the translation of the editio princeps: "so mache den Versuch mit der Veräusserung des Getreides."
26. There was always a market for grain: if Apollonios decided not to buy later, the mother could easily find another buyer.

the "ἀποσπάω clause": its distribution, which cuts across boundaries of local geography, contract type, and transaction type, illuminates the way in which contract as a governance structure organized a particular set of nonsimultaneous transactions in Roman Egypt.

3. The Ἀποσπάω Clause: Definition and Some Hypotheses

In twenty-nine contracts from the first three centuries of Roman Egypt, we find a term by which party A agrees with party B not to remove for a set period from B's effective control a third person, (C), who is legally under A's power (see app. 1; I will refer to contracts with the clause by the number assigned to them there).[27] The clause invariably uses the verb ἀποσπάω and always appears in the penalty section of the document, as in, for example, καὶ μὴ [ἀ-]|ποσπάσειν τὸ παιδίον ἐντὸς τοῦ χρόνου ἢ κα[ὶ αὐ]|τὸν ἐκτίνειν τὸ ἴσον ἐπίτιμον (no. 1, a wet-nursing συγχώρησις from Alexandria, 13 B.C.E.), which translates as "and (the owner agrees) that (he) will not take away the slave child during the term (of the contract) or (if he does) he will himself pay an equal fine.") In all cases, A is a relative, guardian, or owner of C, who is a minor son, daughter, ward, or slave. The occupation and status of B varies: he or she may be a wet nurse, master craftsman, creditor, or (for lack of a better term) employer who wishes to have C under his or her control for a definite period and must therefore get A to agree to forbear from exercising his or her right of repossession for that period. The clause thus appears in contracts that have usually been studied separately according to transaction, that is, wet-nursing contracts, apprenticeship contracts, labor contracts, slave leases, and the παραμονή of minors (loan contracts in which the interest and/or the principal is repaid in labor by a person who promises to "abide by" [παραμένειν] the employer/creditor).[28]

The ἀποσπάω clause is a species of what we may call a "withdrawal clause," variations of which are found in an even wider variety of labor and

---

27. After the late fourth century, one finds similar clauses but different language: see, e.g., Stud.Pal. XX 219.28–35 (Arsinoë, 604); cf. Jördens 1990: 160–61.

28. See Hengstl 1972, a synoptic study from a juristic point of view (cf. Jördens 1990 for the Byzantine era); Rupprecht 1994: 124–26, to which add Bergamasco 1995. The discussion of Jördens 1990: 284–95 on the reality and usefulness of παραμονή as a distinct type of contractual transaction is particularly trenchant; for our purposes here, however, it is probably best to continue to use the term, as it is so embedded in the literature.

lease contracts. Withdrawal clauses specifically subject the unilateral withdrawal of one party from the contract to a penalty, where specific expressions (e.g., εἰ μὴ παραμένω or εἰ ἀπαλάσσω/ἐκλείπω/ἀφίστημι) describe the act of self-withdrawal by the laborer or lessee from the contract. Legally (if not always in fact), a person in Roman Egypt was always free to leave a service contract; hence there was a need to penalize withdrawal.[29] The same held true for dependents one temporarily disposed of through contract: so long as one did not sell the dependent, one retained the right to remove him or her at will. The difference between the clauses is thus rooted in status—namely, whether the party contractually disposed was legally capable of self-withdrawal or lacked legal personality, in which case "withdrawal" was framed as "repossession" by the responsible party.

From the widest perspective, all of these "employment" contracts may be seen as species of μίσθωσις, or "lease": all involve A "leasing" C to B, with the difference being the identity of C (e.g., in a labor contract, C = A, i.e., party A agrees to do a specific task for party B and not to withdraw himself until his obligation to B is fulfilled, subject to a penalty).[30] Crucially, it was not inherent in the concept of μίσθωσις that the lessee was automatically protected from eviction: such protection either had to be specified by contract or specifically implied by law, as may have become the case with land leases in the second century (cf. the discussion of the βεβαίωσις clause in section 2 above). The ἀποσπάω clause—and most withdrawal clauses—were therefore nothing more than specialized guarantees for the "lessee."[31]

A quick glance at the table in appendix 1 shows that the clause was found in all parts of Egypt and in several different types of contracts and transactions. From this, we may conclude that right of repossession, which the ἀποσπάω clause sought to control, was recognized throughout Roman Egypt and that the clause itself was not an idiosyncratic feature of any particular transaction type, contract type, or local scribal formulary. Indeed, we may say that the repossession of a dependent appears to have been a fundamental property right in the province and therefore a potential stumbling block to all nonsimultaneous transactions capable of being framed as the

---

29. Cf. Hengstl 1972: 104–5.
30. Hengstl 1972: 120–24; Manca Masciardi and Montevecchi 1984: 29 n. 80; cf. Rupprecht 1994: 122–24. In the Byzantine era, the language of leasing free humans was finally embraced. See, e.g., Stud.Pal. XX 219 (Arsinoë, 604); SB I 4490 (Arsinoë, 641 or 656). Cf. Montevecchi 1950: 7; Jördens 1990: 149–51, 157–59, esp. 165–67.
31. Cf. Jördens 1990: 160–61.

μίσθωσις of a dependent. We have thus succeeded in isolating a specific structural problem in the institutional landscape of Roman Egypt that appears to have been regularly solved by contract, regardless of contract or transaction type.

If we conceive of this structural problem in terms of TC, the right of repossession presented a definite possibility of *ex post* opportunism by *A*; that is, once *A* had extracted his value from the exchange, he might either exercise his right to remove *C* or attempt to "hold up" *B* for additional value. This possibility obviously depended on *A*'s ability to make a credible threat to exercise his right, a point to which I will return in section 6. Assuming, for the moment, that his threat was credible, the TC associated with this risk had to be mitigated at the outset in order for *B* to proceed. *B*'s basic options were therefore to design a transaction with greater simultaneity—that is, one in which he got his value out of the bargain sooner[32]—or to draft a contract with an equally credible penalty for *A*'s act of repossession. That contracts with the ἀποσπάω clause were regularly written suggests (a) that the risk of repossession was considered real and (b) that the costs of mitigating that risk via a (written) contract (i.e., the TC associated with this solution) were perceived to be sufficiently low for *B* to proceed.[33]

Since the transaction types in which the ἀποσπάω clause appears have been extensively studied, we are now in the position to make concrete hypotheses about the distribution of this clause vis-à-vis the relative bargaining power of the parties (see table 8.1 below). In the μίσθωσις paradigm, the parties in a wet-nursing contract are the parent/owner (the lessor, *A*), the child (the object leased, *C*), and the nurse (the lessee, *B*).[34] Although it is more natural for us to think of the parent/owner as "employing" the nurse, these contracts were structured as μισθώσεις in which the nurse "leased" the child. Furthermore, in the Roman period, the nurslings were typically slaves, and the nurses free women of lower socioeconomic status than the owners, who appear to be raising foundlings—perhaps, in some cases, for sale.[35] Since women need to nurse continuously to maintain their milk supply, nurses

32. Cf. Kronman 1985.
33. Cf. Lerouxel's analysis in chapter 7 of the present volume.
34. For these contracts, see Manca Masciardi and Montevecchi 1984.
35. There is a debate about the origin of the slaves. Manca Masciadri and Montevecchi 1982 suggested that most of the "foundlings" were the children of the nurses, who either sold them or put them up as collateral for cash advances when under economic duress. See, however, Bagnall 1997.

should have preferred, on balance, to have had their access to their infant charges guaranteed for the duration of the contract (typically two years); otherwise, they literally risked having this revenue stream dry up. The slave owner, however, had every reason to retain his right of repossession. Moreover, these contracts typically have the nurse assume the exposed legal position of a "Persian" (a legal fiction, inherited from the Ptolemaic period, by which one agreed to be held liable for personal execution in the event of default), by advancing part of her wages up front. The wet nurses of Roman Egypt thus often found themselves at a double disadvantage: not only did their employers enjoy a stronger initial legal position, as owners invested with the right of repossession, but they were also almost always socioeconomically superior, a position they translated into further legal power by framing the contract as a species of loan guaranteed by personal execution. We should therefore hypothesize that owners would usually attempt to write contracts without the ἀποσπάω clause and that they would be successful in doing so most of the time.

Most labor contracts[36] were also concluded between people of unequal socioeconomic power. Again, as with wet-nursing contracts, many labor contracts were framed as loans, some of which had the interest or principal paid off by personal services. Therefore, in the μίσθωσις paradigm, the parent/guardian/debtor is A, the dependent/laborer is C, and the employer/creditor is B. In these transactions, we should expect the clause to appear regularly, by virtue of the socioeconomic leverage the employer/creditor (B) could exert. In other words, if slave owners would do their best to keep the clause out of wet-nursing contracts, the equally powerful employer/creditors (essentially drawing from the same population) would naturally attempt to have the clause inserted.

Finally, apprenticeship contracts[37] were drawn up because a master craftsman (B) needed to protect his investment in training by ensuring that his apprentice (C) stayed for a full term: only toward the end of the contract did the craftsman recoup his investment and gain the benefit of the apprentice's skilled labor. It also therefore made little sense for a master to pay out an advance. Of course, he might get an apprentice cheaply if he was in a position to make a loan and negotiate what was, in effect, a παραμονή contract.

---

36. For simplicity's sake, I lump together various types of employment contracts. See Hengstl 1972, §§ 4–7; Jördens 1990. Cf. Rupprecht 1994: 124–27.
37. See Bergamasco 1995.

In such cases, we might imagine that he would seek to insert an ἀποσπάω clause and would generally succeed in doing so. Yet, absent financial need on one side or sufficient liquidity to make a loan on the other, we cannot form any hypothesis about these transactions. Basic socioeconomic equality—the elite did not apprentice their offspring to artisans—meant that craftsmen (B) would attempt to insert the clause, while families (A) would attempt to preserve the right or to make the craftsmen pay for their forbearance. Who won the battle turned on the particular circumstances of the parties, not the structural features of the apprenticeship transaction.

Table 8.1 sums up the relative power relations in the transactions discussed above and their hypothetical effects on the inclusion of the ἀποσπάω clause. What makes this clause and the property right it negotiated an elegant test of contract as an institution is not only its geographical ubiquity and independence of transaction and contractual type but also the fact that the contracts in which it appeared do not all embody the same set of socioeconomic power relations. In other words, the structural elements of the underlying transactions meant that the right of repossession resided sometimes with the stronger party and sometimes with the weaker, while it seems likely that there were still other times when it was actively negotiated by parties who confronted each other as equals. These hypotheses also establish an interpretive agenda. If, on the one hand, the clause appears in a wet-nursing contract, we should wonder why. On the other hand, we should be surprised to find it missing from a labor contract and consider the possible reasons as to why it was omitted. The general proposition is that this clause affords us a glimpse into the way in which the institution of contract worked to specify

Table 8.1. Typical relative bargaining power by transaction and hypothesized frequency of the ἀποσπάω clause

	Stronger party	Weaker party	Right of repossession with stronger party	Hypothesized frequency of ἀποσπάω clause
Wet-nursing	slave owner/ parent (A)	wet nurse (B)	Yes	Low
Paramonē/labor	creditor/ employer (B)	debtor/worker (A)	No	High
Apprenticeship	parent (A) or artisan (B)	parent (A) or artisan (B)	?	?

and negotiate a particular property right—namely, that of ἀποσπασμός—by mitigating the TC associated with the transactions for which this right represented a source of "expensive" uncertainty.[38]

4. The Ἀποσπάω Clause: Distribution

The conspectus in appendices 2 and 3 (cf. table 8.2 below) shows clearly that the presence of the clause was a function of not one factor but three: geography, transaction type, and contract type. In the first instance (app. 2), the clause appears in nearly all the relevant contracts from the provincial capital of Alexandria (7 of 8), but it occurs much less frequently in those from the two nomes, or administrative regions, up the Nile, from which most of our documentary evidence survives—46 percent for the Oxyrhynchite (11 of 24) and just 21 percent for the Arsinoite (5 of 24). If we compare the Arsinoite to the Oxyrhynchite directly, we discover a regional subpattern in which transaction type becomes important: both nomes show a strong bias against including the clause in wet-nursing contracts (none in 13 examples)[39] yet diverge with respect to apprenticeship contracts: 10 out of 16 (62.5 percent) of the latter from the Oxyrhynchite show the clause, compared to just 3 out of 12 (25 percent) of such contracts from the Arsinoite.

A third pattern emerges if we turn, finally, to consider document type, "public" versus "private" (app. 3). A public document is any form of document issued and registered by a notarial office.[40] Public documents are distinguished by certain formal hallmarks: for example, they tend to be drafted objectively and dated in particular ways, whereas private documents, like the cheirograph and the so-called "private protocol," are more fluid in form. Private documents could be (and doubtless sometimes were) drawn up privately by the parties themselves or their agents, whereas public documents were drafted in the various notarial offices of the villages, nome capitals (metropoleis), or Greek poleis of Egypt (Alexandria, Naukratis, Ptolemais, and, later, Antinoöpolis). Legally, both types seem to have been equally admissible in court; that is, public documents were (theoretically) not of greater

---

38. Ἀποσπασμός is attested once in the Roman period, in P.Fam.Tebt. 37 (Antioöpolis, 167).
39. We may contrast this with an inclusion rate of 6 out of 7 (86 percent) of wet-nursing contracts from Alexandria.
40. See Wolff 1978; cf. Rupprecht 1994: 135–43 for more recent literature.

probative value for being public.[41] When it came to the transactions for which the right of repossession was at issue, the substantive difference between these two broad categories lay in the act of registration: public documents were registered at the time of execution, and for this (and drafting), the notaries charged a fee (see the discussions by Yiftach and Lerouxel in chapters 6 and 7 of this volume). An important consequence was that private documents were, on average, cheaper in the first instance (e.g., one could subsequently opt to publicize a claim based in a private document by paying a fee, a process known as δημοσίωσις).[42]

The table in appendix 3 illuminates the importance of this third variable, document type. Wet-nursing contracts are overwhelmingly likely to be public, regardless of region (19 to 1), but they only include the clause in Alexandria. Apprenticeship contracts show no such uniformity: in the Arsinoite, they are more likely to be public (9 to 3, or 25 percent private) and to omit the clause (12 to 3, or 25 percent inclusion); in the Oxyrhynchite, they are all private (16 to none) and tend to include the clause (10 of 16, or 63 percent). The pool of labor contracts with the clause is too small to yield a clear pattern.

Table 8.2 represents the actual distribution of the clause. How can we explain this distribution, particularly as it runs counter to some of the hypotheses articulated in section 3? For instance, why was the clause prevalent in Alexandria regardless of transaction type, when it was strongly correlated with transaction type in the other two regions? Again, why were master craftsmen in the Oxyrhynchite so successful in drafting the clause into their apprenticeship contracts, when those in the Arsinoite apparently were not? That this latter difference is also mirrored by one of type (i.e., wet-nursing contracts in both regions are overwhelmingly public, while Arsinoite apprenticeship contracts are primarily public in the Arsinoite and all private in the Oxyrhynchite) suggests that type might also have been a significant factor, at least outside of Alexandria. The orthodoxy as to why people in Roman Egypt

---

41. Wolff 1978: 177–80. This equality, however, was not always understood or trusted by parties; cf. n. 42.

42. See Lerouxel's discussion in chapter 7 of TC and public and private documents in the credit market of Roman Egypt. Public documents and/or registration were required for certain transactions and enforcement procedures (Wolff 1978: 110–14, 174–75; cf. Yiftach-Firanko 2009). On δημοσίωσις and allied procedures, see Wolff 1978: 129–35. We have circumstantial evidence of ancient parties "free riding" by only paying part of the full fare for registration (contracts left partially unexecuted in notary offices, fees unpaid, complaints by officials about this, etc.), which suggests that they were sensitive to price in this regard; see Browne 1974.

preferred one contract type to another is that it was merely a matter of habit, tempered by limitations of access to legal services and/or sensitivity to cost.[43] The pattern identified above, however, seems to show that private forms could correlate, at least in this instance, with more balanced, bilateral (i.e., negotiated) contracts with the clause.

Table 8.2. Distribution of the ἀποσπάω clause by transaction, region, and document type (public or private)

Transaction	Alexandria	Oxyrhynchite	Arsinoite
Wet-nursing	Total: 7 Pub: 100% (7) A: 86% (6)	Total: 6 Pub: 83% (5) A: 0% (0)	Total: 7 Pub: 100% (7) A: 0% (0)
Apprenticeship	Total: 1 Pub: 100% (1) A: 100% (1)	Total: 16 Pub: 0% (0) A: 63% (10)	Total: 12 Pub: 75% (9) A: 25% (3)

Note: A = the inclusion rate for the ἀποσπάω clause; Pub = public contract.

5. Analysis of the Ἀποσπάω Clause Distribution

There is no space here for a systematic exploration of the data collected in the appendixes. I will therefore concentrate on just two aspects of the distribution described in section 4, the wet-nursing contracts and apprenticeship contracts from Middle Egypt.

5.1. Wet-Nursing Contracts in the Arsinoite and Oxyrhynchite Nomes

As we now see, wet-nursing contracts in both the Arsinoite and the Oxyrhynchite nomes were typically recorded in public instruments, and the majority related to the nursing of slaves. Although there are numerous attestations, documents, and contracts related to wet-nursing in Roman Egypt, only

---

43. Cf. Wolff 1978: 137. Three factors worked to make parties conscious of form: (1) state requirements: some forms were mandatory for certain transactions, e.g., notarial documents for land sales and cessions (cf. Wolff 1978: 174–75); (2) an evident tendency to infer from the state's practices that notarial forms were more protected than private forms, even when the latter were registered (see, e.g., *BGU* I 50 [cf. Wolff 1978: 177–79 with n. 35]; *P.Hamb.* I 70 [cf. Wolff 1978: 162–64]); and (3) cost: private forms were, ceteris paribus, cheaper (as discussed above).

four complete contracts survive, two from each region: *SB* XII 11248 (= *C.Pap. Gr.* I 7, 8 BCE) and *P.Bour.* 14 (= *C.Pap.Gr.* I 28, 126 CE), both from Ptolemais Euergetis, the nome capital of the Arsinoite; and *SB* V 7619 (= *C.Pap.Gr.* I 14, 26 CE) and *PSI* III 203 (= *C.Pap.Gr.* I 24, 87 CE) from Oxyrhynchus, the capital of its eponymous nome. The fragmentary contracts suggest that these four are typical for each region and period. No contract, fragmentary or complete, has the ἀποσπάω clause, in striking contrast to their Alexandrian counterparts.

The most significant difference between the Arsinoite and the Oxyrhynchite wet-nursing contracts lies in the absence of the ἀθάνατος clause, or "immortality clause," in the latter.[44] This clause, familiar from animal leases, obliges the lessee to guarantee the number, as opposed to the identity, of the animals or children leased (i.e., the nurse agrees to return *a* baby, not *the* baby given to her; hence the child is "immortal," and the nurse bears the risk of infant mortality).[45] Whereas the Arsinoite contracts typically end with penalty clauses concerning the standards of care and the distribution of the mortality risk via the ἀθάνατος clause, the Oxyrhynchite contracts instead contain an "option clause," by which the owner reserves the right to place another child with the wet nurse on the same terms for the balance of the contract. If the nurse refused, she owed back any unearned wages she had accepted.[46] In the Oxyrhynchite, then, the owners bore the risk of infant mortality (i.e., the nurse's earned wages were a dead loss to the owner if she decided to not exercise the option of nursing a new child).[47] Also interesting for our purposes is the inclusion, in both regions, of an ἀπορρίπτω/προσρίπτω clause, whereby the nurse agrees not to "throw out" or "expel" the child.[48] So

44. For the typical terms of these contracts, see Manca Masciardi and Montevecchi 1984.
45. Hengstl 1979; Manca Masciardi and Montevecchi 1984: 27–29.
46. *C.Pap.Gr.* I 14.21–25: ἐὰν μὴ (*l.* μὲν) τι πάθη ἀνθρώπινον, ὃ καὶ συνφανὲ[ς γέν]ηται, Ι[ἡ ὁμ]ολογοῦσα ἀνέγκλητος ἔστω, ἐὰν μὲν αἱρῆται ὁ Πα<ᾶ>πις ἕτερον Ι [αὐτῆι] ἐγχειρεῖ<ν> σωμάτιον, καὶ τοῦτο θρέψει ἐπὶ τὸν ἐνλείψοντα χρόνον Ι [ἐ]πὶ τοῖς προκειμένοις, ἐὰν δὲ μὴ βούληται τοῦτο ποῆσαι, ἀποδώσει αὐτῶι, Ι [ὃ] ἐὰν φανῇ ὀφείλουσα πρὸς ὃν οὐδέπωι τετρόφευκεν χρόνον (If [the slave child] dies, and the reason is clear, the contracting party will not be called to account. If Paapis [the owner] wishes to entrust to her another slave child, she will raise this one for the balance of the contract on the aforementioned terms; but if she does not wish to do so, she will repay to him [Paapis] whatever she appears to owe with respect to the time she has not spent nursing).
47. Hengstl (1979: 237) posits that employers throughout Roman Egypt could opt to insert an option clause or an ἀθάνατος clause. The ἀθάνατος clause, however, never appears in Oxyrhynchite leases of any sort, and the Oxyrhynchite clauses of equivalent function that Hengstl identifies do not appear in wet-nursing contracts from the nome. Hengstl's reconstruction thus merges two different actual traditions concerning liability into an artificial choice with respect to some ideal type of wet-nursing contract.
48. E.g., *C.Pap.Gr.* I 24.7–8 (Oxyrhynchus, 87); *C.Pap.Gr.* I 28.17–19 (Ptolemais Euergetis, 127);

far as we can tell, then, outside of Alexandria, the contract period was typically never protected on the nurse's part by an ἀποσπάω clause, while the
owner was often protected by an ἀπορρίπτω/προσρίπτω clause. The socioeconomic dynamics of wet-nursing slaves evidently suggested the animal
lease as the most relevant template for drafting wet-nursing contracts (as we
may see from the ἀθάνατος clause), and so, legally, the nurse "leased" the
slave, just as a contract shepherd might a flock; and she did not have the bargaining power to include an express protection of term in the contract, while
the owner could include such protection without having to guarantee the
term of the lease.[49]

Because of imbalances like the one above, these contracts have been seen
as exploitative, and in this respect, the expectations articulated in section 3
vis-à-vis wet-nursing have been fulfilled, at least for contracts outside
Alexandria:[50] the owners translated their socioeconomic position into legal
advantage by drafting boilerplate public documents adapted from animal
leases. There is some negotiation over price, as one finds various rates of pay
and different schedules of advances versus installments, but the contracts
show virtually no negotiation of legal terms, rights, or responsibilities. This
outcome was, in some sense, predictable; but are we to take from this that
wet-nursing contracts were simply legal expressions of exploitative social
power? Or do they have something further to tell us about the economics of
free labor in the ancient world?

Consider contract no. 5, an Alexandrian συγχώρησις of the Augustan period, in which a female Alexandrian citizen (Thermoutharion) engages the
slave of a Roman citizen (Gaius Ignatius Maximus) to nurse the child of her
seemingly incapacitated freedwoman. The child will be cared for in Ignatius's house, and the nurse is required to visit Thermoutharion regularly to
submit the child to inspection. We thus see a clearly exceptional situation
(e.g., the child is not a slave) shoehorned into a run-of-the-mill wet-nursing

---

cf. *P.Amst.* I 41.14–15 (a sheep and goat lease from Ptolemais Euergetis, 8 B.C.E.).
49. Cf. Manca Masciardi and Montevecchi 1984: 29–30; Montececchi 1950: 48.
50. The Alexandrian contracts point to a significant departure from our hypothesis: as noted
in section 4, Alexandrian wet-nursing contracts uniformly include the ἀποσπάω clause.
Alexandrian συγχωρήσεις appear generally balanced in penalty clauses and protections,
which is to say that we typically find unilateral withdrawal penalized on both sides, regardless of transaction and presumed differences in bargaining power. In fact, we see this
in our own wet-nursing cross section. For example, in nos. 1 and 4, the slave owners are
Roman citizens, a sign of power and privilege in Augustan Alexandria; even so, both contracts contain the clause. Its inclusion in the relevant contracts is therefore unexception-
able; *BGU* IV 1058 (= *C. Pap. Gr.* I 4), the one exception, requires explanation.

206 LAW AND TRANSACTION COSTS IN THE ANCIENT ECONOMY

contract, all the more strikingly as Ignatius certainly would have had more claim to repossess his slave (the nurse) in a slave lease than Thermoutharion did her freedwoman's child in this contract. It is particularly interesting for us that the principals were of equal status and that Ignatius, despite receiving a portion of his slave's wages up front, did not (unlike most nurses under contract) assume the demeaning status of "Persian" (cf. p. 199 above). So why did they write a wet-nursing contract instead of a slave lease?

The location of the nursing seems to have been decisive: Thermoutharion temporarily gave up possession of the child in order to have it nursed, while Ignatius remained in control of his slave; hence the deal was framed as a wet-nursing agreement instead of a slave lease. We see the same defining importance of place in παραμονή contracts, where the debtor/worker specifically agrees to "abide by" the creditor/employer. The logic of μίσθωσις turned on the temporary separation of ownership and physical possession, and so the logistics of possession appear to have dictated the particular form of the contract. This suggests that the question we need to ask is, why was the boy, who was free, transferred to Ignatius's house? Why would Thermoutharion not have the nurse move in with her, keeping the boy with his ailing mother and eliminating the need for inspection visits?

The monolithic consistency of the Roman wet-nursing contracts produces an air of inevitability that defies analysis: the nurslings always live with the nurses. The possibility of analysis only opens up when one begins to think in terms of the definite aspects of the transaction and how else one might have structured it. What other possible routes to contract were there? Slave leases (cf. no. 26 and *P.Wisc.* I 5 [Oxyrhynchus, 186]), παραμονή contracts, and nonparamonal employment contracts are all attested forms of μίσθωσις for personal services, but, so far as I know, there is no published example in which the service rendered is wet-nursing. That is, there is no extant contract in which a nurse, in effect, leases herself, as she would do in the other contracts just mentioned, and moves in with the parent/owner, even though this was legally possible.[51] Why should it have been that the children were always placed with nurses rather than the other way around?

It was, no doubt, cheaper to have the nurse stay in her own home, where

---

51. The exception is *C.Pap.Gr.* I 1, our sole surviving Ptolemaic wet-nursing contract. However, this contract is entirely Egyptian in legal conception and language (it is written in demotic), and it is the only contract we have for the nursing of a free child in his own home. We might well wonder what sort of contract Thermoutharion would have written to nurse her own child.

she maintained herself, but we should note that these savings came at a definite price: it made monitoring performance much more difficult (i.e., a version of the agency problem), a fact reflected in the body of wet-nursing contracts, which consist largely of very specific and intrusive stipulations of care (typical requirements included nursing with only one's own, unadulterated milk; not having sex; not getting pregnant; not nursing other children; and taking all due care of one's self and the child—see Manca Masciardi and Montevecchi 1984: 22–25). Thus, the normal wet-nursing contract appears to have had higher TC with respect to the cost of monitoring than other possible contractual arrangements, and monitoring performance was clearly central to these transactions, as we may see from the contracts themselves. Then again, we should imagine that the introduction of a new personality into the home, specifically one over which the owner would have had less than full control—indeed only contractual control—created a significant amount of discomfort and uncertainty, whether it was a slave who had another master, a free woman lodging for a limited time as a paramonal servant, or (worse still?) a free employee. A modern analogy is, to my mind, useful here: my wife and I opted for day care over a nanny for our children precisely because we were uncomfortable being employers in our own home; no mere contract was capable of reducing what we perceived (intuitively) to be the comparatively higher TC associated with recruiting, monitoring, managing, and retaining a reliable person.

My suggestion, therefore, is that we see ancient wet-nursing contracts not as merely the products of status as is usually conceived but, rather, at least partly as the products of the economics of status: they reflect a decision by the employer based on the perceived relative costs of bringing a nurse into the employer's home versus placing a child in the nurse's home. Both scenarios were possible to arrange via contract, so the significance of the lopsided contracts of adhesion we have lies not so much in what they tell us about the exploitation of free workers as in what they tell us about the TC associated with the freedom that kept those workers out of employers' homes (or perhaps even the nurses's power to preserve their freedom and stay in their own homes, avoiding παραμονή arrangments). This conclusion is brought home most forcibly by observing that the one attested transactional alternative to the standard wet-nursing contract was the outright purchase of the nurse herself with the infant slave, a case of ancient "hierarichal integration."[52] It

---

52. E.g., *C. Pap.Gr.* I 4. Cf. Manca Masciardi and Montevecchi 1984: 60; Straus 2004: 267–68,

also pays to bear in mind that whatever the starting positions of the parties, the nurse would be inclined to accept any contract that left her indifferent (in economic terms) between getting the job or not. In other words, these contracts were not signed under duress (other than financial) and were clearly "good enough" for the nurses as written.

5.2. Apprenticeship Contracts in the Arsinoite and Oxyrhynchite Nomes

The majority of apprenticeship contracts in both the Arsinoite and the Oxyrhynchite nomes involve weavers, but, as noted in section 4, we find a sharp difference in type and drafting.[53] The Arsinoite apprenticeship contracts, like the wet-nursing contracts, tended to be public instruments without the ἀποσπάω clause; in the Oxyrhynchite, however, apprenticeship contracts were drafted as private contracts with the clause (see app. 3). Nearly all the Oxyrhynchite contracts come from Oxyrhynchus itself, the nome *metropolis*; and before the third century, nearly all are drafted by fathers for their free sons. In several cases, the fathers are themselves weavers.[54] Looking at the Oxyrhynchite contracts as a body, one thus receives the impression of a well-knit and hierarchically flat community of artisans apprenticing their adolescent sons to each other to get them out of the house, teach them different skills, and create or cement bonds between families.[55] The contracts from the Arsinoite, in contrast, are geographically diffuse, hailing from all corners of the nome except the region's *metropolis*, Ptolemais Euergetis. They are also more likely to be drafted by women for their sons or by owners for their slaves. Finally, all three instances in which parents or guardians in apprenticeship contracts are figured as "Persians" (i.e., debtors, see p. 199 above) come from the Arsinoite.[56] Weavers there certainly were in the Fayyum, but no community of weavers emerges from our documents. This is, of course, at least partly a function of survival, and I look forward to the day when an apprenticeship contract from Ptolemais Euergetis is published, so that we might

---

272–74.

53. See the useful conspectus in Bergamasco 1995: 162–67 (n.b., it contains a few errors).
54. Cf. Bergamasco 1995: 112.
55. Cf. Bergamasco 1995: 150–61, esp. 151.
56. Bergamasco 1995: 111–12; cf. *P.Tebt.* II 385 (Tebtynis, 117).

compare it to those from Oxyrhynchus. In the meantime, it is worth noting that Oxyrhynchus might have constituted a special case: one document suggests that textile production in Oxyrhynchus was quite large; so there might have been a comparatively large body of weavers in the city.[57]

It seems implausible that one could not draft a public apprenticeship contract in Oxyrhynchus: why should this be the case? Whatever might have been the γραφεῖον template, it was not set in stone: for example, no. 26 is a public Oxyrhynchite παραμονή contract that includes the clause. No doubt, the clause could have been included in public apprenticeship contracts had the parties wished. Yet the weavers of Oxyrhynchus did not take this route, and the pattern is too distinct to represent anything other than a choice, especially since wet-nursing contracts from the region are nearly all public (cf. table 8.2 above). The full significance of the choice is unrecoverable, but reading it against the likely socioeconomic background of the contracts suggests a possible answer. The existence of the written contracts shows that the stakes were too high for both parties merely to shake hands: there needed to be a document. But did it need to be registered? What if these private documents represented a backstop for contracts that relied on social pressure for enforcement in the first instance, with individuals leveraging the critical mass of the community in support of their agreements? Membership in the same occupational and social circles may have allowed the weavers of Oxyrhynchus to opt out of relatively more expensive public forms in favor of cheaper, but still legally defensible, private forms.[58] In this scenario, the choice of form and the fact of idiosyncratic content, like the ἀποσπάω clause, were the products of social equality and community enforcement; yet the ability to put these two factors to work efficiently rested at least partly on the state's ultimate promise to enforce written agreements.[59]

The clause disappears from Oxyrhynchite apprenticeship contracts over the course of the second century. Simultaneously, apprenticeship contracts

57. Van Minnen 1986; cf. Bagnall 1995: 80–81.
58. Cf. chapter 7 in this volume, where Lerouxel discusses what he calls "type 1" TC (including drafting and registration) and why certain parties voluntarily bore higher type 1 TC in order to lower enforcement costs associated with default. In this case, I argue the contrapositive: personal and community enforcement were strong enough here to allow parties to save on type I TC.
59. Cf. Terpstra 2013 and the section of the introduction to the present volume, "Transaction Costs and Ancient Law."

grow in duration from about two years to three to five years, usually with a schedule of increasing wages for the apprentice.[60] Most scholars have sought to explain the tiering of wages in apprenticeship generally as the result of negotiations around the increasing economic worth of the apprentice over time.[61] This, however, ignores the fact that tiering is only seen in apprenticeship contracts without the ἀποσπάω clause—not only in the Oxyrhynchite, where longer terms and tiering appear to supplant the clause, but also in the earlier and shorter contracts from the Arsinoite, where the ἀποσπάω clause is rarely attested at all. Perhaps a better explanation of this pattern is to be had in seeing tiered contracts as an alternative response to the possibility of repossession, by incentivizing forbearance, using carrots instead of sticks. In the Arsinoite, which had a weak tradition of the ἀποσπάω clause, this strategy arose early, as masters sought a way to keep the apprentice through the later, more profitable stages of the contract if they could not bind the parent/ guardian as a debtor (recall, from the discussion above, that this is the region from which the only apprenticeship-cum-debt contracts, in which parents or guardians are perceived as "Persians," survive). In the Oxyrhynchite, in comparison, it seems that the socioeconomic circumstances of the (perhaps more concentrated or organized?) weaving industry changed over the second and third centuries such that masters sought increasingly longer terms.[62] Parent-guardians, however, were likely to have been uncomfortable conceding the right to retrieve their children for such long periods (an ancient family's fortunes could change a great deal in five years). Therefore, one side gave on length, while the other gave on the ἀποσπάω clause, with the two compromising on an incentive approach.

Such an interpretation also makes some sense of a notable outlier. Of the third-century contracts from Oxyrhynchus, only no. 28 includes the ἀποσπάω clause. In this contract, Polydeukes places his daughter Aphrodite with the master weaver (ἰστωνάρχης) Thonis for four years. Instead of the usual graduated scale of wages, Polydeukes receives lodging and maintenance for his child (unusual for this period), as well as a lump sum of four hundred drachmas "in advance because of his need" (18–19: ἐν προχρείᾳ εἰς

---

60. E.g., *P.Oxy.* XIV 1647 (late II, missing end), XLI 2977 (239–40), XXXI 2586 (264); cf. *P.Oxy.* XXXVIII 2875 (early III, dealing not with weaving but with house building). Cf. Bergamasco 1995: 157–61. This same period witnesses the clause's first appearance in Arsinoite apprenticeship contracts, in nos. 20 and 22.
61. Bergamasco 1995: 144–47, 157–61. Cf. Westermann 1911: 311; Hermann 1958b: 122–24.
62. Bergamasco 1995: 156–61, following Wipszycka 1965.

ἀναγκαί[ας] | αὐτοῦ χρείας), to be repaid without interest at the end of the term. Polydeukes also promises to have his daughter "abide by" Thonis day and night, agreeing not to "repossess" her until he has repaid the advance.[63] Bergamasco has recently argued that the advance should be seen not as a loan grafting a paramonal relationship onto the apprenticeship but, rather, as a security deposit, which he believes was a regular feature in this period; he points to an identical sum stipulated in a similar clause in *P.Oxy.* XXXI 2586 (264).[64] This latter contract, however, has a graduated scale of wages over five years, with the father bearing the cost of maintenance and with no requirement for the apprentice to stay the night. It also differs from no. 28 in that there is significant vacation time designated for the apprentice (who is male). Finally, as in all other third-century contracts (except no. 28), there is no ἀποσπάω clause in *P.Oxy.* XXXI 2586. As we see from table 8.3, there was little point in stressing the return of the advance in *P.Oxy.* XXXI 2586: the value of the wages the Hermias receives in year 4 of this contract is equal to 684 drachmas; repayment was thus unlikely to be a problem in year 5, since it was worth 912 drachmas, or more than twice the advance sum of 400 drachmas. Whether or not this προχρεία was, as Bergamasco suggests, a standard advance, in the context of no. 28, it became, for all intents and purposes, a παραμονή loan, "with the father in effect sending his daughter to work for the weaver as security for [its] repayment."[65]

More orthodox is Bergamasco's argument that the trade of maintenance for wages was a fair one (2004: 36): indeed, no. 28 states explicitly that Aphrodite is maintained ἀντὶ μισθῶν (15). We may test this assertion with Rathbone's proxy for the cost of maintenance in his calculation of a living wage for the mid-third century, which comes to 420 drachmas per annum (1991: 165). Of this sum, one hundred drachmas is assigned to the cost of housing. If the παραμονή requirement in no. 28 is, in fact, a concession to Thonis, as it almost certainly was, we should not see it as part of Polydeukes's compensation. We thus arrive at a baseline of 320 drachmas per annum as the value of maintenance. According to table 8.3, we see that Hermias in *P.Oxy.* XXXI 2586 breaks even in year 2 between the cost of maintenance and the income

---

63. Lines 21–25: οὐκ [ἐξόντος αὐ]|τῷ ἐντὸς τοῦ χρόνου ἀποσπᾶ[ν τὴν θυ]|γατέρα αὐτοῦ οὐδὲ μετὰ τὸν χρόνον [-ca.?-] | πρὶν ἂν ἀποδῷ τὰς τοῦ ἀργυρί[ου] δ[ραχμὰς] | [τετρ]ακοσίας πλήρη[ς].

64. Bergamasco 2004: 35–39, extending the view put forward in Bergamasco 1995: 147.

65. J. D. Thomas, from the editio princeps, p. 183; cf. Jördens 1990: 275–95.

of wages, and if we graph the total compensation of the contracts against each other (fig. 8.1), we see that Hermias pulls ahead by the end of month 35 or sometime around the last month in year 3. It is, I suggest, no coincidence that two to three years marked the maximum length of most apprenticeship contracts in the century before, where the term was protected by penalties, not incentives. This likely represented the inflexion point at which masters were solidly in the black and needed to start sharing the value of the labor they were extracting from the apprentice. If so, there was every financial reason for Polydeukes to repossess his daughter at any time after the end of the second year, so long as he could scrape up the four hundred drachmas: by this point, Aphrodite knew her trade, and her earning capacity exceeded the cost of her maintenance. While Dioskoros in *P.Oxy.* XXXI 2586 paid a divi-

Table 8.3. Comparison of no. 28 and *P.Oxy.* XXXI 2586

	No. 28	*P.Oxy.* XXXIII 2586
Parent	Polydeukes	Hermias
Apprentice	Aphrodite (daughter)	Unnamed (son)
Master	Thonis	Dioskoros
Duration	4 years	5 years
Lodging	Thonis	Hermias
Maintenance	Thonis, ἀντὶ μισθῶν = 320/year = 5.4 ob./day	Hermias
Advance	400 dr. ἐν προχρείᾳ εἰς ἀναγκαί[ας] αὐτοῦ χρείας	400 dr. ἐν προχρείᾳ
Paid days per year	365	Year 1: ~ 171
		Years 2–5: 342[1]
Wages Y1	0	Mos. 1–6: 0 ob./day
		Mos. 7–12: 2 ob./day
		= 57 dr./year[2]
Wages Y2	0	6 ob./day = 342 dr./year
Wages Y3	0	10 ob./day = 570 dr./year
Wages Y4	0	2 dr. or 12 ob./day = 684 dr./year
Wages Y5	NA	16 ob./day = 912 dr./year

[1] Lines 39–42 are ambiguous: λήμψεται δὲ ὁ παῖς | εἰς λόγον ἀργιῶν ἑορτικῶν Τῦβι | Παχὼν Ἀμεσυίοις ἡμερῶν | ἑπτὰ Σαραπίοις ἡμέρας δύο. The most natural way to take this clause is to see the boy getting a week each in Tybi, Pachon, and for the Amesysia, plus two days for the Serapeia, a total of twenty-three days per year (cf. Bergamasco 1995: 129–30). Nothing about the ancient world generally or this contract specifically encourages us to understand these as paid days off. The given rates should therefore apply to 342 days per year, so my wage totals differ from those calculated by the editor (p. 144, note *ad* 19ff.). Also, since we do not know when these holidays fell in the calendar, I arbitrarily assigned half of them in Y1 to the first six months, in which the boy was not paid a wage (i.e., 342/2 = 171 paid days in Y1).

[2] As per the previous note, I have merely calculated the effective salary at an obol per diem for 342 days.

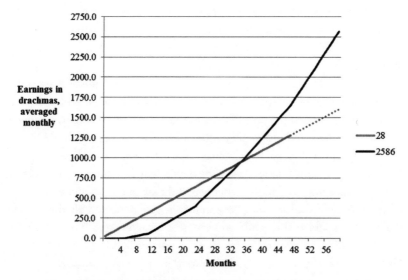

Fig. 8.1. Cumulative compensation of No. 28 and *P. Oxy.* XXXI 2586

dend to keep his apprentice with him, Thonis in no. 28 succeeded in inserting the ἀποσπάω clause in order to extract the full value of the hard bargain he drove. The crucial point is that the right to repossess was negotiated in all these contracts, either expressly, through a penalty clause, or implicitly, through the graduated structure of wages and premiums, but never by both mechanisms.

6. Enforcement

6.1. Transaction Costs, Contract, and Contract Enforcement in Roman Egypt

The existence of contracts with ἀποσπάω clauses in themselves suggests that the right to repossess a dependent was economically meaningful in Roman Egypt and that the uncertainty surrounding its potential exercise was significant enough for parties to bear the very certain costs of negotiating, drafting, and often registering written contracts. These contracts are, in other words, proof that the determinate costs associated with contracting lowered the higher TC associated with the risk of opportunism. The discussion above suggests, further, that the contractual obligation to forbear was similarly meaningful, as parties who could avoid making this concession regularly did so, an example being slave owners hiring wet nurses outside of Alexandria. Again, when the clause was not inserted automatically by boilerplate (e.g., as appears to have been the case in Alexandria), we see the economic value of forbearance measured indirectly by the alternative strategy of tiering wages in the apprenticeship contracts. This value obviously correlated with the credibility of the threat to repossess the dependent. But how credible was the threat of ἀποσπασμός, and in what way did that credibility depend on official enforcement via the state? We should also ask how credible the contractual penalties attached to unilateral repossession were and how—if at all—the state helped to enforce property rights established in private contracts. The answers to these questions are important precisely because they shed light on the larger question of how contract worked as an economic institution in the Roman world. The general topic of contract enforcement in Roman Egypt must await an extended treatment; here I will only adumbrate a few of the important considerations as they touch on contracts negotiating the right of repossession.

It is obvious why the transactions discussed in the previous sections were not likely to be organized through a simple market, like an agora. While markets are useful governance structures for the sale of commodities (e.g., by collocating merchants, they bring down the cost of gathering information related to prices, quality of goods, seller reputations, etc.), they do little to bring down the TC associated with nonsimultaneous transactions. It is less obvious that these transactions could not have been efficiently organized via a hierarchical structure—this was, after all, a world in which one could "integrate" by buying a slave instead of contracting with an apprentice's father (cf. sec. 5.1). It is no answer to say that slaves were "expensive," for this is precisely the point: if contract was not a viable governance structure and if hierarchical integration was too expensive, the alternative was not to transact at all. Contract works by collapsing future performances into present obligations, thereby replacing "expensive" knowledge about the other party and future contingencies with the comparatively cheaper cost of knowing how to enforce your contract in the present. The institutional shape and scope of contract as an economic governance structure thus depends on the modalities of enforcement, and this dependence, in turn, implicates the state as a self-evidently important source of enforcement.[66]

There is a lack of consensus over the role and efficacy of the administration of justice in Roman Egypt. The juristic handbooks, which reconstruct the judicial system and legal procedure, inevitably leave the reader impressed by the significant concern and control evinced by the Roman state over property and contracts. This is nowhere so true as in the discussions of foreclosure, which are based on truly remarkable documents recording the multiple steps involved in debt collection.[67] Yet it is also commonplace in the historical literature to cite the corruption and impotence of imperial justice (cf. Haensch's study in chapter 10 of this volume), nor is it difficult to find evidence for this position.[68] These two perspectives on Roman justice, which I will call the "legal centralist" and the "legal skeptical," have far-ranging implications for our understanding of contract as an economic institution in the Roman Empire.[69] The former tends to see enforcement as properly and exclusively a state function. The latter suggests either, at a minimum, that contracts relied on other entities for enforcement (e.g., the parties or the community) or, in its strongest formulation, that they were merely epiphenomenal to social relations (cf. above, section 2).

An extreme example of the legal centralist view is Taubenschlag's short article on self-help in the papyri: he defined self-help as "when somebody unilaterally secures or satisfies his real or pretended claim . . . , [he takes] the law in his own hands without the permission of his adversary and without the intervention of the court and proceeds against the person or the property of his adversary" (1959: 135). Taubenschlag claims that self-help in this sense was "forbidden in Greco-Roman Egypt," except in certain cases when the prohibition was "lifted" by positive law or contract. This claim is historically incorrect and theoretically confused. A thorough revision of self-help in Ro-

---

66. On the relationship of enforcement to contract design, see North 1990: 61; cf., e.g., Scott and Triantis 2006. On the historical importance of the state to contract, D. C. North (1985: 560) has said that the "most distinctive feature of the cost of transacting in the pre-modern world centered on the cost of enforcing contracts"; cf. North 1981, 1990. The state is not, however, the only source of third-party enforcement. See Ellickson 1991; Greif 2006; Terpstra 2013. On the possibility of community enforcement as an explanation of private apprenticeship contracts from Oxyrhynchus, see sec. 5.2 above.
67. E.g., Taubenschlag 1955: 524–37; Rupprecht 1994: 147–51 (cf. Rupprecht 1997).
68. See, e.g., MacMullen 1974; Lewis 1983. For examples of strategic delay, see Anagnostou-Canas 1991: 229–30. On corruption and misconduct, see Lewis 1954; Crawford 1974 (with Rea 1993). See now also Kelly 2011.
69. "Legal centralism" is not my coinage. See Ellickson 1991: 138–47.

man Egypt is a real desideratum (especially as Taubenschlag's article is still cited—e.g., in Kloppenborg 2006); here, however, it suffices merely to point out that his is, on its face, an inadequate characterization of the relationship of the state to self-help and contract enforcement. Extralegal enforcement could not help but be a vital component to any system of enforcement in antiquity, given the limitations of the ancient state: even if self-help had been proscribed, this would have been a dead letter. That self-help remains important to this day, an era of the vastly more powerful, bureaucratic nation-state, is a potent reminder that any discussion of contract enforcement based solely on the state and its law is irredeemably defective.[70]

To this extent, the legal skeptics have the more compelling model: they recognize the necessary role played by extralegal rules and entities in the formation and enforcement of contracts. They have tended, however, to see the ancient world as an essentially lawless place. Take, for example, Ramsey Macmullen's description of a dispute recorded in a papyrus:

> However majestic the background of Roman law and imperial administration, behold in the foreground a group of men who could launch a miniature war on their neighbor—and expected to get away with it! . . . Brute strength . . . counted for much in the minor quarrels of the village. The only defense lay in one's family. Had government cared more, no doubt their subjects would not have taken the law into their own hands. (MacMullen 1974: 7, 12)

The central irony here is that MacMullen's vision of a virtually Hobbesian state of nature prevailing in the Egyptian countryside is drawn from a petition.[71] If the government did not care, why bother complaining to it?[72] If only brute strength counted, why pay to draft and register the contracts we just studied? At the very least, we must imagine these Roman subjects as buying *something* of value in their contracts, petitions, and trials. What was it? The legal skeptic has no cogent answer.

Legal centralists leave too little scope for the play of extralegal forces in ancient contracting and dispute resolution, while the legal skeptics' tight em-

---

70. See, e.g., Ellickson 1991. Atiyah's discussion of the role of self-help in seventeenth-century England is suggestive of the manner and extent to which self-help is compatible with a relatively strong state and a sophisticated law of contract: see Atiyah 1979: 189–93.
71. See Ratzan, Forthcoming b, on the land dispute underlying this petition.
72. See Kelly 2011 on the sociology of petitions in Roman Egypt. The following discussion was written before Kelly's book appeared and agrees with much of his analysis.

brace of the fact of extralegal power leaves them at a loss to explain the abundant evidence of individual and state investment in official enforcement. In the end, neither camp has an adequate model of enforcement, or one capable of relating and integrating the formal with the informal (e.g., reputational sanctions, social pressure, symbolic vandalism, acts of retaliation, outright violence, etc.). It is only fitting that we conclude with an attempt to show how the negotiation and drafting of the right of ἀποσπασμός in our contracts reflected the enforcement regime and how this regime is more complicated than either the standard positions of the legal centralist or legal skeptic allow. Specifically, I will show that ἀποσπασμός was a self-help right that the state recognized and justified after the fact if the repossession was disputed.

6.2. The Enforcement of Ἀποσπασμός in Roman Egypt

How did the subjects of Roman Egypt "repossess" animals and people, and are we able to read our contracts in light of this practice?

A nice example illustrating the process is found in *BGU* I 46, a petition by the metropolitan Samios to the στρατηγός (the highest civilian officer at the nome level) of the Arsinoite in 193. Reporting that four of his best asses were stolen, Samios requests that his petition be logged, "since I am searching for them wherever I wish, so as to repossess them, should I be so lucky as to find them" (15–19: ἐμοῦ Ι μὲν ἀναζητοῦντος τούτους Ι ἐν οἷς ἂν βούλωμαι τόποις, ὅΙπως, ἐὰν εὐκαιρίας τύχω Ι τοῦ εὑρεῖν, ἀποσπάσω). Moving simultaneously to report the crime and to register his intent to repossess, Samios distinguishes the illegal theft (10: ἐβαστάχθησαν) from his act of lawful repossession (19: ἀποσπάσω). One can easily imagine how looking "wherever he wished" might set off a flurry of complaints. This is one instance, however, in which we need not rely on our imagination: we have a vivid illustration of the pitfalls of self-help in *P.Mich.* VI 421 (Karanis, ca. 41–68), a petition in which a man complains that he and his local constable (ἀρχέφοδος) were beaten and imprisoned just as they were about to seize a couple of thieves from the next town who had stolen his donkeys (17–18: μελλόντων τοὺς αἰτίους καΙταλαμβάνειν παρ' ἑαυτοῖς). Like Samios nearly a century later, this man submitted a report (ὑπόμνημα) before he went out to find his animals.[73]

---

73. Of course, this is not as clear an example of self-help as *BGU* I 46, since the constable ac-

It is not unreasonable to read these two petitions (and others like them) as indictments of Rome's failure to provide basic order and security; but that is to read only for plot. In this context, the medium is the message: these petitions attest precisely to the value of complaining to the state. So important was state recognition and involvement that, in both cases, the "victims" (one should not necessarily take such documents at face value) carefully laid the groundwork for a possible suit if their self-help actions failed or were contested. There is no hint here of any of Roman law's possessory interdicts (e.g., the *interdictum utrubi*) or their equivalents, nor is there any sense in which the plaintiffs were asking for permission to repossess their stolen property. Instead, we see the parties trying to get out "ahead" of any potential dispute, in case it should ever be escalated to the authorities. Properly speaking, Samios's petition and the earlier, unnamed victim's ὑπόμνημα were forms of legal insurance. With respect to the ἀποσπασμός of animals, these petitions therefore suggest the following:

a. one had a "right" to repossess one's animals, such that it was a defense against a charge of theft or assault, presumably contingent on limiting one's actions strictly to what repossession required;

b. the lawful exercise of this right lay in the hands of the owner in the first instance and may therefore be properly called a self-help right; and, finally,

c. the government played a role in authorizing or certifying these recovery actions as self-help, but only after the fact.

Quite by chance, we have a test case that is as near to perfect as one could hope for on this subject, in the trial proceedings preserved in *P.Oxy.* I 37 (Oxyrhynchus, 49).[74] The suit pitted the wet nurse Saraeus against Pesouris and his son, her erstwhile employers, before the στρατηγός.[75] Pesouris had

---

companied the complainant here. One does not get the sense from the petition, however, that the complainant needed the ἀρχέφοδος to come along in order to search for his stolen donkeys. Instead, the constable's presence (and suffering) lends credibility to the complainant's version of events.

74. This famous document has been republished, often with translation and commentary, as *M.Chr.* 79, *Sel.Pap.* II 257, *FIRA* III 170, *C.Pap.Gr.* I 19, and *Jur.Pap.* 90; cf. Rowlandson 1998, no. 91. There are other relevant documents connected to this discussion but for which there is no room here, especially *P.Fam.Tebt.* I 37 (Antinoöpolis, 167), *P.Oxy.* X 1295 (Oxyrhynchus, II–III), and *P.Oxy.* VIII 1120 (Oxyrhynchus, III).

75. On the identification of the Theon who interjects in line 28 as Pesouris's son, see van Minnen 1993: 119.

entrusted a foundling to Saraeus, but during the second year of the contract, he "repossessed" the child, because, as his advocate Aristokles insisted, it was starving (14–15: λειμανχουμέν[ο]υ τοῦ σωματ[ί]ου ἀπέ|σπασεν ὁ Πεσοῦρις). To bolster Pesouris's property claim and justify his act of ἀποσπασμός, Aristokles entered two documents into evidence: the wet-nursing contract (doubtless the standard public Oxyrhynchite contract; cf. section 5.1 above) and the receipt for the second year's wages (12–14, 19–20). In his closing, Aristokles requested that these documents be "preserved," or respected (21: ἀξιῶ<ι> ταῦ[τα] φυλαχθῆ[ν]αι),[76] by which he meant that they should be treated as κύριος, or "authoritative," a common claim for documents in this period.[77] Aristokles thus pressed the στρατηγός to apply a doctrine of strict interpretation to these documents, which identified Pesouris as the child's owner. This strategy was necessary because Saraeus was going to claim that the repossessed child was in fact hers (15–19). Aristokles therefore argued to have the case turn on the probative value of written contracts. What, he might have asked, is the value of documents if they are not authoritative with respect to private orderings, as in this case where one party (Saraeus) has acknowledged (ὁμολογεῖν) the property rights or ownership of the other (Pesouris)?[78]

Hewing to the logic of his attack, Aristokles characterizes Pesouris as a concerned owner moving merely to "repossess" (ἀπέσπασεν) the child for cause (most wet-nursing contracts specified standards of care; cf., e.g., C.Pap. Gr. I 14.16–20 [Oxyrhynchus, 26]; a starving child would constitute breach), while Saraeus bided her time, waiting for an opportunity to break into Pesouris's house and "snatch the child away" (ἀφήρπασεν) in the hopes of "carrying him off" on the specious pretense of his free status (17–19: καὶ βούλεται ὀν[ό]|ματι ἐλευθέρου τὸ σωμάτιον ἀπενέγκασ|θαι). Aristokles thus distinguishes his client's lawful repossession (ἀποσπᾶν) from the nurse's illegal theft (ἀφαρπάζειν, ἀποφέρεσθαι), much like Samios did above.[79] Saraeus, representing herself, acknowledged the receipt of the slave child and her wages, stipulating to the contents of the documents presented,

---

76. For this meaning of φυλάσσω, see Preisigke, *Wörterbuch*, s.v. (3)

77. On the meaning of κύριος in legal documents, see Hässler 1960; cf. Wolff 1978: 145–46.

78. Lines 12–14: ὅτι δὲ ταῦτα ἀληθη<ι> λέγω<ι>, | ἔστιν γράμματα αὐτῆς δι᾿ ὧν ὁμολογεῖ εἴλη|φέναι. Cf. line 28, in which the point is echoed unconvincingly by Theon in rebuttal to Saraeus: γράμματα τοῦ σωματίου ἔχομεν.

79. Cf. also *P.Fam.Tebt.* I 37. Unlike ἀποσπᾶν, which can mean either to repossess or to steal, neither ἀφαρπάζειν nor ἀποφέρεσθαι are ambiguous in legal contexts: see Preisigke and Kiessling, *Wörterbuch*, s.vv.; Taubenschlag 1955: 456 (Taubenschlag is insensitive to mood).

but testified that the slave child had died and that Pesouris and his son now "wished to repossess her own child" (26–27: νῦν βούλον[ται τὸ] | ἴ[δι]όν μου τέκνον ἀποσπάσαι).

Manca Masciardi and Montevecchi (1984: 117) suggested that a violated ἀποσπάω clause might have been at issue in this trial. Yet we may be fairly confident that no such clause appeared in Saraeus's contract, since public wet-nursing contracts from the Egyptian χώρα do not seem to have included them.[80] We should instead see four interconnected legal questions being resolved here: (1) the legal identity or status of the child, (2) the recognition of self-help rights of repossession based on the property rights of parents and owners, (3) the recognition of rights based in contract, and (4) the probative value of documents and the correct theory of their interpretation.

Nowhere is it suggested that either side did anything criminal in repossessing the child: indeed, both sides claimed the right to do so, and these claims are precisely what the state was called in to adjudicate. We should note, in particular, that not even Saraeus disavowed Pesouris's right to ἀποσπασμός or characterized his act as illegal or criminal; she merely claims that he is "repossessing" someone who is not, in fact, his (we should likely hear a note of sarcasm in her use of the term "repossess," echoing the rich man's lawyer). The right of repossession was subsidiary to the more fundamental property right in persons, and so the στρατηγός had only to decide the identity and status of the child in order to resolve the question of repossession.[81] This he did, declaring that the child looked like Saraeus (29–30) and that she could therefore keep him if she and her husband swore out a written oath that the slave child entrusted to them had died and if they returned to Pesouris the unearned wages for the second year.

This decision has been called "Solomonic" by some commentators because of the στρατηγός's rough-and-ready justice,[82] yet this characterization obscures the fact that the decision also had the merit of respecting the rights established by the contract in question. If Saraeus and Pesouris had executed

---

80. As I will argue elsewhere, the ἀποσπάω clause that Vitelli restored in *C.Pap.Gr.* I 24.9–11 should be struck and replaced with a version of the typical option clause.

81. The στρατηγός says that he is following the orders of the prefect (33–34: κατὰ τὰ ὑπὸ | τοῦ κυρίου ἡγεμόνος κριθέντα); cf. *P.Oxy.* I 38 (see below). What he means by this — whether the Prefect gave explicit instructions or merely conferred on him the capacity to decide the case — has been debated: see Anagnoustou-Canas 1991: 27–29; cf. the introduction to *C.Pap.Gr.* I 19 for earlier bibliography.

82. Anagnostou-Canas 1991: 28–29.

a standard Oxyrhynchite wet-nursing contract, which seems highly proba-
ble, it likely contained the standard option clause in which the nurse had the
option, in the event of the original child's death, to nurse another child on the
same terms or return any unearned wages (cf. sec. 5.1). This is precisely what
the στρατηγός enforces: he validates Saraeus's self-help right of ἀποσπασμός
and imposes a solution prescribed by the contract itself (namely, Saraeus opts
to end the contract upon the death of her original nursling and returns the
unearned wages), forcing Pesouris to bear the risk of death, which he had
contractually assumed.

We learn from a subsequent petition to the Prefect by Saraeus's husband,
Tryphon (*P.Oxy.* I 38), that Pesouris "did not wish to abide by the στρατηγός's
decision" and was retaliating by "hindering" Tryphon in his trade (17: τοῦ δὲ
Σύρου Ι μὴ βουλομένου ἐνμεῖναι τοῖς κεκριμένοις Ι ἀλλὰ καὶ
καταργοῦντός με χειρότεχνον ὄντα). Pesouris's recalcitrance has been held
up as evidence of the failings of the Roman system: even when the little man
managed to get justice, he was left at the mercy of his opponent as soon as the
trial ended and the officers departed.[83] This was clearly a problem in the Roman world, but the lesson of this document points in the other direction: Pesouris manifestly did not feel free utterly to disregard the στρατηγός's decision. It is significant, in other words, that Tryphon does not claim that
Pesouris is still trying to enslave his son. The victory was therefore far from
hollow, as the state had put an effective end to Pesouris's open aggression,
leaving him with no other option but indirect harrassment, an utterly reac-
tive and subversive form of self-help—a far cry from the active self-help con-
fidently advertised in the petitions considered above and validated in the
case of Saraeus herself. Of course, we should not minimize the suffering that
the Pesourises of the ancient world caused by virtue of their power, informal
and formal; yet, by the same token, we should not discount the very real, if
ultimately incomplete, effects of Roman justice on the ground.

There is (obviously) much more to say about the relationship of the state
to the institution of contract in Roman Egypt and about the relationship of
contract to property and status, but I will conclude here by noting how this
decision supported the institution with respect to the transactions discussed
in this essay. First, the decision followed what were likely the terms of the
contract with respect to the transaction it embodied against a strict reading in

---

83. E.g., Anagnostou 1991: 230 n. 109; Rowlandson 1998: 117.

service of an oblique and cynical property claim secondary to the main transaction. Second, it upheld the basic right of ἀποσπασμός in a predictable way, rendering it credible and therefore valuable. Third, the affidavit sworn out by Saraeus and Tryphon put an official end to the contractual relationship, extinguishing all rights and claims embodied in Pesouris's documents and, thus, all possible justifications for further acts of self-help, at least as far as the state was concerned. This was an effective way to police this self-help right, as we see from Pesouris's subsequent actions, since he turned to informal means of redress, not to achieve his original design, but to exact revenge and send a signal to others in the community.

7. Conclusion

An NIE focus on transactions and the relative TC associated with organizing transactions via contract is a method well suited to the nature of our evidence from Roman Egypt and, indeed, to the fuzzy, undefined nature of the institution itself. By attempting to define and follow the TC associated with contracting in Roman Egypt, we recover the phenomenon in a way that approximates the ancient experience, forcing us to ask fundamental questions about what the rules were, how the game was played, and what these factors can tell us about the economic agency of individuals, the role and capacity of the state, and, at the furthest remove, the nature of the Roman economy. The preceding case study suggests that contract was a vital and complex economic institution in the Roman world and that we have only begun to understand its full extent and possibilities, its interlocking enforcement mechanisms, its relationship to status and the state, and its connections to the far more intensively studied governance structures of ancient markets and hierarchies.

Appendix 1. Contracts with Ἀποσπάω Clauses prior to the Fourth Century C.E.

	Publication	Date	Provenance	Transaction	Instrument	Reference
1	*BGU* IV 1106	13 B.C.E.	Alexandria	WN	Pub (syn.)	*C.Pap.Gr.* I 5
2	*BGU* IV 1107	13	Alexandria	WN	Pub (syn.)	*C.Pap.Gr.* I 6
3	*SB* XXII 15538	13	Alexandria	AP	Priv (ch.)	Bergamasco 1995: 3
4	*BGU* IV 1108	5	Alexandria	WN	Pub (syn.)	*C.Pap.Gr.* I 9
5	*BGU* IV 1109	5	Alexandria	WN	Pub (syn.)	*C.Pap.Gr.* I 10
6	*C.Pap.Gr.* I 13	30 B.C.E.– 14 C.E.	Alexandria	WN	Pub (syn.)	
7	*PSI* X 1120	25 B.C.E.– 25 C.E.	?	L (παραμονή)	Pub (gr.)	Hengstl 1972: 9, 17
8	*P.Mich.* inv. 931 + *P.Col.* X 249	9 C.E.	Theadelphia (Arsinoite)	L (παραμονή)	Pub (gr.)	Edition forth- coming by Graham Claytor, Nikos Liti- nas, and Elizabeth Nabney
9	*P.Mich.* X 587	24–25	Tebtynis (Arsinoite)	L (παραμονή)	Pub (gr.)	
10	*SB* X 10236	36	Oxyrhynchus	AP	Priv (pp.)	Bergamasco 1995: 6
11	*P.Fouad* I 37	48	Oxyrhyn- chus?	AP	Priv (pp.)	Bergamasco 1995: 8
12	*P.Wisc.* I 4	53	Oxyrhynchus	AP	Priv (pp.)	Bergamasco 1995: 11
13	*P.Oxy.Hels.* 29	54	Oxyrhynchus	AP	Priv (pp.)	Bergamasco 1995: 12
14	*P.Oxy.* XLI 2971	66	Oxyrhynchus	AP	Priv (pp.)	Bergamasco 1995: 18; cf. Kruse 1999
15	*P.Oxy.* II 275	66	Oxyrhynchus	AP	Priv (pp.)	Bergamasco 1995: 17
16	*SB* XVI 12953	70	Alexandria	WN	Pub (syn.)	*C.Pap.Gr.* I 22
17	*P.Heid.* IV 327	99	Ankyropolis (Herak- leopolite)	AP	Pub (syn.)	
18	*SB* XXIV 16253	98–103	Oxyrhynchus	AP	Priv (pp.)	Bergamasco 1995: 21
19	*P.Oxy.* III 496	127	Oxyrhynchus	M	Pub (ag.)	
20	*P.Mich.* inv. 4238	128	Theadelphia	AP	Pub (gr.)	Eckerman 2011

	Publication	Date	Provenance	Transaction	Instrument	Reference
21	*BGU* VII 1647	129	Philadelphia (Arsinoite)	L	Priv (ch.)	Montevecchi 1950: 42–43
22	*SPP* XXII 40	150	Soknopaiou Nesos (Arsinoite)	AP	Pub (gr.)	Bergamasco 1995: 25
23	*P.Mich.* inv. 6665	ca. 150	Oxyrhynchus	M	Priv (pp.)?	Garvey 2010
24	*P.Oxy.* IV 724	155	Oxyrhynchus	AP	Priv (ch.)	Bergamasco 1995: 26; cf. Lewis 2003: 20–23
25	*P.Grenf.* II 59	188	Soknopaiou Nesos (Arsinoite)	AP	Priv (pp.)	Bergamasco 1995: 29
26	*PSI* VI 710	II	Oxyrhyn-chus?	L (παραμονή)?	?	Hengstl 1972: 27 n. 105; Montevec-chi 1950: 48
27	*P.Oxy.* XLI 2988	II?	Oxyrhynchus	AP	Priv (ch.)	Bergamasco 1995: 30
28	*P.Oxy.* LXVII 4596	232 or 264	Oxyrhynchus	AP	Priv (pp.)	Bergamasco 2004: 35–38.
29	*SB* XXIV 16320	293–304	Kellis (Oasis Magna)	AP	NA	*P.Kell.Gr.* I 19a, appendix; Bergamasco 1998

Note: ag. = ἀγορανομεῖον document (the chief notarial office of an entire nome, located in a nome metropolis); AP = apprenticeship; ch. = cheirograph; gr. = γραφεῖον document; L = labor; M = marriage; pp. = private protocol; Priv = private contract; Pub = public contract; syn. = συγχώρησις; WN = wet nursing.

Note: This collection excludes PSI II 203, since the restoration of ἀποσπάω there is incorrect (see n. 80 above). I restore the verb in no. 27. No. 29 is included on the basis of Bergamasco's ambitious reediting (1998). If correct, this would be the latest instance of the clause on record for any contract (cf. sec. 5.2 above). The public document had all but disappeared by the end of the third century (cf. Yiftach-Firanko 2009); hence it is meaningless to characterize no. 29 as "public" or "private."

Appendix 2. Occurrences of the Ἀποσπάω Clause by Region, Transaction Type, and Period

		Alexandria		Arsinoite		Oxyrhxynchite		**Total**	
		T	A	T	A	T	A	**T**	**A**
WN	Augustan	6	5	1	-	-	-	7	5
	Tiberius-Nero	-	-	-	-	4	-	4	-
	Flavian	1	1	-	-	2	-	3	1
	2nd century	-	-	6	-	-	-	6	-
	3rd century	-	-	-	-	-	-	-	-
	Total	7	6	7	-	6	-	20	6
AP	Augustan	1	1	1	-	-	-	2	1
	Tiberius-Nero	-	-	2	-	6	6	8	6
	Flavian	-	-	-	-	-	-	-	-
	2nd century	-	-	7	3	5	3	12	6
	3rd century	-	-	2	-	5	1	7	1
	Total	1	1	12	3	16	10	29	14
L	Augustan	-	-	-	-	-	-	-	-
	Tiberius-Nero	-	-	2	1	-	-	2	1
	Flavian	-	-	-	-	-	-	--	
	2nd century	-	-	3	1	2	1	5	2
	3rd century	-	-	-	-	-	-	--	
	Total	-	-	5	2	2	1	7	3
	Grand Total	8	7	24	5	24	11	56	23

Note: A = ἀποσπάω clause; AP = apprenticeship; L = labor (includes παραμονή and slave leases); T = total; WN = wet-nursing.

The total number of instances (23) does not equal the 29 of appendix 1 because three of our contracts come from regions other than those compared above (nos. 17, 29) or have an unknown provenance (no. 7), while two are marriage contracts (nos. 19, 23). No. 7 likely comes from the Fayyum (Wolff 1978: 86), and its inclusion would reinforce the prevailing pattern for the Arsinoite.

Appendix 3. Occurrences of the Ἀποσπάω Clause by Region, Transaction Type, Period, and Document Type (public or private)

		Alexandria				Arsinoite				Oxyrhynchite				Total			
		Public		Private		Public		Private		Public		Private		Public		Private	
		T	A	T	A	T	A	T	A	T	A	T	A	T	A	T	A
WN	Augustan	6	5	-	-	1	-	-	-	-	-	-	-	7	5	-	-
	Tiberius-Nero	-	-	-	-	-	-	-	-	3	-	1	-	3	-	1	-
	Flavian	1	1	-	-	-	-	-	-	2	-	-	-	3	1	-	-
	2nd century	-	-	-	-	6	-	-	-	-	-	-	-	6	-	-	-
	3rd century	-	-	-	-	-	-	-	-	-	-	-	-	-	-	-	-
	Total	7	6	-	-	7	-	-	-	5	-	1	-	19	6	1	-
AP	Augustan	-	-	1	1	1	-	-	-	-	-	-	-	1	-	1	1
	Tiberius-Nero	-	-	-	-	2	-	-	-	-	-	6	6	2	-	6	6
	Flavian	-	-	-	-	-	-	-	-	-	-	-	-	-	-	-	-
	2nd century	-	-	-	-	5	2	2	1	-	-	5	3	5	2	7	4
	3rd century	-	-	-	-	1	-	1	-	-	-	5	1	1	-	6	1
	Total	-	-	1	1	9	2	3	1	-	-	16	10	9	2	20	12
L	Augustan	-	-	-	-	-	-	-	-	-	-	-	-	-	-	-	-
	Tiberius-Nero	-	-	-	-	1	1	1	-	-	-	-	-	1	1	1	-
	Flavian	-	-	-	-	-	-	-	-	-	-	-	-	-	-	-	-
	2nd century	-	-	-	-	-	-	3	1	1	1	1	-	1	1	4	1
	3rd century	-	-	-	-	-	-	-	-	-	-	-	-	-	-	-	-
	Total	-	-	-	-	1	1	4	1	1	1	1	-	2	2	5	1
	Grand Total	7	6	1	1	17	3	7	2	6	1	18	10	30	10	26	13

Note: A = ἀποσπάω clause; AP = apprenticeship; L = labor (includes παραμονή and slave leases); T = total; WN = wet-nursing.

Bibliography

Anagnostou-Canas, B. 1991. *Juge et sentence dans l'Égypte romaine*. Études de philosophie et d'histoire du droit 6. Paris.

Atiyah, P. S. 1979. *The Rise and Fall of Freedom of Contract*. Oxford.

Bagnall, R. S. 1995. *Reading Papyri, Writing Ancient History*. London.

Bagnall, R. S. 1997. "Missing Females in Roman Egypt." *Scripta Classica Israelica* 16: 121–38.

Beauchamp, J. 2007. "Byzantine Egypt and Imperial Law." In R. S. Bagnall, ed., *Egypt in the Byzantine World, 300–700*, 271–87. Cambridge.

Bergamasco, M. 1995. "Le διδασκαλικαί nella ricerca attuale." *Aegyptus* 75: 95–167.

Bergamasco, M. 1998. "*P.Kell. G.* 19.A, Appendix." *ZPE* 121: 193–96.

Bergamasco, M. 2004. "Tre note a tre διδασκαλικαί." *Studi di egittologia e di papirologia* 1: 31–41.

Berger, A. 1911. *Die Strafklauseln in den Papyrusurkunden*. Leipzig.

Browne, G. M. 1974. "*Ad P.Oxy.* XXXIV 2705." In E. Kießling and H.-A. Rupprecht, eds., *Akten des XIII. Internationalen Papyrologenkongresses, Marburg/Lahn, 2. bis 6. August 1971*, 53–59. Münchener Beiträge zur Papyrusforschung und Antiken Rechtsgeschichte 66. Munich.

Crawford, D. 1974. "Skepe in Soknopaiou Nesos." *JJP* 18: 169–76.

Eckerman, C. 2011. "Apprenticeship Contract for Carpentry." *BASP* 48: 47–49.

Ellickson, R. C. 1991. *Order without Law: How Neighbors Settle Disputes*. Cambridge, Mass.

Finley, M. I. [1985] 1999. *The Ancient Economy*. Updated edition with foreword by I. Morris. Berkeley.

Furubotn, E., and R. Richter. 2005. *Institutions and Economic Theory*. 2nd ed. Ann Arbor.

Garvey, T. 2010. "An Oxyrhynchite Marriage Contract as School Exercise?" *BASP* 47: 67–73.

Greif, A. 2006. *Institutions and the Path to the Modern Economy: Lessons from Medieval Trade*. Cambridge.

Hässler, M. 1960. *Die Bedeutung der Kyria-Klausel in den Papyrusurkunden*. Berlin.

Hengstl, J. 1972. *Private Arbeitsverhältnisse freier Personen in den hellenistichen Papyri bis Diokletian*. Bonn.

Hengstl, J. 1979. "Die 'Athantos'-Klausel." In J. Bingen and G. Nachtergael, eds., *Actes du XVe Congrès international de papyrologie*, 231–39. Papyrologica Bruxellensia 19. Brussels.

Hermann, J. 1958a. *Studien zur Bodenpacht im Recht der Graeco-Aegyptischen Papyri*. Münchener Beiträge zur Papyrusforschung und Antiken Rechtsgeschichte 41. Munich.

Hermann, J. 1958b. "Vertragsinhalt und Rechtsnatur der ΔΙΔΑΣΚΑΛΙΚΑΙ." *JJP* 11–12: 119–39.

Jakab, É. 2009. *Risikomanagement beim Weinkauf: Periculum und Praxis im Imperium Romanum.* Münchener Beiträge zur Papyrusforschung und antiken Rechtsgeschichte 99. Munich.

Jördens, A. 1990. *Vertragliche Regelungen von Arbeiten im späten griechischsprachigen Ägypten, mit Editionen von Texten der Heidelberger Papyrussammlung, des Istituto Papirologico "G.Vitelli," des Ägyptischen Museums zu Kairo und des British Museum, London.* Heidelberg.

Kaser, M. 1959. *Das römische Privatrecht: Das nachklassischen Entwicklungen.* Handbuch der Altertumswissenschaft 10.3.3.2. Munich.

Kaser, M. 1971. *Das römische Privatrecht: Das altrömische, das vorklassische und klassische Recht.* 2nd ed. Handbuch der Altertumswissenschaft 10.3.3.1 Munich.

Kastner, K. 1962. "Die zivilrechtliche Verwahrung des gräko-ägyptischen Obligationenrechts im Lichte der Papyri (παραθήκη)." PhD diss., Friedrich-Alexander-Universität zu Erlangen-Nürnberg.

Kehoe, D. P. 2007. *Law and Rural Economy in the Roman Empire.* Ann Arbor.

Kehoe, D. P., and B. Frier. 2007. "Law and Economic Institutions." In Morris, Saller, and Scheidel 2007: 113–43.

Kelly, B. 2011. *Petitions, Litigation, and Social Control in Roman Egypt.* Cambridge.

Kloppenborg, J. S. 2006. *The Tenants in the Vineyard.* Wissenschaftlishe Untersuchungen zum Neuen Testament 195. Tübingen.

Kronman, A. T. 1985. "Contract Law and the State of Nature." *Journal of Law, Economics, and Organization* 1: 5–32.

Kruse, T. 1999. "Κατάκριμα—Strafzahlung oder Steuer." *ZPE* 124: 157–90.

Kunkel, W. 1932. "Συνγραφή, syngrapha." *RE*, II.4A2: 1376–87.

Lewis, N. 1954. "On Official Corruption in Roman Egypt: The Edict of Vergilius Capito." *Proceedings of the American Philosophical Society* 98: 153–58.

Lewis, N. 1983. *Life in Egypt under Roman Rule.* Oxford.

Lewis, N. 2003. "Shorthand Writers." *Comunicazioni* 5: 19–27.

MacMullen, R. 1974. *Roman Social Relations, 50 B.C. to A.D. 284.* New Haven.

Maehler, H. 2005. "Greek, Egyptian, and Roman Law." *JJP* 35: 121–40.

Manca Masciadri, M., and O. Montevecchi. 1982. "Contratti di baliatico e vendite fiduciarie a Tebtynis." *Aegyptus* 62: 148–61.

Manca Masciadri, M., and O. Montevecchi. 1984. *Corpus Papyrorum Graecarum.* Vol. 1, *Contratti di baliatico.* Milan.

Mélèze-Modrzejewski, J. 1970. "La règle de droit dans l'Égypte romaine." In D. H. Samuel, ed., *Proceedings of the Twelfth International Congress of Papyrology, Ann Arbor 1968*, 317–77. Toronto.

Mitteis, L. 1912. *Grundzüge und Chrestomathie der Papyruskunde.* Vol. 2. *Juristischer Teil.* Part 1. *Grundzüge.* Stuttgart. Repr., Hildesheim, 1963.

Montevecchi, O. 1950. *I contratti di lavoro e di servizio nell'Egitto greco romano e bizantino.* Milan.

Morris, I., R. Saller, and W. Scheidel, eds. 2007. *The Cambridge Economic History of the Greco-Roman World*. Cambridge.

Nicholas, B. 1969. *An Introduction to Roman Law*. Oxford.

North, D. C. 1981. *Structure and Change in Economic History*. New York.

North, D. C. 1985. "Transaction Costs in History." *Journal of European Economic History* 14: 557–76.

North, D. C. 1990. *Institutions, Institutional Change, and Economic Performance*. Cambridge.

Posner, R. A. 2011. *Economic Analysis of Law*. 8th ed. New York.

Rathbone, D. 1991. *Economic Rationalism and Rural Society in Third-Century A.D. Egypt*. Cambridge.

Ratzan, D. M. Forthcoming a. "'Under Contract' in Roman Egypt: *P.Ryl.* II 128 in Context." *Bulletin of the John Rylands University Library*.

Ratzan, D. M. Forthcoming b. "Voodoo Economics: Law, Magic, and Economics in Roman Egypt and the Case of *P.Mich.* VI 423–424."

Rea, J. 1993. "*BGU* I 23: The Dekadarch's Colletion." *ZPE* 96: 133–34.

Rowlandson, J. 1998. *Women and Society in Greek and Roman Egypt*. Cambridge.

Rupprecht, H.-A. 1967. *Untersuchungen zum Darlehen im Recht der Graeco-Aegyptischen Papyri der Ptolemäerzeit*. Münchener Beiträge zur Papyrusforschung und Antiken Rechtsgeschichte 51. Munich.

Rupprecht, H.-A. 1983. "Die 'Bebaiosis' zur Entwicklung und den räumlich-zeitlichen Varianten einer Urkundsklausel in den graeco-ägyptischen Papyri." In *Studi in onore di Cesare Sanfilippo*, 3: 611–26. Milan.

Rupprecht, H.-A. 1994. *Kleine Einführung in die Papyruskunde*. Darmstadt.

Rupprecht, H.-A. 1997. "Zwangsvollstreckung und dingliche Sicherung in den Papyri der ptolemäischen und römischen Zeit." In G. Thür and J. Vélissaropoulos-Karakostas, eds., *Symposion 1995: Vorträge zur griechischen und hellenistischen Rechtsgeschichte (Korfu, 1.–5. September 1995)*, 291–302. Cologne.

Scheibelreiter, P. 2010. "'. . . Apotisato ten paratheken diplen kata ton ton parathekon nomon': Zum sogenannten 'Nomos ton Parathekon' und seinen Wurzeln im Griechischen Recht." In G. Thür, ed., *Symposion 2009: Vorträge zur griechischen und hellenistischen Rechtsgeschichte (Seggau, 25.–30. August 2009)*, 349–76. Vienna.

Scott, R. E., and G. G. Triantis. 2006. "Anticipating Litigation in Contract Design." *Yale Law Journal* 115: 814–79.

Seidl, E. 1932. "Συνάλλαγμα." *RE* II.4A2: 1322–24.

Seidl, E. 1933. *Der Eid im römisch-ägyptischen Provinzialrecht*. Münchener Beiträge zur Papyrusforschung und antiken Rechtsgeschichte 17. Munich.

Seidl, E. 1956. *Ägyptische Rechtsgeschichte de Saiten- und Perserzeit*. Ägyptologische Forschungen 20. Glückstadt.

Seidl, E. 1962. *Ptolemäische Rechtsgeschichte*. 2nd ed. Ägyptologische Forschungen 22. Glückstadt.

Shavell, S. 2004. *Foundations of Economic Analysis of Law*. Cambridge, MA.

Straus, J. A. 2004. *L'achat et la vente des esclaves dans l'Égypte romaine*. Archiv für Papyrusforschung Beiheft 14. Munich.

Swarney, P. R. 1970. *The Ptolemaic and Roman Idios Logos*. Toronto.

Taubenschlag, R. 1955. *The Law of Greco-Roman Egypt in the Light of the Papyri, 332 B.C.–640 A.D.* 2nd ed. Warsaw.

Taubenschlag, R. 1959. *Opera minora*. 2 vols. Warsaw.

Terpstra, T. T. 2013. *Trading Communities in the Roman World: A Micro-Economic and Institutional Perspective*. Columbia Studies in the Classical Tradition 37. Leiden.

van Minnen, P. 1986. "The Volume of the Oxyrhynchite Textile Trade." *MBAH* 5, no.2: 88–95.

van Minnen, P. 1993. "Notes on Texts from Graeco-Roman Egypt." *ZPE* 96: 117–22.

von Soden, H. F. 1973. *Untersuchungen zur Homologie in den griechischen Papyri Ägyptens bis Diokletian*. Cologne.

Watson, A. 1991. *Roman Law and Comparative Law*. Athens, GA.

Wenger, L.1906. *Die Stellvertretung im Rechte der Papyri*. Leipzig.

Westermann, W. L. 1911. "Contracts and the Apprentice System in Roman Egypt." *CP* 9: 295–315.

Williamson, O. E. 1985. *The Economic Institutions of Capitalism*. New York.

Williamson, O. E. 1997. "Revisiting Legal Realism: The Law, Economics, and Organization Perspective." In S. G. Medema, ed., *Coasean Economics: Law and Economics and the New Institutional Economics*, 119–60. Norwell, MA.

Wipszycka, E. 1965. *L'industrie textile dans l'Égypte romaine*. Archiwum filologiczne 9. Warsaw.

Wolff, H. J. 1946. "Consensual Contracts in the Papyri?" *JJP* 1: 55–79.

Wolff, H. J. 1956. "Zur Romanisierung des Vertragsrechts der Papyri." *ZRG* 73: 1–28.

Wolff, H. J. 1957. "Die Grundlagen des griechischen Vertragsrechts." *ZRG* 74: 26–72.

Wolff, H. J. 1978. *Das Recht der griechischen Papyri Ägyptens in der Zeit der Ptolemäer und des Prinzipats: Organization und Kontrolle des privaten Rechtverkehrs*. Handbuch der Altertumswissenschaft 10.5.2. Munich.

Wolff, H. J. 2002. *Das Recht der griechischen Papyri Ägyptens in der Zeit der Ptolemäer und des Prinzipats: Bedingungen und Treibkräfte der Rechtsentwicklung*. Edited by H.-A. Rupprecht. Handbuch der Altertumswissenschaft 10.5.1. Munich.

Yiftach-Firanko, U. 2003. *Marriage and Marital Arrangements: A History of the Greek Marriage Document in Egypt, 4th century BCE–4th century CE*. Münchener Beiträge zur Papyrusforschung und Antiken Rechtsgeschichte 93. Munich.

Yiftach-Firanko, U. 2009. "The Cheirographon and the Privatization of Scribal Activity in Early Roman Oxyrhynchos." In E. Harris and G. Thür, eds., *Symposion 2007: Vorträge zur griechischen und hellenistischen Rechtsgeschichte*, 325–40. Vienna.

Zimmermann, R. 1996. *The Law of Obligations: Roman Foundations of the Civilian Tradition*. Oxford. First published 1990.

CHAPTER 9

Contracts, Agency, and Transaction Costs in the Roman Economy

Dennis Kehoe

In recent years, scholars have used increasingly sophisticated methods to analyze the nature of economic growth in ancient economies as well as the factors that might contribute to it. If we take urbanization as a proxy for economic performance, the Roman Empire achieved an impressive level of prosperity over the course of the first centuries CE, rivaling that of western Europe during the high Middle Ages and even in the early modern period.[1] Although it seems clear that population and technology imposed basic constraints on ancient economies, scholars have also recognized the complex role that law and legal institutions could play in shaping economic activity. In the Roman Empire, under the best-case scenario, the formal legal institutions of the Roman state, including laws and the courts that enforced them, would have lowered the transaction costs involved in doing business, by defining property rights clearly and establishing adequate means of resolving disputes. In this way, legal institutions would have contributed to growth in the Roman economy.[2] But the role of law in the economy is likely to have been much more complex, since it influenced, among other things, the relationship between the urban and rural economies and the distribution of wealth across society.[3]

---

1. For discussion of the phenomenon of urbanism as an indicator of significant economic change, see Scheidel 2009; Wilson 2009; Temin 2006; Temin 2013: 195–219.
2. See, e.g., Harris 2007: 519, arguing that the creation of praetorian remedies in the late Roman Republic "made commercial life more efficient."
3. See, e.g., Bang 2008, 2009. The constraints on economic growth imposed by population and technology are a principal theme of Scheidel, Morris, and Saller 2007, as well as of Bresson, Lo Cascio, and Velde forthcoming.

In this essay, I explore the relationship between law and the Roman economy by examining the governance structures that surrounded the contractual arrangements affecting the economic activities of countless people in the Roman Empire. By "governance structures," I mean the ways in which economic actors understood economic relationships arising from contracts and, on this basis, enforced them.[4] My approach is to examine two areas of the law crucial to the economy, contracts and agency, to analyze the incentives that formal legal institutions created for people involved in significant economic relationships. Contracts, of course, were fundamental to economic activity, since they shaped countless transactions involving virtually every class in Roman society across the empire. Also crucial for the economy is agency, in the general economic sense of agents performing significant economic tasks for principals.[5] Agency as an economic institution is closely tied to contract law. To be sure, in many contractual relationships, one party is the agent for another, but there seems to be a particularly complex relationship between agency and contract law in Roman society, because of the limitations that Roman law placed on the liability of property owners who employed agents entering into contracts with third parties.

I argue that, in developing their approach to contract law and agency, the Roman legal authorities struggled to balance a number of competing concerns. These included generally promoting freedom of contracting, responding to the risk aversion of upper-class Roman property owners, and protecting the property rights of certain key social groups. For the most part, Roman rules can be regarded as "efficient," in the sense that they defined property rights precisely and encouraged bargaining. The formal law of Roman obligations and agency, however, only tell part of the story. Our understanding of the governance structures surrounding contracts in the Roman economy is much better when we consider them in the context of that economy's "informal institutions," including the basic social values that members of Roman society internalized.[6]

---

4. For discussion of governance structures and contracts, see Williamson 1985.
5. Furubotn and Richter 2005: 162–70.
6. Although Boldizzoni (2011) goes too far, in my view, in rejecting "modernist" approaches to the ancient economy, he does make the important point that economic institutions have to be understood in terms of the social values of the societies involved.

Remedies in Roman Contract Law

Let us begin by considering economic incentives created in Roman contract law. In assessing the economic significance of contract law, an essential question is whether a legal system establishes the appropriate incentives for people to abide by contracts, since it is not always economically efficient to do so. The penalties that legal systems develop for breach of contract can have important economic consequences, since they can potentially discourage productive arrangements by imposing inadequately or excessively stringent penalties for breach of contract. To turn to Roman law, it theoretically promoted commercial activity by defining the property rights of the parties to a contract precisely, thus making clear to both parties their rights and obligations arising from a contract. One important element in this process is the way in which the Roman courts would enforce default rules in contracts. Default rules serve to fill in "gaps" in the contract, that is, contingencies that the parties could not take the time to negotiate about at the outset of their relationship, either because they were unforeseen or because it would simply be too costly to negotiate about all possible ones.[7] Modern courts, at least in the United States, tend to impose default rules that are termed "majoritarian" or "market-mimicking," in that they represent the preference of what most contracting parties would have negotiated had they taken the time to do so, not necessarily what the individual people in the contract might have preferred. The other type of default rule would be one "tailored" to the preferences of the parties involved in the contract under dispute. One major advantage of majoritarian default rules is that they spare the courts the task of figuring out the intentions of the parties themselves when adjudicating disputes; likewise, the treatment of contracts in courts will be predictable, so parties will have a baseline against which to negotiate before a dispute ever ends up in court.

In the Roman consensual contract, the default rules depended on the good faith of both parties, which, in turn, revolved around the common meaning of the terms that might be part of a contract. This approach to contract law may find a parallel in testamentary law, particularly in the legacy of a *fundus cum instrumento*, that is, the legacy of an estate, with all of the equip-

---

7.   For default rules, see, among a great deal of literature, Craswell 2000; Schwartz 1992; Ayres and Gertner 1989; Katz 1990: 217; R. A. Posner 2009.

ment and slaves needed to produce an income from it (*Dig.* 33.7).[8] In their treatment of the legacy of a *fundus cum instrumento*, the Roman jurists were concerned that their interpretation of the intentions of testators who sought to pass an income-generating property on to a successor balanced the interests of both the legatee and the heirs. In developing their definitions of a *fundus cum instrumento*, the jurists displayed a range of opinions as to what constituted an income from a farm, but the principle they generally followed—outlined by the jurists Celsus and, earlier, Servius Sulpicius Rufus—was to interpret the wording of a will in accordance with common usage of terms rather than the particular meaning that an individual testator applied to them (*Dig.* 33.10.7.2).[9] Having transparent and straightforward rules made it easier to interpret wills, and the same principle would apply to settling disputes involving contracts and to renegotiating them in response to changing circumstances. When we consider farm tenancy, an institution of fundamental importance to the empire's agrarian economy, the default rules establishing the normative Roman farm lease served to define the rights and obligations of landowners and tenants on matters that they had not negotiated but that might be areas of dispute; as will be discussed below, one potentially contentious issue concerned what would happen when the harvest failed and the tenant could not pay the rent.

To turn to the remedies for breach of contract, an important question, as mentioned previously, is whether Roman law provided appropriate incentives for people to enter into potentially productive contracts and to fulfill their obligations. If the remedies for breach impose too great a penalty on the breaching party or provide too little compensation to the party that has suffered a breach, people will be discouraged from entering into potentially productive contracts. In this connection, it is worthwhile to consider the concept of "the efficient breach of contract."[10] Considering that a contract is only efficient when the gains from fulfilling it outweigh the costs, a contract will be efficiently breached when the gains, or surplus, to be derived from doing so will be greater than the surplus from maintaining the contract. Thus a contract can be efficiently breached when the seller finds someone willing to of-

---

8.   For discussion of such legacies, see Kehoe 1997: 113–23.
9.   On this passage, see Kehoe 1997: 100.
10.   For this concept, see the groundbreaking discussion of Posner and Rosenfield 1977; Schwartz (1992) is skeptical whether courts can apply economically efficient solutions to contract disputes. For more general discussion of the issue, see Mahoney 2000: 118–23; De Geest and Wuyts 2000: 143; Shavell 2004: 338–85; Shavell 2009; R. A. Posner 2009.

fer a much higher price than the original purchaser. Under this circumstance, both the seller and the original purchaser could be better off if the former takes advantage of his new opportunity, as long as he provides the purchaser with appropriate compensation. If the compensation prescribed by the law is excessive, however, the seller will have every incentive to "overperform," that is, to sell to the original purchaser when both could gain if he did not do so.[11] If the compensation is too little, the seller will have too much of an incentive to breach his contract and leave the purchaser in the lurch. Still worse, in either contingency, because of misaligned incentives, many contracts of sale will never be entered into in the first place.

The law of Roman consensual contracts—notably sale (*emptio-venditio*), lease (*locatio-conductio*), partnership (*societas*), and mandate (*mandatum*)— could be viewed as efficient from a modern standpoint, in that all damages for breach were monetary for each contract, with no provision for specific performance.[12] The preference for monetary damages is most apparent with obligations arising from consensual contracts, which were defined as creating in personam claims. Such claims imposed obligations on the parties but did not give anyone a right to a particular piece of property, and a creditor in this situation faced the risk of the insolvency of the debtor, who might have obligations toward other creditors. However, the principle of monetary damages also obtained even in much stronger claims in rem, for example, when a plaintiff sought to vindicate ownership over a piece of property in the possession of another person. In this circumstance, the unsuccessful defendant might pay monetary damages and keep the property, whose value would be determined either by the plaintiff under oath or by the judge.[13] In fact, in certain procedures, the defendant might undertake a *sponsio praeiudicialis*, a formal promise to pay the plaintiff a certain sum of money if the defendant lost the case–for example, in a dispute over the ownership of a slave.[14]

Monetary damages are seen as economically efficient, since they avoid wasteful activity and expenses by compelling someone to perform a contract when there was a greater net gain to be achieved from the contract by breach-

---

11. In this connection, see E. A. Posner 2009, arguing against strict liability in the enforcement of contracts (in American law).
12. For basic discussion of Roman consensual contracts, see Kaser 1971: 545–80; Kaser and Hackl 1996: 369–74 (monetary damages in Roman lawsuits).
13. Kaser and Hackl 1996: 339.
14. See Kaser and Hackl 1996: 346.

ing.[15] For example, in the case of a sale, the court could not compel a seller breaching a contract to deliver the specific item promised to the buyer. In a case involving a farm lease, a court could not compel an owner to fulfill a lease by providing a tenant with a farm; if the owner failed to provide a farm, the only compensation that the tenant could expect would be in terms of monetary compensation. In practice, however, it is likely that many lawsuits for breach of contract or other disputes ended with the plaintiff performing his end of the deal. Thus, even after the "joinder of issue" (*litis contestatio*), when the judge was already appointed and the time for the trial was set, the defendant could avoid an adverse judgment by performing. He might have an incentive to do so if the anticipated damages resulting from the suit were quite substantial or if losing the suit would result in a loss of reputation or in *infamia*.[16]

In Roman law, monetary compensation for breach of contract was designed to make the tenant or another party suffering a breach "whole"; the affected party would often receive his interest in the contract being completed, *quod sua interest*. Precisely what this meant in an individual case could be complex and controversial. The degree of compensation to which a plaintiff in a breach of contract case might be entitled to varied depending on the nature of the action or remedy under which he sued.[17] In a lease for a house, for example, a landlord who failed to provide a tenant with the house specified in the contract had to cover the expenses that the tenant would bear in renting another dwelling (Labeo, *Dig.* 19.2.28.2).[18] But the tenant was not allowed to claim his interest in every case. Thus a lessee of a block of flats, or an *insula*, who commonly sublet the individual apartments to tenants might suffer substantial losses if he lost the lease—for example, if the owner was forced to demolish the property because of its poor condition. In a case discussed by the Augustan jurist Alfenus (*Dig.* 19.2.30 pr.), the lessee would only be entitled to a reduction in rent for the time that his subtenants were not able to live in the building. This lessee would not be able to claim profits lost from sub-

---

15. Shavell 2004: 379.
16. Kaser and Hackl 1996: 371–74; see also Nörr 1993. The penalty for conviction in *bonae fidei iudicia* would make participating in commercial life more difficult, since, among other things, the person convicted was restricted in appearing in court on his own behalf or on behalf of others.
17. See Kaser 1971: 448–501. Contracts of sale often included a stipulation for the seller to pay double if the purchaser were evicted from the property; see Zimmermann 1996: 296–302.
18. On this passage, see Frier 1980: 76–77.

leasing the apartments, and he would remain liable to the subtenants for their loss of habitation. The owner would be liable to the lessee for the latter's lost profits if he demolished the building not out of necessity but for some other purpose—for instance, to build something better.[19] In the law of delict, the jurists recognized that the victim's damages might well go beyond simply the immediate costs of the property and might include lost income (*lucrum cessans*) and future losses (*damnum emergens*).[20]

The compensation resulting from breach of contract in Roman consensual contracts seems to correspond most closely to modern "expectation damages."[21] Expectation damages provide greater compensation than "reliance" or "restitution" damages. Restitution damages awarded to a party suffering a breach compensate him only for what he has provided to the party who has breached the contract. With reliance damages, the party suffering the breach receives this restitution plus any investment that he has made in connection with the contract.[22] Reliance damages do not compensate someone for lost profits, as expectation damages do. Of course, it is by no means completely straightforward to determine what expectation damages actually are, and this area of the law has been the subject of a great deal of litigation.[23]

Providing compensation for breach of contract in Roman law was undoubtedly somewhat more complicated than what I have described, because of the possibility of negotiating penalty clauses at the outset. These were apparently common in contracts throughout the Roman world—for example, in labor contracts in Dacia or in the mining law from Vipasca in Spain.[24] The early third-century jurist Paul (*Dig.* 19.2.54.1) discusses a lease for a *fundus* in which both the landlord and the tenant stipulated to pay penalties for breach: the landlord was to pay a tenant if he expelled him from the farm, whereas the tenant was to pay the landlord if he left the farm early. In many contracts from Roman Egypt, the parties promise to pay a penalty of 50 percent, the ἡμιόλιον, in the case of breach.[25] In the later empire, a constitution preserved

19. See Capogrossi Colognesi 2005: 22–23.
20. On this, see Kaser 1971: 501 n. 20.
21. Craswell 2000: 3; Mahoney 2000; De Geest and Wuyts 2000: 143.
22. Mahoney 2000: 121.
23. See Frier and White 2005: 468–545.
24. Mayer-Maly 1956: 149–51.
25. For literature on contracts in the papyri, see Rupprecht 1994: 120–21. I thank Gerhard Thür for bringing the ἡμιόλιον to my attention during the oral discussion at the 2009 Legal Documents in Ancient Societies conference.

in the ninth-century Byzantine law code known as the Basilica established that both landlord and tenant could end the lease early without an additional penalty clause, unless the penalty had been specifically negotiated at the outset of the contract (*Cod. Iust.* 4.65.34; *Bas.* 20.1.25). This general rule notwithstanding, penalty clauses surely raised the costs for breaching the contract, so they affected the negotiations that parties to a contract would enter into when it was more advantageous to breach. But we might also imagine that such penalty clauses would be included in the contracts when one party or the other felt vulnerable to a breach—in other words, when standard contractual arrangements would encourage too much breaching of the contract. From another perspective, one could regard penalty clauses as establishing *ex ante* what the parties' interests were in not having the contract breached. Penalties could then be regarded as efficient in that they more precisely defined the property rights of the parties to a contract. There was nothing to stop the parties from negotiating around penalty clauses.[26]

In farm tenancy, limiting liability for breach to monetary damages would significantly affect the relationships between landowners and tenants. Roman contract law offered the tenant the protection of what is called a "liability rule," according to which a person breaching a contract would have to offer the other party compensation at an objectively determined price. The alternative to this is a "property rule," which gives a party to a contract much stronger rights. In farm tenancy, a property rule would give tenants rights of possession, so that they could not be forced to give up the land held under lease and could sell their rights as they pleased, at a price they found appropriate.[27] The tenure rights under which *coloni* on the North African imperial estates occupied their land correspond to a "property rule," since they enjoyed perpetual leaseholds with the right to bequeath and otherwise alienate their cultivation rights.[28]

Monetary damages theoretically encouraged landowners and tenants under Roman leases to negotiate to resolve disputes. Likewise, the tenant was entitled to compensation if any improvements he made to the leased property raised its value and potential income beyond the lease period—for ex-

---

26. Berger (1911: 6, 34–36, 43–44) points out that parties are free to establish penalties in contracts preserved on papyri from Greco-Roman Egypt.
27. For discussion of liability and property rules, see Mahoney 2000: 120. Cf. Katz 1990: 189–90; Calabresi and Melamed 1972; Kaplow and Shavell 1996.
28. See Kehoe 2007a: 69–70.

ample, if the tenant planted new vines or installed an irrigation system and would not benefit from those enhancements if he gave up his lease. The tenant's right to compensation for "unexhausted improvements" established a legal endowment for the tenant to enter into negotiations with the landlord in undertaking such investment.[29] In accordance with the Coase theorem, as long as property rights are defined precisely and so long as transaction costs are not a factor, the two parties will reach an efficient arrangement. Of course, in the real world, there can be many impediments to private bargaining, and transaction costs are never zero.[30] In practice, it is likely that negotiations between a landowner and tenant would favor the economically more powerful landowner. Moreover, there was an asymmetry in the effects that a breach of contract would have on a tenant compared to a landowner, since many tenants depended for their livelihood on the farms they were leasing. The monetary compensation to which the tenant was entitled if a landowner decided to lease the farm to someone else or to use it for some other purpose could hardly replace the catastrophic loss of income for one or even many years. One of the criticisms of "expectation damages" as compensation for a breach of a contract is that it is often difficult to measure the losses resulting from a breach. This would be especially difficult in the case of farm tenants, and it is likely that the tenant would place a higher value on his lease than would society as a whole.[31] Consequently, the tenant would be on a very unequal footing when negotiating with a landowner for compensation in order to change the terms of a lease.

The question now to be addressed concerns how the formal rules I have described affected the economic relationships between landowners and tenants in the Roman Empire. The available evidence, primarily from the legal sources, suggests that the Roman legal authorities displayed a great deal of flexibility in adapting the law to the realities of the Roman economy. The Roman legal authorities responded to the needs of upper-class landowners, whose income greatly depended on continued production by their tenants. We can trace this flexibility in the Roman legal authorities' response to issues involving risk in agriculture. Certainly, in view of the droughts that were characteristic of Mediterranean agriculture, allocating the risk for drought and crop failure between landowner and tenant was a crucially important

---

29. Kehoe 1997: 199–200.
30. For the Coase theorem, see Coase 1960; Medema and Zerbe 2000.
31. For the so-called endowment effect, see Curran 2000.

issue.[32] In the classical lease contract, whose basic rules were established in the late Roman Republican by the jurist Servius Sulpicius Rufus (apud Ulpian), the tenant was only entitled to a remission of rent when an unforeseeable disaster (*vis maior*) made it impossible for him to harvest a crop.[33] The types of disasters that qualified as *vis maior* included an invasion of an army, an unusual infestation by predatory birds, or an unforeseeable natural disaster like an earthquake or an unaccustomed heat wave. For his part, the tenant bore considerable risk. Since he paid a rent in cash, he was responsible both for the size of the harvest and for the market price of the crops. The tenant remained obligated to pay his rent when the foreseeable risks associated with agriculture (*vitia ex re*), which might include drought (just not the unforeseeable one classified as *vis maior* in the Servian scheme), diminished his crop. The emperor Antoninus Pius, in a rescript quoted by Ulpian, applied this strict demarcation of risk when he rejected a request for a remission of rent on the basis of a poor crop, or *sterilitas* (*Dig.* 19.2.15.5). In making this ruling, the emperor was enforcing a default contract rule, as he did in a second rescript quoted by Ulpian, in which the emperor characterized as "revolutionary" a request for remission of rent on the basis of the age of the vines on the farm held under lease. In conventional Roman lease law, the tenant could be expected to take the condition of the farm into account when he entered into the lease.[34]

But it is not clear that such a strict demarcation of risk and, thus, the strict application of an untailored default rule really served the interests of landowners, since many types of risk that would reduce the tenant's crop substantially, leaving him unable to pay his rent, were not classifiable as *vis maior*.[35] If the approach of Antoninus Pius accorded landowners more power in the lease, that was a victory of limited value, since landowners often depended on the long-term tenure on the part of their tenants and expected that

---

32. For the frequency and effects of droughts in the Mediterranean, see especially Horden and Purcell 2000: 175–230. This section of the present essay draws on my discussion in Kehoe 2013.

33. On remission of rent in Roman law, see especially Frier 1989–90; du Plessis 2003; Capogrossi Colognesi 2005. Capogrossi Colognesi interprets the landlord's obligation to grant a remission of rent as deriving from his contractual obligations to provide a farm that the tenant can use. Frier, by contrast, sees remission as justified by the impossibility of the tenant's fulfilling his contractual obligations.

34. I discuss this text in more detail in Kehoe 1997: 101–4.

35. See Capogrossi Colognesi 2005: 76–77, 100; Kehoe 1997: 221–34; Kehoe 2007a: 109–19; Kehoe 2013: 197–205.

the tenants would invest their own resources in the continued productivity of the farm.[36] The question is whether the law could provide incentives to overcome impediments to bargaining between landowner and tenant and thus encourage the continuation of productive lease arrangements despite the risk inherent in Mediterranean agriculture.

To some extent, the Roman imperial chancery provided such incentives in the third century, by showing some flexibility in interpreting the rules of leases. Essential to this flexibility were the chancery's recognition that landowners might grant remissions of rent for poor crops out of social considerations and its definition of the rights and obligations of landowners and tenants when the former granted such remissions. Papinian (*Dig.* 19.2.15.4) established the principle that in granting a remission for a poor crop, *sterilitas*, the landowner did not renounce his right to the rent for the entire lease period. In responding to a petition concerning a remission of rent, the emperor Alexander Severus applied the same principle (*Cod. Iust.* 4.65.8, 231), and it has become part of the civilian legal tradition.[37] Papinian and, later, Alexander Severus left undefined what counted as *sterilitas*, and the Roman legal tradition, from medieval times until the early modern period, struggled to define what crop loss was substantial enough to justify a remission of rent.[38] When Roman legal policy accorded the landowner a continuing claim on the rent even after granting a remission, it certainly seemed to recognize his superior bargaining position in relationship to the tenant. At the same time, the policy probably encouraged landowners to grant remissions of rent; at least, it removed a major disincentive to do so, since the landowner could grant a remission without renouncing any contractual claims and could theoretically use the tenants' debt as a bargaining chip against them—for example, to keep them from leaving the land. From the point of the Roman government, this approach supported a socially desirable goal of keeping tenants on the land. Of course, how remissions of rent actually affected the relationships between landowners and tenants depended on many factors, including not just the relative scarcity of tenants capable of cultivating farms productively

---

36. For my argument for this position, see Kehoe 1997: 193–209; 2007a: 95–109.
37. For these texts, see also Capogrossi-Colognesi 2005: 87–90.
38. See Capogrossi-Colognesi 2005; later traditions most often considered the loss of half of the crop to be decisive (but debated whether the losses were to be reckoned in terms of the size of the harvest or the sale price they would bring). Later traditions usually ruled out remissions of rent after the crops were harvested. At that point, the crops were the tenant's property, so all the risk involving them legally fell on the tenant.

but also the broader social values that defined relations between landowners and tenants.

Also essential to the imperial chancery's flexibility in interpreting lease disputes involving the allocation of risk was taking into account the customary rules in a region, which would have affected how landowners and tenants understood the terms of their contract. This approach is explicit in the rescript of Alexander mentioned above (*Cod. Iust.* 4.65.8, 231) and in a later one of Diocletian (*Cod. Iust.* 4.65.18, 290), and modern courts also follow it in interpreting contracts.[39] The flexibility of the third-century emperors in recognizing local custom as representing part of this endowment of rights may be the result of a kind of bottom-up legislation. Caroline Humfress (2007) sees this as characteristic of the law codes in the late Roman empire, and her understanding of that legislation may also be applicable to the way in which the third-century chancery responded to petitions.[40] In any case, this flexibility helped to define property rights more precisely by basing solutions on the reasonable expectations that both parties had about the contract rather than on the traditional allocation of risk in Roman law. We can perhaps gain a better appreciation of the reality behind the contractual disputes addressed by the third-century chancery if we consider two imperial constitutions that seem to recognize that landowners and tenants were often linked in long-term tenancy relationships. In 260 C.E., the emperors Valerian and Gallienus (*Cod. Iust.* 4.65.16) established that in a lease tacitly renewed, landowners were not to raise the rent or otherwise alter the terms of tenure to the disadvantage of tenants. In the Roman legal principle of *relocatio tacita*, a lease was considered to be renewed on existing terms if the tenant remained on his holding and cultivated that land with no objection from the landowner. As I have argued elsewhere, the Roman legal authorities used this principle to describe, in terms of Roman legal conventions, tenure arrangements, often based in local custom, that granted the tenant much more security of tenure than would be recognizable in the classical Roman farm lease.[41] Later, the emperor Constantine made long-term tenure arrangements based on local tradition fully enforceable in Roman courts by recognizing customary rents

---

39. Cf. Craswell 2000: 13.
40. Humfress (2007) argues that late imperial legislation was often in response to some specific problem brought before the imperial authorities, even if the response to the problem took the form of more general legislation.
41. See Kehoe 1997: 206–9; 2007: 125–26.

as legally binding and by providing tenants the capacity to sue landowners who raised their rents without justification (*Cod. Iust.* 11.50.1). The constitution of Constantine underscores the difficulty that the Roman legal authorities faced in subjecting lease arrangements based on local custom and other social considerations to the rule of law and the authority of Roman courts.

The flexibility that the third-century Roman legal authorities displayed in interpreting lease law suggests some of the complexities involved in the interplay between the law and social institutions. Specifically, the jurists and the Roman chancery were concerned to keep an institution so basic to the economy as tenancy under the control of the law, whereas the social reality defined land tenure in terms scarcely recognizable under conventional Roman law. Roman legal policies contributed to making more "efficient," in the sense of defining property rights more precisely, a system of land tenure that landowners found important to their efforts to achieve stable long-term incomes. But this is far from claiming that the Roman system of tenancy was efficient in terms of making the best possible uses of resources. In the theoretical perspective of the new institutional economics, we should expect institutions that no longer function efficiently to fall by the wayside and to be replaced with ones that more closely answer the needs of society.[42] However, as Sheilagh Ogilvie (2007) argues, economic institutions do not necessarily persist because they are economically efficient. Sometimes they endure because they are rooted in a society's basic values—indeed, they can serve to reinforce those values—while at the same time serving the interests of the very powerful in society, providing them with resources, even if at the expense of other groups competing for the same resources or of society as a whole.[43] Indeed, in modern economies, it seems indisputable that a great deal of economic activity is at least partly the product of or "embedded in" social relations, and this would certainly be the case for the Roman world.[44] Legal and economic institutions, once established, have a tendency to develop in such a way as to prolong their existence and even extend their influence, regardless of the economic consequences.[45]

---

42. For this approach to analyzing economic institutions, see especially Alchian 1950.
43. Ogilvie 2007: 661–62. For discussion of the "instrumental" aspect of institutions, see Greif 2006: 153–54, 188, and elsewhere, citing especially Williamson 1985.
44. Granovetter 1985.
45. See Hodgson 1999.

Agency in the Roman Economy

We can trace the influence of social practices in another institution fundamental to the Roman economy: namely, agency.[46] As is well-known, Roman
property owners often relied on social dependents, particularly slaves and
freedmen, to serve as agents in important commercial transactions. As far as
slaves are concerned, providing the slave with some start-up money in the
form of a *peculium* and allowing the slave agent to conduct business on his
own, in exchange for some portion of the profits, helped to protect property
owners against opportunistic behavior on the part of their agents.[47] As a kind
of "residual claimant" (someone with ownership rights in the business), the
slave agent would have every incentive to operate the business properly,
since, absent some catastrophic falling out with his owner, he could be confident of retaining the profits that he generated. The agent would take on much
of the responsibility of running the business, including the monitoring of em-
ployees, many of whom were also slaves.

A series of legal remedies introduced in the third or second century B.C.E.
and later called the *actiones adiecticiae qualitatis* defined the liability of property owners when agents undertook obligations on their behalf.[48] The agents
whose activities were covered under these remedies included shipmasters,
sons in power, and slaves who were operating businesses with the *peculia* set
at their disposal, as well as people of any status appointed to supervise a
specific type of business, or *institores*. Generally, these remedies limited the
liability of the principal; he could be held liable for the *peculium* set at the
disposal of his agent, if the agent were a slave or a son in power, or the liability might strictly be limited to the types of transactions for which the principal gave the *institor* permission to act on his behalf. This approach to agency
provided some protection for third parties doing business with agents, and it
would also have removed possible barriers for them to do so. But in limiting
the liability of the principal, it also seems to have responded to the needs of
risk-averse Roman property owners, who were interested primarily in preserving their property and deriving predictable incomes from it rather than
in taking risks in entrepreneurial activities.[49]

---

46. This section develops ideas presented in Kehoe 2013.
47. Andreau (2004) has a very different interpretation of the *peculium*, viewing primarily as a
    means for the slave to purchase freedom. On specific measures to prevent opportunistic
    behavior, see Ober's discussion in chapter 2 in the present volume.
48. De Ligt 1999; Aubert 1994: 46–91; Aubert 2013; Wacke 1994; Plescia 1984.
49. For the risk aversion of upper-class property owners, see Kehoe 1997. For arguments

This discussion might suggest that the type of commercial enterprises that Roman property owners could undertake might have been limited in scope, given the limited nature of Roman agency law, at least compared with a modern economy. However, William Harris's recent (2006) study of money and credit in the Roman world indicates that Roman businesspeople were capable of managing complex arrangements over great distances around the Mediterranean world. Part of the solution was to rely on social networks to create many business arrangements, as Verboven (2002) and Bang (2008) emphasize in recent studies of commerce in the Roman world. But relying on social networks to create commercial opportunities was only part of the solution; another difficulty involved monitoring the agents who carried out significant transactions on behalf of far-off principals. If the *peculia* or other financial support they received provided agents with incentives to work hard and make profits, property owners still needed some means to enforce appropriate behavior on the part of their agents. Roman property owners were faced with the difficulty of creating incentives that aligned the interests of their agents reasonably with their own.[50] Agents could exploit asymmetries of information, in that the agent would always be better informed about the business he was conducting than would be a principal who was far away or otherwise not in a position to observe the agent's actions closely. An unscrupulous agent would have every temptation to enrich himself at his employer's expense.

The solution to this problem lay in the social relationships between property owners and their agents, which were far more important than any contractual relationship between the two groups. Using social dependents as agents provided Roman society with an institution that performed some of the functions filled in more advanced economies by firms that have their own distinct legal personality (as distinct from the people engaging in a business transaction).[51] With the exception of ones created to collect taxes, Roman partnerships, or *societates*, were, in essence, of short duration, formed for a specific business purpose. They would dissolve upon the withdrawal or death of one of the partners. To be sure, some partnerships, such as that of Cn. Domitius Lucanus and Cn. Domitius Tullus, wealthy and politically

---

that members of the Roman upper classes were more aggressive and enterprising in pursuing profits, see Rathbone 1991 (on agriculture); Wilson 2002 (on investing in technology).

50. See Frier and Kehoe 2007: 122–34; Furubotn and Richter 2005: 354–404.
51. For a similar view, see Mouritsen 2011: 218.

powerful brothers in the Flavian period, might last a long time. These brothers formed a partnership, apparently one involving all of their property, a *societas omnium bonorum*, and managed extensive holdings in land, including clay pits supplying the brick industry near Rome.[52] But the existence of partnerships, no matter how large and of how long a duration, does not change the fact that Roman property owners organized their business activities around the hierarchical structure of the *familia*. So how did the property owners maintain control over a system of organizing commerce that depended on social hierarchies but allowed agents a great deal of freedom in operating businesses?

The ideology standing behind the hierarchical structure of the Roman *familia* played a crucial role. In his groundbreaking study of freedmen in Roman society, Henrik Mouritsen (2011) argues convincingly that this group fulfilled a crucial managerial function for Roman property owners.[53] In Mouritsen's view, property owners had much the same relationship with freed business managers as they did with slaves. If the freedman no longer lived off a *peculium* that was formally the property of a slave owner and theoretically could be withdrawn at any time, he still depended on the financial support of his patron. In effect, the career of a person involved in the management of business affairs for an upper-class Roman might involve serving as both a slave and a freedman; manumission created new rights and a new status for the freedman, but his financial relationship with his former owner and now patron did not necessarily change completely. Freedmen continued work for their patrons and received financial support from them, and they would be part of the circle of people for whom the patron would make provision in his will. Relationships between master and slave and between patron and freedman were, to some extent, defined by law. But patrons had few legal means to enforce the loyalty of a freedman, short of undertaking a complex and probably wrenching process of revoking freedom. Instead, relationships within the *familia* were largely defined by social values that asserted and protected the enviable position of property owners at the top of a social hierarchy. Certainly, a patron could exercise sanctions against an unsatisfactory freedman; these were social rather than legal. The patron might with-

---

52. Pliny, *Ep.* 8.18; Kehoe 2007b: 561–62.

53. Brokaert 2011 (I thank Dr. Brokaert for providing me with this paper) argues on the basis of epigraphical evidence for the widespread use of freedmen as business agents, often working in close cooperation with their patrons.

draw financial support or exclude the freedman from being a beneficiary in his will.[54] But more important was the larger system of social values that made possible the Roman approach toward managing diffuse business interests. The good faith and loyalty of the agent were crucial. For this reason, Roman society developed a set of virtues—such as *fides, obsequium,* and *probitas,* all centering around loyalty—to characterize the ideal freedman.[55] This ideology seems to have enforced loyalty and trust precisely in those situations in which it was very difficult for a patron or principal to exercise any kind of meaningful control over an agent, because of the asymmetry of information and the distances involved.[56]

This system of agency fostered a highly decentralized organization of business characterized by subelite entrepreneurs who disposed of substantial resources. This seems to have been the case whether the resources ultimately came from a wealthy property owner setting up slaves in business or providing financial support for freedmen or from a more modest artisan providing training to a skilled slave and then helping him become set up in business. In the Arretine *terra sigillata* industry, as recently analyzed by Gunnar Fülle (1997), production was loosely organized around master artisans who had slave and freed assistants. Often, the artisans who were slaves would operate in workshops independently from the master, drawing on the resources of a *peculium* allotted to them. The masters provided their slaves training in the ceramic craft and, for a period, benefited from their skilled labor. With time, the slave artisans would set out on their own and pay the master back for their training, eventually earning their own freedom. The dependence of craft industries on individualized training and a kind of partnership between the master artisan and his slaves would tend to keep the units of production modest in size, with little room for vertical integration.[57]

As Mouritsen emphasizes in his study of Roman freedmen, it is quite difficult to evaluate the Roman slave system, at least as far as it pertains to the use of slaves as business managers, purely in terms of economic rationality. It can even legitimately be questioned whether manumission, which has conventionally been understood as the most important reward for good behavior and productive service, can be fully explained in terms of ratio-

---

54. Mouritsen 2011: 149–59.
55. Mouritsen 2011: 51–65, 170, 202, 218, 240.
56. Mouritsen 2001: 206–47.
57. Kehoe 2007b: 559–66.

nally managing a slave labor force so as to provide the greatest possible return for property owners.[58] This is not to deny that Roman property owners gained from using manumission as an incentive to reward particularly loyal or productive slaves. However, other factors also affected the decisions of property owners to manumit slaves. It was a basic value of upper-class Romans to display loyalty and affection toward slaves who had served them well, and many slaves who worked closely with their masters might reasonably expect it. The loyalty and affection that characterized the master-slave relationship would continue to be an essential feature of the patron-freedman relationship. But manumission was so embedded in the Roman concept of the *familia* that it seems inseparable from the Roman method of organizing business. This employment of social dependents as business agents resulted from the efforts of property owners to pursue economic gain in a society subject to overarching social constraints; the slave system basic to Roman society set bounds on the rationality within which Roman property owners could function.[59]

The uniqueness of the Roman approach to agency and its implications for the organization of business becomes more apparent when it is contrasted to the very different system of agency documented in Ptolemaic Egypt on the basis of the Zenon archive, as analyzed by Sitta von Reden.[60] In Ptolemaic Egypt, the institution of agency was much less formal than in classical Roman law. Property owners with significant business interests outside their immediate geographical area relied on so-called traveling agents, who would lend money and enforce obligations on behalf of the principal. But unlike in Roman law, no formal legal relationship established the liability of the principal when a traveling agent took some action on his behalf. Rather, if the traveling agent arranged a loan or collected a debt, he created obligations between himself and the principal and between himself and the third party with whom he might be dealing on behalf of the principal. All of this revolved around close interpersonal relationships—people would deal with parties whom they knew and could vouch for.

---

58. Mouritsen 2011: 174–205.
59. On bounded rationality and the ancient economy, see Kehoe 2007b: 37–39; Frier and Kehoe 2007: 121–22.
60. Von Reden 2007: 239–50.

Conclusion

In this essay, I have attempted to offer a way to assess the role of law in the economy of the Roman Empire by examining the complex relationship between the authoritative legal institutions that the Roman state maintained and broader social institutions. In general, the Roman legal authorities struggled to keep larger economic institutions under the control of the law and courts. Freedom of contract was an essential feature of Roman law, and in the areas of the law with obvious direct bearing on the economy, sale and lease, the Roman legal authorities consistently sought to give precise definition to the property rights of contracting parties and thereby to encourage private bargaining by making the outcome of disputes as predictable as possible. Achieving this goal meant being flexible and adapting to the realities of the Roman economy, as we can see in the doctrine for treating social remissions of rent developed by Papinian and later applied by Alexander Severus. Although it is impossible to quantify its effects, the consistent pursuit of such a legal policy surely lowered the transaction costs that countless people in the Roman Empire faced when they entered into contracts, though few of these contracts resulted in disputes and though few of the ones that did ever found their way into a court. At the same time, as can be seen in the legal institutions surrounding agency, the Roman legal authorities operated within larger social institutions that they could influence but not control, and it seems likely that these larger social institutions affected the interplay between law and the economy more broadly. The introduction of the *actiones adiecticiae qualitatis* certainly did not create agency in the Roman economy but, rather, represented an effort to bring such relationships under the control of the law in such a way as to respond to the needs of upper-class Romans.[61] The Roman legal authorities faced the difficult challenge of maintaining authoritative institutions to regulate contractual relationships within the broad constraints imposed by social values and practices. That the Roman legal authorities persisted in this effort suggests the positive role that the law could play in the economy by defining property rights as precisely as possible and thereby reducing transaction costs.

---

61. See Wacke 1994.

Bibliography

Alchian, A. A. 1950. "Uncertainty, Evolution, and Economic Theory." *Journal of Political Economy* 58, no. 3: 211–21.

Andreau, J. 2004. "Sur les choix économiques des notables romains." In J. Andreau, J. France, and S. Pittia, eds. *Mentalités et choix économiques des Romains*, 71–85. Paris.

Aubert, J.-J. 1994. *Business Managers in Ancient Rome: A Social and Economic Study of Institores, 200 B.C.–A.D. 250.* Leiden.

Aubert, J.-J. 2013. "*Dumtaxat de peculio*: What's in a *Peculium*, or Establishing the Extent of the Principal's Liability." In P. du Plessis, ed., *New Frontiers: Law and Society in the Roman World*, 192–206. Edinburgh.

Ayres, I., and R. Gertner. 1989. "Filling Gaps in Incomplete Contracts: An Economic Theory of Default Rules." *Yale Law Journal* 99, no. 1: 87–130.

Bang, P. F. 2008. *The Roman Bazaar.* Cambridge.

Bang, P. F. 2009. "The Ancient Economy and New Institutional Economics." *JRS* 99: 194–206.

Berger, A. 1911. *Die Strafklauseln in den Papyrusurkunden: Ein Beitrag zum gräko-ägyptischen Obligationenrecht.* Leipzig. Repr., Aalen, 1965.

Boldizzoni, F. 2011. *The Poverty of Clio: Resurrecting Economic History.* Princeton.

Bouckaert, B., and G. De Geest, eds. 2000. *Encyclopedia of Law and Economics.* 5 vols. Cheltenham. Online 1999 edition available at http://encyclo.findlaw.com.

Bresson, A., E. Lo Cascio, and F. Velde, eds. Forthcoming. *Oxford Handbook of Economies in the Classical World.*

Brokaert, W. 2011. "The Demise of Status: Freedmen and Agency in Roman Business." Presented at the Oxford Roman Economy Project European Science Foundation Exploratory Workshop on *Craftsmen and Traders in the Roman World.* Oxford, July 21–23, 2011.

Calabresi, G., and A. D. Melamed. 1972. "Property Rules, Liability Rules, and Inalienability: One View of the Cathedral." *Harvard Law Review* 85, no. 6: 1089–1128.

Capogrossi Colognesi, L. 2005. *Remissio Mercedis: una storia tra logiche di sistema e autorità della norma.* Naples.

Coase, R. H. 1960. "The Problem of Social Cost." *Journal of Law and Economics* 3: 1–44. Reprinted in R. H. Coase, *The Firm, the Market, and the Law* (Chicago, 1990), 95–156.

Craswell, R. 2000. "Contract Law: General Theories." In Bouckaert and De Geest 2000: 3:1–24.

Curran, C. 2000. "The Endowment Effect." In Bouckaert and De Geest 2000: 1:819–35.

De Geest, G., and F. Wuyts 2000. "Penalty Clauses and Liquidated Damages." In Bouckaert and De Geest 2000: 3:141–61.

de Ligt, L. 1999. "Legal History and Economic History: The Case of the *Actiones Adiecticiae Qualitatis.*" *Tijdschrift voor Rechtsgeschiedenis* 47: 205–26.

du Plessis, P. J. 2003. "A History of *Remissio Mercedis* and Related Legal Institutions." PhD diss., Erasmus University Rotterdam.

Frier, B. W. 1980. *Landlords and Tenants in Imperial Rome*. Princeton.

Frier, B. W. 1989–90. "Law, Economics, and Disasters Down on the Farm: '*Remissio Mercedis*' Revisited." *BIDR*, 3rd ser., 31–32: 237–70.

Frier, B. W., and D. P. Kehoe 2007. "Law and Economic Institutions." In Scheidel, Morris, and Saller 2007: 113–43.

Frier, B. W., and J. J. White. 2005. *The Modern Law of Contracts*. St. Paul.

Fülle, G. 1997. "The Internal Organization of the Arretine *Terra Sigillata* Industry: Problems of Evidence and Interpretation." *JRS* 87: 111–55.

Furubotn, E. G., and R. Richter 2005. *Institutions and Economic Theory: The Contribution of New Institutional Economics*. 2nd ed. Ann Arbor. 1st ed., 1997.

Granovetter, M. 1985. "Economic Action and Social Structure: The Problem of Embeddedness." *American Journal of Sociology* 91: 481–510.

Greif, A. 2006. *Institutions and the Path to the Modern Economy: Lessons from Medieval Trade*. Cambridge.

Harris, W. V. 2006. "A Revisionist View of Roman Money." *JRS* 96: 1–24.

Harris, W. V. 2007. "The Late Republic." In Scheidel, Morris, and Saller 2007: 511–39.

Hodgson, G. M. 1999. *Evolution and Institutions: On Evolutionary Economics and the Evolution of Economics*. Cheltenham.

Horden, P, and N. Purcell. 2000. *The Corrupting Sea: A Study of Mediterranean History*. Oxford.

Humfress, C. 2007. *Orthodoxy and the Courts in Late Antiquity*. Oxford.

Kaplow, L., and S. Shavell. 1996. "Property Rules versus Liability Rules: An Economic Analysis." *Harvard Law Review* 109, no. 4: 713–90.

Kaser, M. 1971. *Das römische Privatrecht: Erster Abschnitt, Das altrömische, das vorklassische und klassische Recht*. 2nd ed. HdA 10.3.3.1. Munich.

Kaser, M., and K. Hackl 1996. *Das römische Zivilprozeßrecht*. HdA 10.3.4. Munich.

Katz, A. W. 1990. "The Strategic Structure of Offer and Acceptance: Game Theory and the Law of Contract Formation." *Michigan Law Review* 89, no. 2: 215–95. Excerpted in A. W. Katz, ed., *Foundations of the Economic Approach to Law* (New York, 1998), 189–97.

Kehoe, D. P. 1997. *Investment, Profit, and Tenancy: The Jurists and the Roman Agrarian Economy*. Ann Arbor.

Kehoe, D. P. 2007a. *Law and the Rural Economy in the Roman Empire*. Ann Arbor.

Kehoe, D. P. 2007b. "Production." In Scheidel, Morris, and Saller 2007: 543–69.

Kehoe, D. P. 2013. "Roman Economic Policy and the Law of Contracts." In T. A. J. McGinn, ed., *Obligations in Roman Law: Past, Present, and Future*, 189–214. Ann Arbor.

Mahoney, P. G. 2000. "Contract Remedies: General." In Bouckaert and De Geest 2000: 3:117–40.

Mayer-Maly, T. 1956. *Locatio Conductio: Eine Untersuchung zum klassischen römischen Recht*. Wiener rechtsgeschichtliche Arbeiten 4. Vienna.

Medema, S. G., and R. O. Zerbe, Jr. 2000. "The Coase Theorem." In Bouckaert and De Geest 2000: 1:836–92.

Mouritsen, H. 2011. *The Freedman in the Roman World*. Cambridge.

Nörr, D. 1993. "Mandatum, Fides, Amicitia." In D. Nörr and S. Nishimura, eds., *Mandatum und Verwandtes: Beiträge zum römischen und modernen Recht*, 13–37. Berlin.

Ogilvie, S. 2007. "'Whatever Is, Is Right'? Economic Institutions in Pre-industrial Europe." *Economic History Review* 60, no. 4 (2007): 649–84.

Plescia, J. 1984. "The Development of Agency in Roman Law." *Labeo* 30: 171–90.

Posner, E. A. 2009. "Fault in Contract Law." *Michigan Law Review* 107, no. 8: 1431–44.

Posner, R. A. 2009. "Let Us Never Blame a Contract Breaker." *Michigan Law Review* 107, no. 8: 1349–63.

Posner, R. A., and A. M. Rosenfield 1977. "Impossibility and Related Doctrines in Contract Law: An Economic Analysis." *Journal of Legal Studies* 6: 83–118.

Rathbone, D. 1991. *Economic Rationalism and Rural Society in Third-Century A.D. Egypt: The Heroninos Archive and the Appianus Estate*. Cambridge.

Rupprecht, H.-A. 1994. *Kleine Einführung in die Papyruskunde*. Darmstadt.

Scheidel, W. 2009. "In Search of Roman Economic Growth." *JRA* 22: 46–70.

Scheidel, W., I. Morris, and R. Saller, eds. 2007. *The Cambridge Economic History of the Greco-Roman World*. Cambridge.

Schwartz, A. 1992. "Relational Contracts in the Courts: An Analysis of Incomplete Agreements and Judicial Strategies." *Journal of Legal Studies* 21: 271–318.

Shavell, S. 2004. *Foundations of Economic Analysis of Law*. Cambridge, MA.

Shavell, S. 2009. "Why Breach of Contract May Not Be Immoral Given the Incompleteness of Contracts." *Michigan Law Review* 107, no. 8: 1561–81.

Temin, P. 2006. "Estimating GDP in the Early Roman Empire." In E. Lo Cascio, ed., *Innovazione tecnica e progresso economico nel mondo romano*, 31–54. Bari.

Temin. P. 2013. *The Roman Market Economy*. Princeton.

Verboven, K. 2002. *The Economy of Friends: Economic Aspects of Amicitia and Patronage in the Late Republic*. Collection Latomus 269. Brussels.

von Reden, S. 2007. *Money in Ptolemaic Egypt: From the Macedonian Conquest to the End of the Third Century BC*. Cambridge.

Wacke, E. 1994. "Die adjektizischen Klagen im Überblick." *ZRG* 111: 280–362.

Williamson, O. E. 1985. *The Economic Institutions of Capitalism: Firms, Markets, Relational Contracting*. New York.

Wilson, A. I. 2002. "Machines, Power, and the Ancient Economy." *JRS* 92: 1–32.

Wilson, A. I. 2009. "Indicators for Roman Economic Growth: A Response to Walter Scheidel." *JRA* 22: 71–82.

Zimmermann, R. 1996. *The Law of Obligations: Roman Foundations of the Civilian Tradition*. Oxford. First published 1990.

CHAPTER 10

From Free to Fee?

Judicial Fees and Other Litigation Costs during the High Empire and Late Antiquity

R. Haensch

It is a common assumption in modern scholarship that the costs of obtaining one's rights in a Roman court were high during late antiquity, much higher than in earlier times. One major reason presumed for this high expense were the officially sanctioned judicial fees, which were so costly that many people resorted to episcopal courts or private litigators. The result postulated is that the distance between the Roman state and its subjects became larger and larger.[1] To verify this hypothesis, it is necessary to collect and compare the evidence concerning litigation costs and judicial fees during the high empire and late antiquity.

Up until quite recently, our information on the costs of pursuing a case in court during late antiquity has derived from three main sources. First, there are a number of regulations preserved in the most important law code of late antiquity, the Code of Justinian. These regulations deal primarily with certain privileged groups who were entitled to pay fees at reduced rates.[2] Sec-

---

1. E.g., Di Segni, Patrich, and Holum 2003: 293: "Not many people could have afforded it; those who were less well off—probably the vast majority—resorted to other means . . . such as arbitration and the *episcopalis audientia.*"
2. See especially *Cod. Iust.* 3.2 (*de sportulis*); cf., further, 1.3.32, 3.10.2, 10.11.8.4, 12.19.12, 12.21.8, 12.25.4, 12.28.3, 12.29.3, 12.35.18. See also the hints of a general regulation by Justinian: *Inst.*4.6.25; Theoph. 4.6.24; *Nov.* 17.3, 82.7, 86.9 (cf. 124.3).

ond, John the Lydian, in his account of administrative offices in the Roman Empire (*de Magistratibus*), reveals some important information about what was typical during the first half of the sixth century at the court of the *praefectus praetorio Orientis*, the highest Roman official in the Roman East after the emperor.[3] Third, we have a key piece of evidence in an inscription from Thamugadi in North Africa, dated to the reign of the emperor Julian (361–63).[4] Finally, a fragmentary inscription published in 2003 forms an important addition to our knowledge, providing the most detailed account hitherto known on the costs of judicial proceedings.[5]

The new inscription comes from Caesarea Iudaeae. It consists of nine fragments and records a collection of ordinances issued by the *praefectus praetorio Orientis* Flavius Pusaeus (and others?).[6] Pusaeus probably held office between 465 and 467 and perhaps again in 473. While the editors and the reviewers of the *Bulletin Épigraphique, L'Année Épigraphique*, the *Supplementum Epigraphicum Graecum*, and the *Corpus Inscriptionum Iudaeae Palaestinae* have established a reliable text, the historical and judicial analysis of this important document has only just begun. Before undertaking such an analysis here, it will be helpful to present the text of the inscription and its translation, based on the recent edition in the *Corpus Inscriptionum Iudaeae Palaestinae*:

(Title)

[τύποι] δοθέντε[ς κατὰ τὰ θεῖα διατάγματα παρὰ τῶν ὑπερλαμπρῶν]
καὶ ἐξοχ(ωτάτων) ἐπάρχ(ων), Φλ(αουίου) Πουσέου τοῦ μεγαλο-
πρ(επεστάτου) καὶ ἐνδοξ(οτάτου) ἐπάρχου Ι *vacat* τῶν ἱερ[ῶ]ν
πραιτ[ωρίων --]

(col. I)

[ἐν τ]ῇ ἀνατολικῇ (διοικήσει) τὸν ἐπαρχικὸν τὸν μεθοδ[εύοντα
κ]ομίζεσθαι λόγῳ σπορτουλῶν κατὰ νο(μίσματα) ρ' νό(μισμα) α'
περετέρω δὲ νο(μισμάτων) η' μὴ παρέχεσθαι κ' ἂν ὑπερόγκ‹ο›ς εἴη ἡ
ποσότ[ης.]

3. Schamp 2006; Bandy 1983 (an older, English version).
4. *CIL* VIII 17896 = *FIRA* I² 64 = Chastagnol 1978: 75–88.
5. Di Segni, Patrich, and Holum 2003. D. Feissel makes important corrections (*BE* 2004: 394 = 2006: 718). See now *CIIP* II 1197. The inscription can be found also as *AE* 2003: 1808; *SEG* 2003: 1841.
6. On whether originally one or all *praefecti* were named, see Feissel, *BE* 2004: 394 = 2006: 718 and *CIIP*.

τῷ παραστάσιμον ἔχοντι ἀπὸ τῆς ἀνατολῆς νο(μίσματα) ιβ′
vacat
γνῶσις τῶν τυποθέντων ἀναλωμάτων πά[σῃ κατὰ]
vacat χώραν τάξι·
ὑπὲρ κλητικοῦ μονομερ[οῦς]
vacat πράγ[ματος κερ(άτια) --],
εἰς ἔκδοσιν τοῦ ὑπομνήμα[τος--] *vacat* ἐν χαρ[τ.. κερ(άτια) --]
ὑπὲρ δὲ καθαροῦ ὑπομνήμ[ατος] τοῖς αὐτοῖς [κερ(άτια) --],
ὑπὲρ ἀναγνωσίμου εἰς τ[ὸ] αὐτὸ μονομερὲς Ο [--]
vacat κλητικόν *vacat* [κερ(ατία) --],
ὑπὲρ κομπλευτρῶν *vacat*
παρὰ τοῦ παραβαλλομένου ἄχρι *vacat* νο(μισμάτων) ν′ [κερ(άτια) --]·
ἀπὸ νομισμάτων ν′ [ἕως νο(μισμάτων) ρ′· κερ(άτια) --],
ἀπὸ δὲ νο(μισμάτων) ρ′ ἕως νο(μισμάτων) [ρν′· κερ(άτια) --],
ἀπὸ δὲ νο(μισμάτων) ρν′ ἕω[ς νο(μισμάτων) σ′· νό(μισμα) α′?]

(col. II)
[--]
[? οὐδὲν πλέον ἀπαιτείσθω ?] *vacat* νο(μίσματος) α′.
[-*ca. 26 letters*-]ίοις τετύπωται
[-*ca. 26 letters*-]ΑΖΗ οὐδὲν ἧττον
[-*ca. 29 letters*-] καὶ ἐπὶ τοῖς σινγου
[λαρίοις --] *vacat*
[-- ? καταβά]λλεται τῷ
[-- ? ἡ ποσότη]ς ὑπερβ´αί`ν
[ει? --]Α
[-- παρέχ]ετω νο(μίσματα) αγ′
[-*ca. 40 letters*-]ς νο(μίσματα) α′

(col. III)
[--]
ἐξέπτορσιν ὑπὲρ χαρτῶν· κερ(άτια) ϛ′,
ἐκδοσίμου διαγνώσεως περεωθίσης· νό(μισμα) α′,
εἰ δὲ ἐκλαβῖν βούλοιτό τις τὴν ὑπερτεθίσαν διάγνωσιν,
vacat χαρτῶν μὲν *vacat* κερ(άτια) δ′,

ἐκδοσίμου δὲ παρ' ἑκατέρου μέρους ἐκλαμβάνοντος κερ(άτια) ϛ',
κομπλευ˙σ˙ίμου διαγνώσεως *vacat* κερ(άτια) η',
καὶ ἐπὶ τῶν ἐνκληματικῶν δὲ ὑποθέσεων τὰ αὐτὰ χρὴ παρέ[χειν.]
ὑπὲρ δηκρητοῦ κουράτορος προβολῆς ἢ ἐπιτρόπου γενικο[ῦ ἢ]
ἰδικοῦ· *vacat* ᾧ διαφέρι *vacat* κ[ερ(άτια) --].
ἐκποιήσεως ἕνεκεν βουλευτικοῦ πράγματο[ς κερ(άτια) --],
ἐπιτρόπου δὲ ἢ κουράτορος πρὸς τὴν ἀξίαν το[ῦ πράγματος ?]
vacat ἄχρι νο(μισμάτων) φ' τιμήματος ὁμο(ῦ)·
[ἀπὸ δὲ νο(μισμάτων) φ' ἕως νο(μισμάτων) ψ' ?] κερ(άτια) [--],
[ἀπὸ δὲ νο(μισμάτων) ψ' ἕως νο(μισμάτων) -- ?] κερ(άτια) ιβ',
[? ἀπὸ -- κἂν εἴη μεῖζον (τὸ τίμημα) οὐδὲν πε]ρετέρ[ω] *vacat*
                                            νο(μίσματος) α'.
[-*max. 15 letters*-]ΝΩΝ ˊἐˋκδοσίμο[υ τῶν] δηκρητῶν κερ(άτια) ϛ',
[? ὑπὲρ χαρτῶν ?] *vacat* κερ(άτια) δ',
[-- το]ῦ πραττομένου ᾧ δια[φ]έρι κερ(άτια) γ'.

(Title)
*Edicts issued according to the divine orders by the most splendid and most
eminent prefects; Flavius Pusaeus, the most magnificent and glorious prefect of
the sacred praetoria*

(col. I)
*In (the diocese) Oriens, the praefectianus sent to collect taxes shall receive on
account of sportulae one solidus on each hundred; but beyond eight solidi
nothing shall be exacted, even if the (whole) amount is in excess. To (the
praefectianus) who made appear (in the court) someone from the Oriens (the
maximum permitted is) 12 solidi.*

   *Schedule for the legal costs fixed by law for each office of the province:
   —for a writ of summons ex parte . . .
   —for delivery of a memorandum . . . for papyri . . . siliquae
   —for a clean copy of the memorandum to the same: . . . siliquae
   —for the reading of the same (writ of) summons ex parte . . .
   —for the writing out (of a memorandum) . . .
   —from the party that is sued: up to 50 solidi: . . . siliquae
   —from 50 solidi to 100 solidi . . . siliquae
   — . . . and from 100 solidi to 150 solidi . . . siliquae
   — . . . and from 150 solidi to 200 solidi: 1 solidus (?)*

(col. II)

... nothing must be required beyond 1 solidus

... it is ordered ... nothing less (5) ... and for the singulares ... is paid to the ...
exceeds (10) ... should pay 1⅓ solidus ... 1½ solidus ...

(col. III)

To the exceptores

—for papyri: 6 siliquae

—for issue of a definita causa: 1 solidus

And if one wants to receive (the record of) a deferred trial:

—for papyri: 4 siliquae

—and for the issue from each party who receives (the record): 6 siliquae

—for writing out the record of a trial: 8 siliquae

And in criminal trials the same amounts are to be paid.

For a decree of appointment of a general or a special curator (or guardian)

— (cost) to the interested party: ...

— ... in a matter of sale of property belonging to a decurion ...

— ... and for a (special) guardian or curator according to the value of the
transaction

—up to 500 (solidi) in value, the same

—and from 500 to 700 solidi (??): ...

—and from 700 to ... solidi (??): 12 siliquae ...

... nothing beyond 1 solidus

... of the issues of the decrees: 6 siliquae

—for papyri (?): 4 siliquae

—of the transacted (business) to the interested party: 3 siliquae

(translation Di Segni, Patrich, and Holum 2003, with minor changes)

Most of the preserved regulations deal with the fees for services under-
taken in connection with the court hearings held by governors of the provinces, who were themselves under the supervision of the *praefectus praetorio*
Orientis (hereafter PPO). The first section in column I focuses on the fees
charged in the first stage of a trial, that is, the summons. Under the heading
"For a writ of summons *ex parte*" (I.8–9: ὑπὲρ κλητικοῦ μονομερ[οῦς]
πράγ[ματος]), the text records three different fees, with short descriptions of
what each fee was for.[7] These categories are sometimes difficult to interpret,

---

7. Previous editors have assumed that lines 8–9 represent a separate fee rather than a heading

because the phrases are extremely laconic and highly technical, often using unparalleled vocabulary (the same is true for other paragraphs in the rest of the extant text).

From the inscription, it seems that the party who asked for a summons (thus setting the procedure in motion; i.e., the plaintiff) had to pay for the serving of the summons (I.10: εἰς ἔκδοσιν τοῦ ὑπομνήμα[τος--] *vacat* ἐν χαρ[τ.. κερ(άτια) --]), then for a fair copy of the document (I.11: ὑπὲρ δὲ καθαροῦ ὑπομνήμ[ατος] τοῖς αὐτοῖς [κερ(άτια) --]), and finally for the review of this fair copy by an official senior to the clerk who drafted it (I.12–13: ὑπὲρ ἀναγνωσίμου εἰς τ[ὸ] αὐτὸ μονομερὲς Ο [--]*vacat* κλητικόν *vacat* [κερ(άτια) --]).[8] As the lines following these show, the fees for the defendant depended on the amount of the suit, with three graduated rates.[9]

We thus find two different operating principles governing litigation costs for the same phase of a judicial session, namely, the summons. For the plaintiff, the fees were linked to different parts of the procedure; for the defendant, the fees were determined by the value of the lawsuit. Because the amounts to be paid are not preserved, we do not know which principle resulted in higher costs. Had this information survived, we might be in a better position to understand how both principles operated simultaneously in the same phase, differentiated by party. We also do not know who on the governor's staff was supposed to receive the fees.[10]

The next part of the inscription (column II) is almost completely lost. It likely contained the fees that had to be paid for introducing and then trying a case (*pro introducenda et cognoscenda causa*). Only with column III do we once again have an intelligible text. This final part of the inscription deals with the

---

under which fall the next three fees (i.e., lines 10–13) and have therefore posited a number in the lacuna at the end of line 9. I see no necessity for this assumption or supplement.

8.   In the administrative language of Roman officialdom, ἀναγιγνώσκω meant to check and control each phrase of a document. The argument of the first editors that ὑπὲρ ἀναγνωσίμου should refer to a person "who served the summons by reading it aloud, in case the defendant could not read" (Di Segni, Patrich, and Holum 2003: 283–84) is not convincing. See also Feissel 2006: 718; cf. the commentary in *CIIP*.

9.   How ὑπὲρ κομπλευτρῶν (line 14) is to be understood is an open question. Di Segni, Patrich, and Holum (2003) are certainly right to think of a Greek loanword from the Latin *compleo*. But it is entirely unclear whether the term refers to an office, as they argue (285–86), or a type of document. Feissel (2006) suggests that we see here a *sportula* connected with the act of completing documents.

10.   There is no reason to think—as do Di Segni, Patrich, and Holum (2003: 283)—that the *sportulae* were payable to a group of officials called *exsecutores*. *Exsecutor* was not an official title but a term that designated a variety of different officials who executed judgments (cf. Noethlichs 1981: 161).

fees payable to the shorthand judicial clerks, the *exceptores*, at the end of a trial. As is mentioned explicitly, the fees did not depend on the difference between civil and criminal cases.[11] Instead, the determining factor was the result of the trial. If the trial resulted in a final judgment (III.2: ἐκδοσίμου διαγνώσεως περεωθίσης), each party (?) was charged the maximum rate: one solidus for copying the verdict and a quarter of a solidus for the papyrus necessary to write the case up. But if the trial was deferred,[12] a party wanting a copy of such a verdict had to pay a quarter of a solidus for the writing and a seventh of a solidus for the papyrus. A third of a solidus had to be paid if one wanted a copy not just of the decision but also of the entire proceedings in the record.

The last lines of the inscription list the fees to be paid for the governor's appointment of a guardian, or *curator*, for a minor. The schedule distinguishes three different cases. First, we have the appointment of a "general" *curator*, as was routine for orphans or persons who were deemed to lack legal capacity, such as the mentally ill. In this case, the fee was fixed. It was completely different for the appointment of a *curator specialis* (i.e., one who oversaw his ward in a particular transaction). In those cases, it was stipulated that there should be a differentiation between, on the one hand, *curatores* appointed to supervise property sales of minors who were members of the decurial class and, on the other, those appointed to supervise the sales of minors of any other class. For the former, one again paid a fixed fee; for the latter, one paid a fee that depended on the value of the property to be sold, graded into four brackets. At the end of the inscription, two further fees are listed, apparently also connected with the appointment of *curatores*. They perhaps concerned the papyrus and the fair copy of the decision.

To sum up, in this schedule of the mid-fifth century C.E., two different principles were applied to determine the fees for judicial proceedings. In most cases, the fees to be paid depended on the type of "transaction," but in a number of special cases, the fees were differentiated according to the value of the object of the decision rendered by the governor. We find very similar principles in the other inscription mentioned above, which comes from

---

11. This corresponds to a general observation about the Roman legal system; see, e.g., Crook 1995: 128.
12. In this connection, one should think not only of those times when the judge asked the emperor for legal guidance but also of those cases in which the judge requested further evidence or witnesses; see, e.g., *CPR* I 18.

Thamugadi in North Africa and is dated to the reign of the emperor Julian, about one hundred years earlier.[13] In this case, the ordinances were issued by the provincial governor, an authority lower than the PPO. According to this regulation, the *exceptores* were to be paid differently according to whether they had written down a summons (*postulatio*), a discussion before the bar (*contradictio*), or a whole trial resulting in a final verdict (*definita causa*). The ratio of remuneration was 5:12:20; that is, in the case of a *definita causa*, an *exceptor* received four times as much wheat (or its monetary equivalent) as in the case of a *postulatio*. According to the schedule that follows immediately, the parties involved also had to supply papyrus or an equivalent in cash (?).[14] In the case of a *postulatio*, one "large" (coin or roll, *tomus*) had to be delivered; in the case of a *contradictio*, four; and in the case of a *definita causa*, never more than six. The governor also took this opportunity to establish the amounts parties had to pay the advocates (*scholastici*)[15] who pleaded for them in these same three types of procedures, devising a similar ratio of 5:10:15. Thus this order regulated not only the fees payable to the officials during juridical proceedings but also the salaries of the advocates for the parties.

We find in this earlier inscription a differentiation similar to the one proposed by the PPO above regarding the different stages of juridical proceedings and the fees that one had to pay for the work of the shorthand clerks and writing material. Other parts of the two regulations, however, do not overlap as closely. While the PPO also regulated the fees related to a number of non-litigation procedures (e.g., legal acts associated with guardianship), the concern of the governor of Numidia—aside from the question of fees connected with the judicial proceedings—involved the fees payable to members of his staff who had to undertake journeys in response to the demands of parties involved in litigation. He regulated those fees as well, which had to be paid to the *libellensis*, the official in charge of petitions (in his case, fees had to be paid probably when a petition was submitted or at least if one wanted to be informed about the results of a particular petition).[16]

As different as these regulations are, they have one point in common: in both inscriptions, we find rules that we do not expect in the context of orders

---

13. See n. 4; cf. Stauner 2007.
14. On how line 42 should be read and interpreted, see Chastagnol 1978: 84–86; cf. Stauner 2007: 166–67.
15. *Scholastici* does not mean "legal clerks," as Di Segni, Patrich, and Holum (2003: 284 n. 33) would have it.
16. For the question of his tasks, see also Stauner 2007: 167, 179.

fixing litigation fees payable to court officials. The edicts of Pusaeus, the PPO of 465–67, included a number of legal acts that do not imply litigation, while the provincial governor from the time of Julian regulated not only the fees of his officials but also the salaries of the advocates of the parties. At the very least, that means that these late antique authorities thought about legal fees—what one should consider them to consist of and which ones should be regulated—in ways that differ from modern ones (at least in Germany).

With these last remarks, I have touched on one of the central questions about these judicial fees. According to the *communis opinio*,[17] they were part of the *Sportelwesen* of late antiquity. The traditional argument has been that a system of *bakshish* (tips), bribes, and fees had not only developed in the fourth through the sixth centuries but had run wild in so short a time as to become one of the major problems of late antique government—perhaps even one of the causes of the fall of the Roman Empire. We find, for example, the following statement in Otto Seeck's *Geschichte des Untergangs der antiken Welt*: "So ist jenes Sportelwesen entstanden, das seit dem vierten Jahrhundert sich immer weiter ausdehnt und furchtbar auf den Untertanen drückt" (And so that system of *sportulae* sprang up, which from the fourth century onward spread ever more widely and weighed dreadfully on the imperial subjects).[18]

It is not possible to discuss here the question of when *bakshish* became an officially acknowledged practice in other parts of Roman government—for instance, in taxation or the nomination for posts in the imperial administration. The first examples of officially recognized fees in the field of taxation can be observed in the period of the later Roman Republic.[19] Yet the widely held scholarly opinion is that this was absolutely not the case with respect to the justice system. For example, in the monumental handbook on Roman civil law by Max Kaser and Karl Hackl, *Das römische Zivilprozeßrecht*, the most recent and relevant part of the well-known Handbuch der Altertumswissenschaft series for our topic, we find the following remark about legal procedure in the classical *cognitio* of the first three centuries of imperial rule: "Prozeßgebühren

---

17. See the authors cited in the following notes.
18. Seeck 1921: 104. For a more cautious but similar opinion, see Jones [1964] 1986: 602, 605–6.
19. Cic., *Verr.* 3.78.181–85. In the case of the high empire, we can point, for example, to ὑποκείμενα (= φιλάνθρωπα) ἐγλογιστεία (Wallace 1938: 333), that is, the usual gifts to the central financial accountant, the ἐγλογιστής, of a nome at Alexandria (see, e.g., Haensch 2008a: 96–98). For the fourth century, see, e.g., *P.Oxy.* XLVIII 3424, a προσαίτησις, a list of charges to be collected over and above the sums that had already been taken in. For ὑποκείμενα for the helper of a *decurio* in the third century, see *BGU* I 23; cf. Rea 1993.

an den Staat oder seine Organe sind nach wie vor unbekannt" (Litigation fees payable to the government or its representatives were still [i.e., at this time] unknown).[20] In the case of late antique jurisdiction, however, the same authors write,[21] "Alle gerichtlichen Maßnahmen kosten Gebühren, die, soweit sie den Unterbeamten zu bezahlen sind, als *sportulae* in deren Taschen fließen . . . Das Verfahren ist kostspielig geworden und damit unsozial" (All legal acts required fees to be paid, which, insofar as they were to be paid to officials, lined their pockets as *sportulae* . . . Legal proceedings became expensive and therefore antisocial). Finally, we find these authors saying, "Die Einhebung von Gebühren für gerichtliche Akte wird noch unter Konstantin als Bestechung streng bestraft. In der 2. Hälfte des 4. Jh. wird sie jedoch zugelassen [and in n. 33 they add: "Im CT und den posttheod. Nov. kommen die Gebühren noch nicht vor"] und von Justinian neu geregelt" (The levying of fees for legal acts was, under Constantine, still vigorously punished as corruption. In the second half of the fourth century, however, the practice was permitted—we do not find fees mentioned in the *Codex Theodosianus* and the *Novellae Posttheodosianae*—and regulated on a new basis by Justinian). I am citing Kaser and Hackl's handbook for two reasons: first, it is one of the most prominent authorities with definitive statements on the question of judicial fees over the course of the Roman period; second, we find there the two arguments that have been adduced to support such statements.

Let us deal with these arguments one by one. First, the argument that fees are not mentioned before late antiquity is based on the fact that the Theodosian Code and especially the Justinian Code are, despite their late dates, also our most important sources for the Roman law of the early empire. The assumption is that if something is not mentioned in one of these two collections, it therefore cannot have existed at that time—that is, absence is significant. This argument is not only used by Kaser and Hackl. For example, August Hug, the author of the article on *sportulae* in the *Realenzyclopedia* of Pauly and Wissowa, also made much of the fact that the first mention of *sportulae* in these codes is in *Codex Iustinianus* 1.3.32 (33).5—a constitution of Zeno of 472.[22] But to focus on this is to confuse the codes for complete collections of earlier legislation: the codes were not faithful and complete records of the legal history of Roman law. Rather, they were incomplete collections of earlier decisions and rules, often selected because they were of special interest to the compilers.

20. Kaser and Hackl 1996: 496.
21. Kaser and Hackl 1996: 520.
22. Hug 1929: 1886. See also Bethmann-Hollweg 1866: 200.

Just how unpersuasive these particular *argumenta e silentio* are can be shown by two examples. First, without the evidence given by the inscription of Thamugadi, dated to the reign of Emperor Julian, Kaser and Hackl would never have written that fees became officially recognized in the second half of the fourth century. They would have thought, just as Bethmann-Hollweg and Hug did before them, that such recognition came only in the latter half of the fifth century, a full century later, since all they would have had to go on was the accidental silence of the Theodosian Code on the matter.

Yet we do not even need to concede the silence of the Theodosian Code on this point. At *Codex Theodosianus* 1.29.5, a constitution of Valentinian and Valens, reasons are given for the introduction of the institution of the *defensor civitatis*: "utili ratione prospectum est, ut innocens (et) quieta rusticitas . . . ne forensis iurgii fraudibus fatigata, etiam cum ultionem posceret, vexaretur; dum aut avarior instruitur advocatus aut obsessor liminis maioribus princeps praemiis exoratur, dum acta ab exceptoribus distrahuntur, dum commodi nomine amplius ab eo qui vicerit intercessor exposcit quam redditurus est ille qui fuerit superatus" (In a useful manner, wise provision has been made that innocent and peaceful rustics . . . shall not be exhausted by the fraudulent practices of court trials and be harassed even when they demand satisfaction, while they either provide for a very avaricious advocate or win over the chief of the office staff with very large bribes, as he blocks the threshold, while the records of the case are purchased from the shorthand clerks, and while in the name of a fee, the enforcement officer demands more from the winner of the suit than the loser will pay). First, this passage shows that the Theodosian Code does indeed mention officially recognized fees (*commoda*) and *bakshish*. Second, the passage and the fact that Kaser and Hackl, among others, have overlooked it demonstrate one central problem in all the previous research into such fees: the terms used to designate the fees— *sportulae* (what one got in a basket), *commodum* (the reward), συνήθεια (the "usual" or "customary" additional payments)—are abstruse, indirect, or indistinct, making them difficult to identify. Finally, we also see in this constitution that (a) the salary of an advocate, (b) the *bakshish* that had to be given to the *princeps praetorii* to get a case introduced, and (c) the fees payable to the various court officers (*exceptores* and *intercessores*) were all equated in a manner foreign to our way of thinking about litigation fees.

The problematic nature of such conclusions, which are based on a dearth of evidence, is illuminated by yet another observation. In another volume of the Handbuch der Altertumswissenschaft series, Hans Julius Wolff discussed the private law used by the inhabitants of Egypt in the Ptolemaic and Roman periods, especially the aspect of its "organization and control," as he called it. He based his argumentation on the papyri, that is, an exceptionally abundant body of documentation. In the case of the well-known procedure of ἀνάκρισις of slaves, or their official registration, he wrote that "we do not hear anything about the fees to be paid."[23] He was, in other words, of the opinion that applicants did have to pay for registration but that the particular documentation that survives does not record the fees. This is remarkable precisely because our papyrological documentation is generally rich—in comparison with other sources. Yet this is not the only common procedure for which Wolff made such a remark. For example, in his discussion of the βιβλιοθήκη ἐγκτήσεων, he noted, "Leider ist über Art und Höhe der zu entrichtenden Gebühren nichts bekannt" (Unfortunately nothing is known about the type and amounts of the fees one had to pay).[24] These remarks by one of the foremost authorities on Greco-Roman legal history and juristic papyrology remind us that even in the case of routine procedures that are well documented in the papyri, whole aspects—even ones we should think would have been recorded, like fees—remain outside our ken: documents survive, but only rarely do we know anything about the circumstances in which they were written. A similar problem confronts us with respect to accounts: many survive, but only rarely do we have enough information to understand what the payments were for.[25] (Indeed, for this reason, accounts are often neglected by papyrologists and are doubtless proportionally underrepresented in our published corpora.) Thus there is no way to use *argumenta e silentio* to determine exactly the moment when juridical fees were officially introduced.

To move on to the second main argument on the question of judicial fees over the course of the Roman period, does the constitution *Codex Theodosianus* 1.16.7 from the reign of Constantine offer us a *terminus post quem*, as Kaser and Hackl thought?[26] To be sure, this constitution severely castigates the "rapacious hands of the court officials" (*rapaces officialium manus*), especially

---

23. Wolff 1978: 259: ". . . Käufer, die die Anakrisis betrieben (und wohl auch die Gebühren bezahlten, über die wir allerdings leider nichts erfahren)."
24. Wolff 1978: 229 n. 30. Chalon (1964: 186) also took "frais de justice" for granted.
25. E.g., *P.Sijp.* 12a mentions payments ἀναφορίου (perhaps a petition is meant), προπεσσίωνος (related to a *professio*; one of the most expensive items in the list), and sundry other expenses connected with the use of a ship. All this could point to a trip to Alexandria, but unfortunately we have no more information as to who was paid and why.
26. Cf. Stauner 2007: 177. But see Karayannopulos 1958: 176–77 (followed by Ausbüttel 1988: 183); Palme 1999: 113 n. 142. Cf. already Lécrivain 1911: 1444.

those who controlled the access to the courts of the governors. The emperor threatens them with mutilation and even the death penalty. Even so, the constitution does not prohibit all fees, unless one takes out of context the phrase *semper invigilet industria praesidialis, ne quicquam a praedictis generibus hominum de litigatore sumatur* (The diligence of the governor shall always be on watch lest anything be taken from a litigant by the aforementioned kinds of men).[27] If one reads through the whole constitution, it becomes clear that it has two aims: (1) it categorically forbids fees for access; (2) it orders that the governor's officials be restrained by the *praeses* when it came to fees for the copies of the rulings of the judge (*eorumque, qui iurgantibus acta restituunt, inexpleta aviditas temperetur*), though the emperor does not forbid all fees in this case. One may therefore say the same of the constitution as Sebastian Schmidt-Hofner has said of several of the *sportulae*-related constitutions of Valentinian and Valens: these were issued with a view to eliminating certain kinds of *sportulae* but not *sportulae* as such.[28] Schmidt-Hofner's general thesis is almost certainly correct also in this case: *sportulae* were only considered problematic or criminal if one asked for too much in certain contexts.[29]

In several monographs, we find a line of argument that Schmidt-Hofner has summed up in the following way: "Das Sportelwesen ist so alt wie die Etablierung einer professionellen Subalternverwaltung zur Unterstützung republikanischer Magistrate und galt nie als prinzipiell kriminell" (The *sportula* system is as old as the establishment of a professional staff for the administrative support of republican magistracies and was never in principle deemed criminal).[30] If we take his remarks at face value, we should think of the republican period as the moment when juridical fees were introduced, since we find the so-called *apparitores* already attached to various magistrates at that time. These *apparitores*[31] were professional civil servants (even if not in a modern sense), often drawn from the ranks of freedmen or the sons of freedmen (though some were from free backgrounds—occasionally even of equestrian status) and organized in *decuriae* at Rome. Most functioned as clerks (*scribae*) or other kinds of assistants for years or even decades, until

---

27. See Dillon 2012: 140. Dillon offers an ample discussion of the constitution (139–46; cf. 119, 251, 255), though I do not share all his views.
28. Schmidt-Hofner 2008: 44.
29. Schmidt-Hofner 2008: 41. See also Palme 1999: 114–15.
30. Schmidt-Hofner 2008: 40. For a similar hypothesis, see Hug 1929: 1886; Lécrivain 1911: 1444.
31. Haensch 1997: 711–13; Jones 1968; Purcell 1983; Schulz 1997.

they could sell the office to another person at a reasonable price. But even Schmidt-Hofner did not try to draw this logical conclusion from his general comments. Rather, the footnote belonging to the sentence begins, "See generally for the late antique period . . ." Once more, the reader is confronted with an author who, although he recognizes that judicial fees must antedate late antiquity, supports the scholarly orthodoxy by concentrating his discussion on late antique evidence.

Of course, one may argue that the *apparitores* were not typical Roman officials, because they worked mostly for the old republican magistrates at Rome.[32] From the first century C.E. on, the typical officials working for Roman governors in the provinces were soldiers seconded to administrative duties. From which time on did they—like, for example, the *princeps*, the *cornicularius*, or the *commentariensis*—ask for fees? A. H. M. Jones thought that it was only during the crisis of the third century C.E. "that officials began systematically to exact from the public those fees (*sportulae*) which later became a standing institution."[33] Whether or not there was such a "crisis" in the third century is hotly disputed but is something of a red herring in this case, for how do we account for the more than three hundred surviving, carefully written minutes of court proceedings, the first of which date to the first century C.E.?[34] Are we seriously to believe that the Roman state paid for all the writing and writing material that these records imply? That many if not most of these documents represent copies made not for the administrative purposes of the state but for the private use of parties to suits or even for third parties who used them as precedents makes it only more unlikely that the state footed the bill. As John Crook (1995: 130 n.66) put it, even today legal fees are "under fire" for being too expensive for the poor. But the modern state, even if it has the capacity (unlike the Roman state), does not have the desire to pay for all the costs associated with litigation. The modern solution has therefore been not to forbid fees completely but, rather, to offer different types of "legal aid" to the poorer segments of the population. The ancient equivalent consisted in the practice of the emperor (or other judges) to grant parties a waiver or reimburse them their expenses.[35]

---

32. According to *Cod. Theod.* 8.9.1, the *apparitores* in the fourth century were still interested in continuing their tasks *in civilibus causis et editionibus libellorum*, most likely because they got something out of them.
33. Jones [1964] 1986: 32.
34. Coles 1966 is the only major study dealing with these proceedings until now. But cf. Haensch 2008b.
35. For this practice as a general principle, see *Cod. Iust.* 1.3.25.3 (456?); *Nov.* 17.3, 123.8. For the (generally privileged) groups that had to pay reduced rates, see n. 2 above. For an example,

There is, in fact, some evidence, although not much, that fees had to be paid in the Roman courts of the first three centuries. The highest strata of Roman society in the late republic and early empire considered it unseemly, if not immoral, for advocates to take fees, since advocacy was traditionally a duty that a *patronus* performed for his *clientes* and was meant to serve the political needs of *patronus* and *cliens* alike. The reality was, of course, quite different. From quite early in the republican period, as the *lex Cincia* from 204 B.C.E. suggests (among other provisions, it prohibited orators from taking fees),[36] many advocates made a living from representing people in suits.[37] Even though Augustus confirmed the provisions of the *lex Cincia*, the emperor Claudius was forced, only a few decades later, to acknowledge such fees as basically legitimate, when he capped them at a maximum of ten thousand sesterces—a maximum that continued to be breached.[38] By the turn of the third century, these fees could even be sued for.[39] We should not forget that our sources often give us insight only into the thoughts and the problems of the highest-ranking people in the Roman world, not the commoners and those living in the provinces. Thus we know almost nothing about the income of the advocates lower down the scale, the *iurisperiti*, *pragmatici*, and *scholastici*.[40] The same may be said of notaries or *tabelliones*, whom one finds witnessing the so-called *diplomata militaria* already from the time of Vespasian onward (a major reform occurred at some point during the years 133–138).[41] Their work can also be traced in several different standard legal procedures and acts of the second and third centuries, such as the *professio liberorum natorum*, the *datio tutoris mulieris*, and the *agnitio bonorum possessionis*.[42]

Compared to the advocates' fees, those for drafting and writing material

---

see Marc. Diac. *v. Porph.* 40, 51, 53 (cf. 51): the empress paid the court officials serving during the audiences of the bishops. In this context, one has to ask if the phrase *sportulam dabo* (only in the exterior text of this double document) in *PSI* IX 1026 (= *CHLA* XXV 784), the well-known petition of dismissed legionaries to the governor of Syria Palaestina, with his *subscriptio*, does not mean that the governor would reimburse them their expenses in connection with the petition.

36. Tac., *Ann.* 11.5. Cf. Cic., *Or.* 2.71.286; Cic., *Att.* 1.20.7; Liv. 34.4.9.
37. Crook 1995: 42–43.
38. Tac., *Ann.* 11.5–7; cf. Crook 1995: 129–30. For the situation in the time of Ulpian, see *Dig.* 50.1.13.10–13. Cf. *Dig.* 50.1.13.4. For the time of Diocletian, see *Ed. Max.* 7.73 (one thousand denarii for a day in court). For a payment to such a νομικός, perhaps during the years 345–46, see *P.Oxy.* LVI 3874.ii.39.
39. Ulp., *Dig.* 50.13.10–13.
40. See Wolff 1978: 106 with n. 1, 132 with n. 121a, 179 with n. 36, 254; Kelly 2011: 160–63. See, further, the passages cited in the following notes for fees of private notaries and other kinds of clerks in the high empire. For an example of such a *iurisperitus* in a provincial milieu, see Ap., *Met.* 11.28, 11.30.
41. See Haensch 1996; there is nothing new in Scheuerbrandt 2009.
42. See Haensch 1996: 466–67.

were doubtless minor.[43] This is one area in which we may once again demonstrate the inadequacy of the *argumenta e silentio* relied on up until now, as we have positive evidence that fees for such services were demanded during the principate.[44] Indeed, for at least one of the judicial fees regulated by the PPO in the inscription with which we began this chapter, we can point to a precedent from the times of the high empire. As several papyri from the second and third centuries show, a fee had to be paid whenever a woman requested that she be appointed a *tutor mulieris* in order for her to execute a major financial transaction.[45] We only know this because (in this case, unlike in the registration of slaves) a particular formula concerning the fee had become part of the application for such a *tutor*. In other words, even though the formula is entirely nondescript in its terminology (e.g., *P.Oxy.* XII 1473.30–31 [201]: διέγραφα δὲ τὸ ὡρισμένον τῆς αἰτήσ[εω]ς τέλος, "I have paid the prescribed tax for the request"), it appears in a context from which we can tell what it was for. As above, the problem is more one of context than a lack of evidence for taxes and fees as such: many, many fees are effectively hiding in plain sight, since they were referred to only by such general names as τὰ συνήθεια or τὰ προσδιαγραφόμενα.[46]

In the early third century, we hear of a certain kind of *exceptores*, that is, the shorthand clerks who wrote up juridical proceedings.[47] Unlike other court officials, such as the *commentarienses* or *speculatores*, these *exceptores* did not serve in the army and, for that reason, were not paid for their services by

---

43. Kelly 2011: 40 ("fairly small expense"). In this context, what *litis sumptus* meant during the high empire should also be discussed. Ulpian separates *litis sumptus* from *viatica* (*Dig.* 5.1.79 pr.).
44. Nothing cited by Lécrivain (1911: 1444 n. 25) is convincing. Chastagnol, in his discussion of the inscription of Thamugadi (1978), thought that he could show evidence from the time of Ulpian already hinting that fees were required for writing material. Ulpian states at *Dig.* 48.20.6 that a governor should not tolerate the appropriation of the property of condemned persons either by the *commentariensis* (i.e., the official who supervised the execution of the verdict) or the *speculator* (who executed the verdict). Instead, such property was to be sold, and the money was to be contributed to the so-called *chartiaticum*. According to Chastagnol (1978: 85), this passage offers the first example of "une taxe pour le papier, appelée chartiaticum," known also from *SEG* IX 356 (end of fifth century) and *Nov. Iust.* 8.1. But Ulpian mentions that this *chartiaticum* was part of those things that the governors had the right to acquire (*ea quae iure praesidum solent erogari*) because it had to be used by certain *officiales* (*quibusdam officialibus inde subscribere*). Thus Ulpian's *chartiaticum* appears to have been something quite different from the *chartiaticum* of the fifth and sixth centuries.
45. E.g., *P.Ryl.* II 120 (lines 17–18 [167]: nine and one-half obols); *P.Oxy.* XII 1473, esp. lines 30–31 (201); *P.Oxy.* I 56 (211).
46. See n. 25.
47. *Dig.* 4.6.33; cf. Haensch 1992: 225 n. 44.

the Roman state. Since they had to earn their living, it seems natural to suppose that they did it by collecting fees for their work.[48]

Finally, we have at least two accounts from the second century that list expenses connected with judicial proceedings. The list *PSI* VI 688 r (116, unknown provenance)[49] records payments to an εἰσαγωγεύς, the official who organized the court sessions of a magistrate,[50] and to one or more ὑπηρέται, helpers to a magistrate,[51] in what seems to be accounts related to foreclosing on a dilatory debtor. Unfortunately, we do not know to which representative of Roman rule these functionaries were attached, although it might very well have been the στρατηγός, the chief executive officer of the nome. Even more explicit is *P.Oxy.* XIV 1654 (ca. 150, Oxyrhynchus), an account of expenditure, as the papyrus calls itself (λόγος δαπάνης). This account lists the expenditures of four days in the month of Mesore (= July–August). On the first day, the author of the account records a payment of sixteen obols to some νομογρά(φοι) (writers of legal documents), for the copying of two different proceedings of trials. Further on, he records an additional payment of four obols for papyrus. On the second day, there is another purchase of papyrus, this time worth four drachmas (= twenty-four obols). On the same day, ten obols were paid to an assistant of the library or the archive of the governor (αἱρέτης ἡγεμονικῆς βιβλιοθήκ(ης); the Greek term βιβλιοθήκη can mean both), likely for document retrieval. On the third day, four obols are recorded as being paid to yet more νομογρά(φοι), who were to find two different transcripts of the ἀρχιδικαστής, a middle-ranking officer of the so-called Katalogeion in Alexandria, who had various responsibilities related to contracts. On the fourth day, there was another payment to a νομογράφος, in connection with the acts of judicial proceedings presided over by the governor of Egypt (ca. 150) Munatius Felix. To sum up, this account records the costs associated with the searching, retrieval, and copying of the legal records of two different administrators of Roman Egypt—inter alia, those of the governor— including the costs of papyrus. It is perhaps not a coincidence that the price

---

48. See already Palme 1999: 113 (but I do not see any possibility that *scrinarii* were ever "konzessionierte Gewerbetreibende"; therefore the hypothesis that such a status was the reason for the introduction of *sportulae* does not convince me). Perhaps we should see the slave Chaerammon of *P.Oxy.* IV 724, apprenticed to learn σημεῖα (shorthand), as planning to become such an *exceptor*. This practice continued into late antiquity: see *Cod. Theod.* 8.7.17, from the year 385.

49. I thank David Ratzan for pointing out this document to me.

50. See Haensch 2008a: 91–94.

51. Strassi 1997.

paid for the drafting versus that for papyrus stood in precisely the same ratio (4:1) as we find in the regulation of the PPO three centuries later in the case of a *definita causa*.

To conclude, I have tried to show that at least certain fees had to be paid to the officials of the representatives of the Roman justice system during the first three centuries of the Roman Empire. In particular, I have tried to demonstrate that one had to pay for the drafting and the writing material for private copies of the proceedings of court sessions and judicial decisions. Many of these fees probably began as informal practices, were regulated by custom, and adhered to social conventions, only later becoming prescribed and regulated—that is, capped, at least officially, by law. But I am skeptical that these regulations were only typical for the later Roman Empire and could not have antecedents in the second or third centuries. Generally, the importance of these fees for our understanding of the characteristics of late antiquity has been grossly overestimated. Fees are part of almost all juridical systems—even democratic Athens asked for them.[52] Also, we may feel relatively confident that such fees were only a minor part of the transaction costs of litigation. When considering whether litigation had become outrageously expensive in late antiquity, one should not fixate on the amounts[53] given as *sportulae* to certain officials in the court of the praetorian prefect (according to John the Lydian). Such fees depended on the hierarchical position in the administrative system of the court to which one applied for adjudication. Fees taken by the officials of the praetorian prefect were, of course, considerably higher than those collected by the staff of the comparatively "humble" provincial governor;[54] but if one had a dispute worth pursuing in the second-highest court in the empire, one surely had the resources to afford the fees of the advocates capable of representing clients in such august circles. The fact that litigants indeed pursued their cases, the fees notwithstanding, shows the value of a decision by a praetorian prefect as opposed to that of a (mere) local governor. But the cost-benefit analysis of deciding how and how high to pursue one's legal case was not the creation of the late antique justice system: litigation had always been relatively costly. Finally, if the emperor (or governor) wanted to open his court to lower people, he could exempt them or reimburse them their expenses. For all these reasons, I do not think that the

---

52. See the analysis by Thür in chapter 1 of the present study.
53. Conveniently assembled in Jones [1964] 1986: 591.
54. See already Palme 1999: 114, 117–18.

judicial and litigation costs in the early imperial period were fundamentally different from those in late antiquity.

Bibliography

Ausbüttel, F. M. 1988. *Die Verwaltung der Städte und Provinzen im spätantiken Italien.* Frankfurt am Main.

Bandy, A. C. 1983. *Ioannes Lydus on Powers.* Philadelphia.

Bethmann-Hollweg, M. A. von. 1866. *Der römische Civilprozeß.* Vol. 3, *Cognitiones.* Bonn.

Chalon, G. 1964. *L'édit de Tiberius Julius Alexander.* Olten.

Chastagnol, A. 1978. *L'album municipal de Timgad.* Bonn.

Coles, R. A. 1966. *Reports of Proceedings in Papyri.* Papyrologica Bruxellensia 4. Brussels.

Crook, J. A. 1995. *Legal Advocacy in the Roman World.* Ithaca, NY.

Dillon, J. N. 2012. *The Justice of Constantine: Law, Communication and Control.* Ann Arbor.

Di Segni, L., J. Patrich, and K. G. Holum, 2003. "A Schedule of Fees (*sportulae*) for Official Services from Caesarea Maritima, Israel." *ZPE* 145: 273–300.

Feissel, D. 2006. *Chroniques d'épigraphie byzantine 1987–2004.* Paris.

Haensch, R. 1992. "Das Statthalterarchiv. " *ZRG* 100: 209–317.

Haensch, R. 1996. "Die Verwendung von Siegeln bei Dokumenten der kaiserzeitlichen Reichsadministration." In M.-F. Boussac and A. Invernizzi, eds., *Archives et sceaux du monde hellénistique, BCH* suppl. 29, 449–96. Athens.

Haensch, R. 1997. *Capita provinciarum.* Mainz.

Haensch, R. 2008a. "Die Provinz Aegyptus: Kontinuitäten und Brüche zum ptolemäischen Ägypten. Das Beispiel des administrativen Personals." In I. Piso, ed., *Die römischen Provinzen: Begriff und Gründung (Colloquium Cluj-Napoca, 28. September–1. Oktober 2006),* 81–105. Cluj-Napoca.

Haensch, R. 2008b. "Typisch römisch? Die Gerichtsprotokolle der in Aegyptus und den übrigen östlichen Provinzen tätigen Vertreter Roms. Das Zeugnis von Papyri und Inschriften." In H. Börm et al., eds., *Monumentum et instrumentum inscriptum,* 117–25. Stuttgart.

Hug, A. 1929. "Sportula." *RE* II.3A2: 1883–86.

Jones, A. H. M. [1964] 1986. *The Later Roman Empire.* Baltimore.

Jones, A. H. M. 1968. "The Roman Civil Service." In *Studies in Roman Government and Law,* 153–75, 201–16.

Karayannopoulos, J. 1958. *Das Finanzwesen des frühbyzantinischen Staates.* Munich.

Kaser, M., and K. Hackl. 1996. *Das römische Zivilprozeßrecht.* 2nd ed. Handbuch der Altertumswissenschaft 10.3.4. Munich.

Kelly, B. 2011. *Petitions, Litigation, and Social Control in Roman Egypt*. Oxford.

Lécrivain, C. 1911. *"Sporta."* In C. Daremberg and E. Saglio, eds., *Dictionnaire des antiquités grecques et romaines*, 4.2:1443–45. Paris.

Noethlichs, K. L. 1981. *Beamtentum und Dienstvergehen*. Wiesbaden.

Palme, B. 1999. "Die Officia der Statthalter in der Spätantike: Forschungsstand und Perspektiven." *Antiquité Tardive* 7: 85–133.

Purcell, N. 1983. "The Apparitores." *PBSR* 51: 125–73.

Rea, J. 1993. "*BGU* I 23: The Dekadarch's Colletion." *ZPE* 96: 133–34.

Schamp, J. 2006. *Jean le Lydien: Des magistratures de l'état romain*. Paris.

Scheuerbrandt, N. 2009. *Kaiserliche Konstitutionen und ihre beglaubigten Abschriften: Diplomatik und Aktengang der Militärdiplome*. Großschönau.

Schmidt-Hofner, S. 2008. *Reagieren und Gestalten*. Munich.

Schulz, R. 1997. *Herrschaft und Regierung*. Paderborn.

Seeck, O. 1921. *Geschichte des Untergangs der antiken Welt*. Vol. 2. Stuttgart. Repr., Darmstadt, 1966.

Stauner, K. 2007. "Wandel und Kontinuität römischer Administrationspraxis im Spiegel des Ordo Salutationis Commodorumque des Statthalters von Numidien." *Tyche* 22: 151–88.

Strassi, S. 1997. *Le funzioni degli hyperetai nell' Egitto greco e romano*. Heidelberg.

Wallace, S. L. 1938. *Taxation in Egypt from Augustus to Diocletian*. Princeton.

Wolff, H. J. 1978. *Das Recht der griechischen Papyri Ägyptens in der Zeit der Ptolemaeer und des Prinzipats*. Vol. 2, *Organization und Kontrolle des privaten Rechtverkehrs*. Handbuch der Altertumswissenschaft 10.5.2. Munich.

CHAPTER 11

The Economic Perspective

Demand and Supply in the Reduction of Transaction Costs in the Ancient World[1]

Giuseppe Dari-Mattiacci

1. Introduction

The previous chapters provide an excellent array of interesting case studies in which underlying policy goals related to the reduction of transaction costs can be inductively inferred from actual private and public choices concerning the transfer of property, the design of contracts, and the litigation process. In all these areas, there were attempts by a variety of ancient individuals, organizations, or states, more or less successful, to reduce transactions costs or, more generally, to provide an environment conducive to efficient transactions. In this chapter, however, I will proceed in the opposite direction—that is, I will deduce specific implications from general principles—in order to provide a unitary framework in which all of the issues touched on in the previous chapters can be connected and reexamined. The central aim of this chapter is to show that, to understand the patterns of emergence of measures to reduce transactions costs, it is useful to unpack the characteristics of the demand and supply of institutions to reduce transaction costs in the ancient world. To what extent could contracting parties reduce transaction costs through better con-

1. I may be contacted at the Amsterdam Center for Law and Economics, University of Amsterdam; email: gdarimat@uva.nl; web page: gdarimat.acle.nl. I thank the editors of this volume—Dennis Kehoe, David Ratzan, and Uri Yiftach—for their helpful suggestions on this chapter.

tract design? Under what conditions was the state better placed than the parties themselves to reduce transaction costs? Why were different states unequally effective or willing to reduce transaction costs?

Before addressing these questions, some preliminary remarks are in order about the underlying assumptions of an economic analysis of the role of transaction costs in shaping ancient legal institutions. Although transaction costs are an inclusive and occasionally vague category, the term is used in a consistent and focused manner throughout this book.[2] The individual chapters concern essentially two types of transaction costs: the costs of making a deal and the costs of enforcing it.

Most of the book (chapters 2–8) analyzes contracts for the transfer of ownership or the provision of services and in which parties are asymmetrically informed about some important characteristics of the transaction—for instance, about the existence of conflicting claims on the same asset, the metal content of coins given in payment, or the quality and reliability of service. In some cases, the uninformed party could acquire the relevant information at some expense, which adds to the costs of making the deal (this being the ancient world, there are some cases in which we should imagine that the parties cannot obtain the relevant information they seek at any cost). These are transaction costs associated with making a deal. In chapters 1 and 10, however, Thür and Haensch are concerned with the second category of transaction costs: the costs that private parties bear in order to access the judicial system to obtain, among other things, legal enforcement of contracts in Athens and Caesarea, respectively. In chapter 9, Kehoe touches on both the costs of entering into contracts and the cost of enforcing them.

The costs of making and those of enforcing a deal share an important common feature: if these costs are high, they might forestall some deals.[3] The analysis provided in the previous chapters and my own considerations below suggest that it was in the interest of contracting parties—and, to some extent, of the state—to find ways to reduce these transaction costs and facilitate trade. These attempts also had the effect of shaping contracts (as shown by Ratzan and Kehoe in chapters 8 and 9). Throughout the book, other types of costs are also identified, such as the costs of managing registries, collecting

2.   For a general discussion and a history of the notion of transaction costs, see, e.g., Allen 2000 and the introduction to this volume.
3.   On the interconnection between establishing rights and enforcing them, see Calabresi and Melamed 1972.

taxes, and organizing courts and trials. Although these costs also play a role in parties' calculations and may be seen as transaction costs, I find it analytically convenient to refer to them as administrative costs and to define transaction costs more narrowly as including only the costs of making and enforcing deals.

A second important preliminary remark concerns the meaning of statements such as "reducing transaction costs was in the interest of contracting parties." Does this imply that economic agents in the ancient world were perfectly rational, understood the economic effects of different institutional and contractual arrangements, could calculate expected benefits and costs, and hence acted optimally to reduce transaction costs? The answer is no. Economists have identified countless scenarios in which modern economic actors act in seemingly irrational ways[4] and situations in which economic behavior is strongly shaped by cultural assumptions or priorities,[5] as observed by Kehoe in chapter 9. Assuming a narrow notion of perfect rationality in the ancient world would be holding ancient economic actors to higher standards than their modern counterparts.[6]

Yet the analyses of this book show that some observed contractual practices or institutional arrangements had the effect of making exchange more efficient and, hence, increasing profits for the individuals involved. We may reasonably postulate that higher potential profits led trading parties—who were accustomed to looking for the most profitable alternative—to prefer one arrangement over another. There is also no reason to doubt that the same dynamic nudged contracting parties to invent new solutions or to adapt existing solutions (possibly developed elsewhere or for other purposes) to new functions. In turn, the aggregated effect of individual interests drove the evolution or emergence of at least some of the economic and legal practices observed in the preceding chapters.

The type of rationality and sophistication needed to support this dynamic is no different from the skills that traders displayed in running their businesses. Some private attempts at reducing transaction costs failed while others succeeded, in just the same way that some enterprises, ancient or modern, are more successful than others and set an example for others to imitate.[7] In

4. See, e.g., Parisi and Smith 2005.
5. See, e.g., Guiso, Sapienza, and Zingales 2006.
6. On the use of economic models for the analysis of ancient institutions, see Temin 2001.
7. For an analysis of the Roman market economy, see Temin 2013.

attempting to arrive at economically rational choices, economic actors need not be aware of the underlying model that we use.[8] Formal economic analysis may demonstrate that, say, a particular historical contractual arrangement had the effect of solving a specific information problem and that doing so increased the scope and the profitability of trade. (As I will show below, such analysis is sufficient to draw far-reaching implications about the drivers of the development and the range of measures to reduce transaction costs.) It is a question for historians, however, whether such measures emerged accidentally while other goals were being pursued, were borrowed from elsewhere, or were the result of an explicit economic calculus.

This book reveals that the reduction of transaction costs could be effected by individuals, the state, or both. In chapter 8, Ratzan studies cases in which only private parties are involved: two contractual parties negotiate specific clauses in a service contract, which penalize unilateral exit from the contractual relationship. These clauses may have had the (economic) purpose of, among other goals, reducing the costs of establishing compliance and, hence, of enforcing the contract. Likewise, in chapter 9, Kehoe discusses the spread of penalty clauses in contracts, which functionally tailored the performance incentives to the specific interests of the contracting parties and reduced the costs of calculating damages after the fact.

By contrast, in chapter 2, Ober discusses the law proposed by Nikophon in 375 B.C.E., which regulated the scrutiny of silver coins circulating in Athenian public markets. The law established that an approver had to be present in the Piraeus marketplace so that buyers and sellers could defer to him for the assessment of the metal content of coins if there was uncertainty about their quality or provenance. In this case, while the decision to defer to the approver was left to the parties, the approver was managed and paid for by the state.

Cases in which private coordination failed and transaction costs could only be reduced by state action through the provision of an institutional setting (e.g., an approver or a registry) or through mandating certain types of conduct (e.g., contract formalities) provide valuable insights into the economic role of the ancient state. The failure of private coordination can be interpreted as generating private demand for a state-assisted reduction in transaction costs. The analyses by Muhs, Manning, Yiftach, and Lerouxel in chapters 3, 4, 6, and 7 concern various public registries, a notable example of state involvement.

---

8.   For a discussion of rationality in economics, see Smith 2008.

But was there always an adequate supply; that is, did ancient states react to such private demand by effectively providing such measures? Although ancient states were neither equally effective nor even equally willing to foster or support an environment of low transaction costs, the following analysis will reveal that state involvement in the reduction of transaction costs did not necessarily imply a predatory attitude on the part of the ancient state. Differences between the rather efficient monetary policy of Athens and the seemingly inefficient policy of Ptolemaic Egypt—discussed by Ober and Bresson in chapters 2 and 5—suggest that supply met demand in some cases but not in others. How can we make sense of these different responses?

In the following sections, I will expand on these ideas. In section 2, I will comment on how contracting parties could reduce transaction costs by contract design. In sections 3 and 4, I will explain why private parties in some cases failed in reducing transaction costs through better contractual arrangements. Identifying these failures will, in turn, shed light on the characteristics of the private demand for state intervention. The underlying idea is simply that when the private reduction of transaction costs was more difficult, parties benefited more from state action. Then I will analyze the state supply of measures that reduced transaction costs. In section 5, I will deal with the design of the primary institution to control transaction costs: the judicial system. In section 6, I will identify some political economy factors affecting the state supply of appropriate measures to reduce transaction costs in the ancient world. These factors could explain differential state responses to similar issues.

In a nutshell, the analysis that follows identifies some likely determinants of the private demand for state intervention and of the related state supply, thereby defining the scope of the ideal state policies and explaining the shortcomings of actual state policies. Yet many issues remain open. In section 7, I will conclude with suggestions for further research and a plea for more interdisciplinary scholarship along the lines of the present book.

2. Maximizing Contract Surplus

Contract theory is built on a fundamental principle of bargaining: informed contractual parties will tend to negotiate the agreement that maximizes their joint surplus, irrespective of how this surplus is divided between them, a point stressed by Kehoe in chapter 9. For instance, consider a negotiation between an elite and a peasant over a contract that can be designed in two ways: configuration A provides larger gains for the elite but smaller aggregate gains (gains for the elite plus gains for the peasant); configuration B yields greater aggregate gains at the expense of smaller direct gains for the elite. The elite could force the peasant to choose contract A. However, since contract B generates higher aggregate benefits, the price of the contract can be adjusted (transferring some gains from the peasant to the elite) so that both parties are better off with contract B rather than with contract A. While negotiating an inferior contract harms both parties, negotiations over the price are just a matter of distributing the contractual surplus between the parties. Thus, in principle, it is better for the elite to exploit the power imbalance in order to obtain a more favorable price, rather than to force the drafting of an inferior contract. This principle follows directly from the Coase theorem[9] and implies that both parties have an interest in drafting the contract in a way that maximizes their joint surplus, including reducing transaction costs.

An effect of transaction costs is that not all contingencies can be specified at the time of drafting the contract—contracts are incomplete.[10] One way to solve this problem is to give one of the parties a control right, that is, the right to decide how the contract should be adjusted after an unforeseen contingency materializes. Yet this solution exposes the other party to the risk of holdup and creates costs of its own. In chapter 9, Kehoe discusses two problems with agrarian leases, for instance—one occurring naturally (*sterilitas*) and another manmade (a unilateral increase in the rent by the landowner). Both cases show the risk that the more powerful party (the landlord) exploits the weak party (the tenant) at some point during the lease. The optimal allocation (and limitation) of control rights balances these costs and benefits.[11]

The cases discussed by Ratzan in chapter 8 fit this framework. The essential elements of the transactions are as follows: two parties sign a relational contract by which a party (the owner) entrusts an asset to another party (the receiver). There are three subtypes of contracts. In one subtype, the receiver performs some services for the owner, who pays a price for them; for instance, the owner of a slave entrusts the slave to a wet nurse. In a second set of contracts, the receiver uses the asset for his own interest and pays a price for it; for instance, an owner leases his slave to another party. A third set of

---

9. Coase 1960.
10. Hart and Moore 1999.
11. For an overview of the theory of the firm (starting with Coase), see Milgrom and Roberts 1992; Holmström and Tirole 1989; Aghion and Holden 2011.

contracts features mutual performances, so that the price paid by the receiver discounts the direct benefits to the asset owner; a good example is an apprenticeship contract, in which the receiver benefits from the labor of the apprentice while the owner benefits from the training provided by the receiver.

The default rule in these contracts allows the asset owner to repossess his asset at will. Likewise, the party that receives the asset can return it at will to the owner and hence interrupt the relationship. Yet some contracts contain clauses that put monetary penalties on repossession (ἀποσπάω) or on returning the asset (ἀπορίπτω/προσρίπτω), thereby restricting exit by the owner or the receiver of the asset, respectively. What are the costs and benefits of free exit, and under what conditions is it beneficial to restrict it?

On the one hand, the option to exit at will reduces the risk of moral hazard by the other party. If a party is not satisfied with performance by the counterpart, he or she can simply rely on self-help and interrupt the relationship. For instance, an owner can repossess his slave from the wet nurse if he is not satisfied with her services. Likewise, a lessee can return the leased slave to the owner if the slave is not productive. Self-help will be important when performance by the other party is difficult to specify at the time of drafting the contract or to verify in court, so that nonperformance cannot be easily subjected to specific stipulated penalties. In the wet-nursing case, for instance, many aspects of the nurse's performance are difficult to verify in court—even if parties add lengthy descriptions of the nurse's duties (cf. Ratzan's discussion in chapter 8)—so that repossession is the most expeditious option.

On the other hand, the option to exit at will creates the potential for holdup, as a party can threaten the other with exit and extort a better deal. The problem arises because the parties' bargaining power could change after the execution of the contract. For instance, a wet nurse could threaten to interrupt the nursing unless the owner increases the price. Once the slave has been entrusted to the nurse, the owner becomes dependent on the nurse's services, and an interruption could mean incurring substantial costs in finding a substitute nurse. This might allow the nurse to exploit the situation.

Both moral hazard and holdup generate substantial costs. An optimal design of the parties' exit rights can help reduce these costs and, hence, enhance the value of the contract for both parties. In turn, the optimal design of exit rights depends on the balance between the benefits of free exit in terms of reduced moral hazard and the costs of free exit in terms of holdup. The owner is more likely to retain an exit right if the risk of moral hazard by the receiver is high while the risk of holdup by the owner is low. The receiver can be expected to act likewise. This arrangement maximizes the value of the contract and leaves the possibility of distributing the surplus unequally to the party holding greater bargaining power through the price.

In a nursing contract, where moral hazard on the part of the nurse is a serious problem, it might be efficient for the owner to retain the right to repossess the slave—that is, to avoid an ἀποσπάω clause, which penalized repossession by the owner. But since the nurse is not exposed to the risk of moral hazard by the owner, who often paid at least part of the price upfront, there might be no need to retain the right to free exit; hence the contract might include a ἀπορίπτω/προσρίπτω clause, which penalized interruption of nursing by the nurse. Such a clause also protects the owner from the risk of holdup by the nurse.

Labor contracts might exhibit a different balance of interests. The lessee might need protection against moral hazard on the part of the slave and from holdup by the owner. Hence it might be plausible to expect such contracts to restrict repossession by the owner while allowing interruption by the lessee— that is, to include an ἀποσπάω clause without a corresponding ἀπορίπτω/προσρίπτω clause.

Apprenticeship contracts are more complex to predict, since both parties are exposed to a serious risk of moral hazard. Yet the risk of holdup is more pronounced on the side of the apprentice. The apprentice can hold the trainer up, since the trainer has to make the more substantial investment in the earlier part of the relationship, while the apprentice's performance becomes more valuable in the later part. Increasing payment schedules are likely to accompany these contracts, with very low payments in the initial period, when the apprentice is still inexpert, and higher payments later.[12] In addition, limiting repossession through an ἀποσπάω clause might be desirable, since it protects the receiver from the risk of holdup and enables him to recoup his initial investment.

These considerations offer somewhat imprecise but general predictions for the clauses that we are most likely to observe across contract types. The data reported by Ratzan in chapter 8 are consistent with the prediction that apprenticeship contracts will include an ἀποσπάω clause more frequently

---

12. See the pioneering work in Becker 1962 and related literature.

than wet-nursing contracts. Yet geographical variation can only be explained by reference to specific factors that vary across regions. For instance, different market conditions and power imbalances (as emphasized by Ratzan) might make moral hazard more or less problematic. In fact, holdup is a serious concern if finding a replacement is costly. If there is a large supply of wet nurses compared to demand, an owner will find it less pressing to include an ἀπορίπτω/προσρίπτω clause in the contract to protect himself from interruptions of the service, as he can easily deal with holdup by replacing the nurse. Likewise, the availability of additional ways to deal with nonperformance (including the use of power) might change the function of an ἀποσπάω clause. If repossession imposes a sufficiently high cost on the nurse—since she needs to keep nursing in order maintain her milk supply—an ἀποσπάω clause will not induce moral hazard on her part and will possibly have a beneficial effect in terms of risk distribution between the parties.

Ultimately, the analysis of contractual arrangements provided by Ratzan shows that parties drafted their contracts to reduce the negative effects of transaction costs. They did so with no or minimal[13] assistance by the state. In chapter 9, Kehoe makes a similar point about the prevalence of penalty clauses drafted by the parties to deal with nonperformance in contracts. Yet some form of state intervention is needed in some cases. Kehoe discusses legal doctrines that developed in Rome to deal with the problem of supervening *sterilitas* of a leased *fundus*, so that the tenant could temporarily suspend the payment of the rent. Kehoe also discusses Constantine's policy to limit the possibility of landowners raising rents without justification. Both cases show the emergence of rules that limited the most powerful party (the landowner). As Kehoe remarks, such limits might have advanced the long-term interest of landowners, since they reduced the risk of insolvency by tenants. The existence of these rules also suggests that such limitations were difficult to achieve through private contracting and had to be introduced from above. Likewise, for default contract rules to reduce the costs of making deals in individual transactions, rules concerning the interpretation and the filling of gaps in incomplete contracts have to be provided by the state (directly or through the judicial system). The next three sections examine two additional sets of cases in which we can identify a demand for state intervention.

---

13. For instance, general contract enforcement is provided by the state.

3. Volume Versus Value

A fundamental problem in contracts is asymmetric information, which arises when a party, often the seller, has more information than his counterpart, the buyer. Although the problem is often conceived of as the lack of information per se, it is better formulated as a relative asymmetry of information. As long as both parties are equally uninformed, they could trade the good for its expected value. The possibility that the buyer discovers later that the good is of low value is compensated by a positive risk that the good is of high value. The seller faces analogous offsetting risks.

A problem arises when the seller knows the real value of the good while the buyer only knows what the good is worth on average (or vice versa). The buyer is unwilling to pay more than the average value, but for such a price, the seller will not be willing to sell goods of high value (namely, of value higher than the price). Therefore, the buyer knows that he will only be able to buy low-value goods, and he will adjust downward his expectations about the average value of such goods and hence reduce the price he is willing to pay. But for lower prices, sellers are only willing to sell lower-value goods. This dynamic creates a negative spiral of adverse selection, driving high-value goods out of the market and leaving only "lemons" to be traded.[14]

This outcome harms both parties: if the seller could credibly reveal information about quality to the buyer, the buyer would be willing to pay a higher price for higher-quality goods, which could then be traded. Therefore, parties might be willing to invest resources in order to redress the asymmetry of information and thus capture this otherwise untapped trade potential.[15] The gains from trade are most likely correlated with the value of the asset: because parties are more likely to diverge in their relative evaluations of a large estate than of a goat, gains from trade are likely to be larger in the former case.[16] Therefore, if the value[17] of the asset is large, it is profitable for the parties to sustain relatively large outlays to acquire information. If, instead, the value of the asset is low, such expenditures might not be justified. A direct

---

14. Akerlof 1970.
15. The fundamental mechanisms for information exchange in contract are signaling (Spence 1973) and screening (Stiglitz 1975).
16. Even if the parties' valuations diverge by a constant factor, the larger the value of the asset is, the larger the absolute value of the gains from trade will be. This shows that our contention would also hold if the divergence in the parties' valuations were moderately negatively correlated with value.
17. I am using here a rather inclusive notion of value, incorporating all factors that might affect the parties' valuations, such as durability, productivity, and resale opportunities.

implication of these principles is that it is rational to devote more effort and resources to the correct valuation of high-value assets, which therefore will typically be more accurately valued than low-value ones. Thür stresses in chapter 1 that more resources were devoted to the accurate evaluation of high-value goods than of low-value ones in Athenian court proceedings.

In chapter 3, Muhs explains the development of more efficient registration systems in Egypt with an increased volume and value of transactions. Both factors contribute to making the state's provision of institutions (in this case, a registration system) more desirable: given the largely fixed administrative costs of the institutions, their implementation is economically justified if they deliver greater benefits. Yet volume and value of transaction do not affect this balance in the same way. If the reduction of transaction costs concerns few but very valuable transactions, state intervention has a more limited scope than in the opposite scenario, where the reduction of transaction costs concerns many, small-value transactions or many traders. Coordinating around a private solution to the problem is easier for a few traders than for many parties, so state intervention makes a bigger difference in a case involving the latter.

Economies of scale in the organization and management of institutions make the wedge between private and state action increase with the volume of transactions and the number of parties. The Athenian approver, analyzed by Ober in chapter 2, is a fitting case. The cost of training and managing the slave assigned to this institution was largely fixed and increased only marginally with an increase in the number of contracting parties who needed his services. In addition, the fact that the approver was not paid by any of the parties and could acquire experience and reputation over the long term guaranteed his independence and competence and, hence, made his use more effective than the use of individual experts hired ad hoc by the parties. This suggests that the state was better placed than private parties in the provision of measures that reduce transaction costs for a large number of transactions involving different parties. Thus the volume of transactions can be viewed as a driver of the private demand for state-assisted reduction of transaction costs.

4. Proprietary Rights Versus Contractual Rights

The analyses in chapters 3, 4, 6, 7, and 8 focus on the formalities adopted for different types of transactions. Muhs (chapter 3) analyzes the introduction of more effective and more expensive systems of recording of contracts and title verification for the transfer of property in Egypt, especially during the second half of the first millennium B.C.E. Manning (chapter 4) analyzes the registration of transactions and the use of notary scribes in Ptolemaic Egypt; Yiftach (chapter 6) analyzes the fees applying to contract formalities during the Ptolemaic and Roman periods; and Lerouxel (chapter 7) examines the function of the property registry or "archive of acquisitions," the βιβλιοθήκη ἐγκτήσεων, an institution that fostered the reliability of information about property. Finally, Ratzan (chapter 8) reports on the frequency with which some service contracts were subjected to specific formalities in Roman Egypt.

These studies reveal some regularities in the formalities required for different types of transactions. Contracts concerning the transfer of real property, mortgages, and leases of slaves were often subject to more stringent formal requirements—such as recording through a notary rather than simply through a scribe—than contracts concerning the transfer of other goods or unsecured debts. That registration was made mandatory for selected types of transactions while it was optional for other transactions suggests that, in some cases, the state imposed measures to reduce transaction costs beyond the level that contracting parties would have privately chosen. Although a plausible and somewhat explicit goal was the more efficient collection of taxes (discussed by Lerouxel in chapter 7), I will emphasize and expand, in the following analysis, on a second (possibly implicit) function: the reduction of transaction costs, as noted earlier by Yiftach.[18] Here I will show how it can be used to construct a demand for measures to reduce transaction costs.

The Athenian approver was available at the marketplace, but parties were not obliged to refer to him. The costs of uncertainty concerning the value of coins and the correlated benefits of reducing that uncertainty were entirely private to the contracting parties. After the contract, a seller who accepted debased coins would suffer a loss. Before the contract, a seller anticipating this eventuality might refrain from trading with unknown buyers, thereby passing part of his future expected loss on to them in the form of constrained trade opportunities. Since the costs (including time) and benefits associated with the decision to defer to the approver were internal to the contract—that is, they accrued entirely to the contracting parties—there was no economic reason to make deferral mandatory.

---

18. Yiftach-Firanko 2010.

In contrast, registration of contracts transferring or mortgaging real property or slaves was often mandatory. A plausible reason (in addition to taxation) is that these contracts concerned proprietary rights, that is, rights that have effects beyond the contracting parties.[19] For instance, a double sale or a sale *a non domino* generates a potential conflict between the two buyers or between the true owner and the buyer, respectively. Such conflicts are costly, as they might induce litigation or self-help and might imply that an unwitting party takes a loss as a result. What is important is that these costs are external to the contract.

An illustration comes from the Code of Hammurabi, which contained two different rules applicable to innocent purchases from a thief.[20] One rule concerned "easy" cases, in which the thief could be apprehended and all transactions could be undone. A second rule concerned the "difficult" cases, in which the thief could not be apprehended and, hence, either the buyer or the original owner had to bear a loss.[21] In such cases, not all costs deriving from the transaction were internalized in the contract. This is because, for instance, the escaped thief and the innocent buyer might not feel the loss that the original owner might incur. Analogous external costs emerge in double sales or other cases of conflicts between two incompatible claims. In turn, this is due to the peculiar nature of transactions involving proprietary rights, which have effects for third parties.

At the aggregate level, it makes economic sense to trade off a reduction in enforcement costs after the contract with an increase in the formalities before executing the contract, thus raising the costs of making the deal. We have seen that the state is in a better position than private parties with respect to the organization and management of registries. Here I add that it might be desirable, from an aggregate economic perspective, to mandate registration (along with other formalities). While the increase in the costs of making the deal is internalized by the contracting parties (because it is paid by them), the reduction in the costs of enforcing the deal *ex post* is not (because, as I have emphasized, these costs may fall onto third parties). Hence, the overall effect might be positive, but in each specific contract, private costs might outweigh the private benefits. By mandating registration, the state can assure that the

19. Merrill and Smith 2000; Hansmann and Kraakman 2002; Parisi 2002.
20. Levmore 1987.
21. If property is returned to the original owner, the buyer loses the price paid; if, instead, property is assigned to the buyer, the original owner loses the value of his assets.

externalities are internalized, reduce the overall uncertainty of property titles and contracts transferring property, and hence curb transaction costs and make exchange more efficient.[22]

In a nutshell, the fact that contracts establishing proprietary rights have external effects makes private action insufficient.[23] The contracting parties do not have an incentive to take such external effects into account. Therefore, by imposing certain measures to reduce transaction costs, the state can improve on the failures of private coordination. Note that, at the aggregate level, state action is not necessarily predatory: private parties benefit from the overall reduction in transaction costs. Therefore, the presence of external effects of private contracts provides a second determinant for a private demand of state-assisted reduction in transaction costs.

5. Litigation: Minimizing the Cost of Reducing Transaction Costs

The analysis of ancient judicial systems reveals a fundamental dilemma that still dominates the current policy debate about justice, namely the trade-off between guaranteeing access to justice—thereby reducing the costs of enforcing private deals—and keeping the administrative costs of the system low enough. Ideally, an optimally designed system would guarantee meritorious lawsuits access to the courts while keeping frivolous ones out of the system.[24] Irrespective of how one defines merit in this case, the problem is difficult to solve. Yet this perspective can be useful to explain some apparent paradoxes in the design of legal fees and penalties in the ancient world. Both in Athens (as discussed by Thür in chapter 1) and the later Roman Empire (as addressed by Haensch in chapter 10), legal fees were relatively low. This is clearly in line with the ideal of fostering access to justice, particularly with respect to low-income parties. Yet both systems added correctors.

In Athens, penalties for clearly frivolous litigation were relatively high. If a party could not secure a minimum number of votes in his favor by the jury,

---

22. See Arruñada 2012.
23. See Hermalin, Katz, and Craswell 2007 for a general treatment of the economics of contracts.
24. The registration fees discussed by Yiftach in chapter 6 also indirectly affect the amount of litigation: because low fees induce parties to register their contracts, they reduce litigation. But they were unlikely to have an impact on the selection of meritorious suits.

this was taken as a signal of a clearly baseless claim, for which the plaintiff was sanctioned. In turn, the prospect of receiving a penalty induced parties not to bring low-probability suits (or, for the defendant, not to resist high-probability claims by a plaintiff) and hence allowed the court system to focus on those cases in which a court decision was most needed. The policy of low fees and high penalties kept congestion under control by filtering out unmeritorious suits.

The inscription from Caesarea shows us that the emperor and courts of the later Roman Empire had adopted a different strategy to largely the same end: the sequencing of legal fees. To appreciate the effect of an appropriate sequencing of legal fees, it is helpful to consider the consequences of an inappropriate sequencing. If fees are equally divided between the initial and the final stage of the trial, a plaintiff with a frivolous claim (one that has a low probability of success) might be induced to bring a suit, which under a different sequencing he would have forgone litigating. The key is the relationship of the access fee to the expected pay-off from a successful suit: a plaintiff with a weak case cannot use litigation as a credible threat if the court fee is higher than what he can reasonably expect to gain from litigation. However, suppose that at the initial stage of the trial a substantial part of the fee is paid, which is still less than the expected pay-off, such that it leaves only a relatively small part to be paid at later stages. In this case, after having paid the first installment, the plaintiff's costs of continuing with the trial should be lower than what he expects to gain, especially since the part he has already paid is a sunk cost and should not affect future decisions. Such a regime heightens the credibility of a potential plaintiff's threat to sue and thus increases his leverage in attempting to extract a profitable settlement. Therefore, low-probability plaintiffs might have an incentive to sink some costs into early fees so as to make the threat to continue with litigation credible. If, instead, initial fees are relatively low while later fees are relatively high, this strategy does not work: the defendant can call the plaintiff's bluff since he knows that there is still a substantial financial barrier to the plaintiff with respect to the fee.[25]

Therefore, adopting an increasing schedule of court fees makes the strategic use of the court system by low-probability plaintiffs more difficult and hence screens out unmeritorious lawsuits. Although relying on different methods, policy choices affecting access to justice in Athens (as discussed by

---

25. Bebchuck 1988.

Thür in chapter 1) and the late Roman Empire (as addressed by Haensch in chapter 10) seem to be compatible with the same economic principle. Litigants, ancient and modern, often have varying reasons to go to court. Yet court fees undoubtedly play an important role in their decisions. Fees and penalties implemented in Athens and the late Roman Empire had the effect of limiting the incentives to bring low-value suits, thereby balancing the need to reduce the (transaction) costs of enforcing contracts with the opposite need to keep court congestion and administrative costs at low levels.

6. The Supply of Measures for Saving Transaction Costs

The demand-side analysis of the reduction of transaction costs has illuminated the limits of private action and emphasized the role of state intervention. Yet the desirability of state intervention does not imply that the state will therefore act accordingly. There are striking differences between the highly efficient system for coinage approval in Athens (analyzed by Ober in chapter 2) and the inefficiencies of a functionally similar system in Ptolemaic Egypt (analyzed by Bresson in chapter 5).

   The Athenian solution to the asymmetric information problems created by the existence of "lemons" (coins with low metal content) was remarkable with respect to both the approval policies and the internal governance of the institution. Employing a slave had several advantages over free labor. First of all, the slave could be trained and kept on the job for the long term—with clear advantages in terms of expertise and, hence, accuracy—while simultaneously being subjected to substantial penalties in case of fraud.[26] Moreover, the approval policy was consistent with the maximization of the aggregate value of the Athenian markets. The approver essentially approved all Athenian coins and good fakes (foreign coins with the correct amount of silver) and confiscated only bad fakes (those coins that had been coined abroad and contained an insufficient amount of silver). This system protected the brand value of the "owl" minted on the Athenian coins, without enforcing a monopoly on it.

   If, however, the goal had been to maximize immediate revenues, it would have made sense to confiscate the good fakes as well. This would also have

---

26. Dari-Mattiacci 2013.

increased demand specifically for Athenian coins. Yet this policy would likely have backfired and reduced overall gains. Innocent traders paying with good fake owls would have been unnecessarily punished, which in effect would have levied a highly inefficient tax on transactions and created uncertainty in the market. The result would have been a reduction in the volume of transactions, with obvious overall repercussions on the profits of Athenian traders. In contrast, by allowing the circulation of good fakes, the approvers did what was necessary to enforce the requirements for silver content—confiscation was a heavy penalty on bearers of bad fakes—and hence protected the owl as a signal of quality. This reduced asymmetry of information and fostered trade.

The Ptolemaic solution was different. The ban on the use of any foreign coin effectively enforced a monopoly on the production of coins, with evident short-term gains but diffuse losses due to the inefficiencies such a monopoly created. Plausibly, this was an easy way to tax transactions effectively in proportion to their value, something that could have been prohibitively difficult at a later stage. A way to explain the difference between Athens and Ptolemaic Egypt is to look at the realization of the gains from the two systems. Assuming that the initial decision to adopt one system over the other was motivated by self-interest, one could remark that the Athenian elites were invested in trade and hence considered both short-term and diffuse long-term gains when opting for the approval system, while the diffuse gains were not taken into account by the extraction-driven rulers in Egypt.[27] Studies on the modern period have yielded similar patterns. Countries with limited government and politically powerful traders are able to distribute the gains from trade (and foster democratic institutions), while more autocratic governments focus on concentrated gains and entrench themselves at the expense of the general population.[28]

7. Conclusions

In this chapter, I have distilled some elements of the demand and supply of institutions designed to reduce transaction costs in the ancient world from the analysis of the preceding chapters. In some cases, contractual parties

---

27. Cf. North and Weingast 1989.
28. Acemoglu, Johnson, and Robinson 2005.

could reduce transaction costs, especially the costs of enforcing compliance, by accurately designing contracts. In other cases, the failure of private coordination placed the state in a better position than private parties in terms of reducing transaction costs. I have emphasized two such (by no means exclusive) contexts: (1) cases in which the gains from reducing transaction costs were spread among large numbers of transactions and (2) cases in which contracts have effects for third parties.

Identifying a demand for state intervention raises the question whether the state supplied the appropriate institutions. The main institution for reducing transaction costs is the judicial system. The platform it provides for the enforcement of contracts and the protection of property is more efficient than private violence—self-help is usually subject to legal limits. By adjusting the amount and schedule of court fees and penalties, states could regulate access to the courts, especially by screening out frivolous claims. Moreover, the state offered a menu of default rules that reduced the cost of drafting contracts. Yet the state supply of institutions to reduce transaction costs varied. A political economy perspective suggests that differences depend on the extent to which the state internalizes the gains generated from such institutions.

This book has provided an excellent forum for interdisciplinary research, which I believe will continue to yield interesting insights about the state supply of institutions to reduce transaction costs and about the contractual solutions that private parties adopted to obviate the lack of state action. Unpacking the economic function of certain legal and contractual arrangements could help historians to identify the processes through which certain solutions have emerged and the goals they have served. Likewise, delving into ancient contractual and legal institutions could help economists test and refine their theories.

Bibliography

Acemoglu, D., S. Johnson, and J. Robinson. 2005. "The Rise of Europe: Atlantic Trade, Institutional Change, and Economic Growth." *American Economic Review* 95: 546–79.
Aghion, P., and R. Holden. 2011. "Incomplete Contracts and the Theory of the Firm: What Have We Learned over the Past 25 Years?" *Journal of Economic Perspectives* 25: 181–97.

Akerlof, G.A. 1970. "The Market for 'Lemons': Quality Uncertainty and the Market Mechanism." *Quarterly Journal of Economics* 84: 488–500.

Allen, D. W. 2000. "Transaction Costs." In Bouckaert and De Geest 2000: 1:893–926.

Arruñada, B. 2012. *Institutional Foundations of Impersonal Exchange: Theory and Policy of Contractual Registries.* Chicago.

Bebchuk, L. A. 1996. "A New Theory concerning the Credibility and Success of Threats to Sue." *Journal of Legal Studies* 25: 1–25.

Becker, G. 1962. "Investment in Human Capital: A Theoretical Analysis." *Journal of Political Economy* 70: 9–49.

Bouckaert, B., and G. De Geest, eds. 2000. *Encyclopedia of Law and Economics.* 5 vols. Cheltenham.

Calabresi, G., and A. D. Melamed. 1972. "Property Rules, Liability Rules, and Inalienability: One View of the Cathedral." *Harvard Law Review* 85: 1089–1128.

Coase, R. H. 1960. "The Problem of Social Cost." *Journal of Law and Economics* 3: 1–44. Reprinted in R. H. Coase, *The Firm, the Market, and the Law* (Chicago, 1990), 95–156.

Dari-Mattiacci, G. 2013. "Slavery and Information." *Journal of Economic History* 73: 79–116.

Guiso, L., P. Sapienza, and L. Zingales. 2006. "Does Culture Affect Economic Outcomes?" *Journal of Economic Perspectives* 20, no. 2: 23–48.

Hansmann, H., and R. Kraakman. 2002. "Property, Contract, and Verification: The *Numerus Clausus* Problem and the Divisibility of Rights." *Journal of Legal Studies* 31: 373–420.

Hart, O. and J. Moore. 1999. "Foundations of Incomplete Contracts." *Review of Economic Studies* 66: 115–38.

Hermalin, B. E., A. W. Katz, and R. Craswell. 2007. "Contract Law." In Polinsky and Shavell 2007: 1:3–138.

Holmström, B., and J. Tirole. 1989. "The Theory of the Firm." In Schmalensee and Willig 1989: 1:61–134.

Levmore, S. 1987. "Variety and Uniformity in the Treatment of the Good-Faith Purchaser." *Journal of Legal Studies* 16: 43–65.

Merrill, T. W., and H. E. Smith. 2000. "Optimal Standardization in the Law of Property: The Numerus Clausus Principle." *Yale Law Journal* 110: 1–70.

Milgrom, P., and J. Roberts. 1992. *Economics, Organization, and Management.* Englewood Cliffs, NJ.

North, D. C., and B. R. Weingast. "Constitutions and Commitment: The Evolution of Institutions Governing Public Choice in Seventeenth-Century England." *Journal of Economic History* 49: 803–32.

Parisi, F. 2002. "Entropy in Property." *American Journal of Comparative Law* 50: 595–632.

Parisi, F., and V. Smith. 2005. *The Law and Economics of Irrational Behavior.* Stanford.

Polinsky, A. M., and S. Shavell. 2007. *Handbook of Law and Economics*. 2 vols. Amsterdam.

Schmalensee, R., and R. D. Willig. 1989–2007. *Handbook of Industrial Organization*. 3 vols. Amsterdam.

Smith, V. 2008. *Rationality in Economics*. Cambridge.

Spence, M. 1973. "Job Market Signaling." *Quarterly Journal of Economics* 87: 355–74.

Stiglitz, J. E. 1975. "The Theory of 'Screening,' Education, and the Distribution of Income." *American Economic Review* 65: 283–300.

Temin, P. 2001. "A Market Economy in the Early Roman Empire." *Journal of Roman Studies* 91: 169–81.

Temin, P. 2013. *The Roman Market Economy*. Princeton.

Thür, G., ed. 2010. *Symposion 2009: Vorträge zur griechischen und hellenistischen Rechtsgeschichte (Seggau, 25.-30. August 2009)*. Vienna.

Yiftach-Firanko, U. 2010. "Comments on Andreas Jördens 'Nochmals zur Bibliotheke Enkteseon.'" In Thür 2010: 291–99.

Contributors

Alain Bresson: Robert O. Anderson Distinguished Service Professor, Department of Classics, University of Chicago

Giuseppe Dari-Mattiacci: Professor of Law and Economics, University of Amsterdam

R. Haensch: Direktor der Kommission für Alte Geschichte und Epigraphik des Deutschen Archäologischen Instituts und Ausserplanmässiger Professor der Ludwig-Maximilians-Univerität, München (Director of the Commission for Ancient History and Epigraphy of the German Archaeological Institute and Supernumerary Professor of the Ludwigs-Maximilian University, Munich

Dennis Kehoe: Professor of Classical Studies, Tulane University

F. Lerouxel: Maître de conférences, Université Paris-Sorbonne/AOROC

Joseph Manning: Simpson Professor of History and Classics, Yale University

Brian Muhs: Associate Professor of Egyptology, University of Chicago

Josiah Ober: Professor of Political Science and Classics, Stanford University

David M. Ratzan: Head Librarian at the Institute for the Study of the Ancient World, New York University

Gerhard Thür: Austrian Academy of Sciences

Uri Yiftach: Senior Lecturer in the Department of Classical Studies, Tel-Aviv University

Index

adverse selection, 282
advocates, 39–40, 49, 219–20, 260–61, 263, 267, 270
　See also logographoi
agents and agency, 14, 32, 42–43, 73–74, 125, 206–7, 232, 244–49
agoranomos/ἀγορανόμος, 109–110, 112, 151, 153–54, 157, 159–60, 176–77
　See also notaries
Alexandria, 30, 119–20, 124–27, 129, 131–41, 190, 196, 201–2, 204–6, 214, 223–26, 264n25, 269
anagraphê/ἀναγραφή, 147–48, 154–55, 160
　See also registration
apospaô/ἀποσπάω clause, 31–32, 186–87, 195–210, 213–14, 217–26, 279–80
apparitores, 265–66
apprentices and apprenticeship. *See* contracts
approver. *See* dokimastês
arbitration, 37, 40, 54–55, 253n1
archives, 23, 30, 55, 81, 104, 105n11, 106, 108–10, 111n36, 146, 152n23, 162–80, 188n6, 248, 269, 274, 276
　See also bibliothêkê engktêseôn
Arrow, Kenneth, 5
Arsinoite nome, 148–50, 156, 171–72, 187, 201–5, 208–10, 217–18, 223–26
　See also Soknopaiou Nesos; Tebtynis
associations. *See* networks

Athens, 5, 17, 29, 32, 36–79, 100, 103, 141, 270, 274, 276–77, 283–84, 286–89
auctions, 29–30, 44–49, 99, 103–5, 109, 112, 139, 190n14

banks and bankers, 23, 44, 49, 75–6, 100, 103–4, 110, 122–23, 125, 127, 133, 153, 162n3, 163–65, 167, 173
bargaining. *See* negotiation
bibliothêkê engktêseôn/βιβλιοθήκη ἐγκτήσεων, 12, 18, 31, 146, 162–63, 170n31, 171–80, 195, 264, 284

Caesarea (Iudaeae), 254, 287
chierograph/χειρόγραφον, 152, 166, 179, 201
citizenship, 19, 23, 39, 42–43, 53–55, 57, 188, 205
Coase, Ronald and the Coase theorem, 3–6, 56, 101, 239, 278
coinage
　Athenian, 29, 58–63, 72–73, 119, 124, 129–30, 136, 138, 139–40, 274, 276, 283, 288–89
　counterfeit, 59–71, 274, 284, 288–89
　fiduciary value of, 60, 69–70
　pharaonic Egypt, 90, 92
　Ptolemaic, 30, 103–4, 108, 118–42 119, 288–89
　See also commodity money
collateral. *See* security

295

SB V 7619 (= *C.Pap.Gr.* I 14), 204
SB XII 11248 (= *C.Pap.Gr.* I 7), 204
paragraphê/παραγραφή, 39, 42
parakatabolê/παρακαταβολή, 39
  See also escrow
peculium, 244–47
penalties, 39, 43, 45–46, 49, 55, 65–66, 73–
  74, 76, 80, 108, 175, 265, 286–90
  See also contracts, penalty clauses; fees
  and fines
petitions, 18–19, 46, 84–85, 88, 162, 172–
  73, 216–18, 221, 241–42, 260, 267n35
Pliny the Younger (Gaius Plinius Caeci-
  lius Secundus), 22, 25
Praetorian Prefects, 254, 257, 260, 270
  See also provincial governors
private ordering, 19–23, 219, 249
property rights, 7, 12–13, 17–20, 25, 27,
  29–30, 32, 36, 44, 85–92, 94, 101, 105–
  106, 145–46, 158–59, 169–73, 175–78,
  180, 190–91, 197–201, 214, 219–22,
  231–35, 238–39, 242–43, 249, 290
  See also mortgage; *ônê en pistei*
provincial governors, Roman, 19, 146,
  162, 172, 180, 220n81, 260, 265,
  268n44, 269–70
prytaneia/πρυτανεῖα, 37
  See also fees and fines
Ptolemais Euergetis, 162, 172, 204, 208

quality, determining, 7, 9, 26, 58n9, 63–
  68, 118, 176–78, 274, 276, 282, 289

rationality, economic, 40–41, 43, 74, 247–
  48, 275–76, 282–83
recording. *See* documentation; witnesses
registration, 82, 99, 109–10, 112, 150–51,
  154, 160, 165–66, 176–79, 202, 203n43,
  209, 264, 274, 276, 283–86
remission of rent, 239–41, 249
rent-seeking, 30, 54–55, 66, 68n19, 100,
  103, 105, 139–41
reputation, 10, 20–21, 40–1, 65, 71, 74,
  118, 194–95, 214, 217, 236, 283
risk
  aversion to by upper-class Romans,
  232, 244
  in contracts, 25–27, 31, 44, 46–47, 74,

80–81, 168–69, 179, 195, 198–99,
  204–5, 214, 221, 232, 235, 239–42,
  278–82
  in litigation, 32, 38, 40, 43, 46, 85, 89, 94

sale, 20, 25–27, 31, 44–45, 52, 63–64, 69–
  77, 82, 87, 89–90, 104–8, 110–11, 146–
  47, 150–59, 154–60, 164, 169, 195, 214,
  234–36, 238, 249, 257, 259, 266, 276,
  282, 284–85
satisficing, 11, 54
scribes, 44, 147, 103–4, 108–9, 149–56, 176,
  258–60, 263, 268, 284
  See also notaries
security (real), 41–42, 47–48, 166–69, 171–
  73, 176–79
self-help, 19–20, 187, 215–22, 279, 285, 290
slaves
  as agents, 73–74, 245–48
  public, 73–74, 288
social status
  influencing transactions, 13–17, 85, 100,
  104, 187, 194, 205–209, 218–22, 232,
  239–41, 243, 246–48, 267, 277–78
societates, 245–46
Soknopaiou Nesos, 162, 169n29, 170–72,
  224
sportulae, 253n2, 256, 258, 261–63, 265–66,
  269n48, 270
standardization
  in coins, 58–59, 66n18, 69–70, 119, 124–
  25, 129–32, 136, 138
  of commodities, 9
  in contractual forms, 106–110, 112, 207,
  211
  of legal rules, 54–56, 87, 267
status, 19, 23, 73–74, 108–9, 163, 186–87,
  196–200, 205–9, 219–21, 244–48, 259,
  265, 277–78
  See also citizenship; elites
Stigler, George, 3
stratêgos/στρατηγός, 148–49, 174, 217–
  221, 269
Sulpicii archive, 23–24, 166
surety, 38, 44, 55, 166–67
syngraphê/συγγραφή, 41–42
  See also contracts, written
syngraphophylax/συγγραφοφύλαξ, 150